THE YEAR OF THE PITCHER

The YEAR *of the* PITCHER

BOB GIBSON, DENNY McLAIN, and the
END OF BASEBALL'S GOLDEN AGE

Sridhar Pappu

Houghton Mifflin Harcourt
Boston   New York
2017

Copyright © 2017 by Sridhar Pappu

For information about permission to reproduce selections
from this book, write to trade.permissions@hmhco.com or to
Permissions, Houghton Mifflin Harcourt Publishing Company,
3 Park Avenue, 19th Floor, New York, New York 10016.

hmhco.com

Library of Congress Cataloging-in-Publication Data is available.
ISBN 978-0-547-71927-6

Book design by Chrissy Kurpeski

Printed in the United States of America
DOC 10 9 8 7 6 5 4 3 2 1

For My Mother

CONTENTS

PROLOGUE: HOPE

IN OCTOBER 1968 — A year in which, as we all know, assassins made martyrs out of two good men, young soldiers with no other option waged a faraway war while their privileged peers fought to end that same conflict, and a newly militant citizenry laid waste to their own cities and homes—Detroit Tigers pitcher Denny McLain opened the door of his bright new white Cadillac for Bob Gibson. Gibson was the ace of the St. Louis Cardinals' staff. It was October and the World Series, an event that still mattered to a great many, had begun, and had things gone according to script, these two were to be its stars.

Bob Gibson and Denny McLain had already pitched against one another in St. Louis. Now the two were scheduled to face off against each other again in Game 4 — in what was billed as a World Series marked by pitching prowess the world would remember forever. Yet here they were together, having just finished taping an episode of *The Bob Hope Show* at the local NBC affiliate in Detroit. Paired at the end after absurd appearances by John Davidson and Gwen Verdon and Jeannie C. Riley, the two had been alongside Hope in a painfully unfunny, stilted scene in a medium struggling to stay relevant.

By then, Bob Hope, now 65, had been on television for more than 18 years. Yet it is fair to say that little remained of *that* Bob Hope, who had seemed like a "tot" to one *New York Times* critic when he was first unleashed from the restrictive playground that was radio and surged onto television with the force of an ex-boxer and a dancer, both of which he had been. The radiant Hope, the man who'd held his own with Natalie Wood in dance numbers and brought the movement and speed of vaudeville back from extinction, simply stopped moving at the precise moment in American history when such immediacy and pace seemed the definitive tenor of the age.

As he welcomed McLain and Gibson, Hope looked, and acted, older than his years. Young people weren't interested in him or his skits and jokes anymore. He was now a hardened iconoclast, a symbol of an establishment desperately trying to hold on to cultural power . . . and losing.

Standing to Hope's left was Gibson, a strikingly handsome black man, a perfect physical specimen save for a small gap between his two front teeth. Dressed immaculately in a Nehru jacket and white turtleneck, a gold medallion on his chest, Gibson looked like a man of his time. He was a man of great taste who dressed without equal, according to his friend and catcher Tim McCarver. No one, McCarver would later joke, could wear a pair of pants like Bob Gibson.

McLain should have taken note. Though eight years Gibson's junior, McLain looked worn out. His face was droopy and exhausted, his hair cemented into place. His baby-blue suit seemed to hang off him as his turtleneck bulged at the neck. All season he'd promoted himself relentlessly, appearing on one television show after another, boasting endlessly about a salary increase that, in the era before free agency and arbitration, tight-fisted team management would never approve. He indulged his appetite for a flashy lifestyle and kept apart from his teammates. This was his moment on the big stage, but he was overshadowed by Gibson's cool.

The image of these two that day is unforgettable. Because whether they like it or not, McLain and Gibson are forever linked in our minds and in baseball history as the standard-bearers for 1968, the so-called Year of the Pitcher. That was the year when no less than five starters in the American League finished with an earned run average below 2.00. That year Juan Marichal used his arsenal of arm angles to win 26 games while logging a little over 325 innings, and Gaylord Perry of San Francisco and Gibson's teammate Ray Washburn pitched back-to-back no-hitters in consecutive games against one another's teams. That was the year when Catfish Hunter threw a perfect game and Don Drysdale, in the waning stages of his career, emerged from the shadow of Sandy Koufax to throw 58⅔ scoreless innings.

Even today the numbers seem unfathomable. Seven times that season a pitcher — including Gibson — struck out 15 hitters in a single game. There were 185 shutouts in the National League, and 154 in the American. Hitters were lost, offense nonexistent. It was a disparity so large that after the 1968 season Major League Baseball changed the rules in the batter's favor in an attempt to restore balance. We would never see those kinds of numbers again.

But we'll always have that year. We will always have Gibson and McLain. *Bob Gibson, St. Louis Cardinals: 1.12 ERA. Denny McLain, Detroit Tigers: 31 wins.* In a game where the past is forever bumping up against the present, any conversation about pitching cannot help but return to these two names and the numbers they posted, which were nothing short of remarkable.

It's fair to say that had Gibson not been black, we would regard him differently. He'd be Joe DiMaggio, whose selfish silence played to a great many as the reserve of a dignified, stoic man. Or he'd be Ted Williams, who redeemed himself over the years after a career in which he battled the Boston press and even the fans. We even gave Gibson's contemporary, the reclusive Sandy Koufax, his space. But Gibson's desire to keep to himself, to not play to the press, came off as the mark of the angry Negro, the face of the black power movement that had surged in popularity in the late sixties — even though Gibson himself never believed in any of its precepts.

Then there was Denny. In all the ways Gibson remained aloof, Denny did not. We knew precisely who McLain was and whom he aspired to be. He was a man brazenly out for himself, who spoke openly about his financial interests at a time when ballplayers were still expected to keep quiet about money, to do as they were told, to treat the press politely and behave. His criminal entanglements were still unknown in 1968, but we knew that he lived life on the edge and that, even as he paraded his recklessness in public, he never doubted his invincibility. Like football's Joe Namath, McLain saw his baseball career as just one part of a larger public persona, not the singular thing that defined him. It was Denny, with his playboy antics and lavish tastes, who presaged what lay ahead for baseball and American sport.

It appeared to McLain that at every turn it was "Gibson and Denny." Years later McLain would speak to how ornery Gibson was and could still be — even in old-timers' games. But he understood. Denny believed

that Gibson, like all black players, carried burdens that today seem unfathomable. The abuse would have transformed even the cheeriest of
men.

Perhaps no black player suffered as much as the very first in the major
leagues. Jack Roosevelt Robinson was just 49 years old in 1968, and 12
years into his retirement. Over 10 seasons, from 1947 to 1956, he'd led the
Dodgers to six National League pennants and their only World Series
championship in Brooklyn. But when he walked out of the Ebbets Field
clubhouse for the last time in 1956, he had walked away from the game
and into another life — and what he believed was a more noble calling —
as a political emissary, an advocate for civil rights. By 1968, however, his
family life was in ruin, his health was failing, and the ideals of nonviolence that he'd championed had increasingly lost their currency to the
raised fists of the black radicals, who laughed at Robinson and mocked
him, forgetting how hard he had worked, how much he had given up, to
secure a more equal America. Now, in the midst of personal failure and
public ridicule, he seemed ready to give up.

With his world collapsing, Robinson wrote to a friend, "I can't imagine what else can happen to us this year."

While Robinson was trying his best to stay away from the game, the
pitcher he first faced had spent the same time trying to reinvent it. John
Franklin Sain, born and raised in Arkansas, was on his way by 1968 to
becoming the greatest pitching coach the sport has ever known. Soft-
spoken and forward-thinking, Sain often broke with established practice and focused as much on a player's mental game as he did on the
mechanics of pitching. Everyone was his own man in Sain's mind, and
he treated each pitcher as such. By studying his pitcher's particular
strengths and habits and interests, Sain easily persuaded his pupils to
adjust to new ways of thinking about how to throw a baseball. Thus, it
was probably no accident that McLain, for all his impulsiveness and lack
of discipline, suddenly flourished under Sain's patient tutelage.

Although the 1968 baseball season would always be remembered in
baseball's grand narrative, one can understand why the season has
been relegated to the margins of U.S. history. The bold America that

had emerged from World War II was on the verge of cannibalizing itself from within. To claim that baseball acted as a balm, that it soothed the rage and helped the country heal, is to engage in facile sports journalism, to tell one of the feel-good stories we've been telling for as long as we've been writing about sports. These stories don't reflect reality. From Sixth Avenue, I watched the second tower fall on September 11, 2001, and I can tell you that the Yankees' World Series run, even for this baseball fan, did nothing to assuage the feelings of loss and despair. Not for me or for anyone I knew. Nor can we reasonably claim that McLain's 1968 Tigers, for all their spunk and perseverance that season, did much to stitch back together a city felled by the most terrible race riot in modern memory. We want to believe that the Tigers were playing at a higher level out of civic pride. But this belief comes from the mythos pushed on us by baseball out of its own self-importance. As the game's great pioneer Bill Veeck wrote, "Baseball has sold itself as a civic monument for so long that it has come to believe its own propaganda."

Baseball is a wonderful, poignant game. Its drama captivates us through spring, summer, and early fall, offering us elements of tragedy and elation. But within the rarefied world of sports, baseball was at an even greater remove than most sports from the social unrest of the times. It's true that many ballplayers served in the National Guard. But they didn't board military planes for Saigon. They didn't stand with the tear-gassed students in the streets of Chicago. And while black Olympic athletes struggled to decide whether to participate in the 1968 summer games in Mexico City, whether to represent a country that trampled on their rights, professional baseball players weren't even considering the same level of sacrifice.

There were individual exceptions. Men like Curt Flood and Willie Horton pushed hard for racial progress. The assassination of Martin Luther King Jr. not only delayed the start of the 1968 season but opened the door to wide-open conversations between at least some black and white teammates. When an assassin felled Robert Kennedy, the reactions to it by those who controlled the game came up against a new, muscled internal uprising in baseball, as players felt empowered to stand up to team owners as never before.

A new beginning for baseball was on the horizon. Throughout the sixties, as television raised the profile of football, it became apparent that baseball needed a revamp. But how was that going to happen? Was the future in domed stadiums and a full-on embrace of modernity? How much effort should be put into preserving baseball's traditions? We know now that baseball moved too slowly. It was taking baby steps, making cautious adjustments, when it needed to be bold.

Bold. That wasn't the word one would use in watching Hope with Gibson and McLain. The whole show until this point had been labored — especially the skit where Hope and Davidson played imprisoned hippies. This, however, was far, far worse. Like baseball, television was struggling to find itself in 1968, as Norman Lear and Lorne Michaels and the other visionaries of the 1970s patiently waited to take control.

But this moment still belonged to Hope. He chided the two men by saying, "Now you two are the finest pitchers in the world. Is there any animosity between the two of you?"

"Of course not," Gibson said. "I think Denny's a fine man and great competitor."

"And I think Bob epitomizes great sportsmanship and he's a wonderful human being," McLain chimed in.

Hope prodded them into an argument for laughs, but he didn't have to try very hard. Gibson hadn't been able to stomach McLain's harsh words about the Cardinals before the Series even began. McLain was tired of being seen as the underdog in their World Series matchup. In another time, they might have lunged at one another, but this was still 1968, and still *The Bob Hope Show* in primetime.

"I've never liked him," Gibson said.

"I don't think he's much of a pitcher — he's just very lucky," McLain shot back.

"Twiggy throws a better fastball."

"Brother, I've seen better curves on Phyllis Diller."

More than forty years later, McLain tried to remember opening the door of his white Cadillac, his name splashed across the side, for Gibson after the show. He couldn't recall how he got the car. After all, he said, he had "every car known to man." A Cadillac. A Thunderbird. A Corvette. All were given to him, of course — that year McLain's yard looked like a car lot.

Things would never be this good for either man again. Their careers and their stories didn't end in 1968, but that year was an important milepost in their lives — a year that would come to define both them and baseball. A culmination of sorts, it was a year that would test the limits of baseball's reach, see the end times of old heroes, and feature transcendent moments for others. Americans would learn through Sain and Gibson, Robinson and McLain, what the National Game really means to us, then and in the future.

— Sridhar Pappu
Brooklyn, New York

THE YEAR OF THE PITCHER

1

SILENT FILM

I N THIS SOUNDLESS FILM, it is winter in Arkansas. That much is certain, though the month and day and even the year are unknown. The film was taken after World War II, after Johnny Sain had gone off to Navy flight school, where he grew close to Ted Williams and Johnny Pesky, but not to any real action or enemy fire. Now he is home.

In many ways, this footage, though shot in color, recalls an earlier time. Not much seems to have changed since 1930, or even 1918. The house and garage need paint. A wooden fence looks like it was built in different styles and at different times. The ground is barren. The white laundry flaps gently on the line in the cloudless air.

It all looks austere, though Sain takes no notice. He can only concentrate on his craft. Standing in front of that clapboard white house, he heaves a baseball again and again against a worn card table propped up by two of its legs. This act of repetition has served him well over the years, and watching him is enough to make your own arm grow tired.

You cannot see his eyes or thick eyebrows, or a bulge of chewing tobacco in his cheek. But his focus, his diligence, is undeniable. He's a man at work. In the first reel, there he is in a maroon jacket and gray slacks, raising his arms slightly above his head, then releasing the ball with his leg pointing straight out. As if on a loop, the moment the ball comes back to him he's squared his body in a fielder's position and is ready to begin the whole motion again.

That he is a professional baseball player is not readily apparent, not even in the second reel. Here he has put on his heavy, wool Boston Braves jersey, but his light blue jeans are pulled high above his waist, revealing his white socks. He might as well be an overgrown ball boy.

This all takes place not that far from the auto garage of Sain's father in Havana, Arkansas, a town in the shadow of the Ozark Mountains. That he came from here and became a pro ballplayer still seems improbable. Sain spent most of his youth not on a baseball field but in the garage, whiling away the hours watching his dad take apart machinery and teaching himself to do the same. As he told the great baseball writer Roger Kahn, this was also how he learned to pitch — by watching what others did.

Sain's father had been a minor league pitcher whose career never came to much, but he taught his son how to throw a curveball, how to change speed, how to vary his motion. And when the owner of a local feed store — a man who'd never pitched himself but had seen photographs of great pitchers — suggested that Sain stop gripping the ball with his thumb sticking out, Sain took the man's counsel.

"If I hadn't changed," Sain told a reporter years later, "I wouldn't get a chance to pitch nowhere."

In 1935, at 17 years old, the Boston Red Sox signed Sain for $5 to play for a team in the Class D League. For his first four years, he seemed destined for obscurity — playing for four different minor league teams, he never earned more than $50 a month. Scouts liked his size — at over six feet — and delivery, but not the velocity with which he released the ball. When one minor league manager gushed over Sain's prowess at first base — he batted .315 in his part-time role — the man suggested that Sain make the switch for good.

Then came the war. In 1942, with his pitching staff depleted by the draft, Boston Braves manager Casey Stengel took a flier on Sain and his curveball, using him strictly in relief. Good, but not great.

Sain's baseball career should have ended right there. When his own draft notice came the following season, it would have been easy to predict that Sain, like so many who served, would lose his most productive baseball years and that he would be remembered, if at all, as a fill-in player for a forgettable team.

But Sain slashed his way out of that story. He entered the Navy Air Corps, only to come out a better, more determined pitcher three years later. Maybe it was being around Ted Williams. Maybe it was Sain's rigorous study of aerodynamics, a subject he initially struggled with—it took him 22 months to earn his wings. In later years, he could speak at length about the physics of an object in flight, how it could loop and move, how you could manipulate a ball without having to throw it at ungodly speeds.

Sain was 24 during his rookie season with the Braves and approaching 30 when he was released from the Navy. He knew, as all men that age do, that there was only so much time he would have in the major leagues. Thus, while the other pilots stationed in Corpus Christi did what pilots do—drink, carouse, play cards—Sain would throw. He'd throw to anyone who'd catch him. Short of that, he'd find a wall and throw against it. According to him, he left dents in buildings at every naval air station he was assigned to.

By the time he began playing in exhibition games alongside Williams and Johnny Pesky for the North Carolina Pre-Flight Cloudbusters, he "saw the light" and learned how to focus. And alongside them, he learned how to throw sidearm and how to get the most out of his overhand delivery. Just by watching what his teammates threw, he developed as many as seven different pitches, all varying in speed.

Yet he wasn't able to put them to use when he was up against the most important batter he'd yet faced. Playing against a team consisting of reserves from the Indians and Yankees one afternoon, he stood on a mound in the Bronx waiting for the next batter when he heard the sudden, unbroken applause of over 27,000 fans. Here was the Babe—eight years removed from the game, and five years away from death.

At that moment, his catcher, Al Sabo, came out to speak to him. Sabo told him not to throw Ruth any curveballs since no one wanted to embarrass Ruth, not now. Yet, as Sain said, taking away his curve by then was like "cutting off two of my fingers." Still, this was the Babe. In the

Bronx. Thus, Sain threw one limp fastball after another — five in total — but it was clear that the umpire behind the plate wouldn't call a strike. Ruth took one pitch and eventually walked on five. It was the last at-bat the man who had changed the game would ever have.

While these were the last five pitches Ruth ever saw, for Sain they marked a new beginning. The Johnny Sain who returned to Boston in 1946 was a changed man. Many talented players who returned after being in the service found that their career had been cut short at its peak. But Sain had somehow found his power, his baseball IQ.

At the time the film from Arkansas was made, Sain was throwing as he did during the war, steadily and with purpose. In the coming years, he would instruct the young pitchers he coached — Whitey Ford and Jim Bouton, Jim Kaat and Earl Wilson, Wilbur Wood and Mickey Lolich and Denny McLain — to spend their days off the mound doing the same. He would come to believe in the wisdom of building an arm not through rest but through rigorous and repetitive use. At the time of this film, he was getting ready for spring, when he would again pair with Warren Spahn to form one of the more dynamic pitching duos ever.

During those first heady years after the war, Boston really did rely on the rotation of "Spahn and Sain and pray for rain." From 1946 to 1950, Sain and his gregarious counterpart won 181 games between them, with Sain taking 95. In Sain's first season back from the war, he won 20 games. In one stretch, he pitched nine times on two days' rest. From April 16, 1946, until October 2, 1948, he never left the game during any of his 63 wins. Watching him in his brilliant, but ultimately forgotten, 1–0 defeat of Bob Feller and the Cleveland Indians in the 1948 World Series, Tris Speaker compared him to Christy Mathewson. Cy Young called him "wonderful."

Sain had worked his way to The Show and done well. But during the 1948 season, in the midst of great success, he was ready to walk away from it all. That July, he learned that Braves owner Lou Perini had paid $65,000 for the rights to an 18-year-old pitcher named Johnny Antonelli, who sat on the major league roster. Meanwhile, Sain, who was at the top of his form, was making less than $30,000. Wanting what he was worth, Sain said he'd quit unless he got it — which he eventually did. He wasn't a revolutionary by any means. But it should have been a sign to future employers that the pitchers whom he would later teach would approach their dealings with management the same way. Pitching well deserved a fair paycheck, and nearly all of those who pitched under Johnny were damn sure they fought for what was theirs.

After 1950, Sain's career seems a blur. His arm grew tired during a subpar 1949 season, though he won 20 games the following year. In 1951, Stengel, who'd first brought him to the big leagues, welcomed him to the Yankees, where he spent the better part of five years. Sain was no longer the workhorse who had emerged from the war, but Stengel used him brilliantly, as both a starter and reliever, giving new life to his pitching career. The Yankees eventually traded him to their cast-off team in Kansas City, which was where he ended one part of his baseball life, but was destined to begin another.

Sain could have left baseball behind. He had pitched on pennant-winning teams and performed with great acclaim in the World Series. Another life awaited him at home in Arkansas. There was the car dealership he'd bought with his savings in 1952. There was his wife Doris and the children — they would have four in their time together.

But when the call for a pitching coach came from the Athletics in 1959, Sain left Arkansas again. And in 1961, when Ralph Houk, who had taken the reins from Stengel as Yankees manager, called on him to do the same job in New York, he accepted. Sain was ready for this. In his time away from the game, he had continued to study both the mechanics of pitching and the psychological qualities that drove successful people. He wanted to see how he could apply what he'd learned.

The Yankees had never had a pitching coach like Sain before. No one had. He never came to the mound to talk to the pitcher, and rarely spoke to him on the bench. He never talked of his own past. Unlike other coaches, he never had pitchers running sprints between starts. He gave them books that stressed positive thinking and used a patented device that became known as "the spinner." It was just a baseball mounted on a wooden handle, but a pitcher could try out different grips with it or practice different spins.

Jim Kaat, who immediately took to Sain when he later became the

Twins' pitching coach, initially laughed at the spinner. It looked like a lollipop if you held it up straight. But when Sain used it, he could show the different rotations of the ball — how a curveball or fastball or screwball would spin. The spinner would prove invaluable for an entire generation of pitchers.

The results are without question. Under Sain's influence, Ralph Terry won 23 games in 1962, and Jim Bouton won 21 games in 1963. Sain worked with Whitey Ford, who was having trouble with his velocity, to deliver an "out pitch" that took the strain off his elbow. Each year from 1961 to 1963, Ford won 25, 17, and 24 games, respectively.

But as suddenly as Sain came to the Bronx he was gone. Following the Yankees' defeat in the 1963 World Series, Sain sensed that his relationship with manager Ralph Houk was nearing its end. Yogi Berra was taking over as manager, but Sain didn't think the team would follow him, especially with Houk, ever the general, still dictating affairs from the front office. Sain still loved coaching, but he foresaw an untenable situation.

He had trusted Houk, and believed him to be his friend. But he had learned of Berra's ascent not through Houk but through the papers. In turn, Sain displayed the same cocksure confidence he did in 1948 with Lou Perini. When Sain demanded a contract raise, Houk fired the pitching coach whose team the Dodgers had just demolished in the World Series. He was free.

Even though he'd been dismissed, Sain had made it clear that he — and perhaps he alone — understood the temperament of the modern athlete. He knew how to treat players as independent thinkers at a time when the last thing Major League Baseball wanted was freedom of thought. The dynamics of the player-coach relationship were in flux by the mid-1960s, but Johnny Sain was ready for it. He was even ready for Denny McLain.

Jackie Robinson's story was our story. Or at least, what we wished our story as a country could be. The story of a California housekeeper's son, a four-sport star at UCLA, a veteran who challenged the racism of the Army and then took on something more powerful — baseball. He'd remained silent during those first years in the major leagues, and then, when allowed, he came out as who he really was: a terrific and combative team player who took it upon himself to will his team to win.

In his last years in baseball, the strain of that struggle between the private man and the public pioneer wore on Robinson. In a letter to his wife Rachel from the road, he wrote that he would be "very glad when this baseball is over." He wanted the two of them and their three children to live as normally as they could. Moreover, by the end of the 1956 season, his champion, Branch Rickey, was long gone from the Brooklyn offices on Montague Street. Rumors of the unthinkable — that the Dodgers might be moved west — rattled through the underground lines of Brooklyn. His team had aged with him. He was no longer the whirlwind force who'd changed America. His story, or at least this part of it, was ending, and he was tired.

So he left. He left baseball before he would put on a uniform for the New York Giants, to whom he was traded following the 1956 season. He left ready to take on the role of an executive for the successful Chock Full o'Nuts Corporation at a time when very few black men held such prominent posts. He left, he said, because he wanted to find the normalcy that had eluded him for most of his life.

Jack also had a bigger struggle — with the South and all those still standing behind segregation. As new leaders like Martin Luther King Jr. emerged, Robinson felt the need to join them. Robinson didn't just throw his name or a check at the cause. He was there staring sadly at what remained of the home of Fred Shuttlesworth, cofounder of the Southern Christian Leadership Conference (SCLC), after cowards bombed it in 1956. He was there in 1962 alongside Rev. Wyatt Walker at the charred wreckage of the Mount Olive Baptist Church in Sunset, Georgia, holding remnants in his hands. Robinson was vocal in his support for interracial marriage and against the segregationist Alabama governor, George Wallace. He walked, as millions did, in the 1963 March on Washington. The sit-ins, staged at lunch counters across the South, reminded him of his own life, and he bristled when President Dwight D. Eisenhower called for patience when it came to desegregation.

Baseball had not passed him by. He had left it behind. Speaking at the NAACP convention in Detroit after his retirement, Robinson said that he found it "hard to remember what my life was like just a brief year ago."

"There was a time when I erred in being complacent," he said in another speech before another large NAACP crowd. "I was tempted to take advantages I received for granted. Then I realized my responsibility to my race and my country."

This was the new Robinson. Marching. Speaking. Traveling with a group of athletes, including a young Curt Flood, to Mississippi at the behest of Medgar Evers just a year before Evers was murdered. Robinson enlisted advisers — most notably the NAACP lawyer Franklin Williams — to help him understand the issues as best he could. He also made himself a regular at the expansive Upper West Side townhouse of the prominent African American doctor Arthur Logan and his wife Marian, a singer whom Jackie had met while starring for the Dodgers' minor league team in Montreal; there the Logans hosted the preeminent civil rights leaders of the day. Not long before, Robinson had succeeded in breaking open America's national sport. Now he was working alongside others — preachers, lawyers, entertainers, physicians — to surmount even steeper obstacles.

As others questioned the role that an ex-athlete could play in the movement, Martin Luther King Jr. reminded them who Robinson was and what he had done. In a speech written by King and read by civil rights leader Reverend Wyatt Tee Walker at the Waldorf Astoria one evening in 1962 to commemorate Robinson's induction into the Baseball Hall of Fame, King defended his friend's place in the cause: "There are those, black and white, who have challenged the right of Jackie Robinson to ask these questions. He has the right. He has the right because he is a citizen. He has the right — more rightly — because back in the days when integration wasn't fashionable, he underwent the trauma and the humiliation and the loneliness which comes with being a pilgrim walking the lonesome byways toward the high road of Freedom. He was a sit-inner before sit-ins, a freedom rider before freedom rides."

Robinson did not have to be this public with his views. He could have worked behind the scenes, as the best power brokers do. The NAACP or SCLC could have brought him to functions as a speaker. He could have wielded his influence quietly, whether at the Logans or at the jazz festival he and Rachel started at their home in Stamford, Connecticut. But he chose to be more vocal—hosting a radio show and then lending his name to a series of columns that appeared in the 1960s.

Though ghostwritten, the columns expressed opinions, often caustic, that were entirely his own. At first, they were ghostwritten by William Branch, a Northwestern University graduate and the son of an African American minister. Branch first met Robinson after writing to him in the late 1950s, when Robinson hosted a talk show for NBC Radio, to ask for a job. Branch, who went on to become a playwright of some renown, pointed out that it just wasn't right that a show hosted by a black man had an all-white staff. There were plenty of black men and women who had the credentials—including Branch himself—to serve on his show. In short order, Branch found himself in Robinson's office at Chock Full o'Nuts, and soon after that Branch was directing the program.

It was during this period that Robinson came to him with a request. The *New York Amsterdam News* had asked him to write a weekly column, but since, he admitted, he was "not much of a writer," he wondered if Branch would help him with it.

After thinking it over for a couple of days, Branch came back to Robinson with a proposal. "Well, look, Jack," he said. "If you're interested in doing a column, I would think that there would be more potential in this than just the *Amsterdam News*. Why don't we try one of the major New York papers?" Foremost among them was the old *New York Post,* the liberal tabloid run by socialite Dorothy Schiff.

Branch suggested reaching out to Ted Poston—at the time one of the few black reporters employed by one of the mainstream New York papers. He wanted to see if there'd be interest in it. Robinson agreed and told Branch to check it out.

Poston listened to Branch's proposal with great interest. Within a matter of days, he had arranged a luncheon at the *Post* with himself, Schiff, Branch, and Robinson. Before the meeting, Branch had suggested to Robinson that they have sample columns ready and ask Poston to read them in advance. In a matter of days, Poston contacted Branch and told him that the *Post* wanted to publish the column, under Robinson's byline, three times a week.

Whether Robinson suspected it or not, these columns would help him emerge from baseball for good. Readers would come to understand that the Jackie Robinson they once knew was something more than a ballplayer. He was a man who was unafraid to take on anything, unafraid to hold anything back. No one was beyond reproach. White segregationists, black militants, elected officials — all felt Robinson's wrath. At times he could come across as not just outraged but even hateful.

Robinson was fearless in expressing himself to the public. And once again Rachel found herself explaining to people that no, he was not an angry man. He was passionate and competitive, a man who wanted to be heard and would take risks to ensure that that happened. But at home he was something else.

At least early on, Rachel believed that together they had made the home they wanted for themselves and their children. If either of them was angry, they'd walk away from one another. A quiet would set in, and eventually the two would begin to talk. But there was no shouting. Nothing was thrown — not in Rachel Robinson's house. The enduring image of her husband as an "angry black man" would bother her forever.

Yet Jackie Robinson could be unforgiving — as John F. Kennedy, the champion of "The New Frontier," soon found out. In their first encounter, Robinson glared at the young senator. Robinson remained angry over Kennedy's decision to meet with Alabama governor and segregationist John Patterson, as well as Sam Englehardt, president of the state's White Citizens Councils. When Belford Lawson, Kennedy's adviser on civil rights, took the senator to an NAACP dinner in New York, the two were welcomed with open arms — with one exception.

When Robinson refused to appear in a photograph with Kennedy, the young senator was stunned. Kennedy felt hurt. But, as Lawson explained, Robinson "was a Republican." Moreover, "he didn't matter particularly, being only a baseball player at the time."

Time and again, Kennedy tried to change Robinson's opinion of him, but even Kennedy's meeting with Thurgood Marshall did little to help his cause. Robinson would not be swayed, in spite of efforts by men like Connecticut governor Chester Bowles. Unmoved, Robinson wrote in his column with Branch during the 1960 presidential race that "Senator Kennedy is not fit to be President of the United States."

Perhaps further poisoning relations between Robinson and the Camelot circle was his regard for the "Happy Warrior," Hubert Humphrey. When Humphrey stood before the Democratic National Convention in 1948 — just as Robinson was beginning his baseball career — and boldly said that the "time has arrived in America for the Democratic Party to get out of the shadow of states' rights and to walk forthrightly into the bright sunshine of human rights," he became the white darling of the civil rights movement. At a time when the Southern "Dixiecrats" still held sway over the Democratic Party, Humphrey stood virtually alone. Robinson understandably admired Humphrey, knowing as he did what it meant to take a lonely stance for the sake of the greater good. He was with Humphrey then and forever — campaigning for him in Wisconsin as Humphrey tried his best to defeat Kennedy in the 1960 primary.

After Kennedy clinched the Democratic nomination in 1960, Robinson turned his attention to Dwight Eisenhower's vice president, Richard Nixon, who had befriended him years back. Given the two men's correspondence from the 1950s, it's not surprising that when the time came for Robinson to step out of his role as a corporate executive and part-time newspaper columnist, it was Nixon whom he supported. Yet Robinson's bravery would go unrewarded, his advice unheeded at the campaign's most pivotal point. In the fall of 1960, when blacks across the country watched King being imprisoned on cooked-up charges in Georgia, Robinson pleaded with William Safire, then a Nixon adviser, to have his candidate reach out to King to make sure that African Americans knew on whose side he stood.

Robinson felt strongly enough to fly out to meet Nixon on the campaign trail. After meeting with the Republican nominee, Robinson walked out. He was a tough man who'd endured tough times, but now Safire could see he was crying.

"He thinks calling Martin would be 'grandstanding,'" Robinson said. Then he added, "Nixon doesn't deserve to win."

With this, he ended his role in the 1960 campaign. But Robinson still believed in the promise of the man and did not abandon him, at least not right away. Though he scolded Nixon publicly for not calling King and letting the black vote slip away to Kennedy, Robinson remained loyal far longer than he should have. Robinson didn't truly sever his ties with Nixon until the politician cast his lot with Barry Goldwater, the architect of the conservative movement, which by 1964 seemed to embrace the very same principles as the Dixiecrats. Robinson's misgivings about John Kennedy — now dead — had proved to be wrong.

Robinson also found that the more he spoke out about civil rights, the more alone he felt, abandoned by the very ballplayers whose livelihoods he'd made possible. He could count on men like Bill White and Curt Flood. But as he scanned the ranks of the fully integrated major leagues, he found few players who were willing to stand with him in this new world. As a result, Robinson became increasingly withdrawn from the sport. He seldom watched games on television. He never went to the ballpark. Those who wished to engage him about baseball often found him disinterested.

This was George Vecsey's experience early in his long and prolific journalism career. Robinson's team had been the Vecsey family team. A newspaper family from Queens, the Vecseys were devoted to the progressive causes of their time — integration and fair housing and the promises of the New Deal. The values that Robinson represented were part of their worldview.

But when Vecsey was assigned to write a story for *Newsday* about the absence of black managers in baseball, he felt the wrath of his boyhood idol.

"Well, let me ask you a question," Robinson snapped back when Vecsey called him at home in Connecticut. "How many African Americans are in your sports department?"

"Uh, none."

With that, unfairly, Robinson went off. He had no idea how Vecsey approached race and baseball. White players had seen him quickly engage with black players from the very start of his career. Those in the game knew where he stood. But to Robinson, Vecsey was merely another white liberal, hunting down a quote. In return, Robinson gave the young man "holy hell."

Robinson was often regarded as cantankerous, but he was not entirely disillusioned with the game and what it meant for the country. A couple of years before his terse exchange with Vecsey, in 1964, Robinson had published a book called *Baseball Has Done It,* in which he wrote that baseball had revealed "certain truths about human relations" and served as a "research laboratory and proving ground for democracy in action.

"Integration in baseball has already proved that all Americans can live together in peaceful competition," Robinson continued. "Negroes and whites coexist today on diamonds South, North, East and West without friction, fist fights and feuds. They wear the same uniforms, sit side by side on the same benches, use the same water fountains, toilets, showers: the same bats, balls and gloves.

"Baseball is not only a pastime, a sport, an entertainment, a way of blowing off steam," Robinson wrote. "But it is also the national game, with an appeal to Americans of every race, color, creed, sex or political opinion. It unites Americans in the common cause of rooting for the home team.

"Is it possible that Americans value victory for the home team," he asked, "more than the victory of democracy in our national life?"

Noble sentiments. But were they true? Its own mythos aside, what role did baseball really play in American life? As the decade progressed toward 1968, the nadir of postwar American life, we would begin to find out precisely how much the game actually meant.

2

LOST FATHERS

IKE THE ROBERT TAYLOR HOMES in Chicago, like the Eagan Homes in Atlanta and the Pruitt-Igoe tracts in St. Louis, the Logan Fontenelle Homes and their 556 apartments in North Omaha are gone now. What's left—and these too are fading —are memories of a time when government and public housing projects were seen as active forces for the betterment of society. The families who came here found some degree of good fortune. A new life. A steady income for adults in the meatpacking plants and with the railroads. A chance for children to rise above their impoverished conditions. This was the place that shaped Gayle Sayers and Johnny Rodgers and Bob Boozer. And this was where a young man who initially preferred basketball to baseball, who eventually developed an almost impenetrable aura as a star athlete, found his place in the world. This was where Bob Gibson became Bob Gibson.

Scandinavians settled this part of Nebraska, and then the Italians. By the time they left, the first worker cottages with rooms but no indoor plumbing had been constructed in Omaha, and for the next few decades, as production levels in the packing plants rose and fell precipitously, blacks began to settle in this part of the country. By the time of America's entrance into World War I, the Great Migration of African Americans out of the South had begun, and people seeking work in Omaha found it with companies named Cudahy and Wilson and Armour — all of which operated huge meatpacking plants and needed people. Between 1915 and 1920, as demand skyrocketed, these companies actually looked to Southern blacks for help, advertising a better life for those looking for a way out of the Jim Crow South. In five years, the black population of Omaha doubled, and it seemed that this might be the place where people could put their past and the injustices they had seen behind them. This was an unrealistic but uniquely American dream, built on a belief that place means everything, that a better life and a new start await somewhere else.

It was the packinghouses and their promise of a new life that brought Rodney Wead's family to Omaha. His mother's family came first from the backwoods of Pensacola, Florida, and then his father's family arrived from Helena, Arkansas. What the Weads found, in those years before public housing, was not the gilded dream but a harsh life, made harsher by the falloff of production in the packing plants following the First World War.

A lifetime later, Wead would always cringe at the thought of where they had been *before* the projects. To come to Logan Fontenelle from the squalid rooms with a makeshift kitchen was a "step up." A huge step up. For that, he would always feel fortunate. Things could have been worse. They might have moved to one of the high-rise homes that caused blight in so many sealed-off urban corridors. Yes, they were poor. But at Logan Fontenelle they had athletic facilities close by and nice lawns and good schools. Had they been in some other city, in Chicago or even St. Louis, Wead would wonder if they could even have survived.

And it was there in North Omaha that Wead would meet his best friend Bob Gibson, forming a relationship at the Kellom Elementary School that would last for the rest of their lives. Wead was in fifth grade, Gibson in fourth. Like Wead, Gibson was from a generation that initially found solace and safety in Northern public housing, unaware that it was a precursor to the new American ghetto.

As the historian David McCullough once said of Stephen Hopkins, one of the founding fathers, Bob Gibson was a young man who had seen a lot of life. He was born Pack Robert Gibson, the youngest of seven children and the last of five boys born to Pack and Victoria Gibson. Just months before Bob was born, in Omaha on November 9, 1935, his father died. Had he known what life would be like, Gibson would reflect later, he might have passed on his own existence.

"I was fatherless," Gibson said. "I was poor. I was black."

The boy Pack Gibson never knew was sickly. He had rickets and asthma, a rheumatic heart and pneumonia. There's that story that Gibson often tells. When he was three, he was in the hospital and asked a nurse if she intended on killing him. When the nurse said no, the three-year-old Bob said, "Good. Please don't kill me because my brother Josh told me that if I don't die, he'll buy me a baseball glove."

Both Josh and another Gibson brother served in World War II and on returning seemed haunted by what they witnessed there. But as with all veterans of their time, they returned as heroes. Wead in particular was excited about Josh coming back. He was the man. He was studious, completing a bachelor's degree from what is now the University of Nebraska Omaha and completing graduate work at nearby Creighton. He ran sports programs for the local YMCA, guiding young men like his brother Bob and Rodney Wead beyond the baseball field. As Wead moved through sixth, seventh, and eighth grades, he noticed that Josh always had a book in his hands.

"Take one," Josh told Wead. "Read it and come back after practice."

Which is what Wead did. This became a regular pattern for the two of them. The older Gibson would introduce him to history and literature of all kinds. The thought of Josh would always bring Wead to the brink of tears. To him, Josh was simply "everything."

But Josh, who ended up at a packing plant himself, had time to shape the lives of boys like Wead and Sayers and his brother Bob because he was denied the opportunity to pursue his vocation. That was the cold reality of race. The fact that this man with a degree from a fine Jesuit school could not find work as a teacher seems out of line with how we view America in those years following World War II. The North especially was supposed to provide the sons and daughters of those first refugees from the South with equal opportunities, not only in education but in hiring. Josh Gibson was supposed to be teaching, not laboring in the meatpacking districts. While the South embraced "separate but equal" education, the North had its own way of keeping men like Josh down.

It was this environment that Josh hoped his younger brother might escape, by whatever means he could. After Jackie Robinson, Josh said, the world was wide open to Bob, who, unlike Wead, took to sports, not books. Josh had run up against his own limits by trying to escape through education, and he told young Gibson that he needed to be a "professional man" dedicated to improving his fortunes through sport.

Thus, Bob became his project. This involved, among other things, driving Gibson and Wead and his Y "Monarchs" — the first all-black team to win the state American Legion Baseball Championship — through towns across the Midwest where black people were rarely seen. It meant working on the fundamentals of both basketball and football and drilling Bob with an intensity that inspired both fear and respect. Bob would later internalize his brother's rage and demeanor as his own.

From his conversations with Gibson, the writer Lonnie Wheeler felt that whatever "old school" attitude Gibson had — even in All-Star Games, when he wouldn't speak to others — came from Josh. Barnstorming through the Midwest with his youth teams, Bob Gibson met hostility and a steely reception wherever they went. But Wheeler felt that there was a "combative precedent" that Bob picked up from Josh, whose attitude was, "If you want to be competitive, don't take any shit."

At the same time, Bob was developing a mistrust of those not in his inner circle. Wead felt that it stemmed from self-preservation rather than meanness, a need to erect a wall against those who might seek to harm him and his family. By keeping people at arm's length, the Gibsons tried to shield themselves from those who sought to keep them down. Wead found a silent reserve in all of them. They were a cohesive unit, bound together by both Bob's mother and their own experiences in the projects. They became even more close-knit as the years went on. After high school, Wead felt there was an abrupt change in Gibson. He was quieter — even more so than before. At that point as the two men began to move forward into their early adulthood, Wead could feel his friend change forever.

· · ·

It is said that even from a great distance we can sense when someone close to us has died. Whether Denny McLain really knew his father, a strong-willed man named Tom McLain, was gone for good, he can't say for sure. But he knew something was wrong that day in May 1959. Denny was pitching for Mount Carmel, a Catholic school in the Chicago suburbs where Tom had settled with his family after the war. Tom McLain never missed one of Denny's games, but now here Denny was, age 15, pitching alone, without his father watching, for the first time in a long while.

When he finally made his way home after the game, he heard all of the details. His mother — with whom he had a fraught relationship — coldly told him that his father was dead, according to one account. According to another, he heard it from the neighbors. It didn't matter. Tom McLain — who worked as a truck driver and insurance adjuster, who'd seen his own dreams of professional baseball wiped away — was dead, at age 36, after suffering a heart attack while driving near Comiskey Park in Chicago.

Denny would spend the next three hours crying — the last tears he would shed for years, though he would later recant that account. Tom had been sure of his son's talents. How he knew was unclear. But McLain would always remember Tom waking him up one Saturday morning after reading about tryouts for Little League. Denny was only seven. At the tryout, he took somewhere between five and ten swings and hit one line drive after the next. Afterwards, when they told Tom that his boy had to be eight to play, Tom lied to make sure he did.

That sense of his son's promising future didn't assuage Tom's frightening bouts of anger. Tom McLain was a dark man, one of those fathers who drilled fear into his sons. He drank at home, and he was quick to use his belt if he heard that Denny or his brother hadn't done their homework or practiced piano — the two things he cared about other than baseball. He wanted his sons to rise above the dead-end jobs he found himself in.

"You're going to grow up to be somebody," Tom McLain would scream. "You're not going to waste your life!"

For a time, this kind of discipline had great effect. Denny continued to improve on the organ. His pitching gained a degree of notice. When

Father Austin Coupe of Mount Carmel saw Denny pitch in a play-off game, he recruited him to the school — and immediately inserted him, as a freshman, in the team's starting rotation. Everything appeared to be on track.

And then it wasn't. Over the years, McLain did his best to portray his mother as a co-conspirator in his family's misery. She was the woman who forced her husband to give up baseball, who seemed to take pleasure in the beatings Denny suffered at his father's hands. With her encouragement, Denny believed, Tom McLain took his full frustration out on his kids.

The death of his father was the defining moment of Denny's life. Now, with Tom gone, Denny decided he was on his own. He would make his own rules. This, he believed, was the start of everything to come: the bravado that made him brilliant, the recklessness that would follow him throughout his life. He believed he had to compete more. He felt insecure — both "emotionally and financially." Had his dad been around, perhaps McLain would have stayed under control. But now, with his father dead, McLain was left with a sense of impermanence, the idea that a stable life was not for him. He was a young man burning with the desire to be extraordinary, but with no one to steer him on the right course.

That Gibson would be a great ballplayer was never apparent in those early years. He played very well at multiple positions on Josh's teams, but Wead would remember that, with other pitchers ahead of him, the older Gibson would use him only sparingly to close out games. Negro League players would come in and out of Omaha without giving Bob much thought. The high school coach at Omaha Tech wouldn't even consider him for the team for his first three years there because he was black.

Of course there were signs. Gibson excelled playing American Legion Ball, mostly as a switch hitter. His former teammate Jim Morrison would later say that when Gibson did pitch, you didn't see the ball, you just heard it. It had that kind of speed, that kind of force. Gibson's raw talent drew the attention of the St. Louis Cardinals as well as the Kansas City Monarchs — once the rajas of the Negro Leagues, the Monarchs now ruled over a diminished and largely irrelevant kingdom. It's a truism that one can have all the raw talent in the world, but without the desire to do something with it, it will go to dust. Even then, Gibson had the desire. He was a young man determined to change his circumstances. The question was how.

Basketball. That was how. In Omaha Tech coach Neal Mosser, Gibson found a version of Josh and a new father figure. To start, Mosser was progressive. It was Mosser who had an all-black starting five in the state championship game, and ultimately Mosser who paid the price. In what has become a matter of legend in Nebraska, and dark testament to its racist past, within a matter of minutes during the game's second half all five of those black starters, including Gibson, had fouled out of the game. The game's outcome was determined not by the fast-moving Tech team or their methodical opponent, but by an unspoken edict. Following Tech's one-point loss, Gibson cried — the last time he would do so following an athletic loss. That game taught him something. He had grown up.

Perhaps that was the start. The birth of the calculating Gibson, untrusting and cold toward those not in his inner circle. That steeliness would have been reinforced when he received the rejection letter from Indiana. He'd done his best to attract the attention of Indiana coach Branch McCracken, having Mosser write to the championship coach himself. Eventually he received a response: the Hoosiers were denying him an athletic scholarship because they'd already "fulfilled our quota of Negroes."

Wead felt that Josh took the rejection harder than Bob himself. Bob accepted it and moved on, but "it pissed Josh off immensely." Josh had known hardship, at home and abroad. He wanted his brother to avoid all that. But Indiana — America — wouldn't let that happen. Instead, with Josh's efforts and prodding, Bob would have to settle for becoming the first black ever offered an athletic scholarship by Creighton University — the same Jesuit school where Josh had once tried to better his lot. Now another Gibson would try to do the same.

By the time Denny McLain was a senior at Mount Carmel, he was a self-assured young man with a mischievous, wry smile. He was talented and brash, free of his father's grip and largely unrestrained by his mother or her new husband. He was a young man with little concern for consequences.

Still, he was heeding the lessons of his father. He worked hard at pitching, at playing the organ, at trying to be the somebody that his father had said he would be even while beating Denny half to death. He won 38 games in high school, losing only seven times. And while it isn't uncommon for great high school athletes to hold themselves in high regard, even then his hubris hampered the camaraderie he might have shared with his teammates. His success was his alone.

Father Ben Hogan and his baseball coach, Father Austin Coupe, tried again and again to connect with Denny. Nothing worked. When the team won championships in McLain's junior and senior years, he failed to win the clinching game. By then, Coupe felt that McLain's teammates had grown to resent him. They wanted to win—but they didn't want to do it with McLain.

But Coupe believed in McLain and wanted the best for him, even if his classmates did not. This was never more apparent than when Coupe tried to talk McLain into accepting a scholarship from Notre Dame. Though major league scouts were circling him, offering immediate financial rewards, Coupe tried to tell him, in vain, that "this is a once-in-a-lifetime opportunity."

"You're going to be the number-one guy forever," Coupe told him. "Unless someone offers you a zillion dollars, you gotta go to Notre Dame. You gotta go to Notre Dame. You can always sign after your first year, your second year. It's your decision to make, but I'd sure like you to go to college."

"I can still go to college in the off-season," McLain replied.

"You'll never do it," Coupe said.

He never did. Instead, he and his mother sat in their suburban home waiting for major league scouts to come make their offers. McLain knew that his mother didn't care that he would be the first of his family to go to college. She didn't see what benefit he might glean from being at the grand epicenter of Catholic education. Just as he blamed her for shorting out his father's baseball career, McLain held her responsible for depriving him of a college degree and the opportunities it could have opened up beyond baseball. She was interested in money, he felt, but not him.

Yet who could blame her? They'd long suffered from financial stress. But McLain's mother wasn't interested in the first scout from the Yankees who came to the house, no matter how much money he was willing to offer. She wouldn't say why. McLain had long wanted to play for New York because he loved Mickey Mantle. Hell, didn't everyone? But his mother refused to take the scout's check, leaving the man without a solid reason. Years later, he discovered the reason when he approached McLain at Comiskey Park in Chicago.

"Why didn't you sign with me?" the scout said. "I heard you signed for the same money with the White Sox."

"You had a hole in the bottom of your shoe," McLain told him.

"What?"

"You came in a Cadillac," McLain explained. "You had a beautiful suit on, and when you sat down and crossed your legs, there was a hole the size of a half-dollar in the bottom of your shoe."

McLain's mother believed this detail was telling. If he couldn't afford a pair of decent shoes, how would he make good on his promise? Would the checks actually cash? Did he actually have any money? The next man who walked in, Ed Short—who ran the White Sox organization—arrived with a check in the same amount. But he wore a simple suit, and he arrived in a Buick, not a Cadillac. McLain's mother believed that showed responsibility.

"That's who we're signing with," she told her son. "Take that check." So he did.

There wasn't much to say about Creighton's baseball program when Bill Fitch arrived on the scene in 1956. Like Bob Gibson, he had come primarily for basketball, to work with his old college coach, a man by the name of Tommy Thomsen, who was now the head coach of Creighton's basketball team. Fitch was a country boy who'd grown up in Cedar Rapids. A fine athlete who played basketball and baseball at Coe College, and an almost-priest, he would later become one of those NBA coaches who move from one team to the next, sometimes finding great players to help steer—Larry Bird, Hakeem Olajuwon—and other times just muddling through with some of the worst teams ever seen.

But that life — the arenas, the championships, the Clippers — was still a world away. For now, he was just the assistant coach of a basketball team in the heartland, at a college just blocks from the projects where Gibson grew up. By the time he was a senior, Gibson had already established himself as a star. At six-one, he played with the adeptness of someone much taller, and with speed and an ability to find the ball. As John McPhee once wrote of Princeton's Bill Bradley, he had a sense of where he was on the basketball court.

But already robbed of a state high school championship and a chance to play at Indiana because of his race, Gibson found further frustration closer to home. In one incident he was told, as the lone black player, that he couldn't stay with the rest of the team in Tulsa. Teammate Glenn Sullivan — once his white friend from his old neighborhood — stood up and told his coaches that he would stay with Gibson when the other players would not. But Gibson said no; he wanted to "curse in private."

When Fitch met Gibson, what the coach saw in him wasn't bitterness, but a competitive spirit and tenacity the likes of which he wouldn't see again until decades later. Gibson was a young man who would not accept defeat in anything. In a coaching career that would span well into the late 1990s, Fitch would see only two men who were so fierce, so determined. One was Gibson. The other was Larry Bird.

In later years, one game would come to define Gibson in Fitch's mind. Late in the contest, a couple of players made a racial remark to Gibson, the kind he had dealt with all those years barnstorming in baseball. From that moment, it was over. Gibson, Fitch would remember, outscored the other team for the last two to three minutes. That was a lesson for anyone studying Bob Gibson. Don't mess with him — not like that. If you believed there was a "fire burning" in Gibson, Fitch would later joke, "there's Dynamite there if you roll it the wrong way."

Fitch could see what he had with Gibson the basketball player. But he didn't really know what to do with Gibson during the 1957 baseball season. Gibson has written that he played his most serious baseball in the summers, when he played semipro ball in towns as far-flung as Crofton, Nebraska, and Chamberlain, South Dakota. Gibson's pitching total for his years at Creighton were only 6-2, though in his final season he did bat .333. Fitch always felt he could put Gibson in the outfield, let him man shortstop, or have him pinch-run, since he could outrun any man on the team.

Whenever anyone speaks about Gibson, they speak of his potential to be something else. Meadowlark Lemon, Gibson's roommate in his one season with the Harlem Globetrotters, often felt that Gibson was ready for the NBA — a belief Gibson shared, though he never believed he would be a star. There are those who still wonder what might have happened had Gibson devoted himself to track or, had he been born in another era, to football. Rodney Wead believed that Gibson would have led St. Louis to more pennants had he stayed an outfielder, where he felt Gibson was better suited. Gibson would bristle at this suggestion, of course, but Wead didn't care.

In their brief time together, Fitch and Gibson worked diligently on his pitching and on his control. Fitch believed that young pitchers didn't know how to use the mound or the rubber to advantage. They would come off it — as Gibson did — short and off balance. Fitch showed Gibson that placing a newspaper there, watching where your cleats land, helps establish a body movement consistent with your throwing motion. Those batters in Gibson's major league future who would come to believe he was wild were wrong, dead wrong. He knew where that ball was moving. And he knew that the hitter was scared.

On July 15, 1956, when Gibson was playing semipro ball in Chamberlain, South Dakota, a scout named Frank Fahey wrote out an evaluation card, which is preserved to this day in the Baseball Hall of Fame. After observing Gibson for one game, Fahey described him as a "Colored boy" who had a "Good loose arm" and good arm speed. He said Gibson's hitting was poor, his running very good. Gibson's main weaknesses, Fahey said, were inexperience and lack of control.

"This boy attends Creighton," Fahey wrote. "He has not much pitching experience but has nice loose arm and can throw hard."

According to Gibson, the Yankees said he wasn't worthy of a spot on a Class D ball roster, and the Dodgers scout scoffed at the very idea of him pitching in the major leagues. But Fitch said that Gibson got plenty of attention in those days. Anytime there was a free period, he would see someone "looking at Gib."

Gibson was very much his own man then, a sought-after player whose unorthodox pitching style had an upside that no one had seen the likes of. When scouts would come for a look, Fitch, who had made extra money playing semipro ball himself, acted as Gibson's personal catcher. And each time Fitch caught him, he could see the young man improve with his location, with his control. When a scout from the moribund Kansas City Athletics came to see him, Gibson impressed the scout as well as Fitch with both his fastball and his curve. There was no way, Fitch believed, the A's wouldn't sign him. He could start for Kansas City right now. But no offer came.

An *actual* offer, Fitch would later recall, came from Cincinnati scout Phil Seghi. Seghi—who later, as the team's farm director, signed Pete Rose and as Cleveland general manager would sign Frank Robinson to be baseball's first black manager—liked what he'd seen from Gibson and tried for the hard sell. There was a young, intelligent player Gibson could room with, he said, an outfielder of supreme talent.

"If you come to Cincinnati, we've got a guy at our farm club in Savannah," Seghi told Gibson. "You two would room together, the two of you will be a good combination."

Watching this, Fitch believed, really believed, that Gibson would become a starting pitcher for Cincinnati. Little did he know that Bill Bergesch, the general manager of the Omaha Cardinals at the time, had made a deal with Bob Gibson and his brother Josh. The deal was for a $1,000 bonus, with an additional $3,000 for the season. That money, Gibson believed, combined with the salary he earned in his brief stint with the Globetrotters, was enough not only to start his life as a young married man—in the spring of 1957 he had married his high school sweetheart, a light-skinned, progressive-minded girl named Charlene— but to keep him active in both sports.

That wouldn't last. And after the 1957 season, Cincinnati would trade the diminutive young outfielder Seghi had mentioned, Curt Flood, to St. Louis—where he would indeed change not only Gibson's life, as the Cincinnati scout had predicted, but the trajectory of Major League Baseball itself.

3

RISING

I'M NOT HERE TO STAY," said the handsome, doughy boy when he approached his teammates on the Tigers' minor league team in Knoxville, Tennessee. The first day Willie Horton met Denny McLain, the pitcher was wearing a short mink coat, and with it that sense of invincibility and cockiness that would carry him through life, even after he had lost everything and his gleaming accomplishments had been long overshadowed by darker deeds.

"If you want to get out of here, you better get on my coattails," McLain said to the stunned group that day. "We're going to the big leagues."

Horton thought it was that belief in himself, unwavering and resolute, that separated McLain from other pitchers. It was a quality that turned others off, but Horton admired it even then. You had to trust in your own abilities, your own fortitude, if you were going to get out of the minors. Otherwise, you'd find yourself stuck — or worse, out of the game.

If McLain had been short on talent, that scene — the coat, the proclamation — would have seemed laughable. But that wasn't the case. McLain had everything, it seemed to Horton. He had perfect control from day one. He could tell you to put a matchbox on the ground and then hit it from 60 feet, six inches away. He threw pitches that batters could hit — but not well. McLain believed in the players behind him. With every pitch, he seemed to be saying: *I'm giving my best, now you make me look good.*

In 1962, just hours after his high school graduation, McLain had left home, taking a plane at a time when airplane travel was the transport of the very rich, only to find himself in what seemed like a faraway land, a place that seemed to him wholly apart from modern American life. This was Harlan, Kentucky, where he was reporting to the Appalachian Rookie League. Even on that first day, even as a kid being paid to play baseball, it didn't seem like enough.

Though it should have been. In his very first start for the White Sox affiliate, McLain threw a no-hitter against Salem in hot, humid conditions — heat like he'd never known before. Yet he soldiered on and won, striking out 16. And so it reappeared — that sense of entitled recklessness that had first surfaced after his father's death. In high school he'd been free to do whatever he wanted. Why should he change now?

Soon after that sensational debut, he skipped out on training and drove 15 hours to see a girl he'd started dating in high school, leaving his team in a quasi-panic. He returned just in time for the next game. An average player might have been punished. But in two starts McLain had proven that he was better than average, at least by minor league standards. He had no sense of restraint or responsibility. Even when he was promoted to the team's club in Clinton, Iowa, he refused to stay put or to devote any time to developing another pitch beyond his fastball. His manager, Ira Hutchinson — who saw hitters waiting for his fastball, particularly on 3-2 counts — tried to impress upon him the need to advance beyond the raw materials he'd come with. The hitters in the Midwest League battered him in a way he'd never known before. But he still continued to show the big league team just enough, which he felt gave him license to come and go as he pleased. He was fined for his disappearances, only to disappear again.

"He thought he was king of everything," Hutchinson would say later. "You couldn't talk to him."

Lack of focus and a breaking ball left him vulnerable when he arrived at the White Sox spring training camp in 1963. At the time, teams were forced to put so-called bonus babies — players who'd received bonuses over $4,000 — on the major league roster after only one year of minor league service. The White Sox looked over their roster and saw that they had three such players. All of them were pitchers; besides McLain, they had Bruce Howard and Dave DeBusschere, who would eventually join the NBA. All three showed great talent, if not resolve. From the outset, the club was determined to keep DeBusschere, which left McLain and Howard to face each other in a pitch-off. The winner would stay with the big club, and the loser would be sent down, to serve as fodder for other teams.

For all his self-confidence, McLain came into the game nervous about the outcome. In the days leading up to the game, White Sox manager Al Lopez had taken McLain aside, telling him, "Out of the three guys, you have the least ability."

"Excuse me," replied McLain, whose ability had never been in doubt. "I don't know what you mean by that."

"You throw pretty hard," Lopez said, "but I don't think you'll ever learn how to throw a breaking ball. I'm not sure about your control. But in all fairness, we're going to give you a chance."

That Saturday morning McLain found himself pitching not for a championship but for something far more important: his career. Had he won that contest, had he stayed with the White Sox, he might have become a local boy done good, a Chicago icon. But a home run served to Dave Nicholson and a one-run loss to Howard changed all that. Within half an hour after he'd showered and walked away from the clubhouse, a lost man, he was ready to return home to suburban Illinois.

What kept him from following through was a phone call to his soon-to-be wife, a black-haired beauty named Sharyn Boudreau, the daughter of Lou Boudreau, the player-manager, now retired, who had led Cleveland past Johnny Sain in the 1948 World Series. In truth, Sharyn and Denny didn't have much in common outside of baseball. He was the wild, untamed son of a struggling household. She was the daughter of baseball royalty. But because they were young and because he was charming and confident and because she was already inclined to marry a ballplayer, they fell for each other — despite her mother's ominous warning that she should never end up with a pitcher, because "all you're going to do is worry."

This didn't stop her from accepting his proposal on New Year's Eve of 1962, just weeks after they first began dating. Now, months later, they faced their first test together. He wanted to quit, he said, call it a day, return home. The signing bonus had cost him Notre Dame and a chance perhaps for a fuller, more satisfying life. His baseball career seemed over. He was ready to grow up, to take responsibility, to accept life as a regular man in a regular world. Yet Sharyn would have none of it.

"Don't come home," she said, after Denny had poured out his frustrations. "I won't be here."

"What the hell do you mean by that?"

"I don't want a quitter," she said.

Marrying her, McLain would later say, was "the smartest thing I ever did. Without her, I'd be in real trouble. I'm reckless enough, but she keeps me in line." But no one could keep Denny in line. Had she made good on her promise to leave him, Sharyn might have saved herself a lot of future heartache.

Their real troubles were all in front of them. This was still 1963, when, with one phone call, Sharyn had convinced McLain to stay the course. As it happened, she didn't have to. After Denny left the clubhouse, a White Sox executive told him that someone from Detroit would be coming to get him within the hour. That man was Ed Katalinas, a jowly scout from the Tigers who signed not only McLain but also Hall of Fame outfielder Al Kaline.

"Are you ready to go and be a major league pitcher?" said Katalinas, who'd kept a careful eye on McLain in Clinton.

"Yes, sir, I am," McLain said. Before long, he would be standing in the locker room in Knoxville dressed in that fur coat, and by summer's end he would make good on his promise of making it to the big league club. In time, he would lead Horton and the others who followed him to the majors to far greater heights than any of them could have imagined then.

The traumatic experience of being dropped in an unexpected place didn't happen to Bob Gibson — at first. Following his decision to sign with the Cardinals, Gibson stayed in Omaha with the Cardinals' Triple A affiliate. There he found the man who would help put everything together for him. Johnny Keane, the manager of the Omaha club, had witnessed Gibson's tryout for the Cardinals. Keane and general manager Bill Bergesch had both been blown away by the combination of hitting and pitching skills that Gibson had displayed in his tryout. It seemed unreal the way Gibson could drive the ball over the outfield, and just as unreal was the delivery of his fastball, which even then showed a great deal of movement.

Yet for all his skill, his baseball future seemed unchartable. The game's history is littered with talented players who couldn't perform consistently over a full season. So as an athlete who still vacillated between two sports (he played with the Harlem Globetrotters in 1957), Gibson was fortunate to fall under the tutelage of Keane, a career minor leaguer who nearly entered the priesthood, a man with a great deal of patience and warm feeling toward those he coached. Gibson has called him a perfect human being, a saint among men. At his first practice in Omaha, Gibson threw batting practice, and time and again, even the most seasoned players failed to hit the ball out of the cage. Keane told him to show them his curveball, which had the same effect.

"Should I start throwing hard?" Gibson asked. Keane, clearly pleased, told him that he was doing just fine.

But even under Keane's watchful eye, Gibson got off to a bumpy start. In his first appearance for Omaha, throwing what he called "soft strikes," Gibson gave up three runs. In his next outing, with runners on second and third, Gibson drove the runners in himself with consecutive wild pitches. What Keane saw was a pitcher who was unnerved and needed to focus on the velocity that had led the Cardinals to sign him in the first place. Over the course of 12 games in his first minor league experience, Gibson went 2-1, giving up 46 hits in 42 innings. At that moment, it seemed that the scouts who hadn't seen what Keane and Bergesch had seen in Gibson possibly had a point.

Before the season's end came a demotion to the Sally League and the Cardinals' club in Columbus, Georgia. Why it seemed like a good idea to send black ballplayers to Southern towns still years away from integration is anybody's guess. The abuse was unfathomable. The taunts. The black cats. The threats. Gibson had to live in a YMCA in the black section of town and put up with fans calling him "Gator Bait." He would not learn the vile, racist meaning of this slur until later: it referred to the disputed practice of hunters using African American babies to lure alligators from the swamp.

Like Henry Aaron and other black players, Gibson was willing to deal with anything. As Aaron said decades later, "It wasn't something that you talked about if you were going to make it to the major leagues. You just had to, you know, buck up."

The letters he wrote to Rodney Wead during this time showed Gibson at his lowest point, unsure of himself and his skills. These were dispatches from a desperate man suffused with anger and frustration about his inability to hit with power when he came to the plate, about his total wildness when he pitched. He was at a loss.

Showing little in the way of improvement, Gibson ended this brief, tumultuous run with a 4-3 record. No game illustrated Gibson's ineptitude at that time better than his September start against Cincinnati's Sally League team from Savannah, Georgia, which featured Curt Flood, the small, intense outfielder whom the Reds had plucked from the Oakland ghetto. After recording two outs, Gibson subsequently walked five batters, including Flood, and failed to close out the first inning. It would have been easy to walk away from baseball after a performance like that, to take a job at one of the meatpacking plants and move on. But like McLain, Gibson stuck it out.

The following spring in Florida, Gibson would see Flood again — this time at the rooming house set aside for black players in segregated St. Petersburg at the Cardinals' 1958 rookie camp. The Reds had traded Flood, their talented but seemingly expendable outfielder, the previous winter. Now here he was, alongside Gibson, the man whom Fitch had claimed Gibson might have been paired with on the Reds.

After an interminable train ride from Omaha to Florida, Gibson had walked to the hotel where he thought he'd be staying. He was part of the Cardinals organization, after all, and this was where the Cardinals stayed. But not Gibson or Flood or "Sad" Sam Jones or any of the Cardinals who were black. The same humiliating scene played out over and over again. The arrival at the hotel. The quick declaration that you're forbidden by law from staying with your white teammates. The cab waiting to take you to a rooming house on the black side of town. The discovery of your fellow black players in the same diminished accommodations. The god-awful feeling that despite all of your talent, baseball, supposedly the great American game, has let you down.

"From the time someone made me stay in the colored section when the white kids stayed on the beach," Flood later said, "I felt like a nigger."

While it's often said that Jackie Robinson's integration of baseball was as important an event as any in the modern era of civil rights, the failure on the part of the clubs to fully integrate — to make black players feel welcome at a time when the very best talent on the very best teams all seemed to be black — would cast a dark shadow over the game well into the early 1960s.

That black and white players lived separate and unequal lives was a fact sometimes lost on even the most forward-thinking teammates. When Jim Maloney, one of the top pitchers in the National League during the 1960s, first came to the Reds from California, he was just 19 and admittedly "green around the ears." He didn't know what segregation really was. He thought it was strange that he'd see stars like Vada Pinson and Frank Robinson at the park and then find no trace of them at night.

When told they were staying in a different part of town, away from their teammates, Maloney called his father in California, telling him, "Hey, this is unbelievable."

Maloney would begin to truly understand the experience of black players one night at a dog-racing track between Tampa and St. Petersburg. Robinson had told Maloney and some others that he would see them there that night. The young man was excited. This was Frank Robinson, the man who'd come out of the same impoverished conditions in Oakland as Curt Flood to reach All-Star status in the National League. He wanted to talk to Robinson about the nuances of what it took to not only make a major league roster but to excel on one. But once Maloney arrived at the track, Robinson was nowhere to be found.

After searching out the stands, he asked his teammates, "Where's Frank Robinson? Where does he hang out?'"

"He's over there," someone told him, "on the other side of that fence."

Maloney looked at the scene. Across a chain-link fence, the African Americans were fenced in, separated from the entire grandstand. When he walked over, he found Robinson, the Hall of Fame player to be. Now

one of the soon-to-be great pitchers of his time spoke to one of its greatest hitters — through a physical, dehumanizing divide.

Beyond these social conditions, Gibson had other things to overcome. First was his inability to throw strikes, to make that fierce energy
with which he threw the ball actually work for him. In his first big league
appearance in 1959, against the Dodgers, he pitched in relief and gave up
back-to-back home runs. In 1960, he walked five men for every nine innings he pitched, and his ERA was a god-awful 5.59. He was miserable.
He'd come from the ghetto and had reached the game's highest level, but
he was in a rut — he couldn't win.

Then there was his first big league manager, Solly Hemus. A longtime middle infielder, Hemus had managed to stick around the major leagues for 11 seasons, beginning with the Cardinals in 1949. In the
modern parlance of sport, he might be described as scrappy, a gym rat,
someone whose work ethic and "hustle" helped him overcome his physical limitations. This would be code, of course, for a less talented player,
nearly always white.

Hemus had ingratiated himself with Cardinals owner and beer mo-
gul August A. Busch Jr., or "Gussie." Following his trade to the Phillies
in 1956, Hemus wrote to Bush, gushing over how much he had enjoyed
playing for the team, how the Cardinals really were a first-class outfit,
how he was sorry to leave but hoped that one day he could return. Unfortunately for Gibson, that day came in 1959 when Hemus returned as
a player-manager, the fifth skipper of Busch's eight-year regime.

Gibson felt that he could never trust Hemus. Hemus held meetings
with the other pitchers — the white pitchers — during which they'd discuss strategy, without considering Gibson's input. More than once he
told Gibson and Flood that maybe baseball just wasn't for them, that
they should walk away from the sport altogether. One terrible and telling incident has come to define Hemus. During a game against the Pirates in 1959, Hemus inserted himself into the lineup and was hit by a
stray pitch. He then turned on the Pirates' black pitcher, Bennie Daniels,
calling him either a "black son of a bitch" or "black bastard." Gibson and
others believed that this moment revealed Hemus's truest self as a racist.
That racism blinded him to the talent of his black players.

As some have noted, Hemus was also from an era when managers loomed over their players, believing they could bully them into playing better. But that overbearing, militaristic attitude didn't work with men like Gibson and Bill White, who had gone to college, who had seen more of the world than just baseball, and who demanded to be treated as men rather than 12-year-olds.

Whatever the reasons, Bob Gibson pitched terribly under Hemus and was never really part of the starting rotation. He was pulled back and forth between the minor league team and St. Louis. Hemus, Tim McCarver would later recount, felt that Gibson would never make a big league pitcher because he threw "everything at the same speed."

It was during this time that pitcher Mel Nelson first met Gibson, in Omaha during one of the pitcher's demotions. Nelson marveled at Gibson's arm and believed, as others had, that if Gibson could find some measure of control and discover a way to hit his corners, it would all be over for those who faced him.

Nelson felt there was something going on with Gibson. He noticed that Gibson was closely studying another of their teammates, a man in his early thirties who, at six feet, was a brooding, dark, intimidating figure. Years before, the Kansas City Monarchs had sold Frank Barnes to the New York Yankees along with Elston Howard. While the latter rose to be not only the first black to play alongside the likes of Mickey Mantle and Yogi Berra but also an MVP and perennial All-Star, Barnes languished. He threw no-hitters, but posted only solid, not spectacular, minor league records. In 1957, while with Omaha, Barnes led the American Association with a 2.41 ERA, while throwing 41⅓ innings of scoreless baseball — enough to earn him garbage time with the Cardinals. Though Barnes would have other chances in 1958 and 1960, he seemed destined to stay just below the surface of big league baseball. (Barnes would pitch for 17 years in the minor leagues before finishing his career in the Mexican League at the age of 45.)

Nelson felt that Gibson's interest in Barnes had less to do with how Barnes pitched than with Barnes's demeanor, the anger and intimidation Barnes brought to the mound. Barnes could be unforgiving, Nelson felt, particularly toward black hitters. He would frequently use the brushback pitch, even if it instigated a fight. He had an "old school" attitude: it was a hitter's privilege to play against him, and if the hitter tried to cheat or engaged in any antics, there'd be a price to pay. This was what Gibson took away from Barnes, Nelson felt — a belief in his ownership of the plate.

At a time when National League owners accepted black stars but seldom listened to them, it was Gibson's good fortune to land with the Cardinals. Though St. Louis was late to integrate — this was the team that was rumored to have planned a walkout in 1947 to protest Jackie Robinson's entrance into the game — the Cardinals under Busch made sincere, aggressive efforts to catch up to other teams like the Dodgers and Giants, whose raids of the Negro Leagues had resulted in pennants.

The result was a team that was progressive for its era, one on which black players often led the way. George Crowe, a player who endured unrelenting racism during his nine-year career, took Gibson under his wing and worked tirelessly with all young players, regardless of race, to improve their game. It was a team led by men like Bill White — later a premier broadcaster and then president of the American League — who forced the integration in 1961 of a previously whites-only banquet held by local St. Petersburg businessmen during spring training for the Yankees and Cardinals. While other black players resigned themselves to separate living quarters, black players on the Cardinals forced the hand of Gussie Busch, who solved the problem when a friend bought a local motel and Busch leased rooms from an adjoining one. Whatever one thought of the tyrannical Busch, who initially saw owning the team merely as a marketing tool for Anheuser-Busch, he had made it a model of racial progress in a state that would come to it slowly.

But none of this would have made a difference for Gibson's career had the Cardinals not forced Hemus from their ranks soon after Independence Day in 1961, promoting Johnny Keane to his managerial post. Keane had managed Gibson in Omaha in 1957 and then again in 1958, and as a coach on Hemus's major league staff, he had watched Gibson struggle when he arrived in St. Louis in 1959. The Gibson Keane first saw in that first practice session in Omaha — brimming with potential — was now a player handcuffed by his own insecurities.

Keane picked up where Josh Gibson left off. He told Gibson not to worry, that he'd stay in the rotation, that he'd give him a fair chance to make good. Gibson, in turn, rewarded Keane by going 11-6 for the rest of the year. The writer Lonnie Wheeler believed that Keane didn't make any fundamental changes to Gibson's delivery. Keane believed his job was to show confidence in Gibson, which was never Josh's approach. Josh had driven his brother to a level of competition that possibly no other pitcher could ever match. Now it was Keane's job to coax him, whisper into his ear. Josh got him there, Wheeler would say, but Keane took Gibson to the next level.

As Gibson's catcher Tim McCarver has pointed out, Keane could also be critical and demanding, saying the very same things Hemus probably said to Gibson. But because Gibson trusted Keane, and because the intention behind those words seemed so different, Gibson was willing to listen.

Gibson's sense of confidence — his belief that he not only belonged in the big leagues but could overpower major league hitters — was helped by Keane's conduit, the young catcher Tim McCarver. Over the years McCarver has spoken about the impact on him of his experience with the Cardinals. A Southerner from Memphis, the son of a policeman, and a bonus baby who received $75,000 upon signing with the Cardinals, McCarver had never played "against a black player, much less played with one." Yet Gibson clearly saw something in McCarver, teasing him, yelling at him, both taking him under his wing and admonishing him when he saw fit.

There was the time Gibson tested the young McCarver on a bus trip by asking for a lick of an ice cream cone or a swig of his orange soda, something McCarver could never imagine a black man doing. Then there was an uglier incident, early in their careers together, when Mc-Carver saw a young black boy in spring training jump over the fence to grab a foul ball. Depending on whose account you believe, McCarver called him out as either a "little cannibal" or a "nigger." Gibson recalled getting "right up in McCarver's face" and telling him "what I thought of his language, his mother, his hometown, his catching ability, and anything else I could think of."

Gibson felt comfortable pushing McCarver around, especially early on when Keane would send McCarver out to the mound to try to slow Gibson down. Keane, understandably, believed it was his duty to manage the pace of the game. But Gibson would have none of it, sending Mc-

Carver back before he could even approach the mound, belittling him by yelling, "What the hell are you doing out here? Get the hell back behind the plate where you belong. The only thing you know about pitching is that you can't hit it."

Gibson believed that he wasn't rushing at all, that he was working at his normal pace. The rest of the world, including McCarver, was trying to slow him down. Gibson had a quiet, unspoken way of telling him, "Don't come out here." McCarver did his best to oblige.

But to see McCarver merely as someone Gibson could bully into letting him pitch the way he wanted is to underestimate their shared intensity and desire to win. McCarver grew up in a tough Memphis neighborhood where he watched his classmates and teammates get into "serious trouble" and sometimes end up in jail. He credited his father, whose sternness helped McCarver reach his athletic potential, with enabling him to avoid this fate. Like Gibson, McCarver seemed gifted at every sport he touched. And like Gibson, McCarver brought a great deal of toughness to everything he did — a toughness that led one teammate to call him a "positive tyrant."

"Sometimes we used to consider throwing beer all over him," the player said.

In time, perhaps because of Gibson's admonishments, McCarver came to understand his place as the catcher. Sure, part of his job was to call for pitches based on the batter and the men on base, on the number of outs, and on how well or poorly a hitter had done against his guy, but ultimately the decision to throw a pitch belonged to the man on the mound, and to him alone. McCarver was willing to trust the pitcher "to throw the pitch he wants because it's his ball game."

Besides, McCarver had enough trouble just catching the ball. Gibson's whirlwind delivery would send him flying off to the first-base side of the mound, an exposed pitcher. A player of lesser athletic ability would have compromised his ability to field a ball that might come bouncing up the middle or shooting off to the opposite side. But that wasn't how Gibson saw it. His job was to deliver the toughest pitch to hit. Should the batter actually make contact, the rest would take care of itself.

While Gibson's feverish, fantastic delivery remains something special and indelible in the minds of those who saw it live — as well as for

those of us who watch it now in blurry black-and-white video clips —
in many ways it was a variation on a theme of the great pitchers of that
era. The common denominator was the large windup: the pitcher would
reach high above his head before throwing the ball. Koufax used it. So
did Drysdale and Marichal and Maloney. It was a motion that took a
great deal of physical strength; Gibson's contemporary Jim Kaat believed
that it originated in a more athletic era when all pitchers grew up playing different positions, hitting and running, and so had a variety of motions at their disposal. As a result, Kaat felt, pitchers' deliveries seemed
far more unique and robust than the mechanical deliveries seen today.

In the years following the explosive home run year of 1961, led by
Roger Maris and Mickey Mantle, the big windup helped give birth to
the golden age of pitching. So did the heightening of the mound from
10 to 15 inches off the ground, as well as the expansion of the strike zone
in the National League. Marichal could release the ball from a seemingly infinite number of arm angles, and Maloney was deemed the hardest thrower of the group, but Gibson and Koufax had fastballs without
peer. Koufax's fastball had that rise to it as it approached hitters, while
Gibson's ball moved and sunk in on batters, running into them. As Gibson's teammate and bridge partner Dick Groat described it, both pitchers could "knock the bat out of your hand."

Gibson mastered the pitch that Stan Musial, perhaps the best hitter
of all time, said changed the game forever. This was the modern slider.
And no one — save Gibson's teammate, and pupil, Steve Carlton — threw
a better one than him. At its release, it looked very much like a fastball coming out of the hand, then came the quick break at the end of
it. It wasn't as big as Koufax's curveball, which would fall straight down
in front of a batter; instead, it sailed away from right-handed hitters at
great speed, giving them no chance to make adjustments.

It's often said that Gibson and Koufax were opposites when it came
to pitching style. Yet both were wild when they first arrived in the major leagues. When Bill White introduced Gibson, wearing the glasses he
wore off but not on the field, to Willie Mays in San Francisco, the Hall of
Famer shrieked after finding out who he was.

"Who the hell is that?" Mays asked.

"That's Gibson," White said.

"Gibson!" Mays yelled. "Gibson wears glasses? Why don't you wear 'em when you pitch for God's sake? Shit, man, you're gonna kill somebody!"

Gibson would never wear the glasses on the mound. He was coming into his own, increasing his win total and innings pitched with each year Keane managed. Though he hurt himself late into the Cardinals' pennant drive of 1963, at the start of the 1964 season it became apparent that he was no longer the guy with a potential future; he was the player who could best lead the team to better fortunes.

But throwing strikes and taming his wildness were only small parts of Gibson's maturation into an elite pitcher. Just as important was his on-field persona, which he had been molding since watching Frank Barnes in Omaha and maybe even before. Sandy Koufax too was famously private. He didn't like to sign autographs, and he could be cold to fans who sought him out in restaurants. The way Koufax tried to straddle stardom reminded some of Joe DiMaggio, who let few people into his circle. Even as he dated and married movie stars, DiMaggio longed for privacy and an interior life away from the crowds, who thronged to him and who felt that, by the mere act of watching him hit, they knew him.

Once, sitting at a restaurant following an important win, Marichal completely lost it, according to one writer present. He was coming off a particularly bad stretch during which he'd felt besieged by fans who always demanded great things from him and showed an almost violent displeasure when they didn't get it. Now, with the restaurant cheering him on after his most recent triumph, according to the journalist, Marichal finally "broke."

"Phonies," he said — though he would later deny the remark. "Where were they when I needed them, when I was losing those early games? They were at the park booing me, writing letters saying I'm a bum."

Later, he said that the "trouble with baseball is that always they want more, more, more . . . without thinking of what suffering they bring to a player who happens to be down."

Gibson didn't bother camouflaging his contempt for sportswriters. Long before, his mother had warily looked out from their home in the Logan Fontenelle Projects, and Gibson never truly let go of the same dim view of outsiders, of the potentially menacing forces that sought to

swoop in and wreck everything he had built. What did he owe them after all? He'd conquered his self-doubts, and he'd continued to win and
progress each year under Keane's steady hand. But now he was caught
between two eras — the old era, when the press let you keep your distance if you chose not to speak to them, and the new era, when they
never let you go.

He relished it, his friend Lonnie Wheeler felt. At one point Gibson
made a conscious effort to make a career of noncooperation. Years after
his playing career had ended, Gibson arrived in Cincinnati to talk to the
Green Diamond Gallery, a private club that houses invaluable baseball
artifacts and whose annual dues are $2,400; in fact, it costs $500 just to
be put on the wait-list. Wheeler, who lived nearby, was asked to introduce Gibson to a paying audience there. Profane and edgy, Gibson made
no effort to even fake friendship, though he was paid handsomely. But
that was what he enjoyed. Being disagreeable worked for him.

And that was the older, "mellower" Gibson. As a player, Gibson believed that fraternizing with his opponents would undermine his intimidating presence. Famously, he never spoke to opposing players, even
at All-Star Games — including one in 1965 when he rebuffed his catcher
Joe Torre after Torre insisted that Gibson throw a pitch that Gibson believed was the wrong call. To win, to stay in the majors and reach elite
status, meant barricading himself behind a fierce persona — a pitcher
who glared into the eyes of his catcher, who had no misgivings about
brushing you off or knocking you down should you try to upset his advantage. As close as he was to his teammates, most of whom found him
both funny and introspective, a colleague in the very best sense, he remained an enigma to others — purposeful and haunting, someone not to
cross. That he was black only seemed to make him appear, unfairly, that
much more menacing.

Despite his emergence as a top-flight pitcher, it wasn't until the remarkable year of 1964 that Bob Gibson reached the summit, taking his
place alongside Koufax and Drysdale and Marichal — all of whom had
already played in the World Series. This was the year the Yankee dynasty
died, the Chicago Cubs reconfirmed their curse, and the Phillies simply
laid down in one of the greatest collapses in baseball history. Instrumen-
tal was the Cardinals' midseason trade for Lou Brock, the much-ma-

ligned Chicago outfielder. Brock's speed and daring would help ignite the Cardinals' offense as they overtook Philadelphia for the pennant. But it was Gibson's confidence in his own arm that truly propelled the team toward its historic finish.

It helped that Gibson loved playing for that 1964 team. In a summer when the very best undergraduates from the very best schools in the North traveled to Mississippi to register thousands of disenfranchised blacks, the St. Louis Cardinals looked very much like the integrated America these young people risked their lives for. They were different from other teams at that time: in Cincinnati, for instance, black players occupied a separate orbit from their white teammates, and in San Francisco racial and ethnic factions may have prevented one of the most talented teams of its era from reaching its potential. As Gibson wrote, the 1964 Cardinals "not only believed in each other but generally *liked* each other." They discussed their racial issues in the open and cajoled one another. Gibson later declared that he was never "around a better band of men than the '64 Cardinals."

Whatever warm feelings Gibson expressed toward his teammates, however, he kept hidden from public view. The press — even George Vecsey, who actively sought out black players to speak with — found only the public Gibson. Cold. Untrusting. While Vecsey enjoyed speaking to the team's other African American players — specifically Curt Flood and Bill White and Lou Brock — he desperately wanted to reach out to Gibson, who fascinated him. But he never could.

Had it not been for Gibson, who helped lead the charge to the pennant, and had Philadelphia not folded just as the Cardinals and the Reds began to surge in late August, the Cardinals' biracial success story would have come to nothing. Just another feel-good tale about a team that tried its very best but didn't have what it took to win a championship.

As late as August 23, the Cardinals seemed headed for just such a fate. Morale was low with the dismissal of the man who had built the team, general manager Bing Devine, and very public rumors swirled that the irascible Leo Durocher was ready to step into Keane's spot. The Phillies had an 11-game lead. The Cardinals had every reason to fail, but because the Phillies seemed destined to do the same — losing their final 10 games — the Cards held on.

Gibson began his start on August 24 with a mere 10-10 mark. From then on, Keane began to rely on him more and more, increasingly calling on him to pitch on only three days' rest; Keane would give him that extra day only three more times. In the waning days of the season, Gibson lost an epic game to Al Jackson and the Mets, 1–0, in a game that would have won the pennant. And then, with the Cardinals, Phillies, and Reds all within one game of each other on the season's final day, he returned once more, pitched four innings in relief, and won the game — and with it the National League championship.

Following the game, Vecsey and the gaggle of reporters found a depleted and worn-out Gibson standing on the stairway leading to the clubhouse. In the parlance of Vin Scully, in the year of the improbable he'd done the impossible — but standing there, his expression blank, he seemed unfazed by his accomplishment. His arm, predictably, bothered him. Never in a mood to speak to the press, he seemed to bristle more than usual. After all, what could they ask him now? What he threw in the last inning? Why he agreed to throw in relief? What he expected from himself in the World Series? Was he scared of pitching against Mantle and Maris?

"I've gotta get out of here," he said when he saw the reporters coming toward him.

"How do you feel?" someone asked.

"Like horseshit."

And with that, he was off. Vecsey didn't see Gibson again until he and others were having beers in a restaurant on Euclid Avenue near the Chase Park Hotel. No one expected Bob Gibson, a man who preferred to stay in the shadows, to stop in for a burger — but there he was. This time everyone stayed away from him. Gibson despised them. That much was clear. How he'd fare in the Series, with his arm understandably exhausted, was less so.

He lost Game 2 against the Yankees at home, but in Game 5 Gibson would show the thousands in the Bronx what Keane and others had become accustomed to seeing. Though it was apparent now that the Yankees were fading, this was still the most storied team in baseball, and they would not lose easily, not even in decline.

Now Gibson displayed not only tenacity but also an ability to create his own self-defining moment. In the ninth inning, with the Cardinals winning 2–0, shortstop Dick Groat botched a grounder from Mickey Mantle for an error. Facing the young Joe Pepitone and the prospect of the tying run, Gibson did what he always did — he threw the ball, falling off the mound. Pepitone lined a ball that caromed off Gibson's right buttock. Because of his delivery, Gibson couldn't reach across his body to grab it as it bounded toward the third-base line.

Another pitcher might have watched the ball roll for an infield single. But this was Bob Gibson. In awe, McCarver watched as Gibson hurried to the third-base side, grabbed the ball barehanded, and then, in a single fluid movement in midair, launched the ball toward first base, where the throw beat the hustling Pepitone. Though the next batter, Tom Tresh, would momentarily tie the game with a home run, Gibson continued to pitch well, going the distance and finally earning the win after McCarver hit a three-run home run in the 10th.

Gibson's ninth-inning play may have stunned the national audience, but it did not shock anyone who followed him closely as he rose to prominence in the National League. Before he took control of the Major League Baseball Players Association (MLBPA), Marvin Miller, then an executive for the United Steelworkers union, would take time away from his office in Pittsburgh every time Gibson pitched. He loved not only the way Gibson played the game but his ability to make this kind of play — to come off the mound, pick up the ball, and deliver it with all the grace of the very best third basemen.

In the seventh game, despite having pitched so deep into Game 5, Gibson was again handed the ball by Keane, on just two days' rest. In the ninth inning, with the Yankees trailing 7–3, Keane's directions were to simply throw heat. Gibson gave up two home runs. Any other manager would have pulled his pitcher at this point, but Keane stayed with his man. Gibson proved himself worthy of Keane's trust when he forced the last Yankee batter, Bobby Richardson, to pop out, finishing off the Yankees and ending the Series.

"You can't say enough about Gibson," Keane told reporters afterwards. "He didn't pitch only with his arm; he pitched with his heart.

And he's got lots of heart. He gave it all and more. I went all the way with him because I was committed to this fellow's heart."

Over a two-week stretch, Gibson had showed the world what he could do. He had thrown eight innings in that loss to the Mets, only to come back to win the pennant two days later. In Game 5 of the World Series, he'd gone the distance and beyond, and then, on short rest, he had pitched a complete Game 7. He was now known to the world, then and forever.

With the Cardinals' win, Gibson shut the door on the Yankees and what they stood for. As a team, New York had long taken a hard stance against the integration of the game and won world championships in spite of it. Now — even with black players — having lost to both the Dodgers in 1963 and the Cardinals in 1964, they faced a swift fall into irrelevancy. Players like Bob Gibson were here to stay and here to win.

Approaching Gibson in the locker room after the Game 7 win, Keane — who in the coming days would turn down Busch's offer to remain the Cardinals' manager in order to take the reins of the very same Yankees — told him, "Hoot, you're on your way."

Watching Gibson record that last out from his home in Philadelphia was Gerald Early, then 12 years old. As an adult, he would become one of this country's great African American cultural critics, exploring topics as diverse as war and jazz and baseball. Though black like Gibson, even then Early didn't see Gibson through that racial lens, as others would. Regardless of whether he was black or white, Gibson, to Early, merely seemed the modern athlete personified.

But there was something traditional that ran through Gibson. The truth is that there seemed to be a great deal of the Yankees — the old Yankees — in how Gibson approached the game. The silent resolve of DiMaggio. The work ethic of Gehrig. The athleticism of Mantle. The ability to showcase your best in the grandest of venues during what was then the country's most followed sporting event. The expectation to win and the delivery on that expectation. Later a writer would call Gibson a symbol of a new breed. In truth, he was merely an updated version of an old one.

• • •

"Let's see your fastball," Detroit Tigers manager Charlie Dressen said to Denny McLain in the spring of 1963. McLain was standing with Dressen at the Tigers' spring training ballpark in Lakeland, Florida. He was 19 years old, a castoff from the team that had signed him, trying to regain his confidence and vigor.

He was making a new start. Dressen too was looking to return to form, following less than impressive managerial stints with the Senators and Braves. This was the man who once led the Dodgers to the brink of the 1951 NL pennant, a title denied in the last of a three-game series by Bobby Thomson's game-winning home run as Jackie Robinson stood alone in the infield, making sure that Thomson touched every base.

Dressen had partially redeemed himself by leading the Dodgers to the World Series in each of the next two years. Surely that was enough to earn him a multi-year contract and some degree of stability. But Walter O'Malley was unreceptive to Dressen's demands and replaced him with Walter Alston, who had no misgivings about signing a one-year contract each season — and who led the Dodgers to their lone World Series championship in Brooklyn and to multiple ones in Los Angeles.

Thus, McLain and Dressen, despite their age difference, became kindred spirits. Both had something to prove. And like McLain, Dressen could be excitable and rash. In the dugout, he was known to whistle loudly and curse, as if to make his presence known, and he would spout off about other managers and other teams. Early in his career as a coach, in Brooklyn, Branch Rickey had fired him for spending too much time gambling on horses, then brought him back.

Watching McLain that afternoon, Dressen liked what he saw — at first. Impressed with McLain's fastball, Dressen asked to see his curve. Dressen had spent his formative years with the Dodgers, a team that stressed the use of the overhand curveball.

McLain tried to throw the curve, but the ball didn't move and showed no sign of dropping in front of a hitter, as even the most mediocre curveballs do.

"All I have is a fastball," McLain said. "I can't throw a curve."

"Gimme that ball," Dressen said. "I'll teach you how."

Dressen soon saw that, because of how tightly McLain gripped the ball with his thumb, he couldn't give it the proper spin. Within ten minutes, Dressen was able to accomplish what so many minor league coaches had failed to do—show McLain how to throw the ball with great location and that terrific downward break.

"Good," Dressen said. "I'll give you the chance to try that out against the White Sox on Saturday."

As with Gibson and Keane, there seemed to be something special between Dressen and McLain, an unspoken bond. During McLain's brief and turbulent time within the White Sox system, managers found him uncontrollable and bratty, a player who couldn't be counted on to show up, much less follow instructions. It didn't hurt Dressen and McLain's relationship that Sharyn McLain's father, Lou Boudreau, and Dressen were close friends.

But it went beyond nepotism. Because they shared a rocky past, Dressen took to McLain. And McLain, like Gibson with Keane, found in Dressen a manager he could actually love. McLain felt like Dressen's boy. Again and again, the manager would tell him that he would win a lot of games, "my son."

Despite Dressen's confidence in him, the Tigers still dispatched McLain back to the minor leagues, where he declared with such great resolve that his teammates had better follow him or risk being forgotten. But as he predicted, McLain didn't stay in the minors for long. After brief stints with the Tigers in 1963 and 1964, McLain went 16-6 as a full-time starter in 1965. He was now in the big leagues for good.

By July 1966, a talented threesome of young pitchers had developed within the Tigers organization—McLain, Mickey Lolich, and Pat Dobson. They were so impressive that *Sports Illustrated* ran an article warning the American League, "Here Come the Young Turks." The other two men got a few inches of text in writer William Leggett's piece, but McLain received most of the attention.

Even then, the writer was drawn to McLain's life beyond baseball. Leggett wrote about his signature drink—Pepsi-Cola—and how he sometimes drank over a dozen bottles a day. He wrote about McLain's love of the organ, and how he stayed up playing his Hammond all night after a loss. He'd sought out this kind of attention since his teens. Now he had it.

"I like people," McLain admitted. "I like people to know about me. Some players object to publicity about their private lives. I don't care. In 1965 Joe Falls, who's the sports editor of the *Free Press* here in Detroit, heard that I drank a lot of Pepsi-Cola, and he came and asked me about it. I told him the truth, that sometimes I knocked off as many as 16 bottles a day. Joe wrote about it, and the Pepsi-Cola people read the story, and they sent a truckload over to the house. Now I work for them, and the trucks keep coming, and I still love it, even though I can get all I want.

"I guess maybe all the notoriety affects your personal life in some ways," he continued. "They had my wife on television, and she was terrific. Everyone called in and said how much they liked her, and I was happy for her. Then, of course, I had to bring her back down to earth after she didn't wash the dishes for three days. I enjoy kidding around, and I usually don't mind what people write about me."

By season's end, McLain was more than a mere comer. He'd arrived. He won 20 games by the time he was 22. This was seven years younger than Bob Gibson was when he reached the mark, and more impressively, McLain got there four years sooner than Drysdale and Spahn. He was five years younger than Koufax. Sustained greatness of the kind that all players have forever strived for seemed inevitable.

Yet in the midst of this success, a new recklessness emerged. Charlie Dressen spent a great deal of the 1966 season recovering from one heart attack, and then died of a second one. Just as happened after his father's death, McLain suddenly found himself unmoored, a man set loose upon the world.

More than once, after speaking his mind to a reporter, McLain would say, "[May] God strike me down if I said those things." He invoked it once after telling *Detroit Free Press* writer George Cantor that he wanted to beat Cleveland's Sam McDowell so badly that "my teeth hurt"; he subsequently sought out Cantor and screamed at him, belittling him and demanding a retraction. In 1966, after McLain infamously called the Tigers a "country club team" run by the players and without discipline, Tigers general manager Jim Campbell ordered him to retract the remarks, but he once again said that the Almighty would prove him misquoted. This came in the midst of a season that marked not only Dressen's passing but that of his replacement, Bob Swift, to cancer. Amid all this, McLain called out the Tigers' coaching staff, saying: "With all the managerial problems we've had, you don't know who to listen to, and the coaching of our pitchers has been less than great."

Later, when the press voted him Tiger of the Year, McLain stood at the podium and told the writers who didn't vote for him to "go fuck yourselves."

Willie Horton believed that had Charlie Dressen lived, perhaps Denny would have changed. Dressen would have stayed on him, watched him. He would have done what so many found impossible — made sure of Denny's well-being.

It came with a pop, a terrible sound that McLain didn't pay much attention to, because he was still a kid — just 21 — and still believed he was invincible. Two years before, he'd lost his pitch-off with Bruce Howard, but now here he was in 1965, not only beating Howard en route to his eighth consecutive win but showing the White Sox that they'd made a terrible mistake. Hearing the sound from his shoulder meant nothing to him at that moment.

McLain wouldn't feel the extent of the damage until the next morning. He had pitched without pain or fear of pain through high school and the minors and into the beginning of what seemed a promising major league career. But it was clearly more than a pop — his unhittable arm had been rendered unliftable.

Later that day he learned that the Tigers' medical staff could do nothing for him, that they needed to send him to Henry Ford Hospital, and that something called cortisone would work. At the hospital, a doctor named David Mitchell sterilized McLain's arm, shot him up first with Xylocaine to "deaden" his shoulder, then administered the cortisone. Within four years, McLain was getting injections of Xylocaine and cortisone after nearly every start. Grumbling about the experience after baseball had become mere memory, McLain said, "The name of the game back then was, 'You gotta win one for the Gipper.' Fuck the Gipper."

McLain's bitterness was well earned. Those cortisone shots would cost him his major league career. The myth that baseball players were tougher and more resilient back in the day, that they were willing to endure anything for the sheer love of the game, is just that—a myth. In truth, they were victims of terrible medical advice, merciless management, and unforgiving fans who believed that a worn-out, hurting arm signaled a kind of moral weakness.

In 1969, Jim Maloney was pitching for the Reds and losing his war against constant, searing pain. He still had enough to pitch a no-hitter against the Mets, but in the process he hurt his arm just at a time when the team that would come to dominate the next decade truly needed him. When pitching in another start against the Mets, he simply didn't have it in him to go on. He ached so much that he had the gall to ask his manager, Dave Bristol, to take him out of the game. An enraged Bristol—soon to be replaced by Hall of Fame manager George "Sparky" Anderson—called a meeting with his pitchers and told them that he wouldn't accept pain as an excuse, that they simply had to play through it.

"Listen, if a guy's arm is sore he wouldn't even be able to throw the ball," Bristol said. "Right? If he can throw it up to the plate and get somebody out, then it can't be that sore, so he's gotta stay in there.

"There's only one thing that counts in this game and that's winning," Bristol continued. "Everything else goes out the window: money, pain, sympathy, feelings, all of it. I don't want any individual players on my team. I want team men. If a guy's only interested in his career, I don't want him. The team's the only thing that matters."

Sam McDowell, deemed by many the hardest-throwing pitcher of McLain and Gibson's era, endured similar misunderstanding when faced with a "sore arm" during the 1966 campaign for the Indians. He was the recipient of so much vitriol from fans that he finally lashed out in 1967: "You wouldn't believe some of the awful mail I got. Some of the fans were really on my back. I got mail from all over the country, but the bad mail was from Cleveland.

"How do you convince people how much something hurts?" he said. "How can they judge you when they can't know that? A lot of smart people are awfully smart in their own living rooms."

The toll on pitchers became evident in 1966 to Marvin Miller, then in his first season in charge of the Players Association, when he walked into the St. Louis Cardinals clubhouse during what many deemed the hottest, most unbearable All-Star Game to date. Miller couldn't see the face of Koufax—who had started the game against McLain, pitching three innings— as he sat in a tub of cold water and ice, his back toward Miller. But Miller could see Koufax's arm, which looked more like the "heavy thigh of a big man" than an arm. He'd never seen anything so hideous, so swollen, in his entire life.

When Koufax at last saw Miller and noticed his alarm, the pitcher said, "Don't worry. It happens to me every time I pitch. Just a few innings in, it happens."

The underlying motivator for players not of Koufax's caliber was fear. The fear of not meeting expectations. The fear of general managers and owners looking for any reason to pull you from the starting rotation or, worse, from the team's payroll altogether. That sense of insecurity led McLain's teammate John Hiller, who returned to the team in 1972 following a heart attack, to hide anything that might end his career for good from Billy Martin, the Tigers manager at that time.

For instance, following a collision in the outfield during batting practice that badly injured Hiller's foot, he continued to pitch through it, though sitting in the trainer's room after each ball game, he was nearly driven to tears. He wasn't about to let Martin, or even the pitching coach, know that he was hurt. Hiller wasn't a high-salaried player, after all, and didn't have a multi-year contract. He did what he needed to do to stay in the game.

Upon joining the Tigers in 1967, Mike Marshall was already beginning graduate work at Michigan State, where he would later earn a doctorate in exercise physiology. A pitcher who later went on to win the 1974 Cy Young Award with the Dodgers when he set the record for most appearances in a season—106—Marshall even then understood what cortisone is: not a cure-all for pain, but a corrosive that softens the bone and weakens the ligaments. He could see McLain growing addicted to it. Despite what doctors might have said, cortisone was more of an analgesic than a curative treatment. And ultimately, it would destroy McLain's career.

In time, McLain would understand all of this. But he was young. He believed that the Tigers had his best interests in mind. He had lived his life acting with no fear of repercussions. As one of the best young pitchers in the major leagues, he certainly wouldn't do so now. In an era when their elders chastised young men and women for seeking escape through drugs, these very same people thought it noble that the icons of the National Game misused medications in order to dim their own, different pain.

McLain's soon-to-be pitching coach Johnny Sain understood what separated those who stayed in the majors from those who didn't. As much as he stressed positive reinforcement and mechanics, he knew that mere talent didn't matter. Simply put, Sain said in 1969, the world "wants winners and results. People don't want to hear about labor pains. They want to see the baby."

4

TESTIMONY OF PILOTS

THIS I THINK IS THE ORGANIZATION I've been looking for," Johnny Sain said as he looked out across the Detroit Tigers' practice fields in Lakeland, Florida, in the spring of 1967. "I've seen more good arms in this organization than I've ever been connected with."

Sain was looking at his third new pitching staff since 1961. Once again a baseball club had asked him to do the impossible — to take ordinary, underachieving players and coax from them something extraordinary.

Righting this staff would be no easy task given everything that had happened the season before. Two managers had died, and Denny McLain, flexing his independence, had taken the opportunity to pop off at his teammates. Tigers general manager Jim Campbell had put together an entirely new coaching staff, headed by manager Mayo Smith — a questionable choice given Smith's earlier failures managing Cincinnati and Philadelphia. But Sain was told that Smith was a gentleman, someone he could trust. In time, he'd see it differently.

For now, Sain was not only part of a new start for Detroit but also perhaps under even more pressure than Smith in this reboot. The "Young Turks" lived up to their initial praise, but failed in the ultimate measure of players — their ability to win the pennant. Sain had elevated the pitching staffs of both the Yankees and the Twins to heights previously unimaginable, but there was one reason why things might go differently with the Tigers.

Denny McLain.

At a time when few players took direct aim at management, McLain had done so with malice. As a 20-game winner, McLain believed that he was the team's best pitcher and felt that he had to answer to no one.

Sain knew little about McLain and his teammate and rival Mickey Lolich beyond the fact that both could be temperamental and difficult, but he had readied himself for anything. At that same dinner at which McLain thumbed his nose at the writers who didn't vote for him as Tiger of the Year, McLain sought out Sain. It was the first time the two had ever met. McLain's ego didn't need any boosting, but Sain complimented him on his fastball and remarked that in his time he had never been able to throw as hard. Later McLain referred to the man from Arkansas as "Mr. Sain." As if to tweak his new manager, he referred to Smith as "Mayo."

Detroit writer Joe Falls foresaw the trouble that lay ahead in a magazine piece entitled "Turmoil on the Tigers: Does It Still Exist?" Falls, who'd seen promising Tigers teams fall apart time and again, questioned the team's maturity, its ability to win under pressure, and, perhaps most important, its ability to work together toward a common purpose.

"I don't know about your team," Orioles third baseman and future Hall of Fame inductee Brooks Robinson told Falls. "I can never figure them out. They look so good to me, so good down here in Florida, so good on paper. But your team . . ."

Nevertheless, Falls wrote: "Can these individuals meld into a team? I think so. In fact, I'm picking my Tigers to overcome all adversity this season and win the pennant in early October, which is the hard way. And novel for them."

Sain had joined the Kansas City Athletics as a pitching coach in 1959, hoping to make a new start. But things could never work out in Kansas City, the team composed of exiled, washed-up Yankees or would-be

New York stars. The A's simply weren't interested in winning. Sain felt—and who could blame him—that he was putting far more into the team than the rest of the ball club was. He quit before the end of the season.

So he'd managed his own exit, taking control of his life. He would do essentially the same thing with the Yankees after Yogi Berra was promoted to manager. Sain didn't quit so much as engineer his own undoing when he asked his onetime friend Ralph Houk for an unreasonable raise following the team's defeat by the Dodgers in the 1963 World Series. This perceived insult would forever color Houk's opinion of Sain. Houk would belittle Sain's accomplishments when he pronounced Jim Turner—who served as the Yankees pitching coach from 1949 to 1959 and then again from 1966 to 1973—"the best pitching coach ever."

"A good pitching coach deals only with mechanics," Houk would later grouse. "It can be detrimental to a team if a pitching coach gets too personally involved with his pitchers. He should treat them mechanically. That's why Johnny Sain had his troubles. I've heard a lot of bad things about Sain since he left us. He can't seem to hold a job, can he? Jim Turner's been a pitching coach with the Yankees for years. He knows what I expect of him. We get together, and I tell him how I'm gonna use the pitchers and he does it."

Mary Ann Sain, Johnny's second wife, whom he met while working for the White Sox in the 1970s, felt that this reaction, so common in the aftermath of a Sain departure, betrayed a basic insecurity of his bosses. It was rooted in the belief that Sain wanted the manager's job for himself. But that was never the case. Sain never wanted to be the man in charge. He was happy in the company of his pitchers.

After his rupture with Houk, Sain returned home to Arkansas again, to his 314 acres and his wife and children. He'd sit out the 1964 season, settling into his life as a father and husband, as Bob Gibson defeated his former team. Then another suitor arrived at his door. This was Calvin Griffith, the man who moved the original Senators from Washington, D.C., to Minnesota, where they became the Twins. Griffith was desperate. He'd watched the Twins—a team that boasted both Hall of Famer Harmon Killebrew and Tony Oliva, who was just beginning his celebrated career as one of the great Latin stars of his generation—consistently not play up to their potential, and he was concerned. The desire to win a championship can drive teams to take drastic measures; in this case, it led one of the most conservative owners in sports to hire one of the most progressive coaches for $25,000.

"I have never paid a coach so much in my life," Griffith said in October 1964. "I feel very good about getting Sain. We have a lot of young pitchers. It will be a tough job, but I think we got the best man we could get to do it.

"I told Johnny we have a good young staff with a lot of talent that needs help," he went on to say. "He said that he would like the challenge and that it would be good to get back into baseball. Sain was a smart pitcher himself. He did a good job in developing young pitchers for the Yankees for three years. And he has been both a starter and reliever."

Sain, of course, made no promises, only that he would do his very best in his very own way.

"I don't want to appear as a superman," he said. "All I can do is suggest."

When Sain spoke in depth with Jim Kaat, it was already the third week of March 1965, two-thirds of the way through training camp. Kaat had just been involved in a contract fight with the tight-fisted Twins. But he had worked out with the Rollins College team in Winter Park, Florida, and he was ready to throw.

As a kid who loved baseball, Kaat knew all about the "Spahn and Sain" era, and as a grown man he knew all about how Sain had turned Whitey Ford into a 20-game winner by pleading with Houk to have him pitch every four days. Now, at the Twins complex at Tinker Field in Orlando, he finally got to really speak with the soft-spoken Southerner who had no jaundiced views about contract disputes, having nearly left the game over one himself.

"When can you pitch?" Sain said.

"I can pitch tomorrow," Kaat said.

"How many innings can you go?"

"As much as you want," Kaat said. In that first 1965 spring training start, Kaat threw seven innings. This thrilled Sain, who loved pitchers who could throw deep into ball games.

That was the beginning of Kaat's apprenticeship. One day, standing in the parking lot outside Tinker Field, Sain took Kaat over to his car and pulled out two books—*Think and Grow Rich* by Napoleon Hill and *Success Through a Positive Mental Attitude* by W. Clement Stone. Sain believed that these books had changed his whole worldview. He believed in their power to affect a pitcher subconsciously so that he would stand on the mound with a sense of confidence without knowing where that confidence came from. This was a scene Sain would repeat with young pitchers again and again over the years, and pitchers would come to expect it. But in 1965 Sain's approach was something totally new.

Other pitchers might have found this scene comic—standing with your pitching coach as he pulled self-help books from the trunk of his car. But Kaat, who had already pitched four full seasons in the majors with uneven, disappointing results, knew from experience that talent alone wouldn't cut it. He felt that Sain had a lot to offer. If Sain could help him harness a confident, strong persona on the mound, he was willing to listen.

"I've never run into a pitcher who wasn't interested in an idea," Sain said of his approach. "I don't go up to a guy and say, 'Hey, you're not doing it right. Do it this way.' I say, 'What do you think about this?' And I don't care where they get the idea . . . The idea is to stimulate the imagination."

As Kaat soon discovered, Sain wasn't just tinkering with his psyche but had something more tangible to teach. Kaat bought into Sain's idea of throwing consistently between starts, believing in Sain's precept that "it'll rust out before it'll wear out." Even before he met Sain, Kaat was in the habit of throwing a lot. Other pitching coaches had complained that he threw too much, but Kaat found that working his arm each day strengthened it for his next start.

Later, as a broadcaster for the MLB Network, Kaat watched the Yankees ace C. C. Sabathia struggling. After one poor outing, he went up to Sabathia and said, "You really have good stuff, but it almost looked like it was so good that you couldn't really harness it."

Sabathia chuckled, and then Kaat pressed him further, asking if he wouldn't rather pitch every fourth day instead of every fifth. Sabathia told him he'd "love doing that."

Finding his next batch of eager pupils, Sain introduced them to "the spinner," the tool he'd developed with the Yankees. But Sain also brought with him something Kaat called the controlled breaking ball, a pitch that everyone on the Minnesota staff mastered and put to use during the 1965 and 1966 seasons. Slower than a fastball but faster than the curve, it could be thrown at different speeds and with just enough backspin to trick hitters.

Kaat believed that this was the pitch that forever changed the fortunes of Jim "Mudcat" Grant, who was considered a castoff when the Indians traded him to the Twins for two players and $75,000 in the middle of the 1964 campaign.

Grant was born in Lacoochee, Florida, a lumber mill town. Like Gibson, he was the youngest of seven, raised by a single mother who worked as a domestic. The blacks in Lacoochee were more or less indentured servants — going to the company-paid doctor, living in the lumber mill's housing, sending their children to a small, impoverished, segregated school.

Grant was good enough to play semipro ball for his hometown team as a teenager, and his athletic skills earned him a scholarship to play both football and baseball at Florida A&M. He had planned on becoming a teacher, but the financial needs of his family forced him to drop out of school and move in with his uncle to learn carpentry, a trade he had no interest in. He seemed destined to be *that guy:* the once-great athlete who never got his shot.

Happily, it was a short-term purgatory for Grant. The Braves had tried to sign him to play baseball when he was just 16. When the Indians called, Grant was at a much different stage of his life. He was no longer a kid with other options. This was a second chance to make use of his true talents.

Grant (whose original nickname, "Mississippi Mudcat," was coined at the Cleveland tryout camp in Daytona Beach by a teammate who believed he was from there) was lucky that he never had to play in Southern towns. But the pressures and stresses of being black were never far from his mind. His mother's parting words to him — "Don't be no fool" — stayed with him, guiding him through difficult stages of his early playing career. He felt that it was the wisdom of these words — reminding him to never let anything "penetrate your inner soul to the point where it was going to affect how you compete" — that carried him through.

In 1965, early in their time together with the Twins, Sain turned to Grant—who would become one of his closest of friends—and said, "Mudcat, can I ask you this? How in the hell did y'all do it?"

Sain's "y'all" was a blanket term covering all the black players he'd seen since throwing that first pitch to Jackie Robinson at Ebbets Field in the spring of 1947. At a time when the South had finally burst open over its racial inequities and most whites continued to firmly support its terrible traditions, Sain stood apart from those god-awful views. He had played with and against black players, he'd seen the way they were treated by management and his white teammates, and he'd witnessed the aching anguish of the black players who stuck with it, feeling compelled not only to play but to play well. Sain himself had stuck with the game during his minor league purgatory, though he could have left at any time, but his struggle was something wholly different—dwarfed by the personal, torrid struggles endured by even the most talented black players.

One time with the Indians, when Grant was called upon to pinch-run, his first-base coach, Ray Katt, told him bluntly, "You're the winning run. If you get a tweener, I want you to run like you just stole two watermelons and the man is after you with a shotgun." Grant left the field. There were some frustrations you could hold in, but an insult of this caliber deserved a grand, defiant gesture.

There were darker moments. A year before, on September 16, 1960, as a country preoccupied with the civil rights movement girded itself for its closest presidential election in history, Grant stood in the bullpen listening to the National Anthem.

It had been a summer of great change. America had witnessed the birth of the Student Nonviolent Coordinating Committee (SNCC) and the passage of the Civil Rights Act of 1960. It had also seen four African American students in Greensboro, North Carolina, boldly seek to integrate a Woolworth's lunch counter—a courageous act that spawned countless sit-ins across the South. Grant had remained silent up until this point, but he couldn't keep his feelings bottled up any longer. During the anthem, he felt the need to mock it; he sang either, "This land is not so free; I can't go to Mississippi," or, "How free can it be when I can't go to Mississippi and sit at a lunch counter?"

Whatever his actual words, Grant's intent was clear — at least to his pitching coach, Ted Wilks. Wilks, a Texan, barked out, "If you don't like our country, why don't you get the hell out?"

"Well, I can get out of the country," Grant replied. "All I have to do is go to Texas. That's worse than Russia."

"Well, if we catch your black nigger ass in Texas," Wilks said, "we're going to hang you from the nearest tree."

With one punch to his noggin, Wilks fell to the ground. Grant left the ballpark without telling his manager, Jimmy Dykes — a man he liked — and was suspended for what little remained of the season. Other teams might have sent Grant away, never to play ball again. But Grant apologized to Dykes (though he refused an apology offered by Wilks), and the Indians chose to keep their pitcher, opting to dispatch Wilks to the minors instead.

The Indians liked Grant the man, if not the player. Even after this incident, Grant endeared himself to both black and white fans — and even to John Kennedy. Grant set up a productive friendship with the new president, working toward the betterment of his hometown, whose lumber mill had been shuttered, leaving those put out of work impoverished and desperate. In spite of his clashes with Dykes and Wilks, fans still took to Grant. Amiable and charming, he was a gentleman of the highest order. But as a pitcher, despite intermittent flashes of brilliance, Cleveland never saw him grow into a frontline starter. His talent never quite lived up to expectations.

Grant had already made great strides by the time he met Sain in Minnesota. Following his trade to the Twins in 1964, Mudcat went 11-9, with a 2.82 ERA. But Sain saw the potential for something more.

Sain and Grant became great friends and had long talks about race, about how ballplayers like Grant and Gibson and Mays and Doby managed to survive. Grant often spoke about the inner strength of his family and "the Wisdom of their Survival." His grandmother had endured slavery; his mother had weathered the death of her husband and raised him and his six siblings on her own. The pitcher felt that those experiences had rubbed off on him and that the survival instincts his mother and grandmother passed on to him served as a life raft as he struggled to remain relevant in the major leagues.

What separated Sain from other coaches, Grant felt, was how understanding he could be. Sain had the unique ability to put himself in the shoes of each pitcher—to understand his particular strengths and to know how to improve on them. If you threw a bad pitch and the batter hit a long two-base hit to center, Sain would sit next to you as you sulked, telling you, "Now don't complain when they hit a low-and-away pitch for a double, because that ball should've been a home run." Humor helped. By this point in his career, Mudcat simply couldn't throw as hard as he once did. So when Sain talked to him about throwing strikes that moved and were deceptive in their trajectory, Mudcat welcomed the advice.

In an era when starters were expected to throw a nine-inning game, Sain stressed how important it was to realize that you couldn't be the same pitcher in the middle and at the end of the game as you were in the first three innings. To understand this and adjust your performance accordingly, Sain believed, was crucial if you were going to survive.

The previous year, the Twins had finished in sixth place. At the end of the 1965 season, they'd outlasted the Orioles to win the American League pennant, finishing with a 102-60 mark, easily their best season since they moved from Washington in 1961. Grant led the American League in wins with 21, pitching just over 270 innings and becoming the first black pitcher in the American League to win 20 games. Kaat finished 18-11 with a 2.83 ERA. The success of the Twins' pitching staff led Yankees third baseman Clete Boyer to joke, "When you vote for manager of the year in the American League, whose name will you write in? Sain?"

Though they matched up well against the Dodgers, who'd outlasted the rest of the National League to reach the World Series, the Twins faltered in Game 7. Sandy Koufax, whose arm would finally give way the following year, threw two consecutive shutouts. In the seventh and deciding game, he defeated Kaat 2–0.

Despite their strong season, however, the Twins were very much a team in trouble, filled with combustible elements. Sain and third-base coach Billy Martin were once teammates who won championships together as Yankees, but now Martin bristled at the accolades Sain received for reviving the Twins' pitching staff. So did manager Sam Mele, who had been very close to losing his job at the end of the 1964 season but won Manager of the Year honors following the team's 1965 pennant win.

As had been the case in his last days with Houk, Sain felt he couldn't really talk to Mele. Mele didn't care for the motivational books or for the protective fortress that Sain had built around his men to shield them from the rest of the team. He was willing to put up with Sain's methodology, grudgingly, so long as the team continued to win American League and possibly World Series championships. But that wouldn't happen in 1966, despite Kaat posting 25 wins, the best of his major league career.

Mele and Griffith watched the Orioles, fortified by the presence of Frank Robinson, come into their own as a dominant power, while the Twins slipped back into second. Moreover, it became apparent that Martin and Sain could no longer coexist. Martin, the once-diminutive, overachieving second baseman who went on to manage more teams than can be counted, was Sain's opposite in every way. Short, explosive, perennially angry, he'd clashed with Sain when a mental lapse by reliever Jerry Fosnow allowed a runner to score on a squeeze play.

When Martin lashed out, Sain simply said, "It isn't that all-fired easy." Martin felt that Sain had shown him up in front of the team, an inexcusable offense in the mind of the wiry, Napoleonic tyrant. The next day Sain moved his entire inventory from the coaches' quarters into the players' section of the clubhouse, where he stayed for the remainder of the year.

"I like to be in the clubhouse," Sain said, sitting in another locker room with another team years later. "I like to feel the pulse of the club. I've got to be available, that's my job, and I think they're more likely to come for advice if I'm right there."

As with New York, just as quickly as Sain had come to Minnesota, he was gone. And as with the Yankees, Sain felt a certain sense of relief when he was let go following the 1966 season. Martin had proven to be unbearable. Mele, in his silence, was even worse. Sain had done his job, made good money. He'd helped where he could. But damn if he would stay where he was no longer wanted.

"There's absolutely no reason to work under conditions that are unpleasant," Sain said after he was fired. "Life is too short. If it isn't a pleasant operation and if I find I can't contribute anything . . . I'm gone. Real quick. I'm tickled to death with what I accomplished at Minnesota. There were no hard feelings when I left. Mr. Griffith was good to me moneywise. But money isn't that important to me."

Yet Kaat wasn't ready to let him go. He had just completed a speaking engagement in southern Minnesota and was driving back to the Twin Cities when he heard on the radio that the Twins had fired both Sain and the bullpen coach Hal Naragon. He was so shocked and angry that he had to pull over to the side of the road.

Soon after, Kaat approached the Twins' elder statesmen, Bob Allison and Harmon Killebrew. He told them that he wanted to write an open letter, letting the fans know how wrong this all was, and he asked if they'd consider adding their names. Though both men shared Kaat's sentiments, they weren't prepared to take that step.

Kaat didn't blame them. Sain had been his coach, not theirs. Kaat, who referred to himself as a "stubborn Dutchman," wrote the letter anyway. He hoped that a prominent Minnesota newspaperman, Sid Hartman, would run it, but Hartman did a radio show with Mele, and he told Kaat that he just couldn't do it.

"Well, who's your boss?" Kaat asked with indignation. "Who's the editor of the *Minneapolis Star-Tribune*?"

Hartman told him, Kaat made the call, and the paper ran the letter unedited. He argued that the Twins had handed Sain and bullpen coach Hal Naragon a bum deal, that they had fired the wrong men. He said that the Twins needed to find a manager who had the fortitude to appreciate Sain. If he were a general manager, Kaat wrote, Sain would be his very first hire.

"Allowing him to leave," he said, "is like the Green Bay Packers allowing Vince Lombardi to quit."

Even then, this was an act of tremendous courage. Whitey Ford and Jim Bouton had protested Sain's firing by the Yankees, but this was different. This wasn't a private petition to management, or an off-the-record comment made in a dark corner of a locker room. Just as Bill White had gone public over the whites-only breakfast honoring Cardinal and Yankee players in St. Petersburg, Kaat's letter amounted to a public act of insurrection. It signaled the opening of a new day for players, who were beginning to challenge the established order.

Following the dismissal of the two men, Kaat said with bold certitude, "If Johnny Sain told me to ram my arm into a wall three times because it would help my curveball, I'd do it."

Sain, of course, appreciated the sentiments. He understood the value of independent thinking and encouraged it as a coach. It made you a better player, he believed, and also a better man. Kaat had stood up to management when a lesser man would have demurred. Although there were those who saw Kaat's letter as a rogue act, in truth, it was the beginning of an insurrection.

By this time Sain and Naragon had already settled into their new jobs with the Tigers. Despite their tumultuous departure from the Twins, the two were very much in demand. They believed in their approach, but they were anxious when they first arrived in Lakeland. They'd had one terrific year with the Twins, followed by a regression. When they arrived in Florida, both were impressed by a staff that Joe Falls and others labeled as underachievers. This was a place, Sain felt, where he could pass out those inspirational books and spinners and watch them work.

The program the two laid out, as one reporter described it in 1969, was one of "cautious preparation." They instructed their Tigers pitchers to work toward a state of purposeful stiffness. They would throw one day for over two hours so that the arm would tighten and then feel even tighter the next day, but it would be loose on the third, and ready to go the distance by the time the fourth day came around.

(Years later, the last time Tigers pitcher Daryl Patterson saw Sain at a baseball fantasy camp, the two spoke about sore arms — their causes and cures. By then, Sain had developed a way of working out arm problems. Lying down, he showed Patterson, who was well into retirement, how to rotate his shoulder. Instead of rubbing down his arm, Sain rotated his arm fully 360 degrees several times a day.)

Although he was impressed overall with his pitching staff, Sain saw that much had to be undone. When Charlie Dressen was manager, he had insisted that catcher Bill Freehan call the game. But early on in his tenure, Sain instructed Freehan to believe, following in the steps of Tim McCarver, that "the pitcher throws, and the catcher catches." The pitcher, Sain told Freehan, had the last say. It wasn't a question of Free-han's ability to judge a game, Sain explained, but it was important for the pitcher to develop a positive notion of what he was doing rather than blindly following the signs put down for him. Uncertainty and inability to think for yourself, Sain believed, led to the biggest pitching mistakes.

Moreover, Sain treated all his pitchers the same. While another coach might look around his staff, see someone doing well, and attach himself to that person, Sain seemed inclined to do the opposite. "Guys that are doing well, I just leave alone. I need to talk to the people that are strug-gling a little bit and try and get them back on."

Only *after* a bad outing would Sain seek out a pitcher — most likely the next day. Sain would come up to the Tigers' John Hiller and ask, "Everything okay?"

"Well," Hiller would reply. "I guess so."

"Well, you're back here," Sain would say. "You've got the uniform on. Yesterday's gone."

It was only natural that Sain would seek out Mike Marshall that spring. Sain knew of Marshall's academic pursuits and wanted his in-put about his methodology. Marshall thought the spinner was a bril-liant device, and he was able to explain to Sain the science behind how it worked.

"Okay, John," Marshall explained to him. "What you have here is four seams contacting the air. If the seams are going toward the air mol-ecules, then the top seam is receiving the friction of the air and that causes higher pressure on the top . . . When the seams are going the same direction as the air is, there's less pressure on the bottom and that causes the baseball to move from top to bottom. If you're throwing a fastball, the seams on the bottom are moving forward, so that would cause the ball not to fall as fast as it would have. It doesn't actually rise, but it doesn't fall. It's Bernoulli's flow theory."

This kind of talk was typical of the conversations between the two. Sain was, in Marshall's often harsh estimation, perhaps the most thought-ful pitching coach he'd ever known. He believed that most of them had no idea what they were talking about, but Sain at least had some. Sain was never afraid to approach Marshall and ask him a question, seeking out a deeper understanding of the craft he was trying to teach.

Still, Sain's approach didn't suit everyone. Fred Lasher, a fastball pitcher, felt that the more often he threw the more he lost in terms of velocity, and that he could have used more traditional instruction. Under Sain, he said, the pitchers never sat down to discuss hitters and their weaknesses or any of the tailored tactical approaches a pitcher needs when facing hitters with different strengths. Lasher could throw the ball high and get it out over the plate. What he lacked, however, was an understanding of situational pitching.

Sain, upon his arrival in Detroit, faced a question no pitching coach should ever have to ask of himself: what to do about Denny and his teammate and nemesis Mickey Lolich? They'd come up to the majors within 19 months of each other and had grown to loathe each other. Lolich openly complained that McLain swam against the current, that he was separate from the team. McLain felt that Lolich was jealous of anyone who earned more press.

But Sain and Naragon thought highly of both pitchers from the very start. Despite the two pitchers' reputations for being difficult, the coaches felt they were both hardworking, open-minded ballplayers who were willing to work on the mechanical things that Sain tried to teach them.

Though McLain had won 20 games in 1966, Sain found teaching him a challenge. It wasn't because he wasn't interested. McLain was studious and serious. But the controlled breaking ball, the pitch that Kaat and Grant had used with tremendous success, eluded McLain. Sain taught the pitch to Al Downing and Whitey Ford within one day. For McLain, he said, it took a year.

He just couldn't see it. Then, after a rainout, Sain and Naragon approached McLain and asked him if he wanted to throw. They implored him to work on it, telling him, "We're really close, we're really close."

They were right. The two worked with McLain for over an hour. By the time he left, he "had it." He had it, and would never lose it — not until he lost it all. From that moment, he could "throw that fucking pitch anytime I wanted for a strike. Any time."

McLain needed that pitch, Sain thought. Though he had the overhand curveball, it was hard to control with any consistency since it relied on a dramatic drop. If not thrown precisely right, it gave the hitter enough time to adjust and to launch it far, far into the stands. Sain tried to shorten McLain's pitch and added his version of a slider—the hard curve, or "slurve"—to his arsenal. The short breaking ball was something McLain could control more easily. In addition, Sain helped refine what was already a very good moving fastball.

Sain learned to tread lightly with McLain as well. Since he was the kind of player who could lash out at you at any moment, Sain relied on the power of suggestion with him, making it seem like McLain was forging his own path.

He also worked to establish common ground with McLain, which other coaches and managers had failed to do. Sain didn't play the organ, but he'd been a pilot once, which was something McLain was deeply interested in. So they talked about Sain's struggles in the service, how in desperation he'd once read an entire book on instrument flying into a tape recorder, listening to it again and again until he could recite it by heart. Later on, Sain helped McLain study for his own pilot exams. Sain also knew better than others when to keep his distance with McLain, and he also knew what to say when he was in trouble on the mound to trigger an "automatic physical reaction" that McLain wouldn't even be aware of.

From the outset it looked like 1967 would follow the narrative that Joe Falls had outlined for the team. The Tigers would find solid ground, come together, and win the pennant with ease. Coming off those 20 wins, with Sain and Naragon behind him, McLain would be able to reach back even further, to pitch better than even he could imagine. What no one could have known was that darker forces would gather at the very moment when four teams were trying to best one another in the greatest pennant race in American League history. Racial tensions would run high. And the world would collapse around the Tigers.

5

THE BREAK

THIS WAS AFTER. After the last punches were thrown, after the police had left and tempers — for the moment — had cooled to a mere simmer. It was the evening of July 3, 1967, and Dal Maxvill stood on the mound with his friend and teammate Bob Gibson. Just how long the fight had lasted didn't really matter. It would rank among the worst in the history of the game and in the process help harden Gibson's reputation as the game's great intimidating force.

Now Maxvill watched as Gibson moved his pitching hand, playing with his thumb, shaking it off. Before the fight, Gibson had been throwing a perfect game. Now he had trouble gripping the ball, but he didn't seem to care. Inspecting his hand, he finally said to Maxvill: "That was fun. That was really fun."

Fun? Maxvill thought. *Fun?* Well, maybe. No one missed playing time or was permanently scarred or crushed beneath a pile. Larry Jaster — who had been sent home from the park early owing to his start the following day — had listened in his car to the whole thing on the Cardinals' home radio station, KMOX, feeling remiss for not being a part of it.

Fights were common then, though they weren't usually this intense. In this violent, tense time, however, events like this, George Vecsey believed, mirrored the tensions outside the park. In a country in the midst of civil unrest, how could anyone, he reasoned, escape the tension if the National Game itself embodied our national spirit?

"Nobody can escape the tensions of 1967," the young Vecsey wrote of the increased violence in baseball, "not even a high salaried baseball player accustomed to a good living, to the cheering of fans, to professional pride. He is being bugged, whether he knows it or not. Vietnam is bugging him one way or the other, and the high cost of living is bugging him, one way or the other, and the overcrowding of cities, and race."

Vecsey was reaching. Violence, contrary to the beliefs of those who view the game as a pastoral pastime, has been with baseball since the beginnings. And Gibson, though black, reflected the mind-set of the game's rough traditions. Afterwards, people would put little of the blame on him, but rather overlook the culpability of Lou Brock, who had violated etiquette by continuing to steal bases even after the Cardinals had jumped to a 7–0 lead in the first inning. Brock, who by now had surpassed Maury Wills as the supreme base stealer in the game, was simply padding his stats. The game, as far as the Reds were concerned, was already finished. Gibson was pitching like Gibson. Not yet the Big Red Machine, Cincinnati saw no way of coming back. A steak at Stan Musial and Biggie's (the famous restaurant half owned by the Hall of Famer) or drinks at the Chase Hotel seemed very close at hand.

As far as Brock was concerned, however, the game hadn't ended. He was playing baseball the only way he knew how — mercilessly, with little attention to scores or governance. After Brock tried to steal when he reached base in his second at-bat, it should have come as no surprise when relief pitcher Don Nottebart knocked down shortstop Julián Javier, or when he plunked Brock as he stood at the plate for the third time. Called upon to do his part to avenge these insults, even in the midst of his perfect game, Gibson threw the ball at Reds third baseman Tony Pérez in the fifth inning. It didn't hit Pérez, just sailed past his ear. That, Gibson believed, should have been enough. When Pérez flied out, Gibson seemed willing to let it go — until Pérez, jogging back to the dugout, muttered something indiscernible but incendiary to Gibson, who responded, his teammates believed, with something along the lines of "Fuck you."

That was the beginning. Reds catcher Johnny Edwards called what happened next "probably one of the best fights" he'd ever seen. Soon Gibson and Pérez had moved closer and were eyeing each other, with a sellout crowd looking on, uncertain of what would follow. Certainly they couldn't anticipate that Orlando Cepeda, the Cardinals first baseman, would position himself between the two men in an attempt to break things up — not as a call for the dugouts and bullpens to clear. Nor could they imagine that Bob Lee, a relief pitcher who Tim McCarver said had a history with Cepeda from their time together in winter ball, would charge into the fray, calling out, "I want Cepeda! I want Cepeda!" The man he sought out responded by knocking Lee clear to the ground.

Like others, McCarver later said he'd never seen anything quite like it. It wasn't a traditional baseball brawl as much as a series of individual matches fought in almost round-robin fashion, men paired off against one another, moving from one fight to the next. Behind home plate, Edwards tangled with Cardinals reliever Joe Hoerner, getting his punches in even after Hoerner fell to the ground. A policeman stuck his billy club square into the stomach of Jim Maloney. Pete Rose, who fought Cardinals pitcher Jim Cosman, claimed that Cepeda knocked him in the back of the head three times. Nottebart, whose job it was to pay Brock back for his perceived insolence, emerged from the whole thing with cuts to the face that he blamed on Brock himself. The Cardinals' Bobby Tolan went flying headfirst into the Reds dugout. Gibson said that he ended up beneath a group of Reds players, fighting off Rose and Reds second baseman Tommy Helms, among others. The latter said Gibson had chipped his tooth in the fight. And though he denied it, St. Louis officers claimed that Reds manager Dave Bristol dislocated the jaw of a policeman named Robert Casey — the only person who would actually need hospital care. Gibson, who jammed his finger in the midst of the brawl, finished the game with 12 strikeouts.

Though he would go on to defend Brock in writing, one person who knows Gibson well suggested that Gibson did in fact hold a grudge against his teammate for this kind of recklessness, and that he never liked having to support Brock in these moments. It was unnecessary and put him in a bad spot. With the team clearly ahead, Brock had forced Gibson to do something he would have rather not done. This person would claim that Gibson simply didn't respect Brock in the way he did

Flood. Sure, he admired how Brock made a science out of studying pitchers and stealing bases like he did. But when Brock ignited the temper of other teams, as he did against Cincinnati, Gibson resented the fact that he'd often have to retaliate.

Despite his reputation, Gibson never enjoyed going after people — unless they tried to cheat by leaning over the plate. Gibson told his teammate Dick Groat that he didn't want to knock people down, and when asked to do it he would complain. "Why me? There's nine other pitchers." After all, Groat would joke, Gibson was "wild enough without intentionally throwing at anyone."

Three years had passed since that historic World Series win, when Keane told Gibson that he was on his way to great things. What Keane didn't say was that he himself would be moving on, leaving the Cardinals and Gussie Busch for what seemed like a better arrangement with the Yankees; he told Busch of his intentions only moments before a press conference announcing a contract extension. As it happened, Keane lasted less than two seasons with New York, displaced in May 1966 by the very man who'd hired him, Ralph Houk. Not long after, having taken up a scouting position with the Angels, Keane's heart gave out while evaluating talent in Texas.

When Gibson heard the news that Johnny Keane was dead, at the age of 55, he was shaken. In a moment of uncharacteristic openness, he said that Keane's death "affected me as much as anybody's I've ever known."

In the season following Keane's departure, the Cardinals collapsed, though no one quite knew why. They were a year older, but that didn't seem enough to explain their fall to seventh place and 80 wins. Groat called his '65 effort "the worst year I ever had in my life."

Many put the blame on Busch, who, late in August 1964, made changes that irrevocably altered the makeup of the tight-knit Cardinals. Prior to the Phillies' epic collapse, Busch fired general manager Bing Devine, the man who had built the team and had the steely confidence to trade for Brock at midseason despite others' reservations. Replacing him was Bob Howsam, who traded away the team's veterans, including Groat, Bill White, and Ken Boyer, after the team's 1965 showing. This might have been fine — they were getting creaky after all. But Howsam's rigid management style didn't suit the Cardinals. There were nightly bed checks, rules about how uniforms should be worn, and even, according to Gibson, guidelines for maintaining good posture while sitting in the dugout.

Howsam was, by all accounts, the wrong man for the wrong team at the wrong time. Thus, few of the Cardinal players — and certainly not Gibson — were devastated when Howsam left for Cincinnati following the 1966 season. In time he would help build the Reds into the team that would dominate the National League in the 1970s, fielding the greatest lineup the game had ever seen.

As for the Cardinals, it was left to Gussie Busch to set things right, to repair the damage that he'd caused. Since buying the Cardinals in 1953 — out of a sense of civic responsibility and as an opportunity to lift the profile of his family's company, Anheuser-Busch — he had taken more than a passing interest in the team's inner workings. For a time, he wore a uniform in spring training. He'd run through general managers and field managers. He'd tried, unsuccessfully, to buy stars like Gil Hodges and Ernie Banks. He'd hire then chase away good men.

Though his personal failings and pride would harm the Cardinals much later, at this juncture in 1964 Busch made the right decision. Instead of replacing Keane with Leo Durocher, as many had expected, he chose instead the soft-spoken Cardinal favorite Red Schoendienst, who was just two seasons removed from his stellar playing career. And he installed Stan Musial, the iconic Cardinal, as general manager in Howsam's place in January 1967. No two men seemed better suited to stand back and let the thinking man's team, well, think.

Union organizer Marvin Miller found this unusual shared intelligence apparent when he visited the team in 1966 while touring spring training camps. Lobbying to head the MLBPA, the thin, mustached man would come into team clubhouses and encourage players to open up, to voice their views and concerns. Usually he was met with shyness and silence.

When other players from other teams approached him with questions, privately, he sensed fear. Fear that, should they act like a proper trade union, they would be opening themselves up to an endless series of labor stoppages. Fear that, if the owners didn't care for Miller, the players would face recriminations from those who controlled their livelihoods. After a couple of such meetings, Miller decided that he needed to explain the basics.

Labor-management relations, he told the players, if conducted properly, are inherently at odds. Not in every case, and not on every issue. However, with few exceptions, if the union is acting in the best interest of the players, and the management is acting in what it perceives to be the best interest of the owners, then the two sides will invariably disagree.

"There'll be some things you can work cooperatively on, but just think of some of the things we're talking about that are benefits to you but costs to them," Miller told them. "That's not a common interest, it's just the opposite. So if I do my job properly, it is not likely that the owners are gonna like me, and you have to understand that going in.

"There are situations where the owners and the management officials of the corporation are quite fond of the union representative," he told them. "If that ever happens here, I have some advice for you: fire me. I mean it. It is not in the scheme of things that they should like me. Respect me, maybe, but you've gone too far when you want them to like me."

With the Cardinals, Miller didn't need to make this speech. Unlike most teams, they spoke openly about their concerns, and they understood what it meant to have a man such as Miller represent them. He also sensed a cohesiveness among the blacks, whites, and Latin Americans on the team. After that initial tour, when asked who would win the 1966 pennant, he'd say, without hesitation, the St. Louis Cardinals.

As it turned out, Miller was off by a year. But he wasn't wrong in his assessment of the team's camaraderie. The Cardinals had famously integrated their spring training living facilities in St. Petersburg, Florida, in 1962, a move that irrevocably helped diminish racial hostilities within the club. As Dick Hughes, who won 16 games for the Cardinals in 1967, later said, the warm rapport had to do with a genuine sense among players that they belonged together as a team. Since few players and coaches owned a home in St. Louis, many Cardinals and their families lived in an apartment complex not far from the airport. Players drove to the ballpark together and enjoyed each other's company in the off-hours.

One might assume that Gibson held himself apart from all this, but that wasn't the case. Along with Hughes, he played guitar in a team band, of all things.

To the celebrated cultural historian Gerald Early, then a young man growing up in Philadelphia, the Cardinals could not have looked more different from the team closest to him. As he watched the trials of Phillies outfielder Dick Allen, perhaps baseball's most mercurial black player, even then he could understand the ever-present tension between Allen and the team, the burden of being a black superstar in a less-than-progressive organization and a city where racial tensions were always simmering. To him, the Cardinals seemed special in contrast: smart, determined, jovial, but with the fierceness that fires the best of teams.

Perhaps the most important move Bob Howsam made in his short, tumultuous term with the Cardinals was to bring on Orlando Cepeda. By 1966, Cepeda was no longer San Francisco's dreamy young star and in fact had come to embody everything that went wrong for the Giants, a talented team stocked with talented players who persistently underachieved, winning just one lone pennant in 1962. Like the Cardinals, the Giants were a diverse group. But unlike St. Louis, they self-divided into separate factions — Hispanics and blacks and whites kept their distance from one another, staying within their own separate orbits.

"Our skins might be lighter," Juan Marichal complained to the *Saturday Evening Post*, "but the breaks we get from baseball and the outside are much less than the Negro player gets." (Marichal would quickly deny most of the reporting in the piece.)

Certainly Alvin Dark, the Giants manager from 1961 to 1964, made things worse. He did his best to keep Latin American players from speaking Spanish and even banned Spanish music in the locker room. "We have trouble because we have so many Negro and Spanish-speaking players on this team," Dark said at one point. "They are just not able to perform up to the white ballplayers when it comes to mental alertness.

"You can't make most Negro and Spanish players have the pride in their team that you can get from white players," he continued. "And they just aren't as sharp mentally. They aren't able to adjust to situations because they don't have the same mental alertness." (Dark later disavowed these remarks. Jackie Robinson, of all people, came to his defense.)

As time went on, and as Cepeda began to seem more and more susceptible to injury, he found himself subject to personal attacks. Following the Giants' failure in the 1962 Series, *Look* magazine claimed that the team sought to trade him because: "(1) He doesn't produce the crucial hit often enough. (2) He is not a team man. (3) When things go wrong, he blames everybody but Orlando. (4) He does not rebound and take it out on the opposition. (5) He is a hardy holdout every year." The piece led Cepeda to wage a $1 million suit against the magazine on the premise that the article had irrevocably damaged his standing as a ballplayer.

Things should have improved for Cepeda when the Giants replaced Dark with Herman Franks in 1965, but they didn't. The two, despite an auspicious beginning, began to detest each other. By November 1965, as Howsam began to search the scanner for hitters, Cepeda's knees had given out and he was considered damaged goods. The Giants traded him to the Cardinals for pitcher Ray Sadecki early in the 1966 season.

Ballplayers can find new lives in new places. That's how it was for Cepeda when he joined the Cardinals. Franks and Dark and *Look* were all behind him. The team doctor told him to take care of his hits and the Cardinals, in turn, would take care of him. Now he could begin anew.

"He came here and he took the pressure off all the hitters," Lou Brock said in 1967. "Curt Flood and I are basically singles hitters. Having Cepeda means we score runs and don't have to strain. Then, our nucleus is running. It's a running team that brings out the fire. It brings out the giant within you. The Giants had a nucleus of power. They just waited around for somebody to hit a home run. Our cycle helped bring out the fire in Cepeda.

"Finally," Brock continued, "I think the way he's helped us is with his enthusiasm. He's always optimistic. You can get bugged in this game, you know. But Cepeda is always there, very energetic, full of fire, and it's catching."

By then, Howsam was gone and Musial had stepped in for his brief stint as the Cardinals' general manager, a post he seemed to take on as a kind of civic obligation. It had been five seasons since Maris and Mays challenged each other to break Babe Ruth's single-season home run mark, yet, as Gay Talese noted, their era had passed all too quickly.

Their time was done. Following a hand injury in 1965, Maris lost much of the power that had helped him surpass Ruth and fend off Mantle. Baseball had become a drain for Maris, who even at his height couldn't deal with the New York press. He made it clear to the Yankees that he was ready to end his career after the last game of the 1966 season. But Yankees president Lee MacPhail prevailed upon him to stay active, for reasons of his own.

"Lee, if you have any intentions of trading me, let me know now, and I'll announce my retirement," Maris told MacPhail.

"No, we have no intentions of trading you," MacPhail said. But days later MacPhail did trade him, and Maris, out of spite toward the New York press, which would have vilified him, decided not to retire.

If Maris was initially uneasy about coming to St. Louis, the feeling was mutual. Though the Cardinals knew the tabloids could unfairly malign a player, they did not know how much of Maris's reputation as cold and moody was deserved. Moreover, bringing him in meant moving pieces on the board — like forcing Mike Shannon, by then one of the game's best right fielders, to switch to third base. Maxvill, among others, had pressed Shannon to resist. But in the end Shannon made the move and the Cardinals, as they had done with Cepeda, welcomed Maris into the fold.

"It's been fun since I've been here," Maris said a year into his life in St. Louis. "I've never been in another clubhouse with all the racket of this one, the music blurting out all the time. It's quite relaxing. The old philosophy was, 'In the clubhouse, think baseball.' That's the way it was on the Yankee ballclub. You can win both ways, of course, but you can sometimes overdo the serious stuff."

Now, with Cepeda at center stage and power-stripped Maris finding new ways to help his team, the Cardinals once again took on a new championship form. There were team songs and a new nickname — El Birdos. There was the sight of Cepeda standing on top of a money trunk, leading cheers even after losses.

"We have speed and power, and we have some guys who know what they are doing. One of the few things that sometimes bothers us is that people are in such a hurry to compare us with the Gashouse Gang," Maris said, referring to the Cardinals' 1934 championship team. "We are

El Birdos because Cha Cha named us that [actually it was a Cardinals official, not Cepeda] and that is what we want to be called and remembered as."

Again, one might expect that Gibson would have kept his distance from all the merriment, but he didn't. This wasn't the 1964 team, the one he grew up with and loved. He was older now, the established ace. But he quickly came to love this re-formed version as well. He took part in the cheering, and he forged a lifelong friendship with Cepeda. Once, when the first baseman was late getting to the team bus and the driver was ready to leave him behind, Gibson firmly said, "We're waiting for Cepeda. The pitchers aren't leaving without him."

As the industries that once made St. Louis an industrial force began to recede in importance, a new image of St. Louis emerged — one framed by the Gateway Arch, the steely symbol of grand postwar public works projects. Around the same time, the new Busch Memorial Stadium — the name Busch gave to the old Sportsman's Park when he bought the team and the venue — came rising up from a tract of land in the city's Chinatown, now a long-forgotten place. Built for over $30 million, with $5 million coming from Busch, the Cardinals began to play there in May 1966, less than two years after their first world championship of the Busch era.

In truth, there was nothing special about it. It wasn't the first or second or last stadium of its kind. Washington, DC, leaders christened the structure that would become Robert F. Kennedy Memorial Stadium in 1961. In 1964, Robert Moses's Valhalla, the Mets' Shea Stadium, located on the land where he had hoped to persuade Brooklyn Dodgers owner Walter O'Malley to move his team, rose in Flushing Meadows, Queens. Houston's Astrodome, the wonder of its age, followed in 1965. The Braves moved into Atlanta–Fulton County Stadium in 1966. Soon came nearly identical edifices in Cincinnati and Pittsburgh and Philadelphia. As baseball historian Gary Gillette has said, these weren't baseball parks at all, but structures erected primarily for football.

In time, everyone would come to hate these stadiums. But to walk into something so big, and so beautiful, brought players like Dal Maxvill a great deal of joy. Looking at it for the first time, Dick Hughes could remember the grime of Pittsburgh's Forbes Field, how dirty that stadium was, the dankness and depression of Philadelphia's Connie Mack Stadium, the venue that had once been Shibe Park. Busch Stadium was clean. And Hughes had a job in the major leagues. That was enough.

When Marvin Miller, now charged with leading the Players Association, arrived for the All-Star Game at Busch Stadium in 1966, he felt unnerved. As a boy growing up in Brooklyn, Ebbets Field was what he knew. As an adult in Pittsburgh, he'd known Forbes Field. But here, in this mega-stadium, he felt suddenly claustrophobic. Like thousands of fans, Miller had the sense that the walls of the stadium were closing in on him. Every so often during the game, he would forget that he was wearing a short-sleeve shirt and lean against a scalding-hot metal railing. Players needed oxygen tanks to get through the game. At 94, just one year before his death in 2012, Miller could still hear the loudspeaker calling for medics and stretchers. And he could still remember feeling himself begin to wilt as someone suggested that he ought to find a cool place.

In Tim McCarver's assessment, the Cardinals' new home had its issues. It was too big, he felt. But at the same time, he thought, "a ballpark is a ballpark."

It is and it isn't. Since Busch Stadium was built below street level, the ball didn't carry as much as it did at similar parks, particularly in Atlanta and Cincinnati. Even on a windy day, wind really wasn't much of a factor. It wouldn't push the ball out, helping doubles morph into home runs. At its construction, the stadium's power alleys were 386 feet from home plate and its center field was 414 feet away. In 71 games in its first season in use, batters hit a mere 89 home runs. Hitting a home run here required hitting the ball with incredible force, which of course pleased Gibson. The second Busch Stadium, he later said, was a "pitcher's paradise."

For all these changes, it seemed that very little had changed for Gibson the man. His record-setting World Series effort—he struck out a record 31 batters—didn't generate the cascade of commercial benefits he deserved. He'd seen others taking their places as pitchmen on radio and television, supplementing their incomes in various ways. But these avenues would not be open to Gibson, he quickly found out. No Madison Avenue agency came calling. No trench coat company or sporting goods czar wanted him, such a dark and terrifying figure, to endorse their products. There was nothing save a trip to Pasadena for the 1965 Rose Bowl, where Gibson played catch with McCarver on the Budweiser float during the parade surrounded by papier-mâché figures. Some reward, Gibson felt.

There was also the Corvette, awarded to him by *SPORT* magazine. It was a terrific car, sure. But it felt more like an obligatory gesture than a genuine act of devotion and gratitude. Furthermore, driving it proved problematic. He was a father of two with a family to tow around, not a man about town. The Corvette also attracted unwanted attention from the police, who would routinely pull him over because they couldn't believe that a black man could legally possess it.

And even as the Cardinals were trying to build an inclusive, racially sensitive club, St. Louis itself was not a welcoming place for black players. George Vecsey would later cringe at the thought of Bill White and his wife trying and failing to put down real roots in the area. Once, while sitting with teammates at a local suburban spot, Gibson was told by another customer, "We don't allow niggers in this place." Gibson knocked him down.

Even Omaha — the place of his birth, the city that dedicated a day in his honor following the '64 Series — proved no better for Gibson. Once, he was told he couldn't drink a Coca-Cola in a local bar. With one home, the family endured the indignity of neighbors who, fearing the Gibsons might actually move in, wouldn't let painters finish work on the house. Perhaps more insidious was the reaction when the Gibsons finally purchased a home in a suburban enclave of Omaha; as Rodney Wead would later recall, the aggressive behavior of some of their new neighbors was almost as harsh.

Gibson could have joined his wife and daughters in their protests in front of government buildings calling for fair housing. But that wasn't him. Instead, he channeled his frustration into getting better at what he did best — pitching.

By Gibson's own measure, he didn't truly learn how to pitch until after Keane left the Cardinals, in 1965. When Bob Purkey, the longtime right-hander for Pittsburgh and Cincinnati, came into the St. Louis clubhouse that same year, he spent a lot of time with Gibson. Purkey thought that Gibson could make use of his subpar curveball — a pitch Gibson hated because it often hung there like white linen on a laundry line — against left-handed hitters, who would swing wildly as it came toward them, expecting the ball to sail away from them.

Working with Purkey, Gibson developed what he called a "backup slider." It was a pitch that didn't "break away from a hitter," Gibson explained, but "holds its course and maybe even bends back a little like a screwball." Coming in toward the hitter, Purkey promised, would lead to broken bats and weakly hit balls hit off the fists. In truth, Gibson had been throwing this pitch without knowing it before. When Purkey asked him *when* he had done so, Gibson said it was when he'd accidently overthrown his slider. From then on, he'd occasionally overthrow it on purpose.

This marked the true start of Gibson's dominance. He could throw a sailing fastball by gripping the ball across the seams; by holding it along the seams, he could throw one that sank. Stiffening his wrist eventually helped make the slider unhittable. By 1966, McCarver felt, Gibson knew how to control the outside corner against right-handed hitters, who would indeed either dive after the pitch or freeze up. Gibson understood how to break up a hitter's internal rhythm and get him to open up his front shoulder, throwing off his form. With that, it was over.

There was also what Gibson had created for himself, whatever his internal feelings: the visage of an unfeeling vehicle of annihilation. Through his avoidance of players from other teams, through the glare that he said was not a glower but a squint, his demeanor simply screamed out to everyone — the batter, the umpire, the thousands who came to watch — that he owned the frame to his own story, that this at-bat, this game, was his to control. Everything about Gibson, Roger Angell wrote, looked "mean and loose." Outwardly, in the parlance of the filmmaker Ken Burns, there was an unforgivable blackness to him: he was as dark as the darkest villain, a man pitching from a place of anger, with no remorse.

In his personal life, Gibson could be someone else. When Wead worked with Wesley House, the not-for-profit agency that aided thousands of black residents in Omaha, Gibson would often secretly act in concert with him. In the days before Christmas, swearing his friend to silence, he would tell Wead, "Let's go down and do some shopping for the kids in the projects." Each year Gibson would spend thousands of dollars on presents, telling Wead and his staff that if they told anyone, "I'm not going to do it next year." Later in life, Gibson would be more public, helping Wead establish a radio station, a community bank, and a credit union. These were Wead's ideas, but Gibson helped bankroll them. But in this philanthropic act, he wanted to remain that mysterious figure, the unknown man.

What was no secret at all, however, was that by midseason in 1967, Gibson had become not only a complete pitcher but one capable of sustained greatness. A 20-win, perhaps even 22-win season seemed not only within reach but inevitable. If reached, he would have won 20 games for three straight years, and he knew that level of success would come with off-season spoils. But then came July 15.

It wasn't a line drive, said McCarver, but a hop. A hop, sharp and searing with all the power of a line drive, but a hop nonetheless, one whose malignant bounce might have ended Gibson's season, putting the Cardinals' season in doubt. But what followed next only added to his aura of invincibility and arrogance and will as he emerged as the league's top pitcher now that Koufax, no longer able to pitch with that aching arm, had left the game.

It was the fourth inning. Gibson was squared off against Roberto Clemente, whose brief life and heroic humanitarian efforts have often overshadowed the fact that he was perhaps the National League's most tenacious hitter. With his 40-ounce bat, Gibson's teammate Nelson Briles felt, you never wanted to throw the ball over the plate and down to Clemente, since it would come back screaming like a banshee through the pitching mound.

But that was precisely where Gibson put it, with the Cardinals in first place but still very much in a pennant race with the Chicago Cubs. McCarver had wanted a fastball, then a curve, only to have Gibson shake him off. What Gibson wanted to throw — and who could blame him — was his slider, by now his best pitch. If the slider broke as it usually did,

Clemente would lunge at it ineptly — as so many National League hitters did against that pitch — but he'd be unable to reach it as it hit the outside corner for a strike.

That might have happened had the ball come two inches further. But it came down in the middle of the plate, and Clemente fired it through the pitcher's mound. Hopping with incredible force, it shot through Gibson's right leg. At that moment, everything seemed unreal. At once the pain came rushing up through the leg. Gibson fell to the ground. The ball rolled to the shortstop. Clemente was easily safe at first base.

"I'm fine," the grounded Gibson said as the team trainer came to the mound. "I'm fine."

The trainer could see the dent in Gibson's leg just above the ankle. But Gibson insisted that it was just a bruise, that it only needed a piece of tape. The trainer sprayed the spot with ethyl chloride to deaden the pain so that Gibson could stand up and continue to pitch, which was what he did for the next three batters.

It turned out to be one of the more memorable innings of Gibson's career. He walked Willie Stargell, he popped up Bill Mazeroski, and then, while facing Donn Clendenon on a 3-2 count, he landed hard on the leg Clemente had bashed. Gibson fell to the ground — this time for good. The trainer and Schoendienst came running toward the mound and carried Gibson off the field. Watching the whole thing from his post, Maxvill could only hope that it looked far worse than it was. With Maris and Cepeda on board, the Cardinals had seemed ready to make a charge toward the National League pennant and the World Series. But what now?

After the game, the Cardinals found Gibson, their star pitcher, sitting in front of his locker, wearing a white walking cast. He'd already been to the hospital, where X-rays confirmed that he had a fractured fibula. In his stubbornness, Gibson had exacerbated his injury by insisting on pitching to those other batters.

Gibson's concern, he admitted later, was not only about his team's fortunes but about his own year. Because he'd struggled to add to his coffers through ancillary means, he'd seen this season as a way to earn more income. All of that seemed in doubt now. Sitting quietly with his crutches at his side, he quite characteristically avoided reporters' questions and stared silently at the long cast that encased his leg. In a rare moment of self-pity, he asked himself, *Why me?*

While he recuperated, he'd still be able to throw, team physician I. C. Middleman said — not hard, but just enough so that he would be ready in his return.

"Normally," Middleman explained, "you'd have to think about keeping the cast on four to six weeks. But with Gibby, we should be able to take it off in three weeks. He has big, thick bones."

When Wead traveled from Omaha to St. Louis, he found his friend inconsolable. Gibson played with his model cars and continued to put out his column for the *St. Louis Post-Dispatch,* and he and Wead played cards. But Gibson couldn't hide his restlessness. His team not only stayed in contention but ran away with the pennant — with Nelson Briles taking his spot in the rotation.

During this time, Gibson was a regular at the clubhouse. Once the press had dispersed, he'd walk in wearing dark sunglasses, doing his impression of Ray Charles, weaving his head back and forth, something McCarver later said was the funniest damn thing he'd ever seen. His teammates knew better than anyone that Gibson's great sense of humor was one of his biggest secrets. He was a talented mimic, cracking up his teammates with his impressions not only of the blind Ray Charles but other ballplayers — like Willie Mays, whose high-pitched, nearly tweenish voice Gibson could capture like no one else.

"Get out of the clubhouse!" Maxvill once yelled during one of Gibson's visits. "Put on a uniform or get out! You're eating up too much of our food spread after the game, and you're taking up valuable space on the training table!"

The press hounded him, eager to quiz him about his return. But he had no tolerance for their questions and was certainly not going to be polite about it. He hung a sign around his neck with a menu of possible responses:

1. YES, It'S off!!!
2. No it doesn't HURT!
3. I'm not supposed to walk on it For ONE WEEK!!

4. I don't Know How much longer!
5. ASK Doc Bauman!
6. ASK Doc MiddlEMan!

Later that year, reporter Terry Dickson was assigned to profile Gibson, but nearly backed out. He'd scheduled his appointment the same day Gibson was scheduled to pitch, a day that everyone knew to stay away from him. But Dickson visited Gibson anyway, at the house he was renting in St. Louis. Understandably nervous, Dickson feared that Gibson would be curt. Instead, the pitcher opened up to him, laying out all his frustrations.

"Suppose, for example, you were a garbage collector and every day about 100 people stopped you and asked you how much garbage you collected that day and how much you expected to collect the next day," Gibson said, explaining his attitude toward fans and the press. "I would welcome someone who wanted to come up and talk to me as though I was a person who could talk about something besides last night's game or tomorrow's game."

Leaving Gibson's home, Dickson said, "I'll try to tell it like it is."

"You'd better or I just won't ever talk to you again," Gibson said.

"He was smiling and pleasant," Dickson wrote. "But the message came through."

Gibson made his improbable return on September 7, in a game against the Mets at Shea Stadium. The Cardinals were now 11½ games ahead and had the pennant in hand. Unlike three years prior, when Gibson had led the historic comeback over the Phillies, this time he'd watched from the sidelines as his teammates won the whole thing without him. Lifted after five innings, and with an 8–1 lead against the Mets, Gibson admitted: "I was a little shaky at first with my control, especially in the first inning. That was evident from all the pitches I made—82 of them. I was pleased with myself. I was feeling my way at first, but then I said, 'to heck with it,' and cut loose.

"The only time I've felt it in the last six weeks was when you reporters reminded me about it," Gibson said, when asked about concerns over his leg. "The only thing I was worried about was my control. I wasn't getting enough of the pitches where I wanted to put them."

Four more starts followed. On September 18, Gibson took the mound against the Phillies in Philadelphia, the pennant on the line. The Cardinals had moved slowly with his progress, gradually building his innings as he recovered his strength. But here he was, shutting out the opposing team in a complete game and sealing the title. ("I was never surprised at anything Bob did," McCarver said. "But coming back from a broken leg in the way that he did it and the time that he did it, I don't think that will ever happen again.") The Cardinals finished with 101 wins, 10½ games ahead of the Giants. Now, with Koufax gone and the Dodgers in decline, Gibson had a chance to make the decade his own.

6

INTO THE CITY
OF ASHES

O N   T H E   A F T E R N O O N   O F   J U L Y   2 4 ,   1 9 6 7, several
members of the Detroit Tigers stood on a yacht that had
been docked at a private club in Grosse Pointe, Michigan.
All through the previous night and into the morning they had debated
whether this trip—held on an off day between games in the middle of
the most competitive play-off race in American League history—was a
wise idea. They knew, of course, what was happening across the water.
The day before, while playing a doubleheader in the enclosed fortress
that was Tiger Stadium, they'd seen the white smoke just beyond the
left-field wall—puffs of smoke early in the day, but eventually the sky
turned dark and menacing as the fires raged.

Dick Tracewski and his teammates learned between games what so
many across the city already knew, even in the midst of a citywide news
blackout. After the first game the team's clubhouse attendant told them,
"There's a riot going on right across the street here, on 12th Street." But
there was still a second game to play, so they played it and went home,
without much thought. That evening, along with the rest of the country,
Tracewski and his wife tried their best to understand what was happening as homes burned, stores were looted, shots were fired, and a metropolis came undone.

Teammates called one another asking, "Well, what do you think? Are we still going on that trip tomorrow?" Monday was their day off, and on Tuesday they would face Baltimore, the defending World Series champions, at home. The chase for the American League pennant was taking its toll on everyone. Quite simply, they needed a break.

So they went. That morning, Tracewski and his wife drove from their home in suburban Birmingham down Eight Mile Road, then through a stretch of freeway nicknamed "The Lodge," entering the city. At 9:00 a.m. on a Monday, the road was usually clogged with commuters going downtown. But there was no one on the road that morning. At Grand Boulevard, they encountered a scene from a science fiction movie — fires shooting up high along both sides of the road. They continued on, the only car that dared to keep going.

When they reached Grosse Pointe, many teammates were already there waiting for them, including starting catcher Bill Freehan and Tigers icon Al Kaline. Setting out on the water, looking out across Lake St. Clair, they watched the clouds of black smoke drifting over the fallen city. Eventually Freehan, who was the team's representative to the new Major League Baseball Players Association, got word that the home series planned for the next day against the Orioles had been moved to Baltimore. They'd have to turn around, go home, and get ready to fly east.

Perhaps a month later, Tracewski took a ride down what remained of 12th Street. Once a neighborhood settled by Jews, the area around 12th Street was subsequently settled by blacks who had come to the city, seeking the promise of the North. But the reality was staggering poverty and hardship. Still, with its bustling businesses, there had remained a vibe to the place, the breeding ground for the Motown Sound. Now everything was gone.

It's easy to look back at Detroit before the riots through the hazy lens of history and see it as the model of integration, of reform, of the realization of the promise of 20th-century America. The city's progressive, forward-thinking mayor, Jerome P. Cavanagh, was sympathetic to the needs of the poor and the blacks who increasingly made up large swaths of Detroit. New, gleaming skyscrapers had transformed the skyline. The auto industry still bloomed. Young black leaders, like the promising congressman John Conyers, had risen to power. In 1965, *Fortune* magazine proclaimed that, "of all the accomplishments in the recent history of the city, the most significant is the progress Detroit has made in race relations."

As the city looked inward, it embraced this idea of racial progress. In May 1967, the *Detroit News,* the city's more conservative daily, hailed the rise of the "Negro middle class," saying that their successes "deserve recognition" and offering congratulations. Around the same time, the *Detroit News* launched a series entitled "Urban Challenge," asking in one article, "Can the Cities Survive?"

"A decade or two ago, most people were skeptical," the reporter wrote. "Today, with the emergence of imaginative leadership, the infusion of massive doses of federal aid and private capital, there is a psychological turnabout, a new morale.

"Big Cities," he concluded, "such as Detroit can answer the survival question with a strong 'maybe,' perhaps even 'yes.'"

The national reaction to the Detroit riots was one of disbelief and despair. As the social historian Sidney Fine would later note, in the days following, Eastern media outlets went into mourning. The *Washington Post* deemed the city's situation all the more tragic because "Detroit has been the model of intelligence and courage applied to the governance of a huge industrial city." The *New York Times* lamented that Detroit "probably had more going for it than any other major city in the North."

But for residents of Detroit, there had been signs. The city's murder rate had grown precipitously through the decade. As the historian Thomas Sugrue would write, by 1967 Detroit was really past its prime, no longer "Detroit the Dynamic" or "The Arsenal of Democracy." Two decades had passed since the defense industry called on Detroit to help America win World War II. Large factories used for the production of weapons and military vehicles now stood derelict. Unemployment, particularly for young black males, was reaching untenable levels. The U.S. Justice Department took a dim view of the city's police force and its raids on "blind pigs" — after-hours clubs in the poorest sections of town.

Leading up to July 23, *Detroit Free Press* reporter Mary Ann Weston visited grocery stores in the "inner city" and spoke to the people who shopped in them. What she discovered was a base inequity: despite diminished resources, the poor had to pay more for groceries and the basic necessities of life. It seemed clear to her that the "Model Cities" program, launched as part of President Lyndon Johnson's "Great Society" antipoverty initiative and touted by Cavanagh, had done little to change the lives of those it was meant to help. The day-to-day suffering went on. Little did she know that before the summer was out, those very same stores she visited would no longer exist.

The riots began in the early hours of July 23, when the police force's riot unit—entrusted with preventing what had happened in Buffalo and Watts, in Newark and Cleveland—was off duty. A raid by white police officers on an after-hours club on 12th Street, the epicenter of poor Detroit, set off five days of violence. Most of the more than 80 people who were in the club at the time had gathered to celebrate the return of two soldiers from Vietnam. Over the next few hours, they were loaded into paddy wagons—not through the building's locked back entrance but through the front doors, where a crowd had gathered to watch—and taken to the holding cells of Detroit's 10th Precinct. At some point, a bottle was thrown, then another and another and another. By 6:30 a.m., the first fires were set, and the firefighters who were dispatched to put out the fires were stoned. At 11:30 a.m., Conyers, the bright young man who many felt represented the new Detroit, stood on top of his car at the intersection of 12th and Clairmount Streets. Holding a bullhorn, he pleaded with the gathering mob to "stay cool."

"We're with you!" he said. Many in the crowd responded by shouting: "No, no, no!" When someone launched a rock at Conyers, it seemed all was lost. A city. A dream. A future.

By late afternoon, as the Yankees-Tigers doubleheader continued, Cavanagh asked Governor George Romney to bring in the ill-prepared Michigan National Guard. It wouldn't be enough. As July 23 became July 24, Vice President Hubert Humphrey assured Governor Romney that federal help was forthcoming, but the U.S. Army wasn't mobilized until much later in the day. Lyndon Johnson, who was poised to take on Romney in the 1968 presidential election, blamed the Republican governor for his incompetence in action. Before it was all over, 43 people were killed, over 1,100 were injured, and, by Fine's account, 2,509 stores had been looted, burned, or otherwise destroyed.

In his first autobiography, written with ghostwriter Phil Pepe, Bob Gibson grossly misread the significance of the kind of violence taking place in cities like Detroit when he likened the riots to a pitcher taking action against his opponent.

"Negroes have been mistreated for years," Gibson wrote. "They are getting tired of being mistreated, misused, and misunderstood, and the only way they can rebel is to stage riots. If you're getting pushed around, if they're knocking you all around the lot, you're going to protect yourself. You're going to brush him back from the plate.

"You're going to riot and get him to think a little," he continued. "Blowing up places and rioting are, in my opinion, just like a brushback pitch. The reason for the riots is to point out to the people that these things are going on and they should be changed, something should be done. The white man sits back expecting the Negro to fail. The Negro can succeed. All he needs is a little help like everybody else has had."

He would go on to say that he believed things "are getting better, but they're not getting better fast enough. I'll tell you one way they'd get better faster in Omaha — if they start blowing up downtown Omaha instead of their own homes in the ghetto."

Whatever their cause, the national riots would forever change how Americans viewed their urban centers. The images captured in 1967 of an American city in flames remain with us to this day. Of the many indelible images from that time, one still stands out — that of the handsome young reporter William Serrin, his head and white shirt almost entirely covered in blood. Serrin, who was born in Saginaw, had worked his way up from papers in Flint, Ann Arbor, and Ypsilanti, and then Toledo, Ohio, before going to the *Free Press* in 1966. He was 28 years old at the time; already a widower and the single father of a young daughter, he lived with his late wife's parents in Pontiac. As one of the first reporters on the scene, he could tell that things were about to explode. People told him to leave, but he found a phone and called his news desk, telling them, "This is a full-scale riot, you'd better get some people out here; it is starting to go." Before he knew it, people were throwing objects, any objects, through the air—bricks, bottles, anything they could find. Not long after, Serrin was at the hospital, but then he headed back to the newsroom and out into the field again.

Soon he found himself standing next to a general with the National Guard.

"Serrin," the general said, "do you know how you kill niggers?"

"I don't know."

"Machine guns and tanks," he answered. "Tanks and machine guns."

By this time, people had abandoned any hope that all this could be contained by peaceful means. Although there were those who saw the riots as an assertion of black power and a response to repression, in the days that followed some 77 percent of black residents surveyed felt that the police had acted too slowly, and over two-thirds shared the view that they should have acted "more firmly." At first the police, instructed to act without weapons, stood by, according to one account, as 11-year-old boys brazenly looted stores.

Now, as looters raided homes, houses burned, and snipers allegedly fired from rooftops, police and Guardsmen seemingly fired at will. Afterwards, in their Pulitzer Prize–winning investigation, Serrin and a team of *Free Press* reporters not only delved into the systemic issues that had led to the riots but discovered that many of the 43 people killed were actually victims—civilians felled by police officers or poorly trained Guardsmen who were utterly unprepared for what they faced. They were collateral damage in a five-day war that changed the perceptions and realities of Detroit. No longer a beacon, a model city, it was the poster child for social and racial dysfunction.

Some 20 years later, Barbara Stanton, whose brilliant reporting for the *Free Press* had headlined the newspaper's 1967 Pulitzer effort, solemnly articulated an "inescapable reality": there was actually "far more destruction and violence in Detroit in 1987 than in 1967.

"It is as if the riot had never ended but goes on in slow motion," Stanton continued. "Instead of a single, stupendous explosion, there is steady, relentless corrosion. It is happening now, a riot without end, a tragedy still without resolution."

• • •

With all of this unfolding, there remained baseball at Tiger Stadium. Those who were there on July 23 — players and broadcasters, ushers and fans — all have their own stories about what they knew when. Broadcasting the game with Ernie Harwell — the soothing and Southern-born radio voice of the Tigers — was Ray Lane, who saw the smoke beyond left field. Lane and Harwell couldn't see the fires, just smoke, and they didn't think much of it. But then their engineer's phone rang, and he had a message to convey: Tigers general manager Jim Campbell "does not want you to refer to that black smoke at all, so don't even mention it." So they didn't. The Tigers lost the first game and won the second while neither Lane nor Harwell nor the public-address announcer told the crowd about what lay beyond the stadium. After he left the stadium, Lane sat listening to his car radio, awaiting news, any news, but there was nothing. No talk of riots, no mention of a flame-engulfed city, just a passing remark about civil disturbances that had popped up around Detroit.

Everyone else who left the stadium had the same experience. They exited without warnings, with no words of caution from the public-address system, with only the announcement: "For Detroit, seven runs, twelve hits, no errors; for New York, three runs, nine hits, and one error. Winning pitcher, Hiller. Losing pitcher, Petersen. The Detroit Baseball Club has been advised that the Grand River, Linwood, and Fenkell bus lines will not be operating this evening. Please drive safely."

It was as if baseball occupied another world and Tiger Stadium was "The Shire." Writing for the July 25 edition of the *Free Press,* sports columnist Joe Falls spent his column inches waxing lyrical about a sailing trip he'd taken. A year later, Falls explained why. His publisher, he wrote, "told me that I wasn't to write a single line about what was happening in our streets. He told me that I should go on as if nothing was happening. He said we needed a point of reference in our newspaper, something to keep things in balance — something the people could understand.

"I never felt more inept in my life," he wrote. "I felt as deeply as anyone else about what was happening in my city and yet, I couldn't say a thing about the happenings."

That evening Denny McLain returned to his home in Woodcreek Farms, a suburb just off the Northwest Highway. Several family mem-

bers, including his aunt and uncle and his mother, were staying with
Denny and Sharyn that night, worried about rumors that "they" were
spreading out past the city's borders and into the suburbs. Each of the
adults took turns staying up with a Winchester handgun, terrified by
what had happened and fearful of what was to come.

Meanwhile, McLain's teammate and fellow pitcher Mickey Lolich
had retired to the Tiger Stadium locker room a frustrated man. He'd lost
in the opening game that day—his 10th straight loss. It didn't help that
the Tigers team behind him that day was listless, scoring just two runs.

He was helpless. He could have stayed around, sat with Sain, but to
what end? There was nothing to do but go home, riding the motorcycle that Campbell hated to his sprawling red brick colonial on 240 acres
in Washington, Michigan. His loss behind him now, Lolich planned on
barbecuing some ribs.

Then came the call. In the myth of the moment, Lolich changed out
of his baseball uniform and into his National Guard uniform at the stadium. In truth, it wasn't until he arrived home that he received his or-
ders to trek back to Detroit in full gear. Joining his unit, he watched
the prisoners coming into the police station one after another, some of
them, he said, "in really bad shape." Assigned to patrol the streets in
a deserted part of downtown and worried about snipers, he told one
writer that the situation was "ridiculous. I'd rather get shelled by line
drives any day than by bullets."

Though Lolich didn't know it, Willie Horton, then the team's left
fielder, was also in the streets. Thickly built and with a boyish face, Horton was the youngest of 21 children. Like millions of blacks who went to
cities like Omaha and Detroit, Oakland and Chicago, his father, Clinton,
had gone to Detroit in search of economic stability after he'd lost his job
as a coal miner in Virginia. By the time he was nine, Willie was living
in the Jeffries Housing Projects, close to The Lodge. Life was a struggle
for the family, but Horton was a standout baseball player from a young
age, and the Tigers kept their eye on him. He and Bill Freehan played
together as teenagers on a sandlot team. By the time he was a starter
for Northwestern High School, it seemed that everyone in the city had
heard of Willie Horton.

Horton has been credited with helping to build a bridge between the

Tigers and black fans. Armen Keteyian, who wrote perhaps one of the most sentimental and factually flawed documentaries of sport ever produced, *A City on Fire: The Story of the 1968 Detroit Tigers,* has said that "Willie Horton was the single greatest reason that there was a beginning of a unification in that city." In the same spirit, George Cantor said that when Horton joined the Tigers, "it was like the connection had finally been made between the black population of Detroit and this ballclub."

The early years were difficult for Horton. There were death threats, and he sought out security for his young children. Yet on the evening of July 23, Horton walked out of Tiger Stadium, still in full uniform, and headed to the epicenter of the unrest. He drove down 12th Street, along the same stretch where he once delivered papers as a kid. He climbed on top of his car, much as John Conyers had done some hours before, and pleaded for calm. It looked to him like the end of the world. Decades later he would still hear them — the voices beseeching him to get down, telling him there was nothing he could do. There was nothing baseball could do.

"I've never lived in Detroit but it always has been a very interesting city to me," Johnny Sain told one reporter early in the season. This comment was made upon his first return to Minnesota, where Twins pitchers had already expressed, with little fear of recrimination, how much they longed for him to appear once again in the players' section of the locker room, as though still lamenting a lost love. By now, Sain was refusing to comment very much about his departure, saying only that he'd felt that the Twins manager needed someone he could talk to, and that person could never be Sain. It might have made sense to strike out against his former bosses, but he refrained. The Yankees and Twins were his past now — Detroit was his present.

"Would you trade the Detroit staff for any other staff in the league?" Sain said. "I wouldn't."

However, the outsized personalities of his pitching staff, which he had been warned about, were on display from the outset and threatened to disrupt his work. Even before the season's start, Earl Wilson, who had struggled as one of the few black players on the Red Sox, openly lobbied to start on opening day in Anaheim, and openly groused when the slot went to McLain. Within two days, though, Wilson recanted, saying, "Every time Denny wins he puts money in my pocket."

"I'm going to build myself up for this one," McLain said in anticipation of that first start, which he would lose. "Now if I can find my fastball someplace."

All spring long, Sain had worked with McLain on his fastball, stressing the idea of rotation and movement, with little in the way of results. Still, Sain never wavered in his support or in his belief in the power of positive thinking.

Sain by then had established a pattern of separation—earning the separate trust of his pitchers even at the risk of alienating the man actually in charge of the team. Detroit would prove no different. While most of the Tigers' pitchers—especially the starters—took to Sain, the team as a whole seemed dismissive toward their new manager, Mayo Smith. As the season went on, the team weathered strange injuries as close observers spoke of dissension in the ranks, with younger players pitted against more seasoned ones.

Nevertheless, the Tigers remained close in the pennant race, falling in and out of first place throughout the summer. Despite their physical ailments, collectively they scored the second-most runs in the American League. And when McLain took the mound at Baltimore's Memorial Stadium on July 27, just four days after the start of the riots, he threw a seven-hit shutout against the American League's perennial power. The win was his 12th of the season, and his next start—with Lolich still on National Guard duty—would take place on two days' rest.

"I think we're ready to make our move now," said McLain, who had openly criticized the decision to move the series from Detroit to Baltimore, citing his fear for his family's safety.

Less than two months later, things looked remarkably different for McLain. As he would tell it, after a debilitating loss to the Red Sox on September 18, he kicked his locker in frustration, injuring his ankle. Later that night, in one of his retellings, he fell asleep in front of the television and was startled awake by a sound in his garage. In rushing to investigate, he claimed, he further injured his ankle, though at that moment he didn't think much of it. By the following morning, he was unable to put any weight on his foot — much less, with just 11 games left to play, help a team deadlocked with three others in a pennant race.

"I don't know if anyone will believe it," McLain said at the time, "but that's what happened."

He was right. *No one believed it.* Even the injury — was it an injured ankle or dislocated toes? — seemed to change depending on the story you read. Speculating about the actual cause of McLain's injury became something of a pastime among his teammates even as they tried to fix their gaze on an American League championship, which was still within reach in the last days of the season. By now, the Tigers had grown weary of McLain, of his brash predictions and his tendency to sidestep matters of fact.

When one reporter asked Mayo Smith who would start for him should the team manage to pry the pennant away, the oafish skipper said that he would put his faith in Lolich and Earl Wilson and Joe Sparma, provided "none of them falls off a sofa."

Within the clubhouse, Tigers broadcaster Larry Osterman heard the chatter. There were rumors of what had happened, but no proof. What was evident to him, though, was the anger directed at Denny, at what he'd done to himself and to the team's chances for the pennant.

There were also rumors of McLain's unsavory dealings with unsavory people. But no one knew much. It wasn't until early in 1970 that a detailed account emerged in *Sports Illustrated,* outlining McLain's supposedly illicit activities and revealing a possible real cause of his injury. It was a story of deceit and deception, one that depicted McLain as someone whose sense of invulnerability and brazen entitlement got him in way over his head, a victim of his own making. According to the piece, in early 1967 he'd invested heavily in a bookmaking outfit run out of a restaurant called the Shorthorn Steakhouse, where he could often be found playing the organ. The story alleged that McLain had partnered with Syrian mobsters. When one gambler won big — $46,000 — the bookie he counted on told him that he didn't have the money, that he'd have to collect from one of his partners, including McLain. When the gambler called another mob boss, Tony Giacalone, to intervene, Giacalone reportedly summoned a frightened McLain to his "boatwell," where he threatened him and, with the force of his heel, crushed and dislocated McLain's toes.

McLain admitted fully to sinking $15,000 into the bookmaking operation, along with a Pepsi executive, Edwin Schober, and two others. Schober had befriended McLain when he learned that the pitcher drank up to 25 bottles of his product a day. The two were regulars at the Shorthorn, where, having lost with some consistency in their own bets on college sports and horse racing, they decided to go into business for themselves. But McLain would contend that, at the time of the $46,000 claim, he and Schober were already out of the business, that he never met with any Giacalone, and that none of this had anything to do with his injury.

Over the years, McLain's friend, radio and televison cohost, and ghostwriter Eli Zaret has prodded McLain again and again, asking him, "Look, this is between you and me. What the hell happened? Come on now.

"Hey, look, Denny, if it's the truth, that's a great story," Zaret would say to him. "You could really benefit from that. You could take that one to the bank. There's a book right there." Yet with each plea from Zaret, McLain would maintain his version of events, telling him and others that it was a terrible accident, that everything — the mob, the threats — was "all bullshit." He would stick to the story that the injury was just an accident. An embarrassing, dubious accident — but an accident nonetheless.

Yet, before the injury, McLain was certainly distracted. He was pitching without his usual self-assurance, that singular driving instinct born of equal parts anger and ambition. For perhaps the first time since the death of Tom McLain, Denny was, well, scared. Scared about potential exposure, scared of violent reprisals, fearful of an unfriendly hand tapping him on the shoulder, demanding that he pay up or else.

When *Free Press* columnist Joe Falls arrived at McLain's house in Woodcreek Farms on September 28, it had been more than a week since McLain spent time with his teammates. He was home with his family celebrating his daughter Kristin's birthday.

"How about coming out and kicking some field goals?" Falls asked when McLain first opened the door.

"Yeah," he said, "now I can kick field goals. Come on in."

McLain tacitly acknowledged how difficult it would be to return to the team. Everything Falls had predicted for the Tigers that season was now in doubt. And many blamed Denny.

"How many people dislocate their toes when their foot falls asleep?" Falls wrote. "Some, maybe. How many dislocate their toes when their foot falls asleep in the middle of the greatest pennant race the American League has ever known?

"Only Denny McLain."

In an unlikely turn of events, it was Lolich who, following that loss on July 23, had emerged as the Tigers' most dependable starter. He'd been embarrassed — forced to return a Mercury Cougar that a local dealership had given him at the start of the season after the owner feared bad publicity. Overcompensating under pressure, he was overthrowing his fastball and attempting to get his curveball to break harder than was possible. It was his good fortune to have Sain's counsel, since the pitching coach had seen this sort of thing before: a loss of faith, the strained striving for perfection. Meeting with Lolich after he returned from National Guard duty, Sain didn't talk about movement or spin or the breaking ball. Instead, he told Lolich that, at 5-12, he didn't have much to lose. Sain didn't want him to try anything new. He just wanted him to stay focused on the present, not looking forward or back.

It was simple advice that proved effective. In a two-month stretch, from August 11 through the end of the season, Lolich won nine games, losing only once. On September 8, he beat the White Sox to draw the team even with Minnesota in first place. In his last start of the season, during back-to-back doubleheaders at Tiger Stadium, he shut out the Angels. The riots, the ten losses — it all seemed a world away now. With McLain distracted and underperforming, Lolich and Wilson bravely picked up the slack.

With Detroit's World Series hopes again lifted, one person speaking for the Greater Detroit Board of Commerce predicted "at least" a $6 million windfall for the city, adding that this figure was a "conservative estimate." He figured the World Series would draw 15,000 people to the city — a delusional idea, if not totally absurd.

If the Tigers' clubhouse was not always harmonious, the Twins were going through their own internal crises. The team had fired Sain's nemesis,

Sam Mele, just 50 games into the year. In his place, they promoted Cal Ermer, a career minor league manager who failed in every way to connect with his talented and troubled team. During one road trip, Ermer fined one-third of the team $250 each after they were absent during bed checks. One of them was Mudcat Grant, who, scheduled to start the next day, had gone to the lobby to ask for a room with air-conditioning. When Ermer found him absent, he fined Grant. Soon after, Mudcat demanded a trade.

Ermer had lost control of the Twins. During one bus trip, at the end of an exhausting day that had involved two plane rides and too much alcohol, pitcher Dave Boswell started playing with a pistol, declaring, "I'm gonna shoot out this window." Grant told him to put the gun away. Tony Oliva did the same.

"You Cubans play with guns down there," Boswell said to Oliva. "We got a right to play with guns up here." The racial tensions could only grow worse from there.

And yet the Twins hung on, dropping in and out of first place like the Tigers. The charge was led by Kaat, who had risked his standing with the club and the league by speaking out about Sain's departure. After beginning the year with one win and seven losses, he entered September with nine wins and 13 losses. Yet, like Lolich, he found his form again, winning seven straight starts and averaging nine innings in each.

In the last days of the race, the White Sox should have had the upper hand. They had a doubleheader scheduled against the A's and would finish the season against Washington. Yet they were knocked from contention when they managed to lose three straight games. At the start of the day that Saturday, September 30, the White Sox collapse had put the Twins in first, but Boston and Detroit also still had a shot at the title. The Red Sox needed to win both Saturday and Sunday at Fenway Park to have a chance.

The Red Sox faced Kaat on Saturday and Dean Chance in the season finale. Whatever troubles Kaat had early in the season were now behind him. He was in the midst of the best month of his career. But in the third inning Kaat injured his elbow, in what would turn out to be a season-ending and career-damaging blow.

Knocked out of the game, Kaat looked on as the Twins lost on Saturday and then again in a terrific tumble on Sunday as Boston won at least a part of the American League pennant. After the final out, as fans rushed the field in frenzied celebration, the players listened to the radio inside the Red Sox locker room, fully expecting Detroit to win both ends of its doubleheader and praying and clapping as the second game progressed.

The day before, Lolich had once more done his job, winning his game of Saturday's twin bill. To force a play-off game for the pennant, however, the team would have to win both games of Sunday's doubleheader. The Tigers won the first. But in the second game, handed a 3–1 lead, McLain simply lost it, leaving the game in the third inning with the score tied, 3–3. Smith used a series of relief pitchers — including Lolich again, just one day after his shutout performance — but it was all for naught. When Dick McAuliffe, who had hit into just one double play all season, did so in the ninth inning, the Tigers ended their season with an 8–5 loss, one game short of the pennant.

Then chaos. Not all of the 38,000 fans rushed onto the field, hatred in their hearts, but it sure seemed like it. While the team moped inside the locker room, angry fans destroyed chairs and equipment, water coolers and benches. They ripped out home plate and tried to do the same with the pitching rubber, but it was bolted to the ground. They smashed lightbulbs, attacked ushers, and charged policemen, who were once again caught ill prepared by a riot.

William Serrin, the man who'd risked his life to cover the real riot, was left to write the epilogue. He talked of the agony and "unparalleled despair," writing that no city "needed a pennant like Detroit. And for a while all troubles were forgotten — the riots, the strikes, the crime rate. Then the bats of the Angels thudded."

With an eye on the bigger picture, Serrin continued: "But there was delight in despair," he wrote. "The fans had dreamed dreams and the dreams were worth the admission. The beer was cold, the peanuts were fresh, the dogs were hot. The vendors were in voice, birds flew in the sky. There was the crack of bats, the slap of putouts. There were home runs, strike-outs, fine catches. For much of a sunny afternoon, thousands of Detroiters had fun."

• • •

In the immediate aftermath, as workers began to repair what remained of Tiger Stadium, speculation had already started about McLain's future. He'd pitched a total just over 16 innings following his win on August 29 and didn't post a win when his team most needed it. Lolich and Earl Wilson, the latter of whom won 22 games, had established themselves as the team's best pitchers.

McLain, for his part, felt helpless. All he could do was pout. Following his injury, doctors tried everything — including injecting the ankle with Xylocaine, which they thought could numb the pain for up to five innings. Instead, his foot had felt as if it weighed 80 pounds. It was entirely his fault, he would lament years later. Had he been healthy, with his mind straight, he could have led his team to the World Series, if not the world championship.

In spite of everything that happened, there was a flash in 1967 of something special to come. Late in the season, while playing the Tigers, Kaat had gone to visit with Johnny Sain in the bullpen. McLain wasn't starting that day, just throwing — as Sain's students did — but Kaat could see that he was starting to master the controlled breaking ball that he and Mudcat Grant had used to take Minnesota to the World Series two years before. Kaat knew all about the Dodgers-style overhand curve that Dressen had taught McLain, and he knew about his fastball. Despite McLain's incompetence of late, both Kaat and Sain could see that something had begun to change with McLain, that something special was happening.

Finally, Sain turned to Kaat and said, "Watch out for him next year."

7

A BLACK MAN WINS
IN BOSTON

I T HAD BEEN MONTHS SINCE Nelson Rockefeller sent Jackie Robinson as his emissary to Buffalo in the wake of the race riots there at the end of June 1967. This wasn't Detroit. It couldn't be. But it had all the same trappings: battle-ready police, looting, and fires and damage estimated at around $100,000. The governor had believed, perhaps naively, that Robinson could use his powers of inspiration to help ease tensions.

It hadn't worked. Robinson delivered Rockefeller's promises to the disaffected black youth, but with many looking at him as an out-of-touch emissary for an out-of-touch governor, his visit failed. Even so, in late September, Robinson returned to Buffalo, this time to address a meeting of the city's chamber of commerce. This audience — consisting of well-heeled businessmen — was arguably more on his wavelength than the angry young crowd he'd met with at the YMCA that summer.

But whatever they'd asked him to speak about that day — urban renewal, unemployment among the city's black youth — invariably fell away as discussion turned to the game he'd left behind more than a decade earlier. He was still a baseball icon, after all, and the audience wanted to hear from *that* man, not the public servant. The last truly great pennant race was in its final stretch, and of course someone asked him for his thoughts.

Who won was of no concern to him, Robinson said, but he hoped the Red Sox would fall short. The team's owner, Tom Yawkey, Robinson said, "is one of the most bigoted guys in organized baseball."

Word got out. Upon hearing about Robinson's comments, an outraged Massachusetts-based Rockefeller supporter called on Alton Marshall, a member of the governor's inner circle, to lean on Robinson to retract his words. But not only did Robinson refuse to take back what he said, but he promised to repeat it all over again if asked.

"I am sorry but in my opinion Yawkey is one of the worst bigots in Baseball," Robinson wrote. "I do not go around saying things for the sake of saying them . . . I once tried out for the Red Sox and was rejected. I was informed that Yawkey would not hire Negroes regardless. His record indeed proves what I said to be true."

Even in 1967, more than two decades after that "tryout," the humiliation of his experience with the Red Sox still gnawed at Robinson. He'd been sent to Boston to try out at Fenway Park with the grumbling Red Sox, who had consented to hold a tryout for black players only after being repeatedly pestered by sportswriters like Wendell Smith of the African American *Pittsburgh-Courier* and the *Boston Record*'s Dave Egan. Adding his voice to the chorus was the Jewish Boston politician Isadore "Izzy" Muchnick, who believed that the bold move of desegregating the game "should begin in Boston, where abolition was born."

It was Muchnick who put pressure on Eddie Collins, the Hall of Fame second baseman who had become the team's vice president and general manager, until he finally gave in. But when Robinson and two other black players arrived at Fenway Park to take part in something that had all the looks of a real tryout, it was anything but. The three hit against minor league pitchers and showed what they needed to in the field. Someone took notes on index cards. Collins promised that he'd be in touch. But it was clear to Robinson from the outset that it was all a charade. The Boston Braves had opened up their ranks to black players in 1950, but the Red Sox, given the chance to sign not only Robinson but later Willie Mays, would inexplicably wait.

Writing in his column in the *New York Post* with William Branch in May 1959, Robinson took aim at Yawkey and the Red Sox. At that moment, the Massachusetts Commission Against Discrimination was looking to take action against the last team in the National and American Leagues to field a black player. Addressing the charge that the Red Sox were guilty of racial discrimination, Robinson wrote: "Truth speaks for itself, and there has never been any question in my mind that the Red Sox management is prejudiced. I can't in the least tell you why, since the Red Sox themselves are the ones hurt most by limiting their choice of players on the basis of skin coloring rather than ball-playing."

By 1967, of course, black players had been signed by the Red Sox organization. But Yawkey was still in charge, and there remained an indelible whiteness to the Red Sox and the city they played for. Perhaps no one felt this more keenly than the Boston Celtics, who, from the arrival of Red Auerbach in 1950, showcased black players like no other team in the NBA. Bill Russell was a player-coach for the Celtics at the time, but like his teammates, he felt estranged from his city even as Boston fans pulled for the first team in the history of the NBA to start five black players.

To even these championship players, the city remained closed off and racist in its dealings. Sam Jones, who enjoyed a Hall of Fame career with the Celtics from 1957 to 1969, might be welcomed to Boston nightclubs if Sammy Davis Jr. or Johnny Mathis was playing. But Jones liked Sinatra, and to see the Chairman live he had to face unwelcoming stares, if not intimidation.

Moreover, the Celtics were taken for granted. The city had grown used to their championship banners, expecting a new one at the end of each season. Thus, in a city that had gone generations without a baseball pennant—much less a true championship—the Red Sox victory over the Twins at Fenway Park on that last day of the regular season, putting them in a tie for the American League pennant, set up a frenzied scene that very few had seen the likes of. With the final out, thousands of fans descended onto the field, many seeking out pitcher Jim Lonborg. Hoisting him high above their heads, they tore his uniform to shreds before policemen helped him to the safety of the Red Sox clubhouse. Outside, fans continued the mayhem. Signs fell. Firecrackers went off. Grown men climbed the screen behind home plate. Although this was chaos in triumph — unlike what would follow hours later in Detroit — it was chaos all the same.

From their own clubhouse, more than 900 miles way in Atlanta, the Cardinals solemnly watched this spectacle unfold on television, having settled their affairs in Philadelphia long before. Gibson and his team-mates had wanted the Twins to prevail. Now they rooted for the Tigers to win that last game, to secure, at the very least, a Detroit-Boston play-off. The reason was quite simple. At a time when players' World Series checks were calculated based on overall attendance, Fenway's intimate size meant drastically diminished returns.

Yet, late the next day, there they were — pulling into their lodgings at the Quincy Motor Inn on the outskirts of Boston. Reportedly no hotel in Boston proper would take in the team, citing lack of accommodations for the Cardinals' "large entourage." They were met by hundreds of Sox fans chanting, "Welcome No. 2!" Gibson, decked out in a smart suit and thin tie, simply held up one finger on his way to his room — where the temperature was set at a not-very-welcoming 80 degrees.

There, holding court with Boston reporters, he grew increasingly ag-itated. A reporter handed him a paper showing a headline with Carl Yas-trzemski's prediction that the Red Sox would take the Series in six. At seeing this, Gibson only said, "Huh," before dropping the paper to the floor.

"What's the matter?" someone said. "You worried about Yaz?"

"I don't fear anybody," Gibson said. After his wife Charlene tried to cool his temper, Gibson went on to tell the assembled press, "I mean it. You guys asked for two minutes. I gotta unpack."

That evening before the first game, Bill Russell invited Gibson and other Cardinals to his home to hear jazz artists like Nat and Cannonball Adderley, eat well, and enjoy themselves. Pitcher Nelson Briles was the lone white person in the group. He would say later that he'd never had so much fun in his entire life. There was music and food as the champagne and conversation flowed. But the bonhomie masked an ulterior motive. Celtics stars K. C. Jones and Wayne Embry confessed to their guests at the end of the evening that they had brought them out as a way to throw the Cardinals off their game.

Years later, neither Jones nor Embry could remember this act of civic sabotage—and their teammate Sam Jones was incredulous that defeating St. Louis was the basis for the event. Embry, in 2012, then a senior basketball adviser for the Toronto Raptors, could not recall the party or the reasons behind it. Ellen Jones, K.C.'s wife, said her husband had no recollection of it as well. And Sam Jones contended there were too many black players on the Cardinals. They were—at least for that period in the '60s—black America's team. Embry and K.C. might have played in Boston, but it seemed unrealistic that they'd root for the Red Sox to win.

And it couldn't have been a view shared by Bill Russell. His allegiance was to the Celtics, not to Boston. Russell described the city as a "flea market" for racism, going as far as to say that he'd rather be in a "Sacramento jail than be mayor of Boston."

By 1967, Russell was a towering figure in the black power movement. He had proudly marched on Washington in 1963, but now he understood the power of Malcolm X. He openly supported Muhammad Ali's refusal to be inducted into the U.S. Army. It was a decision that cost Ali, for the moment at least, the heavyweight championship of the world. Russell and Jim Brown saw this as an act of great courage, a view not shared by Jackie Robinson. In backing Ali, Russell demonstrated his willingness to take a stand and embrace an unpopular viewpoint, regardless of the risk to his athletic career. Five years later, Russell, never one to seek the adoration of fans, would insist on having the team retire his number in an empty Boston Garden.

Russell was nearing the end of things . . . as a player at least. But when the Cardinals went to Boston for the 1967 Series, Gibson was still a man seeking to define his own place in the game. He was not yet seen as the equal of Koufax or even Marichal. He had much to prove in this Series. The cockiness that he perceived in the Red Sox, and especially in Boston fans, only fueled the flames.

Those looking at the front page of the *Boston Globe* would have seen news capturing the fast-changing future of the Republic. Montana senator Stuart Symington, a onetime hawk, had called for an all-out end to military action in Vietnam. A former Ohio state representative, Carl B. Stokes, had beaten a two-term incumbent mayor of Cleveland in the Democratic primary in his bid to be the first black man to lead a major city. But dominating the front page was Bob Gibson, standing alongside

Boston pitcher José Santiago in a posed photograph above the fold. San-tiago, for his part, looks nervous — his roundish face peers down at the baseball he's holding. Gibson, standing next to him with his hands at his hips, wears a wide red collar beneath his buttoned-down jersey and is smiling wryly. The Red Sox had beaten the very best the American League had to offer. Now they'd have to face him.

That afternoon, when Tim McCarver walked out onto the field at Fenway before the start of the game, he shared Gibson's confidence. Fen-way still lacked a darkened batter's eye, but McCarver believed that the white shirts on fans in the center-field bleachers would still give Gibson the advantage. Gibson had proven himself unhittable at times with a black background behind him. How could he fail to make an impact at a venue where the hitters would be half-blind?

In a country in which the '60s generation was coming into its own, Fenway itself seemed trapped in another time. In two years, the United States would send a man to the moon, yet in 1967 the National Game's great showcase was set to be played in a venue that many saw as an-tiquated and outdated. Just one day before Game 1, the *Globe* ran an editorial calling for public leaders to "Start the Stadium Now," arguing that with the possibility of four World Series games, the park would be turning away as many as 100,000 customers, losing up to a potential $2 million in revenues. The newspaper called for a new park to be built — "preferably a domed one." Days later, the chairman of the Massachusetts Turnpike Authority said that a 52,000-seat, $60 million domed stadium could very well be in place by 1970, adding, "I hope the Legislature will act as soon as this World Series is over."

It seemed somehow reasonable. No one knew what the game would look like in the 1970s. For all its charm, Fenway seemed staid compared to the other new multi-use stadiums in America. Baseball felt that it had to adapt to the times, even if that meant reinventing the game itself — beginning with the very surface on which it was played. Cit-ies watched as the Astrodome and other cavernous stadiums opened to wide-eyed crowds. This was the future, and Boston wanted to take part.

But for now, there was a World Series to play. Jim Lonborg admitted that the tense last weeks of the Red Sox season had kept the team from spending much time thinking about who they'd play next. They were just hoping to survive the pennant race, which, until that Sunday, had been very much in doubt. What they knew of the Cardinals came from scouting reports, hastily compiled in September.

They knew, of course, about Lou Brock, whose spectacular hitting and tenacious base running had broken the will of so many teams in his own league. In Game 1, he opened with a single in the third inning and would score the first run. In the seventh, with the game tied 1–1, he singled again, stole second, and scored again — helping Gibson seal a 2–1 win.

Lonborg, however, was more worried about Gibson. The Red Sox knew about his reputation as an intimidating, aggressive pitcher. They knew that he'd broken his leg midseason, so they expected that, with the forced respite from the wear of the regular campaign, he'd be coming back "pretty fresh and strong."

After watching him in the first game, Lonborg believed that he'd seen one of the most terrifying and intimidating pitchers he'd ever seen. Gibson was just *that* good. Lonborg and his teammates remained confident in themselves and their bats, but they knew that getting to Gibson early remained key. To fall behind was to stay behind.

Still, Carl Yastrzemski, for one, refused to give Gibson his due. Following Game 1, in which he went hitless, Yaz stood on the field taking batting practice.

"I don't like a couple of days off," he said. "I don't feel right at the plate. My six-year-old son could have got me out.

"Gibson threw hard," he continued, "but we've got pitchers in our league who throw hard too . . . The greatest asset Gibson had was his ability to move the ball around. I can't wait to face him again. I feel great now. I wish we were playing a doubleheader Thursday. But in this game, I had slow hands. I didn't swing the bat the way I should."

Following that first effort against the Cardinals, Boston's survival seemed very much in doubt. The pressure was on Jim Lonborg — who, until that season, had shown only flashes of promise — to keep the Sox in the Series, to be their Bob Gibson.

It was a tall order. Gibson's ability to manhandle hitters through both technical prowess and intelligent intimidation was unmatched. In fact, the two pitchers couldn't have been more different in how they handled themselves both on and off the field.

From the time he came to the Sox, Lonborg had earned the nickname "Gentleman Jim." A tall, dreamy-looking bachelor with an easy temperament and a degree in biology from Stanford, he at one point contemplated walking away from baseball and becoming a doctor. (In later years, he'd become a dentist.) But the Red Sox signing bonus proved too tempting for the earnest and handsome young pitcher. For their part, the team believed that Lonborg could help bring an end to the decades-long misery of being denied a championship.

His photogenic good looks seemed at times to overshadow his pitching. In an era when it was unheard of for athletes to pose in expensive suits in the pages of general interest magazines, Lonborg (who broke his leg in a skiing accident following his Cy Young season) appeared in a 1968 photo spread projecting an image of unflappable cool. One photograph shows him in a blazer and checkered slacks at an Eastern Airlines counter, a stewardess gazing longingly at him. In another, he's wearing a plaid sport coat and gold pants while chatting with a pretty companion. The photos seem less like staged photographs than scenes plucked from real life. It was certainly easy then to imagine him stepping off the pitching mound and into a scene with Mia Farrow or Ann-Margret, holding his own with the starlets of his day.

Nor did it hurt his stock that even when struggling to find his form early in his major league career, Lonborg always maintained friendly relations with the Boston press. Unlike Gibson, who sidestepped reporters, Lonborg was always amiable. Sportswriters had their jobs, and he had his. He understood how they needed each other.

Moreover, he liked them. He found reporters to be intelligent, bound by a kind of honor code: things said off the record stayed off the record. He never had to worry about whether a remark he made at dinner or in a bar would wind up in a column. The relationship seemed absolutely perfect.

Yet it wasn't until Lonborg understood what it meant to be mean, at least on the mound, that he made the transition from pressman's favorite to an ace. Many, including manager Dick Williams, attributed this change to an early season loss to the Angels in Anaheim. Holding a 1–0 lead into the bottom of the ninth, Lonborg gave up two singles and let California tie the game. Looking around, he saw two men on, with two outs. He'd let the hitters dive over the plate, taking ownership of the space that was rightfully his. When he threw a wild pitch to score the winning run, he left the field wondering what might have happened had he not let the hitters position themselves as they did. He decided from that point forward never "to give a batter a break."

Williams believed that Lonborg had turned the corner with that game, that he'd needed a "jolt" to understand that baseball had a toughness to it, however genteel a sport it might appear to be. As Gibson and Drysdale and others had learned far earlier, a pitcher had to develop meanness to win, whether it expressed his true nature or not.

Lonborg now felt the same way. Before that Angels game, he felt he hadn't really challenged hitters — certainly not as Gibson did. Perhaps, he thought, it was simply a matter of not understanding his own strength, his own power. Perhaps he was being too timid. Regardless, he knew he wouldn't lose a game that way ever again. He would challenge hitters from then on — which he did.

Over the course of the next nine games, under the tutelage of Sal Maglie, he would throw at and hit six different batters.

By 1967, Maglie had become a pitching coach, and throughout that summer he taught Lonborg what Gibson and Drysdale already knew: that success depended on establishing himself on the outside part of the plate. To achieve this, he'd have to keep hitters on the inside part, always aware that should they lean in or lunge at pitches on the outside, the consequences would be painful.

However, it was Sandy Koufax, now in the early stages of a short-lived and ill-advised television career, who approached Lonborg near the batting cage before Game 2 with words that would change his life. The reserved left-hander asked Lonborg how he prepared for a game in the bullpen, what he did to warm up. Lonborg told him that he just threw fastballs and curveballs until he felt ready to come in. Koufax said he needed to do more.

"Have you ever thought about putting their lineup as imaginary hitters at the plate when you are warming up?" Koufax asked. "So that, when you come out on the field and actually play the game, you psychologically have visualized getting all of these hitters out?"

This advice stayed with Lonborg for the rest of his playing career. And while one could argue about its immediate impact on Lonborg's pitching, the fact was that his performance that day was Gibson-like. Lonborg stuck to what Maglie had taught him, never giving Brock or any other Cardinal hitters the opportunity to extend their arms. During his 5–0 shutout in Game 2, he retired the first 19 consecutive batters before giving up a walk in the seventh and allowing just one hit — a double in the eighth. Nelson Briles, however, won Game 3 for the Cardinals, 5–2, and Gibson won Game 4 to put St. Louis within one game of winning the Series at home. But Lonborg matched him the following day, allowing just three hits and one run, in the bottom of the ninth, to bring the Red Sox a 3–1 victory in Game 5.

While the Red Sox focused on Brock, Lonborg believed he had an advantage against the right-handed-heavy Cardinals lineup. They were high-ball hitters whom Lonborg knew he could challenge if he kept command of his pitches in the lower part of the strike zone. In his first two Series starts, he had not only that control but an awareness of what he was trying to do. He would later call those games the kind of "perfect moments" that seldom come.

Through six games, he and Gibson circled each other like prizefighters. Having staved off elimination once again in Game 6 behind the work of three pitchers, the Red Sox would have a chance to win their title at Fenway Park. In Game 7, Gibson would pitch for the third time in the Series, on three days' rest. Williams would call upon Lonborg once more, after just two days.

Gibson had "honestly" felt that the Cardinals would do him a favor and win the Series before he had to pitch again. Instead, he would be facing his second Game 7, and his sixth World Series start. Of course he could have used more rest. But he'd been here before. There was something about these games that gave him a "little extra."

"What do you want me to do? Be excited?" he said. "I'm not. I'm not trying to prove anything. I just want to win it."

That same evening, when *Boston Globe* writer Will McDonough visited Lonborg at his apartment, he found that the Red Sox pitcher didn't share Gibson's outlook. Lonborg was staring at a large photo of the moon that he'd hung in his living room. He admitted that, after winning the American League pennant, he didn't think he'd ever experience anything as thrilling again.

"But I was wrong," he said. "Pitching the seventh game of the World Series will be greater."

The apartment's hallway was crowded with paper bags filled with letters and postcards, notes from well-wishers thanking him for what he had accomplished. Anything seemed possible now. The once-unfathomable championship was suddenly within reach.

"I'm not going to kid myself about it," Lonborg said. "I'm not going to be as strong as I'd like to. But I'm just going to give it everything I have. Why save it? There's nothing after tomorrow."

At the park the following day, Lonborg sensed early on that he wouldn't be the same pitcher he'd been in the first two starts of the Series. Still, he hoped that he'd be able to locate the ball with greater precision, to force the Cardinals hitters to swing at pitches they'd normally lay off of. And he desperately wished that his teammates could accomplish what they hadn't been able to in Games 1 and 4 — score early, forcing the Cardinals ace from the game.

Lonborg had hoped for two things: that his teammates could get to Gibson early and that, working on two days' rest, he'd have a cushion to work from. Neither happened. In fact, things quickly got out of hand when Dal Maxvill — the wiry shortstop with little power — hit a triple in the third inning, staking the Cardinals to a 2–0 lead. When Gibson came up to bat in the fifth, he blasted a home run that hit the ledge of the left-center-field wall. None of what Lonborg had banked on — an early lead, undisciplined hitting from the Cardinals — came to pass. The Cardinals won the game going away, 7–2. Boston's "Impossible Dream" was over.

Gibson would later admit that he too had worried about how much he'd have in reserve after only three days' rest. He could pitch six innings, he was sure of that. As the game progressed, his body and his arm grew more tired with each pitch. But unlike Lonborg, he had the early runs to work with. After the eighth, with a large lead and his stuff diminishing, he didn't think he could finish. But he managed to cobble together whatever was left to complete his third complete-game win of the Series.

It had been a storied day that began less than auspiciously. That morning Gibson and his wife joined the McCarvers and the Maxvills for breakfast in Quincy. While everyone else was served, Gibson's breakfast of scrambled eggs and toast, for whatever reason, never arrived. The story would go through several iterations, but the bottom line was that Gibson boarded the Cardinals' bus to Fenway with an empty stomach and a toothache to boot. It was *Post-Dispatch* columnist Bob Broeg who would jump off the Cardinals' bus to hunt down a couple of egg sandwiches for Gibson.

Born and bred in St. Louis, Broeg had followed the Cardinals since birth. He was every bit the company man, cultivating close relationships with Musial and Schoendienst. But like Gibson, he was hot-tempered and quick to throw whatever was at hand whenever the University of Missouri Tigers or any of the other teams he followed fell behind.

To future *Post-Dispatch* columnist Rick Hummel — who, like Broeg, would go on to win the Baseball Writers' Association of America's J. G. Taylor Spink Award for baseball writing, awarded each year during the Baseball Hall of Fame induction ceremony — this shared temperament made them ideal for each other. Broeg, Hummel felt, was never afraid to challenge Gibson when he grew sullen. He fought back. Hummel surmised that each appreciated the tenacity in the other; perhaps that was what endeared them to each other well beyond Gibson's playing days.

Hummel, who began covering the Cardinals in 1973, freely admitted to feeling trepidation when he first approached Gibson. But Gibson, for whatever reason, took a liking to him. While other veteran players — Joe Torre and Tim McCarver and Reggie Smith — gave the newbie a hard time, Gibson did not.

He never understood why. Gibson was ending his career just as Hummel was beginning his, but the two never shared a cross moment, though a Gibson with diminishing skills had every reason to remove himself further from the press. They enjoyed each other's company, and

Hummel felt that he got along with Gibson as well as anyone — certainly better than those perceived by outsiders to be less cantankerous.

Boston writers couldn't say the same. Perhaps they mistook Gibson's confidence for indifference, his aloofness for anger. Bob Sales of the *Boston Globe* wrote that Gibson was "blasé about his job. He does not show the enthusiasm for his work that some of his cohorts do. It is in his makeup."

Of course, nothing could rattle Bob Gibson. One comment, though, in particular worked on him: the words in a Boston paper announcing Dick Williams's plans for the seventh game — "Lonborg and Champagne." Watching Gibson studying those words, his teammate Joe Hoerner knew how much they would fortify Gibson's resolve. It wasn't that he needed any extra motivation to win his fifth consecutive World Series game, but that smug headline, combined with the perceived slight at breakfast, would bolster Gibson's belief that he needed to prove to the world that he was capable of anything.

In Game 7, Gibson allowed only two runs with three hits, striking out 10 and winning the World Series MVP once again. As Williams walked to the visitors' clubhouse to offer his congratulations, he could hear his own words being mocked — "Lonborg and Champagne! Hey!" Then Williams saw what millions at home were seeing on television — Cardinal players chanting in unison, stomping their feet, spraying each other with champagne.

Gibson sat off to the side — drinking, not spilling, champagne. The night before, he'd gone to hear Les McCann play jazz piano. Now McCann entered the locker room, his fist raised, yelling, "Black Power!" Gibson had little use for such sentiments — his power was his, and his alone — but he'd showed them what Jackie Robinson and Willie Mays and scores of Negro players could have accomplished had they teamed up with Johnny Pesky and Ted Williams. Gibson may have been reticent about speaking out on social issues, but his actions spoke louder than his silence — a black man could win in Boston.

Less than two weeks later, with the Cardinals back in St. Louis, Jackie Robinson himself returned to the city that had once spurned him. He'd come to speak at Boston University. But first he held court at the George

Sherman Union, surrounded by many of the same reporters who'd covered the Series. Speaking on a range of topics, he retold the story of his Red Sox tryout. It was too bad that the Red Sox had lacked the foresight to recognize that he and other black players were the game's future, he said, because "we could have helped them a little bit." He was pleased that Boston fans, and even Yawkey himself, had taken to players like George Scott and Reggie Smith.

"I always felt a bigot who sees the light is our best friend," Robinson said of the Red Sox owner.

Just down the hall was BU's newspaper office, where a photo of Muhammad Ali now hung. Robinson's feelings about Ali were complicated. There were moments when he'd stood up for Ali, whom he always called by his Christian name. This was not one of them.

"I don't think in a country such as ours that you can reject your responsibilities," Robinson said of Ali's refusal to be inducted into the armed forces. "Everybody thought Cassius Clay would be a big martyr. It worked out just the opposite. I think he was tremendously misguided in this area."

With the black power movement ascendant, Robinson's thinking may have been out of step with the times. But after the riots that summer, he sensed that something dangerous was simmering.

"Young people nowadays are learning to hate," Robinson warned. "We've got to show them that moderate leaders can accomplish something. That's the problem with Negro leadership today. We're losing. Kids today are looking for success. They're looking for achievements. The kids aren't like we were. They're not fearful. They're not afraid of dying."

Little did his audience know how prophetic these words would be.

8

WINTER OF
RECRIMINATIONS

H AVING FAILED TO WIN THE PENNANT in the very last inning of the very last game of the 1967 season, with pitchers like Earl Wilson and Mickey Lolich at the center of his rotation, Tigers general manager Jim Campbell decided to take action. Specifically, he had to do something about McLain. He no longer had any use for Denny and his antics, and like the rest of the team, he simmered in the off-season over McLain's mysterious foot injury that had prevented him from pitching in the final weeks of the season.

Campbell never forgot this failure. In his office in Tiger Stadium, he'd hung a handsome wooden plaque listing the pennant standings for that year. He was determined to finish what the team had started the previous season, and the first step toward that goal, he believed, was to trade Denny McLain.

Though Campbell denied it when asked about it late in the 1968 season, there's no question he'd put a deal in place during the winter meetings in Mexico City. He was interested in the Orioles' shortstop Luis Aparicio, who for seven seasons with the White Sox had teamed with Nellie Fox to form the best double-play combination the game had ever known. His best years were now behind him, but Aparicio was still unmatched in the field and added a true bat to the Tigers lineup. A three-team trade was arranged with Baltimore and the Yankees, but it fell apart when the Yankees demanded a minor leaguer (who'd never amount to much) from the Orioles whom they were unwilling to part with at the time. Thus, Campbell was stuck with a headache for which there seemed no cure.

Inexplicably, Campbell had made plans to trade McLain without consulting Johnny Sain. Had he asked Sain or his bullpen coach, Hal Naragon, what they thought about trading McLain, they would have strongly advised against it, for both believed that McLain was on the verge of something great. Despite Denny's pedestrian 1967 record and his troubles late in the season, Sain had seen steady improvement. To give up on him now, Sain believed, would be a grave mistake.

But McLain would never be Campbell's man. Campbell was an ex-marine who wanted to fill his roster with players who did their jobs and kept their mouths shut and didn't create sideshows for the team. By the end of 1967, it was apparent that McLain — despite his efforts to keep his mob affiliations secret — had exhausted Campbell's patience. The organ playing. The Pepsi endorsements. The avid interest in aviation. It was too much.

Campbell had his supporters. Broadcaster Larry Osterman said that he found Campbell candid and honest with members of the press, a man who'd never lie when asked a direct question. And Willie Horton developed an almost filial relationship with Campbell, particularly after the death of Horton's parents.

But by most accounts, Campbell was tight-fisted, even cheerless. When Bazooka held a bubble gum blowing contest for major league players, he forbade the Tigers from taking part — though a good deal of the money raised was to go to charity. In the early 1990s, when the team's new management had the gall to fire Ernie Harwell, the broadcasting voice of the Tigers for three decades, Campbell berated the voice of the team. He blamed Harwell for the bad press the Tigers were getting in the wake of the dismissal, telling him, "You've hurt this ballclub more than you realize."

"Do you still want to be my friend?" asked the soft-spoken Harwell.

"We'll have to see about that," Campbell said.

Detroit News writer Jerry Green saw Campbell as a reactionary, someone who might have fit in very nicely as a baseball executive in 1900, but not in the 1960s. With the exception of Al Kaline — whom Campbell christened as the team's first $100,000 player — he bullied players, forcing them to sign contracts that both sides knew were below market value. And of course he hated agents.

Once, in a caustic contract negotiation with second baseman Dick McAuliffe, Campbell accused him of "blackmailing" the team. Another time, Campbell decided to trade Elliott Maddox, a promising young outfielder. Maddox was at his parents' home in New Jersey when his father walked in holding a newspaper that broke the news to him. The phone call Maddox expected from the Tigers never came.

Nor did Campbell welcome Marvin Miller when he took charge of the MLBPA. Campbell expressly told his players that he wanted the Tigers' player representative to be a minor actor, preferably a rookie pitcher or bench player — certainly not his starting catcher, Bill Freehan. When Freehan told Miller, Miller explained that Campbell was breaking the law, that he could file an unfair labor practice suit. But Miller wanted to talk to Campbell first.

"It's my club," Campbell said in his meeting with Miller. "I'm the general manager, and I've always done this."

"Mr. Campbell," Miller told him, "I don't know what I can say to get you to understand, but the law specifically says you may not interfere in an internal union matter. Who represents the union from your club is an internal matter. Therefore, this is an unfair labor practice."

"What's that?" Campbell said.

After explaining to Campbell what "that" precisely meant, Miller could see him calm down considerably. Campbell said he simply didn't know any of the things Miller had told him.

"I believe you," Miller said. "You've had no occasion to."

But because of Miller, Campbell, like the rest of the established order of baseball, would find his total control of his team slowly erode. Miller was intent on bringing in a new, more equitable era in baseball — one that would be irreversible. In a matter of years, who was designated as each team's player representative would be of little consequence as Miller grew perhaps the most powerful labor organization in America.

A lone motorboat glides through the mucky brown water of the Everglades. There is no one else in sight. Whoever controls the boat has come to this spot seeking solitude. This is the image that millions of Americans saw when they turned on their televisions on February 4, 1968, and tuned in to an episode of *Gentle Ben,* a show about a boy (played by Ron Howard's brother Clint) and his pet bear.

As the camera draws closer to the boat, the viewer sees its pilot. Dark-complexioned, wearing a light blue mock turtleneck and a captain's hat, he occasionally looks back at his motor. Suddenly the boat gets trapped in algae and begins spinning round and round. The pilot, thrown off balance, falls into the water. We see him with his head just above the surface, his eyes wide with fear. An alligator looms nearby. When a hydroplane driven by a wildlife officer comes to his aid, he clumsily climbs aboard and splays out on the deck.

"You know, we haven't met someplace, have we?" the man's rescuer, Tom Wedloe, played by a young, clean-shaven Dennis Weaver, asks. "You look familiar."

After Wedloe introduces himself, the man, his wet khakis clinging to his body, replies, "Bob Gibson."

"Bob Gibson?" Wedloe asks. "You mean the . . . say, you're not the St. Louis Cardinals pitcher who won three games on the Red Sox in the World Series?"

Looking down in embarrassment, Gibson mutters, "Yeah, well, me and eight other guys, we beat the Red Sox."

The point of this episode — of the whole show, really — is unclear. Perhaps it was simply meant to provide an antidote to real life. Just days before, the whole facade of the Vietnam War had come crashing down with the Tet Offensive, awakening the nation to the realization that the war could not be won. Through the lens of Associated Press reporter Eddie Adams and a television cameraman for NBC News, Americans had seen the image of Major General Nguyen Ngoc Loan pointing a pistol at the head of a slight, unarmed Viet Cong prisoner and firing into his skull on a Saigon street — a cold-blooded execution by a man we considered an ally.

In this age of television, though, Gibson's appearance made perfect sense. The man who'd won the World Series MVP had earned a right to appear in an episode of a half-hour family drama. The famous athlete comes into the lives of an ordinary family and sticks around to provide some moral guidance. As it happens, Wedloe's son, Mark, is a pitcher — who's discovered that not playing fair can yield great results. It's up to Gibson to set things right.

Sitting with Mark on the bleachers, wearing a cutoff gray sweatshirt and his Cardinals cap, Gibson listens as Mark describes his bag of tricks, the staples of "inside baseball." Among them is the "old brushback," something Gibson himself had mastered. But Gibson tells Mark that he's never heard of the brushback and asks him to explain.

"Well," Mark says to Gibson, "the old brushback. A batter crowds the plate, you uncork one right at his belt buckle — brush him back, you know?"

"No, I don't know," Gibson says. "When you throw a ball deliberately at the batter, it's against the rules."

"Not right at him, Mr. Gibson," Mark says. "Just in close. That's not against the rules. Is it?"

Pausing for a moment, Gibson says, "Well, no, it's not against the rules, but the rules are just a guideline. After that, there's a thing called sportsmanship."

Gibson's words seem to make an impression. In the championship game, which Gibson himself umpires, Mark actually behaves with honor. He doesn't throw the ball when he sees that the batter isn't ready, for instance. But by not resorting to "inside baseball," Wedloe gives up the game-winning home run. Head down, Mark stomps off the field. Back at the house some hours later, when Mark emerges from his room, his uniform untucked, his face still puffy from crying, he finds Gibson sitting in the living room. Gibson then pulls out a signed baseball that reads "To Mark Wedloe, a real sportsman — from Bob Gibson."

"You know what that means, don't you, Mark?" Gibson asks.

"Yes, sir," Mark says. "Not pitching when the other fella can't see."

"That's right."

"I don't deserve this, Mr. Gibson," Mark says. "I lost."

"You didn't lose," Gibson says. "You won."

It was television at its worst. Whoever wrote the episode whitewashed Gibson, stripped him of competitive drive, and neutered his personality for public consumption. This Gibson — a person who's patient and easygoing, who'd rather do the right thing and lose — masks the real man and what made him great.

No, the real Gibson was the one who was approached by a stranger as he walked down a street in Omaha that winter. The man said that he hated baseball, but added, "If my boy finds out I ran into you and didn't get your autograph, he'd kill me."

"Why tell your boy you saw me then?" Gibson said in a way only he could. "He'll never know." With that, Gibson turned away and was gone.

The Sporting News, a St. Louis institution, had long tired of this Gibson, observing in an editorial that he "could use some lessons in the art of cooperation with the press and the public." The weekly bible of baseball went so far as to say that Gibson was first in "just about every department you could name — except patience and affability."

Following his victory in Boston, Omaha again honored Gibson, a native son, with a special day. There were visits to his old grade school and high school, a luncheon at Creighton. He was named honorary governor of Nebraska and honorary mayor of Omaha. Creighton made him honorary president. There was a heartfelt visit to an elementary school in the heart of Omaha's Near North Side ghetto. But the entire spectacle — save the appearances at the schools — left him unmoved.

"I wasn't particularly touched by any of this," he said later. "All they're saying is I'm a 'special' Negro. That's the only reason some neighbors accept me. I'm 'special.' It makes me want to vomit."

Yet things had turned around for Gibson. The endorsements he'd sought earlier in his career were now his. The White House invited him and Charlene to a state dinner honoring the premier of Japan. He met Norman Hahn, the Omaha businessman, who helped him develop financial interests beyond baseball. He signed with the sports marketing agency headed by Marty Glickman — the famed Jewish athlete who'd been denied his chance at Olympic triumph during the 1936 Hitler Olympics and who'd go on to become the preeminent sports announcer of his time.

As a result, suddenly Gibson was everywhere. There he was with Pat Boone on his television show, making an appearance on *To Tell the Truth,* or dropping in on *The Joey Bishop Show.* With Koufax gone and Marichal's fighting Giants aging out of contention, Gibson had finally reached the summit. He'd broken his leg only to come back stronger. He seemed unstoppable.

This was the man the sportswriter Phil Pepe met in Manhattan that winter. Pepe had covered Gibson before — in the 1964 World Series — for the *New York World-Telegram & Sun,* one of the once-proud broadsheets that had struggled to stay alive in any way possible, only to slip into a lonely, desperate death by mid-decade. Now Pepe was out of work with a family to support. So when a man named Zander Hollander, who matched books with authors, called and asked him if he wanted to write a book with Gibson, Pepe couldn't afford to say no.

Pepe wasn't the first choice of anyone involved. He was a last-minute option, his collaboration the by-product of a vanishing that would trouble one man's family for years. Pepe and Gibson were thrown together by the events of a Saturday evening, the dark aftermath of which became a great mystery in the history of modern New York.

John Eric Lake disappeared on the evening December 10, 1967. He was 37 years old at the time, six feet tall, 180 pounds. There's not much else in the way of physical description — he was a white male with a small scar on his chin who may have been wearing a navy blue blazer with a striped lining when he disappeared.

At the time, Lake was the much-respected sports editor of *Newsweek.* Born in upstate New York, he attended Syracuse University before joining the Navy. He married a woman named Alice after being stationed at Pearl Harbor for four years. In time, there was a house in Teaneck, two small children, a comfortable job. Tall and thin, with a large face and his trademark thick black-rimmed glasses, Lake looked the part of the tenacious journalist pounding away at his typewriter.

Eric Lake felt that his father was "on his way" by late 1967. He'd written three cover stories for *Newsweek* that year — on Lew Alcindor in February, Mario Andretti in May, and Carl Yastrzemski in October. There was a *New York Times Magazine* piece profiling New York's two star quarterbacks — the unassuming Fran Tarkenton and the brash and electrifying Joe Namath. He'd finished a book manuscript for Random House on the Olympic runner Jim Ryun — a deal he'd gotten with the help of Hollander. Now he would take on the difficult task of cowriting Bob Gibson's autobiography.

Despite his professional success, however, Lake's personal life was unraveling. He'd tried and failed to reconcile with his wife twice, and he had moved into a studio apartment in the Village. In the account pieced together by his son, Lake's drinking had gotten out of hand as he coped with financial and relationship stress. The dissolution of his marriage and financial troubles had taken their toll. He no longer enjoyed his work.

On that Sunday — the last day he was seen alive — Lake had pleaded with Sandra, a nurse and a friend of a colleague at the magazine, to go out with him that evening. Twice, she said, she'd said no. She finally relented, and they ate at a restaurant near 58th and Second Avenue, where Lake became increasingly intoxicated. In an account Sandra gave to a private detective agency, by the end of the evening he'd dropped his wallet on the floor. When Lake left Sandra at her apartment in Midtown, she suggested that he take a taxi home. He said he'd take the subway instead.

Authorities would say they had no idea what really happened to Lake. Among the personal items that Lake left at his then girlfriend Jean's apartment — his Phi Beta Kappa Key, cuff links, tie clips, and clothing — were several tapes of interviews he'd conducted with Bob Gibson after the 1967 World Series. Lake had gone to see Gibson in Omaha to collect material for a ghostwriting project that Hollander had helped arrange after Lake completed his book on Jim Ryun.

By the time Hollander reached out to Pepe to complete the project that Lake had started before his disappearance, months had gone by and Gibson had already received his share of the money. A deadline loomed. Although Lake had spent a considerable amount of time talking to Gibson, he hadn't written a word. When Pepe first met with Gibson in

Manhattan, Gibson, unsurprisingly, was not eager to open up again to a complete stranger. No matter what he tried, Pepe simply couldn't break through—he couldn't earn Gibson's trust. Desperate, Pepe tried to find something that would resonate with Gibson. He told Gibson that he'd starred in sandlot baseball, that he covered him in the World Series for the *World Telegram & Sun*. Gibson wasn't impressed. He thought that Pepe was trying to take total control of the book.

"Tell that guy it's my book, not his!" Gibson told Glickman.

Even so, Gibson eventually decided to cooperate. In time, Pepe was able to draw him out on the subject of race and life in Omaha, on Solly Hemus and his teammates. Pepe got enough to cobble together a book on time. In the process—his first stab at ghosting—Pepe felt that he *became* Bob Gibson.

Yet despite everyone's best efforts, the book, titled *From Ghetto to Glory: The Story of Bob Gibson* and released later that year, falls somewhat flat. Gibson felt "unburdened" when it came out, and Pepe considered it a "trailblazer," since it was one of the few books to deal with race straight on. But it feels restrained. As with *Gentle Ben,* it just doesn't read like the Bob Gibson we know. Yes, Gibson opens up about growing up in the projects in Omaha and the inspirational people in his life—his brother Josh and Johnny Keane—and he speaks his mind about race relations in this country. But something is missing. Unlike his relationship with Lonnie Wheeler, with whom Gibson would go on to write three books, Gibson wasn't in position to be himself yet. When he collaborated with Pepe, he was more publicly diffident, a feeling he would lose over time. In the years and books to come, Gibson would feel more liberated, Wheeler felt, to "be the asshole" he truly enjoyed being.

One day late in 1967, Howard Cosell called Jackie Robinson at home at 6:30 in the morning. Cosell wanted to know how Robinson felt about the proposed boycott by Negro athletes of the Olympic Games set for Mexico City the following summer. Robinson, without giving it much thought, said he opposed the idea.

But over the course of that day, his opinion changed. As he wrote with the help of his new ghostwriter, Alfred Duckett, in his new column in the *New Amsterdam News,* he was moved by the comments of San

Diego State sprinter Tommie Smith, who at one time would have given anything to win gold at the Games, but now felt that he'd give it all up — the medal, the adulation — should it somehow move the needle on racial conditions in America and end the exploitation of the black athlete.

"Maybe we, as Negro athletes have 'been around' too long, accepting inequities and indignities and going along with the worn-out promises about how things are going to get better," Robinson wrote. "If this is the way the youngsters feel, believe me, I can sympathize with their point of view."

In an even more startling turn, he cited the late Malcolm X — whose tactics and beliefs he'd so bitterly opposed in the past — in his remarks. Robinson had written nothing when Malcolm X died about his assassination, about his sacrifices and self-transformations. Now Robinson referred to him as a brilliant leader who'd once said to him, "Jackie, in days to come, your son and my son will not be willing to settle for things we are willing to settle for."

"I am certain this is correct," Robinson wrote, "and this is the way it should be."

Still, even though he didn't come out and say it, Robinson was torn. He understood and admired these young athletes for the sacrifices they were willing to make, but he also knew that their participation in the Games could bring great power. After all, where would *he* be without baseball, without the distinction of being the man who broke the color barrier in America's favorite sport? Would Eisenhower have ever brought him to the White House? Would he have his column? His job with Rockefeller? Would he ever have risen to a place of political power?

Not long after Cosell's call, Robinson agreed to appear with Harry Edwards on the radio show that Cosell hosted in New York. Edwards, the sprinter turned scholar and activist, had been the organizing force behind the Olympic Project for Human Rights (OPHR), the organization that had called for the boycott. In the green room for half an hour before the show and again in the limo afterwards, Robinson and Edwards spoke at length about racial inequality in sports. He told Edwards he was dissatisfied with his public image. The press, he complained to Edwards, had made him out to be a passive person because of his willingness to "turn the other cheek" during those first years in baseball.

There were those who used the example of Robinson's career to declare victory over racism in sports. But the Robinson whom Edwards spoke with was much more ambivalent about the progress that had been made than the Robinson who'd compiled the celebratory *Baseball Has Done It*.

Edwards, like so many black athletes, grew up in poverty, in East St. Louis. He used his athletic prowess to eventually earn an athletic scholarship in track and field at San Jose State, the premier program of its day. (He also served as cocaptain of the basketball team.) Edwards excelled at San Jose State, but would quit the track team. In many ways he was an anomaly—a man who understood early on that the belief (still prevalent today) that the only way out of the ghetto was through sports was a myth. Edwards knew that, as soon as a school or team was through with you, it was back to the ghetto.

By the time he met Robinson, Edwards was already a disruptive force in the world of sports. While still working toward his doctorate in sociology at Cornell, he returned to San Jose State as a visiting professor and helped prevent a college football game from taking place between San Jose State and the University of Texas at El Paso in 1967. The Olympics, draped in the sham purity of amateur athletics, seemed like the perfect platform to protest the bondage of the black athlete. Here were young men and women training to represent a country that cared little for them outside their medal count. Edwards understood this, as did the athletes who supported his cause.

Baseball was another matter. Edwards put little effort into the recruitment of players to address concerns within their own sport, though he knew of the inequalities that ran through the game. In 1966 and 1967, he had called out baseball for its appalling lack of black managers, but never bothered reaching out to black players to ask them, "Hey, don't you know this is something that you should be standing up for?" To Edwards, who understood the conditions that players still toiled under, any such outreach was a waste of time.

By mid-December 1967, the OPHR had specific demands. Standing alongside Martin Luther King and fellow civil rights stalwart Floyd McKissick, and with the pledged support of a number of athletes, including Bob Gibson, Edwards called for the restoration of Muhammad Ali's heavyweight boxing title and the desegregation of coaching and administrative staffs across the country. He demanded that the apartheid nations of South Africa and Rhodesia be banned from Olympic competition, and that Avery Brundage, the racist head of the International Olympic Committee (IOC), be removed from his post. (Later, Gibson, in a forthright interview with *Los Angeles Times* reporter Dwight Chapin, said: "I can't really say what I'd do if I were in their shoes but I admire the guys who are involved in the Olympic boycott. They're taking a terrific chance — risking an awful lot. I don't know what their goals are but if they feel that the country has been kicking them in their rears for 50 years, then I agree with them.")

Most immediate among the OPHR's demands was the boycott of the annual indoor track and field meet held by the New York Athletic Club in February. The NYAC, with its whites-only membership policy and persistent discriminatory practices, was an easy target for Edwards, who drew the support of the Anti-Defamation League and the NAACP. Thousands of people, white and black, including athletes, gathered outside the new Madison Square Garden to protest the event, while others walked wearily through those doors to compete. Things could have easily turned violent, but Edwards and his supporters managed to keep the peace.

It wasn't fair that Jackie Robinson was dragged back into all this. He'd done enough. His eyesight was failing. Diabetes increasingly crippled him. At 49, he had the look of a man 20 years older. Yet here he was, taking a stand, just as he had in the aftermath of the Selma march in Alabama, after King was arrested during the 1960 presidential campaign, in Buffalo when Rockefeller needed him, in Mississippi alongside Medgar Evers.

In February 1968, he stepped forward . . . again. Holding court before reporters as the spokesman for the American Committee on Africa, he represented two dozen athletes in declaring his support for the NYAC boycott and the exclusion of South Africa from the Olympics. While Robinson still seemed torn over the boycott itself, he was "proud of these fellows willing to sacrifice something dear to them."

"When I was an athlete," Robinson said, "things were coming in good and we didn't see other problems. But the kids today are taking a better look because in many places you'd be in trouble if you didn't get in-volved. It was different in my day; perhaps we lacked courage."

Robinson's views surprised some who simply didn't know better. Af-ter all, Jesse Owens, a teammate of Robinson's brother Mack on the 1936 Olympic team, had come out against the Olympic games — asserting that politics had no place in athletics. But Robinson believed in the in-dividual act of courage. Thus, in spite of his unwavering support for the war in Vietnam, he respected the boldness it took for Eartha Kitt, King, and Ali to speak out against it.

Yet those who give their lives for the sake of progress, who are com-mitted to righting history and rerouting our future, seem always to do so at great and terrible personal cost. At one point in her teens, Robinson's daughter Sharon had hung a poster of Black Panther Huey Newton — whose calls for racial separation her father abhorred — in her bedroom at their home in Connecticut. Yet that was nothing compared to her de-cision to marry, in April 1968, a young basketball star who — unknown to Robinson — had hit her during their courtship. She was just 18.

Even Chip Logan — Arthur and Marian Logan's young son and the ring-bearer at the wedding — was aware enough to know something wasn't right. By all accounts, it was a typical wedding. Robinson walked his daughter down the aisle. There were hopes — genuine hopes — that despite age and reservations and the families' natural fears, things would work out for the best. But young Chip could feel a lack of warmth toward the young man and a lack of enthusiasm for the spectacle itself. This was a ceremony of diminished expectations. The marriage lasted a year.

This troubling development only added to a larger one the month before. On March 4, a reporter seeking comment called Robinson in his office. The reporter told him that early that morning police had broken up a drug sale in downtown Stamford in which shots were fired. His son, Jackie Jr., was arrested for possession of large amounts of heroin and marijuana, as well as a .22 caliber pistol.

Robinson vowed to stand by his son, but Jackie Jr.'s troubles exacted a physical toll. Answering questions later in a near whisper in front of the jail, Robinson was visibly shaken and broken.

Asked if he knew about what was going on in his son's life, if he'd had any idea that his firstborn had fallen to such depths, Robinson recounted everything that had happened to his son: Dropping out of high school. Joining the Army. Being wounded in Vietnam. When he saw his namesake, Jackie had calmly asked, "Are you all right, son?" But he clearly was not. The elder Robinson couldn't help but see in his son his own failure as a father and wondered if perhaps he'd had "more effect on other people's kids than my own."

Standing in front of the jail, Robinson, a man who had endured a life of personal and professional struggle, told reporters, "God is testing me."

That moment would stay with him — and by extension, Rachel — forever. They were simply words of heartbreak, after all. The young man in jail was not the young Jackie Jr., who can be seen in photos snuggling his mother, his face rubbing up against hers, a seemingly happy boy whose life, from its start, would be lived in public. Rachel believed that Jackie Jr. had been born too soon — that he was ill suited to the limelight, to growing up as the son of a great man whose great responsibilities would take him away from his family for long stretches. As he got older, Jackie and his father grew distant. He dropped out of high school. In 1964, without his parents' permission, he joined the Army just as U.S. involvement escalated in Vietnam. He witnessed horrific atrocities. In an explosion that killed two of his fellow soldiers, he sustained such severe shrapnel wounds that he was sent home. He came back a damaged man.

By the time of his arrest, Jackie Robinson's namesake had done unthinkable, unspeakable things. He'd done cocaine and LSD and now struggled with heroin. He carried a gun because it was part of the image he wanted to project: "being tough and fighting and this whole thing being what manhood was all about." Now he had two choices: rehabilitation or prison. He chose the former.

He had entered the decade as a man leading a righteous charge for integration, for the inclusion of black people in both political parties, but Jackie Robinson now found himself submerged by events at home over which he had no control. Of course, had he looked around at the millions of fathers in millions of homes across the country, he would have found kindred spirits — parents who believed that they'd done their best, given their children chances they'd never had themselves, only to have something go wrong. The disconnect between young and old in the '60s was a whirlwind that would change American family life forever.

Their public life in 1968 was of little concern to Rachel then. Her elder son had come back from war entirely lost. Her daughter's marriage was already collapsing. In May, the death of Jack's mother, the woman who'd saved him from the South, had left the family without its fighting, moral force. The political and public life, she felt, would have to wait.

Jackie Robinson remained baseball's link to the greater world, but now, like so many fathers of his generation, he faced tumult at home. The coming months would test him—physically, emotionally, spiritually.

Near the end of his life, Robinson went to Nelson Rockefeller's offices on West 54th Street in New York to meet with Gerald McLaughlin. Robinson was forming a committee of black community leaders to support Rockefeller's initiatives, and McLaughlin had been assigned to work alongside Robinson on the presser. Watching him, McLaughlin thought that Robinson still had the look of a man of great stature in spite of family tragedy and deteriorating health. He wore a fine suit, his tie in a Windsor knot. When he took off his jacket and rolled up his sleeves, McLaughlin remembered, Robinson still had the forearms of the athlete he once was—muscular, unbreakable.

They spoke for nearly an hour. The press release, the names, the vitals, were merely pro forma. What Robinson spoke more freely about was Rockefeller, how he still believed in the governor's vision, in the bravery he showed in walking out of the Republican Convention in 1964. He asked McLaughlin if he had a family. "Yes," said McLaughlin, "I've got a son who's five and a little girl who's about a year old."

"Nothing like family, Mac," Robinson said.

9

THE SILENT SPRING

S PRAWLED OUT ON THE GROUND following his very first at-bat of spring training in 1968, Tommy Agee honestly believed he'd gone blind. In one retelling, he hadn't seen the ball coming high and behind him, as it struck him in the head. In another, he'd seen the path of the ball, but just couldn't move out of the way quickly enough. Regardless, as the team medical staff sprinted toward him and lifted him onto a stretcher, he doubted whether he would ever see or play baseball again.

Since Agee's trade from the White Sox in the off-season, the press around St. Petersburg — where the Mets and Cardinals both trained — heralded his arrival as a new beginning for New York. The Mets team he'd joined — young, brimming with promise in its lineup and pitching staff — seemed far removed from the expansion franchise Casey Stengel first fielded in 1962. Those Mets had filled their roster with ex–New York Giants and Brooklyn Dodgers, players who were in the twilight of their careers. These Mets were a year away from the impossible.

Having watched the Yankees fall into irrelevance, there were some in New York who rightfully saw the Mets as the future of New York baseball. Agee, a thickly built center fielder who was all of 26 years old, was to be its centerpiece. But suddenly, at Al Lang Field — with more than

6,200 spectators looking on and even more watching on television in New York — that future seemed in doubt.

As it turned out, Agee didn't lose his sight or even sustain a skull fracture. But he had become part of a bigger moment — a Bob Gibson moment. Many believed that Gibson had tired of all the Agee talk, that he'd had enough. Legend has it that after he threw the pitch — a high, inside fastball — and Agee went down, Gibson yelled something along the lines of: "Welcome to the National League."

His catcher, Johnny Edwards, would swear to this story. Edwards had just come from Cincinnati, and this was his first game as a Cardinal. Decades later, Edwards could still see Gibson plunking "him good," followed by that historic howl from Agee, batting third. Edwards and his teammate didn't talk about what happened until years later, at an old-timers' game, when Edwards brought it up. Gibson flatly denied yelling those words at Agee. But Edwards knew what he'd heard, that he could still hear that yell.

However it played out, the Mets weren't taken by surprise. Ed Charles had warned Agee before his at-bat that Gibson would "introduce himself to you." And after it happened, outfielder Cleon Jones told his Mets teammate Ron Swoboda, "I told you he was gonna do it. I knew he was going to do it."

Not that Swoboda was shocked. Gibson, he felt, was the "most violently aggressive person" he'd ever faced in the game. The way he moved, the way he acted, expressed an anger in him. Forget about trying to bunt. In all his at-bats, Swoboda never felt comfortable with him — not with the way Gibson could move the ball at any point within the strike zone. Even with the passage of time, Swoboda feared him: late into his sixties, he still felt that if Gibson entered the room, he would once again feel that dread.

Gibson would never waver in saying that hitting Agee was simply an accident. He lost control of the ball. Agee's closed-in stance, he claimed, left the hitter no way to get out of the way of the pitch. He just wasn't the headhunter people made him out to be. (Statistical evidence backs him up. Gibson hit 102 batters in his 17-year career — one batter for every 157.5294 batters he faced. By contrast, Don Drysdale hit one batter for every 91.5389 batters he faced.)

"Indiscriminately hitting men is a form of pouting," Gibson told one magazine reporter in 1968. "A pitcher who hits batters because the other team is knocking him all over the lot is acting babyish. He's pouting. I did it once. When I was with Omaha, the other team was beating me something awful. I knocked the next guy down. Johnny Keane, who managed Omaha, came over and said, 'That's not the way to do it.' He chided me. I've never retaliated like that again. But I do hit the opposing pitcher when he's deliberately hit one of our men."

Yet, as much as Gibson has insisted that he loathed throwing as an act of retaliation, there's no denying that when he threw at a batter, he did it intentionally. When San Francisco rookie Jim Ray Hart dug in against Gibson in his first at-bat, in 1963, Gibson took aim at him, breaking the young man's left scapula. Late in Gibson's career, after his first marriage was over, San Francisco catcher Dave Rader attempted to make small talk with Gibson while he stood at the plate, asking about his wife and kids. Gibson responded by hitting Rader square in the ribs in Rader's next at-bat. During his rookie season with the Braves, Dusty Baker saw Gibson deliberately hit his teammate John Milner in spring training. When Baker and Hank Aaron and Gibson went out to dinner that evening, Aaron wasn't shy about addressing the issue.

"Hoot, why'd you hit that young kid?" Aaron asked Gibson.

"Because I heard he could hit and I wanted to get him in line," Gibson said.

In fact, Baker had outhit Milner in the minor leagues and was considered a far better prospect. He hoped Gibson wouldn't catch on to that. Because if he did . . .

Despite everything Gibson had done to soften his image in the off-season, when George Vecsey approached him that spring he found Gibson even more withdrawn than in the past. Instead of a sign around his neck that preemptively answered reporters' questions, Gibson took out an index card with four replies: "yes," "no," "horseshit," and "none of your business." When Vecsey asked how his knee was, Gibson pointed to "horseshit." When Vecsey asked if he'd be ready — really ready — by opening day, Gibson pointed to "yes."

Even Phil Pepe, his hardworking first ghostwriter, wasn't spared his wrath. When they were working on the book together, Gibson had told Pepe that he never talked to reporters the day he was scheduled to pitch. But given their history, Pepe felt he was different. After landing a real job with the *Daily News* in 1969, he approached Gibson at Shea Stadium. Gibson, of course, didn't or couldn't hold back.

"How dare you!" Gibson said. "You oughta know better than anybody I don't talk to anybody when I'm pitching that day!"

Gibson's attitude seemed a part of everything Vecsey felt that spring. All he felt was cold, an undeniable chill that had stuck around since winter. Maybe it really was the temperature. But Vecsey felt something else at work—a collective despondency that could not be ignored. He'd covered the boycott of the NYAC games in New York and H. Rap Brown laying out the new militant vision for the civil rights movement. He could feel the relentlessness of the Vietnam War draining any remaining good feeling between white and black, between young and old. And Vecsey couldn't stop thinking about Otis Redding, the singer who'd died in a plane crash in early December. Since then, the saddest song in the world—"Sittin' on the Dock of the Bay"—had been playing on an endless loop. One magazine in its baseball preview issue had declared 1968 "a year of transition, a year of momentous decision, a year of high promise." To Vecsey, it seemed anything but.

That spring Vecsey could very much identify with the pain of Redding's ballad of a man looking out on a world that was moving without him. That man was motionless, wasting time, watching the water and the world move past him. Vecsey could hear it, feel it, all of it. "Sittin' here resting my bones / And this loneliness won't leave me alone." Redding's words would stay with him for 1968 and for the rest of his life.

Redding was, of course, merely a vehicle for Vecsey's malaise. Through this death, he found form for the feeling he shared with millions of others—a sense of a terrible trial, an inability to move on with life, a chasm of despair. When, he asked, would spring—the true spring of rebirth and all the overused adjectives that come along with it—actually come? Or would it ever?

For Vecsey, that year, it never would. His hands would remain cold in the open press box. He felt himself shivering while standing around the batting cage. As the season wore on and his sense of malaise built, he'd ask himself, watching one 1–0 game followed by another, "Why can't these motherfuckers hit?"

There was something about it for him that fit into the national narrative. Nothing seemed right. Nothing. Otis Redding had died. A war went on without end. Assassinations would take the lives of fine men. A president would slink out of office. Vecsey would never truly feel warm that year.

Johnny Sain knew he hadn't delivered. In 1967, he'd helped Earl Wilson win 22 games, and he'd replenished the confidence of Mickey Lolich following his ten consecutive losses. But his pitchers hadn't led the team to the World Series. McLain looked like a man in a full regression, someone whose hubris simply outmatched his actual talent—even before his fall. That Denny's mind wasn't completely in it, that he was pitching scared, was still unknown to Sain. But Denny was his guy, and he believed in him.

Sain had his starters. But what he found when he arrived in Lakeland in 1968 was a team packed with relief pitchers. There were untested rookies, some ready for major league play, and some—like Mike Marshall—still years away from greatness. Apparently management believed that the problem, outside of McLain, was with the team's bullpen and what was needed was more bodies. The relief corps had been deemed the weak link—the problem that had kept the team from taking the pennant the previous fall.

This was the environment that rookie Jon Warden stepped into. Looking around, he saw what looked like about 20 pitchers all desperate for their time on the mound. There were men with years of game experience, and there were others working their way back from injury. There were those who'd come up the previous year and seen their share of the pennant race. Warden, who'd moved up only as far as the Carolina League within the Tigers system, saw pitchers who'd done their time in Triple A and earned their right to come up. What possible chance did he have?

Then one day Sain quietly told him he'd be throwing an inning of work. Sain was low-key and unobtrusive, but Warden knew that the pitching coach could see everything, and he understood that this was his inning to win or lose. Regardless of how well he performed, Sain wouldn't berate him or dispense advice unless Warden approached him first.

That's not to say that Sain didn't understand when someone was in trouble. In one outing, Warden delivered a pitch that thundered off the hitter's bat. It turned out to be a "loud out," the last of the inning. But when Warden returned to the dugout, he seemed dejected and rattled, even though nothing really had gone wrong.

Looking at Warden, Sain knew that this was his time to step in. Sain had last pitched in the majors in 1955, but he'd never lost his ability to read youth, to understand a player's point of view. He knew Warden needed something — now he wanted to know what.

"Come here," Sain said. "What's the matter?"

"Oh man," Warden replied. "Did you see the way the guy hit the ball?"

"Well, it was an out," Sain said. "Great pitch. If it was an out, it was a great pitch. Don't worry about stuff like that. They're gonna hit balls like that and they'll be outs, and then they'll hit a little dribbler and it's gonna be a hit. Keep your level head, don't let them worry you, just go out there and throw your game."

Some managers felt that Sain lacked attention to detail, that he concerned himself more with self-help mantras than with the actual business of coaching. He also had a reputation for not caring much about physical fitness. He believed that in order to make a living throwing, you had to, well, throw. But Sain did believe in the importance of training — up to a point.

"Boys," Sain would say to his staff, "as far as running and conditioning, you're on your own. But I'm gonna tell you this: I've never seen a man run the ball across home plate. In order to pitch nine innings, you've got to pitch nine innings."

However, Sain added, "You've got to take care of your legs because if your legs go with your body, you're done in any sport. I don't care what you're doing: tennis, bowling, golf, football, basketball. If your legs go, you're out of business."

Late in the 1967 season, Sain had told Jim Kaat that 1968 would be Denny's year. Few in the Tigers organization believed it. The team had failed to trade McLain to Baltimore in exchange for a Hall of Fame shortstop. According to one reporter, when McLain arrived in Lakeland that spring, he was sporting orange hair and had traded in his thick glasses for contacts. He'd spent the off-season in bowling alleys, throwing thousands of frames. McLain honestly believed that all the bowling had strengthened his arm and that he was finally ready to become the pitcher Sain believed he could be.

What Tigers broadcaster Ray Lane discovered on his first day at camp was not the embittered team that had sulked in the Tiger Stadium clubhouse the previous October. They had moved on from their devastating loss. Everyone on the team, from Mike Marshall — who would not make the roster that season — to Al Kaline, believed that this was his moment.

Since November, when a teamsters' strike stopped the presses of the two great broadsheets of Detroit, reporters had been left to ply their trade any way they could. There were television shows. There were strike papers, staffed with out-of-work writers and their own delivery boys. Unlike the *Free Press,* the *Detroit News* remained free to operate in the shadows, filing reports that the paper collected in bound books as its staff went through the motions, free to do as they wished.

Jerry Green, then a football beat writer for the *News,* began spending more time around the ballpark, reading the out-of-town press and taking notes that would later form the definitive diary of the team. Green too felt that the Tigers had emerged from the wreckage of their lost season somehow fortified by failure. From the second game of the regular season — in which Gates Brown, perhaps the best pinch hitter of his day, hit a game-winning home run in the team's final at-bat — he sensed that they were on to something big and that he'd better follow the team as best he could, just in case.

But that moment was deferred by the god-awful event on the evening of April 4. We can still see him in the photo taken the night before he was assassinated — a weary yet somehow tireless Martin Luther King Jr. speaking to the striking sanitation workers at a rally in Memphis on April 3. He's drenched in sweat as he delivers what would be the last speech. Even those not yet born then have heard, again and again, those final calls for progress through nonviolence. We know the defining, final words — "I've seen the Promised Land. I may not get there with you. But I want you to know tonight that we as a people will get to the Promised Land." We know these words. We know them by heart.

What happened the following day would become part of our story, never to be forgotten. The story comes back to us through the grainy black-and-white images. The panic on the balcony of the Lorraine Motel. The assassination of a leader. The idealism that marked the beginning of the 1960s gone for good.

That evening in St. Petersburg, Tim McCarver was supposed to have dinner with third baseman Mike Shannon and Roger Maris. It was Maris, coming down from his room, who told them the news. McCarver's brother had marched with King in the procession through their hometown.

To watch the aftermath of the assassination with white teammates was one thing. To speak about it with Bob Gibson was quite another. By Gibson's own account, he and King had crossed paths in the Atlanta airport not long before, though Gibson hadn't approached the civil rights leader. In their conversation the following day, Gibson told McCarver that he couldn't possibly understand what he felt as a black man, that it was impossible for a white man to step into that same place. Yet so much had changed since the pitcher and catcher first met. They'd not only won championships together but formed a bond that would last forever. None of that seemed to matter now. McCarver was a white Southerner, from Memphis no less. McCarver argued that he himself was living proof that integration could change people. He'd come to the Cardinals never having known a black man. Now a black man was his best friend.

In Houston, Jim Kaat was riding in a car with Johnny Roseboro, the Twins' black catcher, and Roseboro's wife, who was at the wheel. The Twins had played an exhibition game against the Astros, and the three heard the news on the radio. What was there to say? Kaat knew King's death meant a great deal to Roseboro and America. Now he fumbled for the right words.

Gabby — as Roseboro's teammates called him — settled the matter quickly by leading the conversation to safer ground. He said he liked what Kaat had shown with his new grip on his slider. What these two men had together in that moment was baseball. And that would be enough.

After King's assassination, Marvin Miller fielded phone calls that started off in the typical way, broaching some topic related to player-owner relations, but that invariably shifted to King. Miller found himself in the role of counselor. Even before his election as head of the MLBPA, he'd taken it upon himself to listen, really listen, to players' concerns about what it meant to become a real union. Players felt comfortable confiding in him, sharing their fears and misgivings. Black players called him, but so did whites — Rusty Staub among them. They wanted to talk things through with someone who would listen without judgment — and that person was Miller.

Among players' immediate concerns was opening day. The season was set to start around the two leagues on April 8 and April 9, but since April 9 was the day of the King funeral in Atlanta, Commissioner William Eckert urged the team owners to postpone their starts. Riots were raging in over 100 cities. An angry populace that once had faith in King's vision of nonviolence now believed that his vision for change would never be realized.

There was a great deal for baseball to consider. Of course safety was a priority. But for once the feelings of the ballplayers themselves, typically of secondary importance, were taken into account. Empowered players felt emboldened to act. Gibson and his teammates opposed a regular start to opening day. So did the Pirates — most notably Roberto Clemente, Dave Wickersham, and first baseman Donn Clendenon. Clemente and King had spent time together in Puerto Rico, and Clendenon had known King as a young man. It was King who'd convinced him to attend Morehouse College in Atlanta. Following a unanimous team vote not to play, Clemente and Wickersham issued a joint statement: "We are doing this because we white and black players respect what Dr. King has done for mankind."

It should be noted, of course, that the rest of America didn't stop during this time. Men and women went to jobs in high-rise buildings, took their shifts at what was left of industrial towns. Children went to school. Grocers stocked their shelves.

But baseball waited. Those normally tedious days between the end of spring training and the opening pitch dragged on. The ticket takers and vendors, the general managers, the players, the patriarchs eager to refill their coffers — they all waited.

It was in this atmosphere of angst and recrimination that Jim Bouton stood on the mound in Yankee Stadium throwing to George Vecsey. They were alone there — a pitcher in a precipitous decline and a sportswriter beginning to question the relevance of the very thing he wrote about and loved.

It was a strange sight. But on a morning when sportswriters would normally be heading to the ballpark for their first game story of the season, in that waning era when sportswriters and ballplayers could still be friends, Vecsey had gotten a call from his friend. Jim Bouton, like the rest of Johnny Sain's protégés, had never forgotten Sain's precepts, and he was feeling the need to throw.

Bouton — who later would dedicate one of his victories to Senator Eugene McCarthy, the peace candidate who'd chased Lyndon Johnson out of the presidential race and the chance to win a second full term as president — told Vecsey, "I need to work out."

So Vecsey went to Yankee Stadium. There Bouton waited for him with a catching mitt — most likely one belonging to bullpen coach Jim Hegan. Bouton was trying out a knuckleball that day in the hopes of resuscitating his career. His velocity had fallen off so precipitously that Vecsey felt no pain from anything Bouton threw to him.

At the same time, Jackie and Rachel Robinson were making arrangements to travel to Atlanta for King's funeral. It had been less than five years since the Robinsons and their three children had taken part in the March on Washington. Afterwards, Robinson said, he'd never felt prouder to be a Negro, and he had never been more certain that King was the right man to lead the cause. Although Robinson and King were openly at odds over Vietnam, Robinson never wavered in his support.

Robinson knew what King meant to the civil rights movement, and he worried about King's safety. Following the murder of Medgar Evers in 1963, he'd called upon President John Kennedy, whose seeming lack of commitment to civil rights once led Robinson into the arms of Nixon, to protect King and others as they attended Evers's funeral. In a telegram, he had implored Kennedy, "in the spirit of your recent magnificent appeal for justice to utilize every federal facility to protect a man sorely needed for this era."

"For to the millions Martin Luther King symbolizes the bearing forward of the torch for freedom so savagely wrested from the dying grip of Medgar Evers," he wrote. "America needs and the world cannot afford to lose him to the whims of murderous maniacs."

When the Robinsons arrived at the Logans' Manhattan townhouse on the evening of April 4, the salon that had been a place of anticipation and optimism, a place where the great leaders of the cause plotted their next moves, had been transformed into a mourning bunker. The Robinsons had just come from visiting Jackie Jr. at his treatment facility in New Haven. They were feeling lost. Now they wanted to be with the Logans, to share in their grief.

Among those gathered at the Logans' that evening was Lee Murphy, a white radio broadcaster, who'd sprinted over from his own home nearby. The Logans were busy reaching out to people as well, arranging transportation to Atlanta for the funeral. Murphy could feel the vast undercurrent of fear that everything those at the gathering had worked for, risked their lives for, had suddenly been thrown into doubt.

Rachel Robinson, like her husband, understood the consequences. They'd lost a friend and a confidant, a kindred spirit whose intentions they'd never questioned, even when they disagreed with him. The Robinsons felt acutely that they'd lost not only a family friend but also a higher cause. Now that cause looked to be in danger.

For Rachel, as for so many others, the grief went beyond the personal. She now shared in the loss for the country. The funeral service and the other gatherings held in King's name were of no use. They were simply a reminder of what had happened — and their inability to prevent what had happened. These dark ceremonies only left her asking, "What are we going to do now?"

At the time of King's assassination, almost one-third of major league ballplayers were members of the National Guard, often at the urging of the clubs themselves, which couldn't bear the thought of signing prospects and developing them, only to have them drafted and shipped off to war. Pete Richert, whom the Senators had traded during the 1967 season to the formidable Baltimore Orioles, now found himself back in uniform just outside the D.C. Stadium — albeit in a different uniform from the one he'd expected to don on opening day.

When he first joined the Guard in 1962, Richert never imagined they'd call him up like this. Yet as the war in Vietnam dragged on, the reservists within baseball's ranks found themselves called upon to serve more and more often. Red Schoendienst spoke glowingly about McCarver's tenacity during the 1967 season: on very little sleep, he'd leave his National Guard post to take up his position behind the plate — just in time to catch the likes of Bob Gibson — and, as if that weren't enough, he batted his way to a second-place finish in the NL Most Valuable Player voting.

Richert had by now gotten used to juggling baseball and his Guard duties. As a Senator, he'd helped establish a program that brought American League teams to Walter Reed Hospital to visit with Vietnam veterans. He knew how close his own unit was to being called up for active duty, and he appreciated how lucky he was. By October his service would be done. He just had to get through the summer.

Like everyone else, Richert was scared. Baseball and the excitement of playing for a new team could not have been farther from his mind. He'd seen Washington, D.C., burning. In the first two days of rioting after King's assassination, his squad was responsible for securing city blocks so that firefighters could get to work putting out the fires. In the evening, he would return to the high school auditorium where his unit spent the night. Because Richert knew Washington, he'd go out with local police into the city for a couple of hours to speak to children at schools, to play his part as an athlete role model, before returning to his Guard duties.

This went on for days. At the end, everyone was exhausted — those who had rioted as well as those who'd stood in their way, the men charged with protecting the city. Finally, they were able to retreat back to their lives.

Armed personnel stationed outside a baseball stadium was a sight that American ballplayers never expected to see — maybe when playing winter ball in Nicaragua or Venezuela, but not on their home turf. But here it was, happening in the nation's capital no less. Players coming to Washington were told not to leave their hotel rooms and to take their meals on-site. The Athletics stayed far away from Baltimore when they came to visit, and when the Cubs arrived in Cincinnati to begin their season, they also found themselves confined to their hotel. Jim Kaat felt uncomfortable through it all. He felt embarrassed — embarrassed to be a white man playing baseball.

These precautions served only to physically protect the players. Senators relief pitcher Dave Baldwin felt that the team's management didn't really appreciate the significance of what had happened or understand the state of shock and fear players continued to feel even when the season began. When opening day came, it didn't really feel special. It was merely the first game of the season, something to get through. As it turned out, that would be how the whole season felt for him — something to simply finish and get through.

It didn't help that the Senators were terrible and would continue to be terrible until they decamped for Texas following the 1971 season. For other ballplayers, despite the external distractions — the obligations of Guard duty, the racial strife in neighborhoods surrounding ballparks — there was still a season in front of them, paychecks to earn, games to win. Looking around the Indians' locker room, pitcher Sam McDowell felt that there wasn't a single person there who wasn't upset about what had happened. His teammates respected the hell King had endured, but just as with a death in the family, after the initial grief, McDowell felt, there comes a moment of recognition that life must go on.

In this period of national darkness, the season finally began. There was no indication that the season would be any different than any other year, that it would forever change the rules of the game. King was dead, and Lyndon Johnson would not seek reelection. Denny McLain was still a member of the Tigers, and Johnny Sain was still his pitching coach. Bob Gibson was about to have a chance to build on his end-of-the-season comeback. It was 1968. And there was baseball to play.

▲ JACKIE'S NEW LIFE: Jackie Robinson, along with boxer Floyd Patterson (far left), meets with Martin Luther King Jr. in May 1963. *AP Photo*

◄ THE SAVIOR ARRIVES: Johnny Sain demonstrates his teachings to his pitching staff in his first spring training with the Tigers in 1967. *AP Photo*

▶ THE BREAK: Bob Gibson on the mound following the hard hop off Roberto Clemente's bat that broke his right leg on July 15, 1967. *Bettmann/ Getty Images*

◀ THE DETROIT RIOT: An aerial view of burning Detroit on July 24, 1967. *AP Photo*

▼ DENNY IN MOTION: Denny McLain pitching during a troubled 1967 season, his first under pitching coach Johnny Sain. Sporting News *Archive/Getty Images*

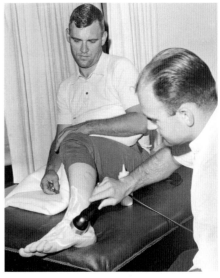

▲ DENNY'S CHECKUP: A physiotherapist treats Denny McLain following the mysterious "accident" that sidelined him in 1967. *AP Photo*

▶ MARVIN MILLER IN ACTION: Marvin Miller, the man owners feared —with good reason— upon taking the reins of the Players' Association, meets with members, including Don Drysdale (far left), during pension negotiations with ownership following the 1968 season. New York Daily News *Archive/Getty Images*

▲ THE DEATH OF A DREAM: Robert Kennedy, speaking at the Ambassador Hotel after midnight on June 5, 1968, following his win in the California primary, began with a congratulations to Don Drysdale on his shutout streak. *Dick Strobel/AP Photo*

▼ THE SALUTE: Just days after the conclusion of the World Series, on October 16, 1968, U.S. sprinters Tommy Smith (center) and John Carlos (right) give the Black Power salute during the playing of the "Star-Spangled Banner" following the 200-meter race at the Mexico City Olympics. *AP Photo*

▲ THE DYNAMIC DUO: Sandy Koufax, now retired, congratulates his friend and former teammate Don Drysdale after his record streak of 58²/₃ scoreless innings came to an end on June 8, 1968. *AP Photo*

▶ DENNY AT THE ORGAN: Denny McLain shown with his Hammond organ, the vehicle he hoped would lead him to a musical career beyond baseball. *AP Photo*

◀ FINALLY: Denny McLain surrounded by teammates after they rallied to give him his 30th victory of the season on September 14, 1968. *AP Photo*

▶ THE TIGERS TAKE THE PENNANT: Denny McLain and Tigers outfielder Al Kaline celebrate the Tigers' first American League pennant victory since 1945 on September 17, 1968. *AP Photo*

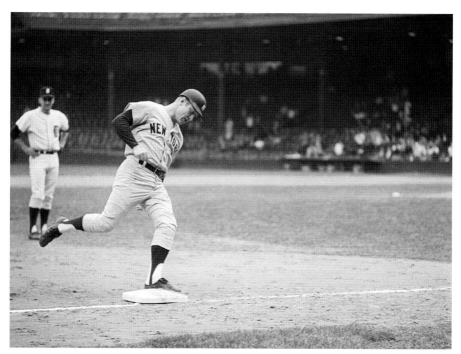

▲ MANTLE AT DUSK: Mickey Mantle circles the bases in what would be his final home run at Tiger Stadium on September 19, 1968, against Denny McLain, eclipsing Jimmy Foxx's total of 534 career home runs. *Bettmann/Getty Images*

▲ DENNY AND BOB: Denny McLain pitches to his counterpart Bob Gibson in Game 1 of the 1968 World Series. *Bettmann/Getty Images*

◄ BOB GIBSON IN THE NINTH: Gibson faces Tigers first baseman Norm Cash in the ninth inning of Game 1 of the 1968 World Series.
AP Photo

▶ BOB GIBSON WITH JUBILANT TEAMMATES: Bob Gibson heads to the locker room following his masterful performance in Game 1.
Sporting News *Archive/ Getty Images*

◄ JACKIE AND HUMPHREY: Jackie Robinson attending Game 4 of the 1968 World Series with vice president and Democratic presidential nominee Hubert H. Humphrey.
Herb Scharfman / Sports Imagery / Getty Images

► LOU BROCK AND DENNY McLAIN: St. Louis left fielder Lou Brock hits Denny McLain's second pitch of Game 4 of the 1968 World Series for a leadoff home run.
AP Photo

◄ GIBSON IN MOTION: Gibson's motion on full display in Game 4 of the 1968 World Series.
Bettmann / Getty Images

► THE BLOCK: Cardinals left fielder Lou Brock colliding with Tigers catcher Bill Freehan in the fifth inning of Game 5 of the 1968 World Series.
AP Photo

▲ GRAND SLAM: Tigers outfielder Jim Northrup comes home to jubilant teammates following his grand slam in Game 6 of the 1968 World Series. *AP Photo*

▲ CURT FLOOD AGAINST THE WALL: St. Louis Cardinals center fielder Curt Flood leaps against the ivy of Wrigley Field in 1962. *AP Photo*

▼ TIGERS TRIUMPHANT: Catcher Bill Freehan lifts unlikely hero Mickey Lolich following the final out of Game 7 of the 1968 World Series. *Bettmann/Getty Images*

10

8:45

I T WAS 8:45 ON SATURDAY, and the big guy had done it."
Dwight Chapin, then in his second year as a reporter for the
Los Angeles Times, wrote these words in the press box of Dodger
Stadium on the evening of June 8, 1968 — just three days after an assassin shot Robert Kennedy following his win in the California Democratic
primary. Only a short time before, thousands of people had lined the
route from New York to Washington, watching Kennedy's funeral train
pass.

In Chapin's wonderful portrait of this strictly baseball moment,
Donald Scott Drysdale, "the big guy," had broken a 55-year-old pitching record once thought unbreakable. Chapin describes Drysdale's posture — perfectly erect — and that whip-snap sidearm motion with which
he delivered the baseball. He mentions the catcher — Tom Haller. The
count — 0-2. The batter — the Phillies' Roberto Peña. He describes how
the ball bounced high and took a slow hop to third baseman Ken Boyer,
who, "ever so slowly looking at his feet, checking it seemed to see if he
dropped his glove," fielded the ball and threw it over to first baseman
Wes Parker.

Chapin, most notably, takes note of the black armband on Drysdale's
left, nonpitching arm. This is what stood out — not the "string of pearls,"

Vin Scully's term for the zeros posted on the stadium scoreboard indicating scoreless innings. The armband was a reminder on this momentous and happy night for baseball that something terrible had happened. The outside world had seeped in.

In the not-too-distant past, Drysdale had been petulant, prone to uncontrollable outbursts. But time and success had mellowed him. He'd helped bring championships to this city, and Los Angeles loved him. He'd grown into his wide-set frame, and his face no longer seemed doughy and malleable, but somehow set. He was his own man.

And yet he could never quite shed his association with Sandy Koufax, his onetime counterpart, who stood that night in the runway leading to the Dodgers' dugout, quietly watching his friend. They had to be together for this, even if Koufax had walked away from the game. They were the terrific twosome of Los Angeles who, working off the clifflike pitching mound at Dodger Stadium, set the tone for the type of baseball that would come to define the National League of their time.

Although they were very much the odd couple, their stark differences in temperament, style, and mechanics while working together had made them unbeatable. Koufax was the cerebral headliner, serene in his outlook, with a dramatically dropping curveball and a fastball that today's hitters would find impossible to catch up with. Drysdale, "Big D," was voluble with reporters but also willing, like Gibson, to do what was necessary when he saw hitters encroaching on the plate.

Drysdale would prove more violent than Gibson. Drysdale hit 154 batters over the course of his career. Gibson, who faced close to 2,000 more batters, hit 102. But both men would forever point to the time in 1965 when Sandy Koufax reportedly lost his cool as evidence of Koufax's own meanness. In the first inning of a game in Los Angeles against the Cardinals, Lou Brock — in typical Lou Brock fashion — reached base on a bunt, stole second and third, and came home on a sacrifice fly. According to one account, Koufax warned Brock that he'd come after him — something that Koufax denied. In any case, when Drysdale saw Koufax seething on the mound, he turned to his teammate Jim Lefebvre and said, "Frenchy, I feel sorry for [Brock]."

The next time Brock was up, Sandy hit him in the back — the one and only time he hit a batter on purpose. Over the years both Drysdale and

Gibson used this episode to deflect attention away from their own aggressiveness on the mound, as if to say, *Look! Sandy did it too!*

It had been two years since Koufax, at the height of his pitching prowess, walked away from the game. Before he retired, after the 1966 season, Koufax and Drysdale had been the centerpiece of a team that also boasted great speed and a strong defense. They had the brash base running of Maury Wills and the dominant hitting of Tommy Davis and Willie Davis. Without Koufax, however, the Dodger dynasty had collapsed, and an epoch had come to an end. All that remained was Big D.

By 1968, Drysdale was the last player still active from the Dodgers team that once called Brooklyn home. Not only were the players gone, but Ebbets Field had been leveled and reconstructed into public housing. Drysdale took his Brooklyn days with him in the form of the lessons learned from Sal Maglie (later Gibson's teammate and Lonborg's pitching coach), who'd taken a young Drysdale under his wing when he arrived in Brooklyn in 1956. Maglie's lessons were simple and tough. Watch a hitter's feet and how he moves during an at-bat. Have a sense of where your fielders are at all times. Pitch to your opponent's weakness. And most important, move a hitter away from the plate, even if it means knocking him down.

Pitching inside wasn't meant to make batters swing at pitches close to them. Rather, it was meant to prevent them from diving at the outside corner of the plate, where all great pitchers earn their keep. Both Drysdale and Gibson believed in keeping a hitter honest.

"Unless you get used to looking at this guy," Willie Mays lamented, "you'll swear that every pitch is going to crack you on the head."

Like Gibson, Drysdale thrived on his fearsome reputation. According to Gibson's ghostwriter Lonnie Wheeler, Gibson always maintained that Stan Williams — not Drysdale — was the meanest of the Dodgers staff. But it was Drysdale who harnessed that meanness into success, earning more victories than any pitcher in Dodger history at the time of his retirement in 1969.

Unlike Gibson, however, Drysdale was able to leave that image of meanness at the ballpark. There's no doubt that race played a part. Both men went out of their way to scare the bejeezus out of hitters. Yet it was Gibson, with his dark complexion and steely gaze, who played into

America's fears of angry black men. With his slicked-back hair and wholesome good looks, Drysdale could be menacing on the mound and then leave that persona behind.

Marichal he was not. Drysdale didn't vary in his delivery. Instead, he relied on a fastball and a curve, thrown at a three-quarters arm angle that looked like a sidearm motion and gave him great movement. With his arm behind him, Drysdale would hook his wrist behind his body and then come across, a motion that made it difficult for a right-handed batter to hit him. This delivery also allowed him to throw a tailing fastball that right-handed hitters had trouble moving away from and that reached the corner of the plate against left-handers.

When the Dodgers first arrived in California, there was little indication that Drysdale would reach such prominence. At the Los Angeles Memorial Coliseum, a venue that hosted two Olympics but was in no way suited for baseball, Drysdale pouted about the inane playing conditions. In particular, he struggled with the Coliseum's short left field — 250 feet — which he believed caused him to lose more games than he won.

The ballpark's dynamics brought out Drysdale's infantile tendencies. He accused his teammates of heckling him while he was on the mound. When the National League hinted that it might suspend him for hitting batters, he threatened to sue National League umpires.

Watching this, Fresco Thompson, then the vice president of the Dodgers, wondered whether Drysdale had advanced too quickly to the major leagues. He had never experienced the struggles of minor league life — the dirty uniforms, the terribly hot bus trips, the god-awful hotels. He had never known how "the other half" lived.

Drysdale might have been, Thompson conceded, "a little spoiled."

But by 1968 the tempestuous brat was gone. That came with winning, and with the pitcher-friendly conditions at the new Dodger Stadium. Drysdale had also found his comfort zone in Los Angeles. Not long after he arrived in California, he met Ginger Dubberly — a former Rose Bowl Queen and aspiring actress — on a quiz show. They married, and by 1963 the William Morris Agency had signed the two of them, along with their young daughter Kelly, to a package deal.

It didn't hurt that he had a light touch with the press. Chapin felt that

Drysdale was not only cooperative but something else as well. He was a man who understood the media before he would become a member of the media himself.

And suddenly he had it all. A rambling ranch in the Hidden Hills. A restaurant. A record with Frank Sinatra's Reprise label. Racehorses. Commercial endorsements. Roles on *The Rifleman* and *The Lawman* — and later on *The Flying Nun* and *The Brady Bunch*. Ginger and Kelly mixed in quite easily at charity events with the likes of Donna Reed and Tippi Hedren. It was the good life. Drysdale had found wealth and celebrity outside of baseball — but he never lost sight of his primary responsibility.

If there was any doubt about his focus, he made sure the world understood early in the 1968 season. His work was with the Dodgers, he told one reporter. His paycheck was signed by Walter O'Malley. Everything else that came with success was secondary. He could devote himself to those things later. Right now he intended to pitch, and pitch well.

We remember the ends of streaks, not the beginnings. We don't remember Drysdale at Wrigley Field beating the Cubs 1–0 or his start against the Astros when he left the bases loaded in the ninth. And we certainly don't remember when he told reporters afterwards, "I've had it. I couldn't throw another pitch. Stick a fork in me, I'm done."

But of course he wasn't done — not nearly. There was another shutout against the Cardinals and Bob Gibson, and a second against the Astros. By then, he'd pitched four complete games without giving up a run. Only then did the league and the city seem to come alive.

By most accounts, Drysdale remained unaffected by the attention to the streak of scoreless innings. He rarely brought it up when he spoke to his sister and parents. He went about his business as usual. He still didn't shave on game days. As a matter of superstition, he still never stepped over the chalk lines on his way to the dugout. With his team's anemic hitting, he needed to keep other teams scoreless simply to survive.

Drysdale had already matched Luis Tiant's four-game shutout mark from earlier in the season, and like Tiant, he was poised to tie and then surpass the record set by G. Harris "Doc" White, a long-retired White Sox pitcher who'd pitched five straight shutouts over six decades before.

At the time, White was 89, bedridden, and living with his daughter Marian in Silver Spring, Maryland. Marian conveyed her father's good luck wishes and said that, if he was able, Doc would be rooting for Drysdale, just as he did for Tiant, not just to tie his record but to break it. It was time for someone to finally surpass him.

It was late in the morning on May 31 when Drysdale woke up. The Dodgers had sent him home a day early from their road trip so he could decompress and calm his nerves before the next game. For several hours, however, he thought only about how he could break White's mark against the aging, but still tenacious, San Francisco Giants. This was not the group of young upstarts that Orlando Cepeda had starred for. But they still had Willie Mays and Willie McCovey, and they'd be hungry to win. Breaking the record against this team, in this year, would be a capstone to his career — which, as Drysdale openly wondered, might be drawing to a close.

Very seldom does sport follow the narrative we expect. Yet that night everything went according to script. Over 46,000 people — including 30 of Drysdale's friends and family members — came out to watch. Before the start, Minnesota senator Eugene McCarthy, then in the midst of a raucous battle with Robert Kennedy in the California Democratic primary, played catch with Mudcat Grant, who supported his rival.

The Dodgers managed to score three runs, and Drysdale was able to keep the Giants off balance and scoreless through eight innings. His manager, Walter Alston, had put in his best defensive players to begin the seventh. The record, it seemed, was tantalizingly within reach.

Great collapses in baseball, perhaps more so than in other sports, seem to unfold in slow motion. At the beginning of the ninth, Drysdale walked McCovey, then allowed Jim Ray Hart to single, and walked Dave Marshall. Up next was the big-eared Dick Dietz, the Giants' catcher, who worked the count to 2-2. Anything would have ended Drysdale's shutout. *Anything.* A base hit, a wild pitch, even a fly ball. The writers in the press box scrambled to write alternative endings for their stories. Epitaphs seemed in order. Drysdale had had a fine run. But now it was over.

Of course, the Dodgers and the Giants have shared many remarkable moments over the years. Bobby Thomson's 1951 home run to mark the Giants' improbable comeback against Brooklyn to win the 1951 pennant. Joe Morgan's 1982 home run to keep the Dodgers from winning the National League Western Division. Juan Marichal using a bat to attack Dodger catcher Johnny Roseboro in 1965. Yet Dietz's at-bat against Drysdale stands out as perhaps the strangest moment of all between the two teams.

For most of the evening, Drysdale had used his slider, along with his sinker and fastball, with great effect. Yet the slider he threw to Dietz simply got away from him. Instead of sailing away from Dietz, as it was supposed to, it hit Dietz squarely on the arm. Drysdale's streak should have ended right there, but it didn't. Dietz wasn't permitted to take first base because umpire Harry Wendelstedt ruled it a ball: he claimed that Dietz hadn't made an attempt to get out of the ball's path. He was invoking an official but rarely enforced rule — especially in such a high-stakes situation. After enduring the wrath of Giants manager Herman Franks, Wendelstedt called for play to resume. Drysdale, who threw 150 pitches that night, brought Chavez Ravine to fever pitch as he cobbled together the next three outs. (When Dietz passed away in 2005, one headline for his obituary read, "Dick Dietz, 63, Who Didn't Try to Avoid a Drysdale Pitch, Dies.")

Walking into the clubhouse after the game, Drysdale saw a sign taped to his locker: DRYSDALE FOR PRESIDENT — SHOO-IN IN CALIFORNIA PRIMARY. Drysdale's catcher, Jeff Torborg, said Wendelstedt showed "real guts" in not awarding the base. Alston admitted that he'd never seen that call before, but added that he'd never seen anyone deliberately try to get hit by a pitch either.

Meanwhile, Chapin and other writers waited, notebooks in hand, outside the visiting team's clubhouse. It wasn't the first time that a team, piqued by their performance, had left beat reporters waiting. But this was too much.

At last Chapin pounded on the door. The door opened ever so slightly — and a catcher's shin guard sailed past. When the Giants finally allowed them in, the writers found a sullen bunch. Dietz was showing anyone who was interested the red welt on his left arm. When Chapin approached Franks, the manager accused Drysdale of a great many things and spit tobacco juice on Chapin's shoes.

"It was the worst call I've ever seen," Franks said. "If Drysdale breaks the record now, he and Wendelstedt should share it. Hell, put Wendelstedt's name on the trophy first."

June 4. The eyes of California, and Los Angeles, were not on Drysdale but on Bobby Kennedy, who held a slim margin over Gene McCarthy in the primary that Drysdale's teammates thought he himself could take. In previous days, Kennedy, who had faltered badly against McCarthy in Oregon, had worked his way back into contention by campaigning tirelessly at shopping centers in Sacramento, in the ghettos of Watts, in San Francisco's Chinatown.

That day Drysdale woke at noon. As the hours wore on, he began to feel uneasy about facing a young Pittsburgh team. He tried listening to Frank Sinatra and Dean Martin. He and Ginger went to the restaurant they owned and ordered the same meal they'd had during the four games of the streak. He felt far more nervous than he'd been against the Giants. He just wanted the whole thing done with.

He won the game handily, 5–0. There was no drama this time. Yet, like the Giants, the Pirates accused Drysdale of cheating: he was using Vaseline on his ball, they said, making his sinker more effective and forcing his already formidable fastball to drop, much like a curveball, in front of batters.

Drysdale, for his part, was in high spirits. Not only had he broken White's shutout streak, but in the second inning he'd bested Carl Hubbell's National League record of 46⅓ scoreless innings. By Chapin's account, Drysdale was "simply unbeatable" from that point on.

Afterwards, as he dodged questions about the next mark—Walter Johnson's major league record of 55⅔ innings, a record that had lasted over 50 years—Drysdale wryly asked, "How's the election coming out?"

It was after midnight on June 5, a time when the Dodgers and the beat writers had left Dodger Stadium, now a quiet and darkened ballpark set amid the lights of the country's most maddening metropolis. Kennedy, the triumphant winner of the California primary, had left his spot at the podium of the Palm Terrace Room at the Ambassador Hotel. Now

Ken Gaydos, a radio newsman who'd run out of paper for taking notes, rushed to the podium where Bobby had left a crumpled piece of paper.

On the paper were last-minute notes Kennedy had scribbled before he took the stage. It was a list of people Kennedy wished to thank — including labor organizer Cesar Chavez and track legend Rafer Johnson. At the top, though, in heavy ink was this notation: "Drysdale — 6 straight."

"I want to first express my high regard for Don Drysdale, who pitched his sixth straight shutout tonight," Kennedy famously began. "And I hope we have as good fortune in our campaign."

It was a moment of triumph, one that would remain with us forever. There was the impassioned victory speech calling for Americans to work together to create a more compassionate society, to achieve peace in Vietnam. Then there was the final call of "on to Chicago," to bring home the nomination. And then the shrieks, the scurrying reporters, the frantic calls for a doctor. Another shooting, the end of an 82-day campaign, and the final death knell for a decade that had begun with the optimism of a young country, now grown dispirited and older and lost.

Drysdale heard it all transpire while driving home from the stadium that night. Millions would claim they knew Robert Kennedy, but Drysdale actually did. They had met through the Job Corps program, run by Kennedy's brother-in-law, Sargent Shriver. Drysdale — along with Chuck "The Rifleman" Connors — had spent time at Kennedy's expansive compound, Hickory Hill, outside of Washington. The two would sometimes spend time together in Los Angeles when Kennedy came to town. And now, because of the words on the piece of paper left on the podium, the two men would be linked with each other forever.

At that same moment of collective shock, Drysdale's teammates Mudcat Grant — traded from the Twins after the 1967 season — and Ted Savage were also driving, on their way to the Ambassador Hotel. Like Drysdale, Grant claimed a personal connection with Kennedy, dating back to the time when Jack Kennedy was president and Grant was a talented, though erratic, pitcher for the Indians.

The two had met in Detroit. When the president learned that the team was staying at the same hotel where he was, he invited Mudcat to breakfast, during which they spoke about many things. Foremost on Grant's mind was the state of his hometown in Florida. It was still seg-regated, without a real school, and its black residents were confined to living in the workers' living quarters left over from a defunct lumber mill. Grant would later boast that, with Kennedy's help, the town got its school, better housing, a park, and some other infrastructure. And it was through JFK that Grant met Sargent Shriver and Bobby.

Grant and Savage had seen Bobby again only a few days before the California primary, and they had wanted to be there at the hotel with him that night as he squeaked out a narrow, desperately important win. But they were too late leaving the ballpark.

Nothing at that moment seemed real. The world, for the second time in a matter of months, had come undone, and Grant was asking him-self, as were so many others, *What the hell is happening to our country?* Should they press on, they wondered, to the Ambassador, where they could only serve as witnesses to another dark part of history, be by-standers to a nightmare?

They realized that driving to the hotel was out of the question. Both men were at a loss for thoughts, even for speech. They pulled to the side of the road. Looking at each other, they simply had nothing to say. It was time to turn around and go home.

Before Don Drysdale's next start on June 8, Dodgers broadcaster Vin Scully opened his broadcast as only Vin Scully could: "They say the eye of the storm is the quiet part, and here, Dodger Stadium, has suddenly become the eye of the storm. A large crowd, approximately 50,000, and the winds of all kinds of emotions swirling around the ballpark. Cer-tainly there are still the winds of sorrow; what a dreadful, drab and heartbreaking day it has been. But as the gray skies now slowly start to disappear to night, so, too, the feelings in the ballpark are turning. And from almost the pits of despair, we concentrate on a child's game — a ball, a bat and some people hitting it, throwing it and catching it, and particularly Don Drysdale's big night in baseball."

Drysdale had spent the day as millions of Americans had — in front of his TV watching the funeral service from St. Patrick's Cathedral in

New York. Now, on his big night, he was at the ballpark, where the mood was buoyant. Thousands of fans who'd hoped to see him pitch had to be turned away at the ticket booths, creating a long stream of cars leaving the ballpark before the game had even begun.

Drysdale's black armband was the only reminder of what had taken place.

Yet something was off about Drysdale that night. With rare exceptions during the streak, he'd kept men off base, walking only 13 batters, one intentionally. But that night he threw seven of his first eight pitches for balls and seemed to toil through the first two innings. At the end of two, he had tied Johnson's streak.

In the top of the third, the diminutive shortstop Roberto Peña tried to bunt but fouled off the pitch. Now Drysdale stood tall, raised his arms in a demonstrative windup, bringing the ball back beneath him, and then let it loose. Peña hit the ball hard toward third base, where Ken Boyer grabbed it easily and threw it to first. Drysdale had officially kept teams scoreless for 56 innings. As of 8:45 that evening, the record was his.

For some 20 seconds, Drysdale chose not to face the next batter, but took a moment to compose himself. He turned his back on the mound, folded his arms, and stood as he always stood—perfectly erect. The cheers were deafening.

He'd passed the mark, and now he was trying to keep it going. At the end of the Phillies' third inning, and again before the top of the fourth, umpire Augie Donatelli stopped Drysdale to check him for the Vaseline that he'd been repeatedly accused of using. Then a Phillies infielder named Howie Bedell hit a sacrifice fly to drive in a run in the fifth—the only run he'd drive in all season—and the streak was over at 58⅔ innings.

"It was bound to happen sooner or later," Drysdale said. "This was one of those nights, the kind when you just run out of steam."

What Drysdale couldn't know was that the streak marked the last significant achievement of his pitching career. He finished the season with a terrific earned run average—2.15—but just 14 wins. At times his velocity wavered. The following year he went on the disabled list with a torn rotator cuff, then tried, with the help of pills, to pitch through it, but had little success. When he announced his retirement in August 1969 at age 33, the era of Drysdale and Koufax was officially brought to a close.

Drysdale would thrive in his new career as a broadcaster, both nationally and for several teams, including the Dodgers. His marriage to Ginger would end in divorce, but he'd find love again, with the basketball standout Ann Meyers, with whom he'd have three children.

Don Drysdale reached the summit in June 1968, having done what no man had been able to do in 55 years. But at that very moment an insurrection was happening within the game, one that would change the dynamics of all sports for good.

11

OUT THERE

YOU GUYS ARE WRONG. I'm telling you," Milt Pappas said to his Cincinnati Reds teammates in the clubhouse of Crosley Field, "there's no sense in having a players' association if you go out there and play."

It was Saturday evening. Less than five years had passed since NFL commissioner Pete Rozelle made the ill-advised decision to play the Sunday following John Kennedy's death in Dallas. Now Major League Baseball commissioner William Eckert, who'd already made one decision that season about whether to play following an assassination, faced another. The funeral in New York for Robert Kennedy had been scheduled for Saturday, and President Johnson had declared the next day a national day of mourning. Eckert canceled some games in some cities, but allowed other games to begin after soldiers had put the younger Kennedy—the political insurgent who entered the race only after it was clear that Johnson was in free fall—to rest at Arlington National Cemetery.

For a sport that had long prided itself on strong leadership from its front office, the decision would reveal a moment of weakness. While some teams had gone along with the plan, others had not. At issue were two days: the funeral on Saturday, and the day of mourning on Sunday.

Baltimore had called off its Sunday doubleheader at home against the Athletics, and Kennedy's team, the Red Sox, had wiped out a twin bill at Fenway against Chicago. Elsewhere the decision was not so straightforward.

Following the assassination, Tim McCarver, the Cardinals' player representative, had remained a stalwart voice, reminding players that they owed it to the country not to play that weekend. He called for baseball to act as a group and rightfully asked why some clubs could cancel while others could not. By majority vote, the Cardinals had decided they wouldn't play their scheduled doubleheader so long as their opponent, the Cincinnati Reds, agreed to do the same. The Reds had voted 25–0 in favor of not playing, but Reds executive Dick Wagner, a lieutenant to Reds (and former Cardinals) general manager Bob Howsam, was indignant when Pappas, the Reds' player representative, told him how the players voted. The doubleheader would go on as planned, Wagner declared. Reluctantly, both teams agreed to play—albeit with objections.

"Why don't they call off all the Sunday games?" McCarver asked. "We have a moral obligation not to play on the day of mourning." Yet, as a member of a team in pursuit of its second straight pennant, he also said, "We don't want to play, but we don't want to forfeit the games either."

McCarver's views were similar to those of Pappas, who observed succinctly, "If they did it for Dr. Martin Luther King, then why not for Bobby Kennedy?"

Pappas had already become something of a punch line in baseball history. Following the 1965 season, he'd arrived from Baltimore in exchange for Frank Robinson—a trade considered nearly as unbalanced as the Lou Brock–Ernie Broglio trade in the midst of the Cardinals' 1964 championship season. Broglio was a solid, if not spectacular, starter who would go on to pitch only two more seasons—winning one game in 1965 and two in 1966. Meanwhile, Brock would play well into the 1970s, be a pivotal member of championship Cardinals teams, and earn a well-deserved space in the Hall of Fame after retiring as the most prolific base stealer of all time.

The Reds would long be haunted by their costly decision to trade for Pappas. While Robinson surged ahead with his Hall of Fame career, winning the Triple Crown in 1966, Pappas struggled, tussling with teammates, including the beloved future radio announcer Joe Nuxhall, who openly questioned his aptitude.

Regardless of players' desires, the Reds' management never wavered in its intention to play that Sunday. As far as management was concerned, they'd fulfilled their duty by moving the start of Saturday's game from the afternoon to the evening, just as Eckert had requested. Upon hearing that the players unanimously decided not to play on Sunday, the indignant Dick Wagner insisted that the club had "an obligation to the fans, to the industry, and to the players" to go ahead.

Roger Maris, the Cardinals' right fielder, now in his final season, shot back, "And they call the players greedy at contract time."

But no one foresaw that Saturday's game plans would be thrown into flux as well. Kennedy's funeral train was slowed by the thousands of mourners who stood on platforms and between railway tracks, in overgrown, empty fields and along dirt roads, to pay their respects as it left Manhattan and made its way to D.C. Indeed, Kennedy's body didn't arrive at Washington's Union Station until after nine o'clock that night. And even then, the funeral procession paused at the steps of the Lincoln Memorial, where the Marine Corps Band played "The Battle Hymn of the Republic," before continuing on to Arlington National Cemetery. The motorcade arrived at Arlington at 10:30 p.m. — more than three hours after the game time set by Eckert.

As afternoon turned to evening, no one showed up for fielding or batting practice at Crosley Field. The players had gone along with the commissioner's directive to hold off playing until the burial was over at Arlington. As it became obvious that there was no chance that would happen by 7:00 p.m., McCarver and Pappas spent a considerable amount of time in each other's clubhouse determining what to do.

Players on both teams were unwavering. It wasn't that they didn't want to play. They did — that was why they were there. But they'd been dealt a bad hand. Whatever agreement had existed no longer mattered. They'd relented and agreed to play the two games on Sunday. How much more would they give?

Unsurprisingly, the Reds' management held firm. Howsam said the team had consulted with Eckert, who'd agreed to let the Reds and other teams walk away from the original compromise. The Reds anticipated a capacity crowd that night demanding what they'd paid for—professional baseball. But they needed the players to get on board.

Pappas did his best to assure his teammates that management couldn't suspend them or release them or hold back their paychecks if they refused to play. As a team, they voted at least twice not to take the field. Following what he believed was the final decision, Pappas said he walked from the Reds' clubhouse to the Cardinals' clubhouse, and then to the umpires' quarters, to inform everyone of the Reds' decision. His job, he believed, was done.

When he got back to his clubhouse, Pappas found Reds manager Dave Bristol and a member of the Reds' management team speaking to his teammates. Shooing them both from the locker room, he told them that the players had voted and that they weren't going to play. But by now, the players had become wary. Many of them called for another vote even as Pappas told them not to be intimidated. When the results of the new vote came back the same, Pappas again relayed the news to the Cardinals and the umpires. However, when he returned to the clubhouse this time, he saw that some of his teammates were getting dressed.

"What are you doing?" Pappas asked.

"Well," one of them replied, "we're going to play."

The turn of events had been mainly instigated by Bristol. The Reds manager had gone as far as to prepare a series of lineup cards, made out to list whichever nine players decided to follow him to the field. He asked for nine fellows—any nine fellows—to come along with him so they could start the game, albeit 45 minutes late.

"Get your glove, Maloney," Bristol said to the Reds' ace, who was still pitching despite persistent pain. In this particular lineup, he wasn't the starting pitcher but the third baseman—though Maloney would later say he'd been penciled in to play right field. Whoever agreed to play would play, no matter what their regular spot on the roster. Bristol knew that playing out the game under these circumstances would have been a farce. The fans would have known it too. But by driving a wedge among his players, Bristol knew he'd regain control of his team and put an end to the insurrection.

Maloney felt an obligation to play. After all, with his fellow Reds ready to play out of position, he'd be able to tell his children and grandchildren in later years that even as one of the game's elite pitchers, he'd once started a major league game as a right fielder. Moreover, he saw no reason not to go ahead. It wasn't that he had anything against Robert Kennedy. But he had signed up to play and was willing to go ahead with the game if it came down to it.

Bristol believed that if he could field a starting lineup, the rest of the roster would follow. And they did. Maloney did not start as a right fielder or third baseman — Pete Rose and Tony Pérez took those spots. When the 7:00 p.m. game began 45 minutes late, the Cardinals, as both McCarver and manager Red Schoendienst promised, had stepped out into the dugout and bullpen with their full roster. When it became apparent that all the hours of deliberation had been for nothing, Pappas found himself permanently estranged from his team.

"If nine guys go out there and play, then we'll all go," Pappas said. "We won't give them the satisfaction. But if we play, you guys will have to find yourself another player rep."

Pappas understandably felt drained and underappreciated. It seemed ridiculous that management could still coerce players despite his assurances that "they can't do a damn thing to you" under the circumstances. Watching his teammates put on their uniforms, Pappas felt helpless. But since there was nothing more he could do or say to persuade them to do the right thing at this moment, he dressed too. Pappas would pitch in relief in both games of the doubleheader the following day, each time enduring boos. Before the week was out, the Reds would trade him to Atlanta.

"Our position is that we had scheduled this game in good faith at a time about an hour and a half after the burial was scheduled," Howsam said afterwards. "We would have waited if the delay had been a short time, but we felt an obligation to our fans who were in the park — many after long drives to see the game. We did all we could in good faith."

Howsam was certainly not alone in his failure to understand the whirlwind of emotion blowing through baseball in those days after Robert Kennedy was assassinated. The day before the debacle in Cincinnati, on Friday, June 7, the San Francisco Giants had released their own passive-aggressive statement: "In deference to the memory of the late Senator Kennedy and in the belief that it would not be in the best interest of baseball and the public to have a game decided by forfeit, the Giants have canceled the game with the New York Mets that was to have been played tomorrow afternoon. The Giants sincerely regret the disappointment of thousands of young fans who had intended to attend the Bat Day game tomorrow and are compelled now to rearrange their plans."

It was the Mets, they wanted to make clear, that had forced this decision on them, depriving fans of their special day. The Mets had voted twice not to play their game as scheduled on Saturday — once in Chicago and then upon arriving in San Francisco. When initially informed of the Mets' decision, Horace Stoneham, the Giants' owner, had pointed out to Gil Hodges, the Mets' manager, that Saturday wasn't just any day but Bat Day, and that there had been advance sales of up to 30,000. Hodges relayed this information to his team, and upon arrival in San Francisco, the Mets sat aboard their plane deliberating for two minutes. They didn't change their minds. When Hodges conveyed their final decision to Giants officials, he was told that Stoneham was willing to move the game to 4:00 p.m. Pacific Coast Time. But the Mets wouldn't budge — even though they faced the prospect of a forfeit. Unlike Bristol and Howsam, however, M. Donald Grant, chairman of the Mets' board of directors, and Hodges himself supported and took pride in their players' position.

As the Mets' player representative, Ed Kranepool, said, Kennedy had been their elected senator and represented their fan base. And even though the match they were set to play was some 2,900 miles from New York, they still saw it as their civic duty to sit this day out. The Giants' starting time concession meant nothing.

"We're from New York," Kranepool said. "It's a matter of respect.

"If we did forfeit, so what?" he continued. "It's only one game. It's better than playing, I think."

After much consternation, the Giants issued their statement — releasing the players from both teams to do as they wished. Thus, on Saturday afternoon, while Hodges spoke about taking time to pray in church and some Mets players walked through Haight-Ashbury, George Vecsey and some other sportswriters traveled to Tiburon, the hilly enclave in Marin County north of San Francisco, where they wanted to look out at the Pacific at the continent's edge. After all, there was no game to cover — the

Mets had made sure of that. It was a lovely day in a lovely place, and the writers had some time for themselves.

And that's what they got. After seeing what there was to see, Vecsey and the others sat down to a brunch of eggs and orange daiquiris. Despite everything that had happened that week, it was still an off day to enjoy, a day to act and do as they chose. *That poor bastard Kennedy,* Vecsey thought when they raised their glasses to the slain senator for giving them this respite from the business of a beat writer's life, made possible only by his death. They would be working again soon enough, with a doubleheader to cover on the actual day of mourning the next day — the Sunday that the Reds and Cardinals had fought so hard against playing on.

Like the Reds, the Houston Astros had voted 25–0 not to play the scheduled doubleheader, against the Pirates, on Sunday, June 9. Their general manager, Spec Richardson, was livid and warned that there would be repercussions should they follow through with their threat. In the end, 23 of the Astros played and two — Rusty Staub and Bob Aspromonte — did not. Neither would Pirates infielder Maury Wills, who refused to leave the clubhouse and chose to spend the time reading a book by Kennedy himself. Roberto Clemente did not want to play but finally relented, regretfully, and went along with the rest of his team. Like Pappas, Staub and Aspromonte were traded at the end of the season, the Pirates left Wills open to the expansion draft, and all three were fined.

Catching flak for his decision, Spec Richardson responded that the games had to go forward because Robert Kennedy "would have wanted it that way."

Of course there were journalists who supported the position of owners and management that the games should be played in spite of players' objections. Addressing Kranepool and his teammates, Dick Young wrote in the *Daily News:* "Each man worships within his heart. Each man feels grief within his heart. No man, nor group of men, has the right to tell another man when to mourn, any more than he has the right to tell another man which God to worship, if any. I must wonder about the brash young Mets, who ordain when they will play ball and when they won't."

But many of his peers didn't share Young's viewpoint. Most journalists would have agreed instead with Young's friend Red Smith.

"The refusal of the Mets to play in San Francisco on the day of Robert Kennedy's funeral was one of the few heartening aspects of a weekend of shame," Smith wrote. "The rascals of Shea Stadium may be young and callow and 'brash,' but they recognized something that seems to have eluded the understanding of most grown men in sports.

"When Dick Young suggests that grief is a private thing which each man must express or conceal in his own way," Smith went on, "he is absolutely correct — provided he means the grief of the private individual. It is something else entirely when it involves a public demonstration of respect or callous indifference."

Kennedy aide Frank Mankiewicz wrote telegrams of thanks to Milt Pappas and the ballplayers who refused to play, as well as to Gil Hodges on behalf of the Mets, expressing his "personal admiration for your actions. Senator Kennedy indeed enjoyed competitive sports, but I doubt he would have put box-office receipts ahead of national mourning."

Eckert, who wisely hadn't suspended players who sat out spring training games after Martin Luther King's death, wasn't willing to be as understanding this time around. When Marvin Miller, the union leader, heard about Eckert's plans to suspend players who chose not to play that weekend, he warned the commissioner, "You're going to get the worst adverse publicity you ever saw.

"These players are not acting so they can go on a picnic," Miller told him. "They're really feeling this assassination, and you're acting as if they decided they're going to go swimming instead of playing ball." In the end, perhaps seeing the growing influence of Miller and his union, the commissioner did nothing.

Many professional athletes felt a connection to Bobby Kennedy, but he and his campaign had also reached out to them and tried to include them in the political process. It had been Rams defensive lineman Rosey Grier and Olympian Rafer Johnson, acting as Kennedy's bodyguards (along with journalist George Plimpton), who had subdued and disarmed the gunman Sirhan Sirhan at the time of the assassination. Following Jim Lonborg's 22-win 1967 season, Bobby and his wife Ethel had befriended the pitcher, inviting him to a host of family functions, including a touch football game, at Hickory Hill. Oscar Robertson and Bill Russell, Vince Lombardi and Dave Bing and Gayle Sayers, Bob Cousy and Hank Aaron, Bobby Mitchell and Sam Huff—all these men had supported Robert Kennedy in one way or another.

As Robert Lipsyte wrote in his *New York Times* column, Bobby's campaign had created a special group of "National Sportsmen for Kennedy," publicly led by Stan Musial. Lipsyte reported that the campaign had explicitly sought out athletes—like Musial, who had stumped for John Kennedy in 1960—who were perceived as being on the rise and particularly influential.

"Kennedy supporters spoke often of the identification athletes felt with the Senator," Lipsyte wrote. "He had energy, ambition, perseverance, physical courage and a sense of his body. He appealed to the younger men of the country, and athletes are young. Also, athletes were attracted by the Kennedy camp's glamour and will-to-win, two of the intangibles that had brought them into sports in the first place.

"In amassing perhaps the largest group of committed athletes to support a contender for candidacy," he wrote, "the Kennedy camp was criticized for appealing to younger voters and black voters in an emotional and unreasonable way . . . Although athletes have supported and actively campaigned for every one of the other major candidates, only Kennedy went out of his way to include them in as a group, and only Kennedy provided an instant expression for the growing political involvement of athletes."

If Robert Kennedy's campaign awakened their political awareness, his assassination showed ballplayers where they stood within the sport. Year after year, they had fought for one-year contracts, which often came with pay cuts. Ownership was not willing to cut them any slack— no matter the cause—and treated them like cattle. There was a great deal of anger simmering beneath the surface.

"We want a voice in schedule-making," Bill Freehan, Denny McLain's catcher and the Tigers' player representative, would lament. "Baseball is not just a game and a business. It is an entertainment. The fans come out to be entertained, and we ought to be able to perform at our highest level. The schedule does not permit us to. Not when you play 20 days straight, in July and August, when you're doggone tired. That is the true peak of the season, when teams get eliminated. It is unfair for a team to be knocked off, because it has to play 20 or 30 games in a row without a break."

Freehan's statement underscored a burgeoning understanding by players of how much they were really worth and what they should expect. Having negotiated their first collective bargaining agreement that February, they now understood the strength of the collective. Marvin Miller could sense they were ready for more.

It had taken considerable effort for Miller to get to this point. Sam McDowell, whose father had worked as a steelworker in Pittsburgh and who had seen the spoils that unions could bring, bristled when Cleveland manager Birdie Tebbetts repeatedly referred to Miller as a Communist. The Yankees were just as relentless, warning Jim Bouton and his teammates that if they elected Miller, they would be putting an unrepentant rabble-rouser in charge and paving the way for a future filled with "picket lines and bicycle chains and baseball bats and labor goons and violence."

Then they met him. Miller was slight in stature, quiet, respectful. He was happy to address the players' questions and concerns and was never dismissive of the way they felt. Dal Maxvill, who would later take his turn as a player representative, decades later could still see Miller walking into the clubhouse with his disfigured right arm, smoking a cigarette. Here he was, the man whom they'd been warned against even listening to, telling them how happy he was to be part of their "wonderful" group, promising that he would do his best to improve their fortunes, but more important, that he would always be honest with them and keep them fully informed during negotiations. At the end of Miller's presentation, Maxvill was completely won over, nodding in agreement when others said they'd found the right man for the job.

Players in Boston felt the same way. Jim Lonborg immediately felt a new strength and confidence among his teammates, who now seemed ready to act as a group, without cowering. They'd all been aware of the inherent discrepancies in baseball, and now they'd found someone who could articulate it and who understood how to fight for their rights, to help them earn what was rightfully theirs. The players eventually voted

489–136 in Miller's favor. Over time, Lonborg felt, Miller's demeanor and the care he took in working every angle, pursuing every measure, to protect and better their lives made him feel a part of the family for a great many ballplayers.

In the days after baseball's bungled response to the Robert Kennedy assassination, one sportswriter after another decried Eckert's laissez-faire approach — letting clubs decide for themselves whether their teams should play — as an act of cowardice. Deemed the "Unknown Solider," Eckert, with his impressive military credentials, was exposed as a weak leader who was out of step with the times.

Speaking in his own defense, Eckert said later that he and the clubs had done their best. In setting the start of their Saturday games well beyond their initial starting times, their "intentions were proper." Fans, after all, had come to the ballpark, and the teams felt it would be unfair to ask them to wait any longer. (Never mind that fans were routinely expected to wait through weather delays so clubs could "get games in.")

Team owners, for their part, were just as set in their paternalistic ways. Gussie Busch, the Cardinals' overlord, infamously and publicly berated his players during spring training in 1969, telling them that they'd grown selfish. Other sports — including soccer — had grown in their reach, he said, while baseball players seemed indifferent. He was a man, like other owners, whose attitude toward the people who worked for him would ultimately cost him and his brethren. But for the time being, Busch remained his team's unchecked ruler — and nothing he believed would change that.

This was apparent in 1970 when Steve Carlton, Gibson's heir apparent, asked for a pay raise. Busch didn't like his attitude and couldn't understand how the players could view owners as "tight-fisted." He was "fed up."

"I just can't understand what's going on, on the campus and everywhere in our great country," he said. "I only hope some of the other owners have the guts to take the stand I have and get this thing back to normal." (Busch battled with Carlton again before the 1972 season and demanded that the team trade him, no matter how good his fastball was or how persuasive his slider was about to become. Carlton would go on to end his career with 329 wins, winning four Cy Young Awards while earning his place in the Hall of Fame.)

By then, however, the definition of normal had changed — owing in large part to Miller. Late in life, Miller recalled a conversation he had early in his tenure as head of the MLBPA with Joe Cronin, who was then president of the American League. Cronin — the onetime manager and general manager for the Red Sox who had passed on signing Willie Mays — had been a player himself once, and a great one at that. But now he reminded Miller of an Irish politician protecting his ward.

Cronin said to Miller, "You know, young man, I want to tell you something that you oughta know and you oughta keep it in mind as you go along.

"The players come and go," he said, "but the owners stay on forever."

Miller was at a loss for words — but not for the reasons one might think. If Cronin was right, if the owners did stay on indefinitely, set in their archaic ways, he would come to know their weaknesses and it would be that much easier for him to deal with them. Year after year Miller would take advantage of that knowledge — using the owners' hubris against them. They had acted badly in the aftermath of Kennedy's death. In the coming years, he would make them, quite literally, pay.

To claim that Bobby Kennedy's assassination marked a turning point in player-owner relations might be overreaching. But it is true that the following December, 150 players — including Mickey Mantle, Bob Gibson, Willie Mays, and Al Kaline — announced that they wouldn't sign their contracts for the upcoming year without a new benefit agreement. By then, anyone could see that a challenge to the reserve clause, which bound a player to a team for the entirety of his career, was coming. Before the start of the 1968 season, the MLBPA negotiated its first collective bargaining agreement, raising the minimum salary to $10,000 from $7,000 — a figure that had been in place for three decades. The agreement also called for a "study committee" that would examine not just the length of the season but the reserve clause itself — something Miller had been pushing for since the summer of 1967. Maybe Miller intended that provision as a warning. He understood the importance of the reserve clause, and he was willing to play the long game with regard to its repeal.

Yet the reserve clause moved rapidly from something spoken about in hushed tones to an issue that players were willing to speak about openly. In a roundtable discussion late in 1969 among athletes speaking on the direction of sports in the next decade, Denny McLain said, "There are a lot of things wrong with baseball that I'd like to see fixed in the 1970s. The reserve clause, for one thing, which binds a player to one team for life.

"It doesn't give the athlete enough freedom," he said. "We can't negotiate with anyone but one person on one team. But as far as testing it, I don't think it will ever be tested in baseball . . . 'cause I'm not going to do it."

In the same discussion, McLain said of Miller: "Well the owners hate him and despise him, which is a good sign. It means we've finally got a man who will negotiate for us. I think Marvin Miller is going to do a great deal for the Baseball Players' Association."

In just a few years with the Players' Association, Miller had created something that took on a life of its own. Before the start of the regular season in 1972, just as teams were gearing up to play, he found himself sitting with a group of players in a meeting held at the Dallas–Fort Worth airport. At issue was the pension plan put forth by the owners, which the players felt was insulting. In all of his years in organized labor, Miller said later, he'd never been to a meeting quite like this one. The players were furious — not only with ownership but with Miller himself. They were on the verge of the very first fully organized strike in the history of professional baseball. And they were willing to go through with it whether or not Miller believed it was a good idea.

"You're underestimating us," one player said. "You don't really know how we feel." At that point, they wrested control of the meeting from Miller and forced him out of the room as they voted nearly unanimously to strike.

The meeting was eye-opening for Miller. As much as he'd done to educate these men about their rights and their collective bargaining power, it wasn't until this moment that he understood how far they'd come in the six years since he'd stepped into their lives. Whether they realized it or not, by exercising their will that weekend in 1968, the owners would come out a weakened lot, outflanked within a matter of years by the newly emboldened group of players — who would take control from them and keep it.

12

UNCLENCHED FISTS

IN THE SUMMER OF 1970, the editors of *SPORT* proclaimed that the "political awakening of the American athlete, we believe, began with the murder of Bobby Kennedy." Had they asked Roberto Clemente—a man who seemed to feel things more strongly than many of his peers—he would have told them that their belief wasn't based in actual fact.

Clemente would have told them that what he saw in the clubhouse following Kennedy's death was not a political awakening but just the opposite: apathy. Clemente ultimately played in the two games on Sunday that were the subject of so much hand-wringing—but he did so reluctantly and uncertainly. Many of his teammates, he said, simply "didn't care whether they played or not."

SPORT magazine shouldn't be singled out here. Its editors were not alone in making sweeping generalizations that linked sports to important national moments and argued that baseball somehow served as a reflecting pool for the country's woes. One could point to the Mets and their decision against participating in Bat Day and the handful of ballplayers who refused to play on Sunday, June 9, as representing a poignant moment in baseball history. But by the same measure, it should be noted that when the Astros arrived in Chicago during the Democratic National Convention in August 1968—which was marked by violent clashes between Mayor Richard J. Daley's police thugs and antiwar demonstrators—the players didn't get involved. No one ventured outside. They remained in their cocoon, like baseball at large, sealed off from the political and social unrest.

Those in charge of the game could always make the point that they were running a business, not unlike the stores that stayed opened for customers regardless of the political climate. Fans did come to games —on the day of mourning for Robert Kennedy, on the evening of the funeral, even on the day after his assassination. When Cleveland relief pitcher Billy Rohr asked, "Has the whole world gone crazy?" he wasn't referring to Kennedy or King or a society in upheaval, but to the behavior of fans in Tiger Stadium. That night there were fistfights in the stands and everything from fruit to empty whiskey and beer bottles to eyeglasses were being thrown out onto the field. Beer flowed into the Cleveland bullpen. One umpire called the situation the worst damn scene on a ball field he'd ever seen. Indians outfielder Tommy Harper wore a batting helmet in the outfield in the ninth inning for protection. Of course, the world *had* gone crazy, but the fans in Detroit weren't reacting to that. They were merely drunk.

"Baseball's function is not to lead crusades, not to settle sociological problems, not to become involved in any sort of controversial racial or religious question," then baseball commissioner Ford Frick said in Jackie Robinson's 1964 oral history *Baseball Has Done It,* a collection of interviews about integration in the sport.

"The function of baseball is to produce the best games possible and to pick its players solely on their ability to run, hit, throw, to play the game," Frick continued. "And that is the way this integration situation was really approached."

It's not such a big leap from Frick's point of view to the opinions espoused by Avery Brundage, the International Olympic Committee president who had controversially opposed the boycott of the so-called Hitler Games back in 1936. His own racist tendencies aside, Brundage was a firm believer in the sanctity of the Games, in keeping them divorced from all political sentiment, regardless of what was happening in the world. There's no question that he was responsible for making the Olympics what it is today — a jingoistic display of national one-upsmanship meant to showcase the cities of the world while simultaneously draining their coffers.

In supporting Harry Edwards and the Olympic Project for Human Rights, many prominent black Olympic athletes believed that they were part of a progressive movement that would expose the truth about what was happening socially and economically in America — namely, that the rise of the black athlete had little to do with the advancement of black Americans. As amateurs, many black Olympians saw themselves as mere gladiators toiling for the Olympic propaganda machine.

There were also black athletes — like Rafer Johnson, the same man who helped restrain Sirhan Sirhan, and long jumper Ralph Boston — who disagreed with Edwards and opposed the boycott of the 1968 Olympics in Mexico City. And they were not the only ones who questioned how boycotting the Games could possibly bring about a sea change in race relations in America after decades of social and economic inequality.

But Edwards, in his beret and dark glasses, was a galvanizing figure who understood how to use the press. And he had help. Kareem Abdul-Jabbar, then Lew Alcindor, declared that the United States was "not really my country" and abstained from taking part in the Olympic trials for basketball — forfeiting his only chance at a gold medal as the most dominant college player of his day.

Edwards also had the support of white liberals. The all-white Harvard crew team, slated to represent the United States in Mexico City, said that, if their black teammates on the U.S. team decided not to travel south, they would stand by them.

"It's certainly regrettable we have to take this stand," one Harvard crewman said in a prepared statement while the team stood alongside Edwards in Cambridge. "But everything about the plight of the black man in this country is regrettable. And, in a sense, our stand is an expression of brotherhood with our black teammates and that's my idea of the spirit of the Olympics, at least the original plan of the Olympics.

"We've invested all our efforts in athletics for so long, and we've worked so hard, that I think we've earned the right to use our main area of interest to express our main concerns," he continued.

"It is not our intention or desire to embarrass our country or to use athletics for ulterior purposes. But we feel strongly that the racial crisis is a total cultural crisis. The position of the black athlete cannot be, and is not in fact, separated from his position as a black man or woman in America." (Afterwards, under tremendous pressure from the United States Olympic Committee [USOC], seven of the nine crew members signed a halfhearted apology — saying that they would not participate in any "demonstration of support for any disadvantaged people in the United States" — even as they continued to try to find other white athletes to join the boycott should it come to pass.)

In the end, the Harvard crew team and even the most outspoken supporters of the boycott — sprinters John Carlos and Tommie Smith — did go to Mexico City. Just ten days before the start of the Games, on October 2, Mexican troops slaughtered an unknown number of student protesters. The exact circumstances that led to the massacre, as well as the final death toll, are still unclear. The Games went on anyway.

It would prove an exhibition of American athletic power. Bob Beamon smashed the world record in the long jump. Dick Fosbury won the gold in the high jump with his "Fosbury Flop." Sixteen-year-old swimmer Debbie Meyer won three individual gold medals. A young George Foreman pranced around the ring waving an American flag following his championship effort. In the 200-meter dash final, Tommie Smith broke the world record to clinch the gold medal, with Australian Peter Norman taking the silver and John Carlos finishing third.

The last event would be overshadowed forever by what followed — Smith and Carlos on the victory podium raising black-gloved fists during the playing of the National Anthem, their heads bowed, defiant, as Norman stood by in silent support. Brundage was furious. He demanded that the USOC throw Smith and Carlos off the Olympic team and bar them from ever setting foot on the Olympic stage again. Their athletic prowess was immaterial. Because they had gone off script, using the Olympic spotlight to make a political statement, Brundage destroyed them.

Meanwhile, the two great black pioneers in American athletics stood at odds with each other on the issue. Jesse Owens — the greatest Olympian of all, who had shown Nazi Germany and the rest of the world what a black man could do — strongly disapproved of Carlos and Smith's actions, yet Jackie Robinson, whose brother Mack was a teammate of Owens's in 1936, later expressed his pride in Carlos and Smith — in what they had done and what they had given up.

Robinson's words might have surprised many. He had spoken out against the black power movement, and in his 1949 congressional testimony, he denounced the actor and singer Paul Robeson for his supposed anti-American rhetoric. But now Robinson called the sprinters' protest "the greatest demonstration of personal conviction and pride I've ever seen."

"I take pride in their proudness in being black," he said when he appeared on a televised panel of black sports figures that included Edwards, Arthur Ashe, and Bill Russell. "What they did had nothing to do with shaming this country.

"Sometimes I wish we had done the very same thing when we were playing ball," he continued. "If we had stood up, I doubt very seriously that the youngsters would be having the kind of troubles they're having today."

It was the golden age of the black athlete in baseball — the age of Hank Aaron and Willie Mays, Bob Gibson and Dick Allen. But with a few notable exceptions — such as the brave stands taken by Allen, Bill White, and Curt Flood — baseball players remained largely silent during the battle for civil rights. The point of view prevalent among ballplayers could be summed up by Mays himself. A Birmingham native, Mays chose not to take part in the Birmingham civil rights campaign in 1963, saying: "I don't picket in the streets of Birmingham. I'm not mad at the people who don't. Maybe they shouldn't be mad at the people who don't."

What happened? For years baseball had mirrored the country's progress on a parallel track. After the war, Jackie Robinson came on the scene just as black men who'd fought for the freedom of others abroad began to fight for their own freedoms at home. As millions of Americans moved out west, so did the game. But now baseball seemed static, frozen in time. How could the two major sporting events of October 1968 — the World Series and the Olympics — be on such different wavelengths?

For journalist Robert Lipsyte, the difference lay with two things: race and college. Those who sought to express themselves at the cost of their athletic careers, as Ali had done, were black athletes on college campuses — young men and women who often lived in the same dorms and walked on the same campuses as empowered student bodies. These athletes worked without pay and were systematically oppressed, always uncertain whether maintaining muttonchops or dating a white girl might cost them their scholarship. Seeing Ali stripped of his title in 1967, they were left to believe that, "if this could happen to the heavyweight champion of the world, it could happen to any of us."

One rare exception in professional sports was the freethinking Jim Bouton, then at the low point of his baseball career. He was no longer the Johnny Sain protégé with so much potential. The Yankees demoted him in 1968 and then left him exposed to the expansion draft — perhaps the best thing to ever happen to him. Instead of being remembered as a promising but ultimately middling pitcher, Bouton would become one of the game's great memoirists. In 1969, during his time with the Seattle Pilots and the Houston Astros, he had the audacity to keep a baseball diary, chronicling with clarity and honesty what went on in a major league clubhouse and exposing the crude excesses of Mickey Mantle. This became the tell-all sensation *Ball Four*.

But in 1968, as Bouton's time with the Yankees was drawing to a close, he received the same letter all major league baseball players did: a request for a signature in support of a United States boycott of the Games should the still-segregated South Africa be allowed to compete. Many ballplayers, black and white, ignored the letter. Bouton signed on.

That's how Bouton, along with his teammate Rubén Amaro and the black South African soccer player Steve Mokone, first came to be in Mexico City, discussing their feelings at a press conference about the Olympic boycott and the possibility of readmitting South Africa to the Games. Six days before the start of the Games, Bouton was in Mexico City again to lobby against South Africa's participation.

He had one main task: to find American members of the USOC — and specifically the committee's president, Douglas Roby — to argue the case. He was accompanied by Mokone, the activist and former cricket star Dennis Brutus, and the white South African weight-lifting champion Chris de Broglio. After delivering a letter to Roby's mailbox, the two would soon meet. When Roby argued that South Africa had "made some progress and should be allowed to participate," Bouton fired back with statements from the country's prime minister that his country's black athletes would never be allowed on the same track as whites.

"We can't tell South Africa what to do," Roby finally told Bouton. "Just like in our own country, everybody wants changes overnight. You can't move too fast on these things." In the end, when one African nation after another threatened to withdraw, everyone agreed that it would be best for South Africa to stay away.

Bouton didn't think he was risking much by taking this stand in Mexico. Even though his baseball career was floundering, as he began to make the transition from a traditional pitcher to a knuckleball specialist he felt that whoever he ended up playing for wouldn't care that he'd lobbied on behalf of the black athletes in South Africa. Everything would be fine as long as he could do his job, as long as he still got guys out. If he couldn't do that, then his association with South African activists wouldn't matter anyway.

But still, Bouton was largely alone in taking a visible political stance. Yes, he and his teammates were aware of the daily antiwar protests, the war in Vietnam, the splintering country. But what remained important to them was simply today's game. It was the most important thing in their lives — not just the source of their livelihoods but the end product of what they'd spent their entire lives trying to build. Everything else seemed to occur in another world, if not another time and place. And even Bouton, with his flashes of insolence and activism, felt that he couldn't let that other world in.

The vast majority of clubhouses existed in a bubble. And why not? Most other Americans didn't suddenly stop what they were doing and walk off their jobs in response to Harry Edwards's call to action or Richard J. Daley's brutal policing methods. Why expect more from ballplayers? Though Frick's comments about integrating baseball may seem coarse to us now, he correctly read the pulse of the game. Players were not prepared to take on the mantle of social justice — even if baseball had let them.

Perhaps it's unfair to characterize clubhouses as dens of ignorance, closed off from the outside world. After all, with roughly one-third of all players serving in the National Guard in 1968, plenty of players were out in the world, missing games in order to serve their country stateside. Clubs had to adjust to the frequent absence of players like Mickey Lolich and Pete Richert, who were called up three different times that spring and summer. And players did get involved politically, campaigning for both Republican and Democratic candidates.

Still, the clubhouse was not then — and would never be — a source of political and social activism. When the sportswriter Arnold Hano profiled Bill Freehan, the Tigers catcher wouldn't discuss the war or race relations or the frightening events in France or Bolivia. His most overtly political statement was to stick up for the "long-hair kids playing in a band," who he thought got a bad rap from adults. Baseball, Hano wrote in his piece about Freehan, "is what he does, what he knows, and what he lives for."

When pitcher Dave Baldwin, early in his career in the minor leagues in Durham, voiced his opposition to the war in Vietnam, he was taken aback when his teammates went on the attack. They'd reflexively swallowed the official dogma about communism running rampant and spreading to New Zealand and Australia. Needless to say, that debate didn't last long. What would be the point? Very quickly Baldwin learned that he had little to no chance of changing these men's minds, no matter how rational and grounded his reasoning. Over the years, he frequently encountered overt racism in clubhouses. Baldwin felt that his manager in 1968, Jim Lemon, couldn't hide his contempt for his black players. It was out in the open for everyone to see, but no one had the courage to speak up for fear of getting into a "difficult situation."

By 1970, George Vecsey, now covering the Yankees, had grown uneasy in his role as a sportswriter. It felt like the clubhouse walls were closing in on him, and he was nagged by self-doubt, wondering, *Does any of this actually matter?* He certainly wanted it to. It had been his dream since he was a boy to be a sportswriter. His father had helped him secure his first job with the Associated Press when he was just a teen. While still in college in 1960, he had joined the sports section of *Newsday*. The editors there recognized his intelligence and talent and took him under their wing, bringing him to games, assigning him to cover high school sports at first. Before long, he would move on from the high school gyms of Long Island and land at the *New York Times*.

Vecsey knew he was lucky, of course. But he couldn't shake his malaise, the ambivalence he felt about his job. The press box no longer seemed like a worthwhile place to sit. After all, how important was his subject matter given what was going on in the world? When he left *Newsday* in 1968 for the *Times*, he knew that being a sportswriter wasn't going to be enough for him, that he'd eventually leave his beat. The only question was when.

As 1968 wore on, Vecsey grew increasingly restless, feeling more and more disconnected from the athletes he was assigned to cover. He needed only to look at the paper's front page to see young people, not much younger than himself, who were willing to face tear gas and billy clubs and prison for their political convictions. Vecsey admired their "spunk," their courage. He stuck it out for the next couple of seasons, until he finally told himself, *I've got to get out of this.*

The real end for him would come in the spring of 1970. By then, Richard Nixon had risen to power. The war seemed like it would never end. National Guardsmen had just killed four unarmed students at an antiwar rally at Kent State University in Ohio — firing 67 rounds in 13 seconds. *67 rounds. 13 seconds.* Vecsey approached the two Yankees he thought would be most affected by the events in Ohio — his friend the infielder Gene Michael and catcher Thurman Munson. Both were from Ohio and both had attended Kent State. Vecsey had become accustomed to ballplayers espousing conservative beliefs, but what Munson had to say shocked Vecsey. Not only did Munson side with the National Guard, but he told Vecsey: "They should've gotten more of them. Get those hippies."

And that was that. Vecsey knew then that he'd overstayed his welcome, that he didn't belong there. Not anymore. He'd return to sports later, coaxed back after a ten-year hiatus. But for now, he was done.

The absence of liberal voices among the game's stars was not lost on young players just starting out in baseball. As an undergraduate at the University of Michigan, Elliott Maddox — soon to join Denny McLain on the Tigers' roster — was critical of black ballplayers, especially Willie Mays. As a black youth, Maddox couldn't bring himself to idolize the great center fielder the way millions of fans did. He appreciated Mays as a player, of course, but Maddox couldn't understand why the greatest ballplayer of his generation didn't speak out about racial injustice when he had such a rapt audience.

Later, when Maddox joined the Mets while Mays was the hitting instructor, he'd come to understand why. Mays wasn't cowering or shirking his responsibilities. He was a perfectly decent man who simply didn't feel comfortable speaking out. He couldn't make himself into someone he wasn't, and he wasn't an activist. His friendship with Mays taught Maddox a basic human truth: when we judge someone from afar, often we know nothing.

In 1968, Maddox, drafted by the Tigers that June, fit perfectly the description of Lipsyte's activist athlete. He was black and had attended college at Michigan, where the Students for a Democratic Society (SDS) first came into being in 1962. He readily took part in student protests, to the consternation of his coaches. Later, as a member of the Senators, he posted photos in his locker of Huey Newton and Eldridge Cleaver as well as a Free Angela sticker—a reference to the Communist civil rights leader Angela Davis, who was wrongfully blamed for the murder of a judge in California. Management, interpreting his display as an affirmation of black power and radical ideology, demanded that he take it down. Noting that all the other players had photos and keepsakes in their lockers, Maddox said, "I'll take mine down as soon as everybody takes theirs down." This response only made things worse.

Harry Edwards of all people might have been expected to reproach major league ballplayers for their lack of political engagement, but he didn't. Edwards understood that they were at a different place in their lives. They weren't caught up in the student movement because they weren't students. They had struggled to escape minor league ball, and they had married young and had financial obligations—to their families and to their employers. To ask them to risk everything for a political cause was unreasonable. Why would he ask a black baseball player in Pittsburgh what he thought of Ali's decision to not fight in Southeast Asia? After all, no one would ask Don Drysdale or Roger Maris or Johnny Sain the same question.

Like Edwards, cultural critic Gerald Early was willing to forgive baseball players for not taking a stand. Unlike track and field, baseball was a team sport, and it was understandable that black ballplayers didn't want to "rock the boat." For a long time, he believed, African Americans had to rely on those in popular culture — not just athletes but singers and musicians — to be political actors, carrying out the unusual burden of speaking out for an entire race.

And for all those who did travel to Mississippi, who did sit in at lunch counters, and who marched with King, Early would later say, we must remember that the vast majority of black people didn't participate in the movement. Like ballplayers, like millions of other Americans, they went on with their lives, striving for what we all want: a decent life. They wanted their youngsters to go to school and build a better existence for themselves, not get sidetracked by political crusades. Even Early, as he made his way out of the Philadelphia ghetto, had to answer to his relatives about his decision to get involved in politics — to side, as they saw it, with the "trouble-makers."

But what then of Bob Gibson? He'd been to college, endured injustice, and helped direct change within the culture of the Cardinals. He was smart and — when he chose to speak — eloquent. Nor was he ever afraid: he feared neither the press nor the blowback from offending a sportswriter or fan. When he did speak out, he usually confined himself to what his ghostwriter and friend Lonnie Wheeler would describe as "an angry quip" and leave it at that.

But at times Gibson would respond to prodding and speak on the racial issues of the day as well as any of his peers. Aside from his blunder in describing the riots that decimated American cities as equivalent to a "brushback pitch," he was articulate on matters of race and the reality of being poor and black in America. After all, not that long before, he'd been just that. He was eloquent about the need for "open housing" and life in the Northern ghetto, and however cool he remained to its leaders, he understood the new militancy of the civil rights movement.

"It's justified," he told a reporter at the time. "This crap has gone on for years and years.

"In the past," he went on to say, "not enough people were willing to voice their opinion. Now the young Negroes are concerned. They're not afraid to speak out. They have no jobs, no families to support, nothing to lose by speaking out. Their parents don't like what's going on either, so now they're speaking out, following the kids. They've got to speak out. The older I am, the more bitter I get about the whole darn thing."

Yet there were things that perhaps he should have left unsaid. Even as he correctly addressed questions of race and overrun slums, he stood up for the ongoing war in Vietnam, still trusting leaders who, with each passing day, were revealing themselves to be masters of deceit—men who sought out the wrong conflict at the wrong time with the wrong enemy. But Gibson continued to believe that there "must be some purpose in it.

"I feel they know what they are doing," he said. "If I had to go, I'd go." Then, in an unfortunate use of baseball terminology to describe the war abroad and the antiwar movement at home, he added: "A player feels good when he plays at home and the fans are behind him. The same thing with the war. The soldiers must want to feel the people back home are behind them."

These comments were published at the beginning of the 1968 season but would ultimately be overshadowed by what he was doing in his professional life. It was clear from the opening days of the season, even before Drysdale's streak, that 1968 would be the Year of the Pitcher. Now it was time for Gibson to make sure he would be not merely a bit player but baseball's true star.

13

PRESIDENT OF
THE WORLD

WHAT WOULD IT TAKE—how many wins—for others to see Denny McLain as the exceptional pitcher he believed himself to be, as one of the handful of elite pitchers of his day? That was the question McLain put to Johnny Sain early in their time together. Sain thought it over for a minute, then said, "As many as you want. You know what that fellow Napoleon Hill wrote in his book, don't you?"

McLain had never heard of Hill or the author's best-selling *Think and Grow Rich*, published in 1937 and one of the most influential self-help books of its era. But as always, he was willing to hear Sain out.

"Anything you can conceive or believe," Sain paraphrased, "you can achieve."

By mid-August, it was obvious that McLain had taken Sain's and Hill's counsel to heart.

Detroit Free Press reporter Mary Ann Weston, part of the Pulitzer Prize–winning team who'd covered the Detroit riots the previous year, had been assigned to write a piece about the Tigers from a "woman's perspective." The newspaper strike by the *Free Press* and *Detroit News* that had lasted for over 260 days had finally come to an end. Journalists who had scrambled to cover events throughout the year with strike papers and self-produced television shows were finally allowed to return to work. The King and Kennedy assassinations, the rise and fall of Eugene McCarthy, the end of George Romney's political career, the resurgence of Richard Nixon — it had all passed them by.

And they had missed out on a big sports story that had captivated Detroit. Early in the season, the Tigers had charged into first place and then had stayed there, in no small part because of Denny McLain. He was well on his way to winning 30 games — a feat unmatched in 34 years, not since the Cardinals' Dizzy Dean did it in 1934.

Weston was a newcomer to baseball, but she was a good reporter. She knew that the success of her story depended on McLain's cooperation. But Denny was proving impossible to talk to.

As they traveled on the Tigers' team bus through New York, Sain did his best to shield Weston from the players' crass banter, trying to distract her with his own conversation. At a time when women were absent not only from the dugout and the playing field but even the press box, the players had some fun at her expense, ramping up the vulgarity. Weston listened as the Tigers carried on — gawking at leggy women they passed on the street, singing bawdy songs, using language they thought would shock her. It would all end up in her notebook and ultimately in her story.

Weston, who had reported from Detroit's worst neighborhoods, was not so easily unnerved. What she needed help with, however, was getting access to Denny. The Detroit papers were beneath him now. He had been featured in *Time* and *Life*. He had appeared with Steve Allen and played his organ on *The Today Show*. Why should he waste his time talking to a non-beat reporter for the *Free Press*? McLain would put her off: "Later. Later. I'll talk to you later." Of course he never did.

Despite a tepid start to the season and two no-decisions, by June 13 McLain had 10 wins against two losses. When Tom Loomis from the *Toledo Blade* remarked that he was well within reach of 30 wins, McLain, with uncharacteristic humility, said, "I've got a helluva shot at eleven." When a blown call cost him a no-hitter against Boston, he didn't complain; when a reporter suggested he'd gotten a lousy call, he replied that those were his words. At Jim Campbell's request, McLain was making an effort to be more diplomatic in his dealings with the press.

Wins, it seemed, came easily to him. That season the Tigers won 40 games after trailing in the seventh inning, often saving McLain from a defeat or no-decision. In May, while McLain was pitching his third straight complete game, his teammates bailed him out in the eighth when, with the score tied 2–2, second baseman Dick McAuliffe hit a triple, then came home on a sacrifice fly by outfielder Willie Horton. In another outing, with the Tigers behind 4–3 in the eighth inning against the last-place Senators, a pinch hitter batting for McLain hit the game-winning single, earning Denny his 19th win.

That's not to say that McLain didn't work some of his own magic. In his 25th win, with no outs in the sixth inning and the Red Sox leading 2–0, McLain struck out one batter and then the 1967 MVP Carl Yastrzemski. When Mayo Smith—who came to the mound instead of Sain—suggested he walk Ken Harrelson, McLain insisted that he wanted to pitch to him. He threw three straight pitches, all of them sliders, all of them strikes, and Harrelson fell as Yaz had, ending the Red Sox rally. The Impossible Dream was becoming a distant memory.

Four starts later, this time against the Orioles, Boog Powell—once McLain's nemesis but now just another batter—slapped a ball hard toward McLain. With the Tigers leading the game 4–3 and two men on base, the ball seemed destined to find its way into the outfield, allowing Baltimore to score the tying run and then the go-ahead run. But McLain lunged at the ball and threw it to the shortstop covering second base, who in turn sent it back to first base, where Frank Robinson was scrambling to return, to no avail. It was a triple play, something many major leaguers go their entire careers without seeing. McLain was just going about his business—and pitching his way to his 27th victory.

With each win, Sain began to take note of McLain's outsized ego. Once during the 1968 season, Sain and his pitching staff got into a debate about the best pitchers, past and present. Someone mentioned the high-kicking Juan Marichal. Earl Wilson offered up the "Monster," Dick Radatz, who in his first two seasons with the Red Sox was as dominant as any relief pitcher of his time. Sain put in a vote for his onetime teammate "old Spahnie." When someone suggested they ask McLain what he thought, Sain couldn't help it. "Don't bother," he said. "He'll only tell you it's himself."

By the time Weston arrived in New York to do her story, McLain believed he had every right to boast. He was a winner again. Detroit fans loved him, despite everything he'd said about them back in May during a Tigers' losing streak. He'd called them "the biggest front-running fans" in the world. Their affection was forever conditional. They'd booed McLain and slugger Norm Cash last season. Now they were going after Al Kaline, who was on his way to the Hall of Fame. McLain even blamed them for the Tigers' collapse in 1967: "There were certain guys on this club who didn't want to go out and play last year because of the fan base."

McLain quickly realized that he had gone too far and tried to backpedal, quickly telling Tom Loomis to clarify that he had been talking about just 1 percent of the fans. But the damage had been done. Soon enough, everyone heard about his remarks, including Tigers general manager Jim Campbell.

Campbell called him the following morning and asked, "Why the fuck did you say this?"

"What did I say?" McLain said. Campbell repeated McLain's tirade.

"Oh Jesus," McLain said. "That's not what I said. Jim, I said some of these fans are front-runners in the city of Detroit to be booing Kaline and Cash. I never said everybody. What difference would it make if I said everybody or just some of them? Who would know who I was talking about?"

"Well, that's the problem," Campbell said. "Everybody thinks you were talking about them."

Those manning the phones at Tiger Stadium were overwhelmed by complaints from angry fans. McLain appeared with broadcaster Ernie Harwell to clarify his comments, only to be roundly booed when he returned to Tiger Stadium. McLain's wife found a smoke bomb beneath their car. Another time, after a win, McLain said of Tiger Stadium: "They can take this park and throw it into the Atlantic Ocean."

Even after he started winning and fans' anger turned to adulation, McLain was still resentful. "I get an ovation when I warm up," he told a *Life* reporter. "It feels great. Of course that'll only last as long as I win. Fans are basically hypocrites."

• • •

Broadcaster Paul Carey believed that one could learn a lot from watching Denny that season. He didn't try to pitch around batters. He pitched fast and threw strikes and was confident even as they put the ball in play. He was confident in his teammates' ability to back him up. He threw quickly and had people swinging, keeping the ball active as much as he could. In that game against the Orioles, it should have come as no surprise that his shortstop, Tom Matchick, was ready for the relay from him and that first baseman Norm Cash was there to triple up Robinson. Because of McLain's pace, they were always ready.

It's a simple idea — pitch to contact and hit your corners — but difficult for even the best pitchers to execute. In 1968 McLain still had the traditional straight, over-the-top fastball. But now there was more in his arsenal. Because of his high leg kick and compact, straightforward throwing motion, he was able to be effective with his controlled breaking ball, turning the ball over just enough to fool hitters with its big break. His fastball came in one of three ways — overhand, sidearm, or with a three-quarter turn. He used the overhand pitch to get the ball to rise on its way to the plate, while the three-quarter motion would "tail into" a right-handed batter. With his sidearm delivery, he'd make the ball sink.

Sam McDowell, whose promising career would be derailed by alcoholism, always felt that McLain was one of the strangest pitchers he'd ever seen. McDowell ranks as one of the fastest pitchers in the history of baseball. But he had no control — though in 1968 he had a 1.81 ERA. McLain threw hard too, if not as hard as McDowell, but he could place his fastball two inches outside the corner, while McDowell was forever struggling to get within two feet of the plate. To McDowell, what made McLain's curve devastating was that, with his overhand delivery and the right velocity, he threw it perfectly. McDowell and his teammates would call it "the yellow hammer."

"Control is God-given," McLain told one writer. "Like a good arm. You don't develop it, and I thank God he gave me both."

Johnny Sain, to whom many gave credit for McLain's success that season, remained largely silent during this run. He watched from a distance, letting McLain enjoy the attention. The year before, Sain had been the go-to guy for interviews. His track record of turning around the fortunes of struggling pitching staffs had made him a rock star. He was also someone who could be counted on to be candid and not fly into a rage when asked a difficult question. Late in 1968, however, one reporter noted that Sain was now a "forgotten man" who would go weeks without being approached by a reporter for his thoughts on what was happening or what went wrong.

That's because little was going wrong. The Tigers were easily winning their way to the pennant. By September, the team's ERA had dropped one full run from 1967. Meanwhile, McLain had come into his own. Sain felt that McLain understood instinctively when to throw a rising fastball instead of a sinking one, or a curveball when a changeup seemed best. He loved McLain's motion, which one writer described as beginning with a high leg lick that mirrored Juan Marichal's, followed by bringing his leg around and squaring his toe toward home plate — his movements as graceful as a ballet dancer's.

As spring turned to summer and McLain's star shone brighter and brighter, he admitted privately to a teammate, shortstop Roy Oyler, that "fucking yeah" he thought he could win 30. It was a mere "chip shot now." But he did his best to keep his ambition in check publicly. After his 24th win of the year, against Cleveland, he initially told the *Detroit News,* "You can't satisfy everybody no matter what you do. If 30 games come, it's all right with me. But the pennant is first. We've fought too hard and too long to do without it."

But then he couldn't keep up the pretense any longer. This had been his 21st complete game. His record was 24-3. Surrounded by no less than five photographers and magazine reporters, as well as baseball beat men stretching from Detroit to Cincinnati, McLain admitted that there was no point in hiding from the truth.

"Aw, why try to kid about it anymore?" he said finally. "Sure I'm thinking about 30 games. Who wouldn't? That's what I'm shooting for. It's what I've been after since Number 15."

McLain had all of Detroit in his thrall. In one *Free Press* cartoon entitled "Would You Believe 35 Wins?" McLain is portrayed as Superman flying above the city. He's grinning widely, with a white streak running through his hair. At his side is a pitching glove. The bystanders below are peering up, shouting, "Look up in the sky . . . it's a bird . . . it's a plane . . . no, it's just Denny McLain!" A couple of days later, another cartoon showed McLain in an astronaut suit walking toward an Apollo space-craft and further toward his final destination: "MVP Award/Cy Young Award/pennant for Tigers/100,000 '69 salary and points north."

"Denny is their boy, their hero of the hour," *Free Press* columnist Joe Falls wrote, "and nothing or no one can say anything wrong about him." But the press was well aware of his darker side, of his shiftiness. Falls re-counted an exchange in which McLain told a wire service reporter that the only way he could escape the public glare was to go up in his air-plane, to "lose himself in the sky." But he wasn't sure if the Tigers knew this, and he admitted to not having a license. Later, when another re-porter asked McLain where he flew, Denny shot back, "Who says I fly an airplane?" He protested, "I never said any such thing."

McLain could give one person one answer and in a matter of min-utes tell someone else something totally different. He had little regard for the truth, and a reporter was never sure if he was getting a scoop or a tall tale. When asked about it, McLain would explain that everyone needed a story.

He could also be petty and desperately immature. McLain claimed that the Detroit newspaper strike actually helped the Tigers because the sportswriters weren't around to demoralize the players. In September, in the visitors' clubhouse in Anaheim, he was steamed about a profile that ran in *Life* that showed him sleeping in the dugout during his nonstarts and lounging in his hotel bedroom in New York after an evening out on the town. He felt that the writer unfairly portrayed him as an undisci-plined playboy—even though in life he was more than willing to play the part.

For instance, the piece in *Life* (which ran a sanitized version of the event) recounted that, while sitting in the convertible of *Life* reporter David Wolf, McLain spotted a car driven by a pretty young woman, to whom he yelled, "Hey Honey, how'd you like to fuck a five-game loser?"

The pitcher from Detroit had catapulted himself onto the national stage through his craft, but his preoccupations hadn't changed. He con-tinued to talk about his addiction to Pepsi—he drank 60 to 70 bottles a week — and the importance of his organ playing. He also spoke openly about his plans to use baseball as a springboard to a second career, something that would provide financial security once his arm gave out.

In one interview, he unabashedly expressed his desire for a Lear jet — not to fly necessarily, but just to have at his disposal. He wanted Drysdale's life, and then some. Though Drysdale and Koufax could hold their own in the company of movie stars and studio heads, they were still outsiders in that world. Drysdale especially felt that the horses, the ranch, the bit parts on television were all secondary to his vocation as a pitcher. McLain didn't see it that way.

"I'm a mercenary," he said. "I admit it. I want to be a billionaire."

Monetary aspirations aside, McLain honestly enjoyed playing the organ. Nothing, he said, made him happier than sitting in front of a keyboard. Not pitching. Not gambling. He put together a band with a drummer and a guitar player. He believed that his organ — a Hammond X-77, a hulking machine with two levels and 61 keys — would be his second act. And why not? Capitol Records signed him to a deal. He booked shows at the Riviera in Las Vegas. The music was important to McLain, but he was also seduced by wealth.

He took the gigs that came to him, largely around the Midwest — in Michigan and Illinois and Indiana. Above all else, he wanted people to take him seriously as a musician. He could read music, he could make his own arrangements and do his own scoring. What bothered him was that he could never rise above the shtick. He got calls to perform with Mudcat Grant, a great singer in his own right, and for one-off appearances. But he wanted more, and no one seemed willing to give it to him.

Of course, he wasn't easy to work with. Producer and journalist Dave Dexter, who traveled to Detroit to record the Capitol album, found McLain to be "a pain in the ass." He had sent McLain around 25 songs he saw as commercially viable, and McLain had turned down all of them. The two men nearly came to blows. McLain insisted on keeping his album moored in the past with such ballads as "Lonely Is the Name," "On a Clear Day," "Nice 'n' Easy," and "Cherish." Of the 60,000 records Capitol eventually issued, Dexter would write, one-third were returned.

What McLain didn't understand was that no one was interested in him as an organ player, regardless of his ability. As William B. Mead pointed out, he wasn't the guy with the guitar or the mike, sweating and gyrating before crowds of squealing fans. Who was Denny McLain to the younger generation? Someone their parents watched on *The Today Show*? McLain's foray into music coincided with the complete ascendancy of rock, which had become that generation's preferred medium for social commentary and sexual longing. Despite his contract with Capitol Records, McLain would never achieve the musical relevancy he so desired.

And as McLain's catcher Bill Freehan observed, "Denny says he's an organist first and a baseball player second, but without baseball he would be — well, how many organists can you name?"

Although McLain didn't have the money — far from it — he seemed determined to mimic the life of the super-rich. During the three-day All-Star break in Houston — an All-Star Game in which he didn't start — Denny and Sharyn, accompanied by Freehan and his wife, traveled to Vegas in a borrowed Lear jet. All of Sunday night and Monday morning, according to one account, McLain stayed at the craps table. On Tuesday, McLain pitched two shutout innings, and then he and Sharyn reboarded the jet for another round at Vegas and a quick trip to Detroit. From there, McLain hopped back on the plane once again to rejoin his teammates in Minnesota. By now, though, his luck seems to have run out. As he sat in the plane, eating a sandwich with his legs propped up, the door inexplicably blew open. With nowhere to land, the pilot was forced to fly the plane the rest of the journey at 10,000 feet. McLain and the pilot walked away unharmed, but this incident was emblematic of McLain's incredible run of luck, which fed his sense of indestructibility and gave the green light to all sorts of reckless behavior.

Surprisingly, McLain's antics didn't bother his teammates. Yes, he wasn't around for long stretches, but when he was around he won. Freehan believed that McLain could "turn on his valve" differently than the other members of the team. In his diary, published after the 1969 season, Freehan wrote about how hard it was to understand McLain. He wondered how McLain managed to focus on so many different things outside of baseball but was always present, ready to do his job, when he stood on the mound. The two often quarreled about how to handle different hitters. Still, Freehan would write, "I've never caught a better pitcher in my life. When Denny goes there and puts his mind to it, he's the best pitcher in the world."

McLain had a penchant for winning following a Tigers loss. In return, the team averaged five runs during his starts, while leading the league in both home runs and runs scored. Unlike other pitchers, McLain didn't think that he had to win the games alone. No team, he believed, played better with a lead than the Tigers did that season, and no team could come from behind so effectively.

As the time dwindled away before the start of one game in Cleveland, the entire team waited for McLain to show up at the ballpark. Then suddenly he was there, twenty minutes before he was scheduled to start. The Tigers were mad at him, but McLain regained their affection by pitching a complete game. Between innings, he told his teammates how little he actually had in his arm that day. It didn't seem to matter, though, because he delivered.

Although McLain generally seemed uninterested in socializing with his teammates, he could also be unexpectedly generous. Dick Tracewski could no longer count the number of times McLain would join him and infielders Don Wert and Dick McAuliffe for lunch, have only a cup of coffee, walk away, and pay their tab on his way out, as they'd discover when the check came. Whether the check actually cleared was another question.

As a rookie, Jon Warden tried to pay when he was out with McLain. He'd reach for his wallet only to have Denny tell him, "You're not buying anything. You're making shit." Warden was young and nearly broke, and McLain would take him out in different cities to hidden places with secret back rooms where there'd be gambling tables and women. Walking in with him, Warden could see that McLain knew everyone he probably "shouldn't know." At the time, Warden was in awe. But as the years passed, he began to think, *Who was I running with?*

That question would remain for years. Relief pitcher John Hiller saw McLain as a loner without close friends. During the 1968 season, as the team was closing in on the pennant, Paul Carey often found Denny alone in the back of the clubhouse, not in the bullpen, as was the custom, or in the dugout. For someone who courted fame and attention, McLain liked being by himself. Infielder Tom Matchick and the rest of the Tigers never knew where McLain was or what he was doing. All they did know was this: "Denny was Denny."

McLain wouldn't have been able to pull this off without an enabler. His manager, Mayo Smith, allowed Denny to be Denny so long as he kept his team in contention. One evening when Lane and Smith and a couple of other coaches were sitting around a bar in Oakland after midnight, McLain and another pitcher walked in. Curfew had long passed. Smith said, "Hey, you two — it's past curfew. You're fined $500 each."

"Oh, skipper, you can't do that. You just can't do that," McLain's counterpart said.

"Oh yeah?" Smith replied.

"You can't do that to us because we've won 17 between us," he said. "He's won 15. I've won two."

After he finished laughing, Smith said, "Just get to bed!"

For all his intellectual shortcomings, Smith understood what McLain meant to the team's prospects. McLain was special, Smith felt, and he gave the pitcher his space. He just needed to keep winning.

Like many great managers — Sparky Anderson, Casey Stengel, Tony La Russa — Smith never had a big major league career of his own. He spent 18 seasons in the minors with only a short stint with the Athletics in 1945. For several years, he managed in the minor leagues. But when finally given the chance to prove himself on the major league level — first with Philadelphia and then with Cincinnati — he failed . . . badly. He did, however, show his baseball acumen as a scout with the Yankees when evaluating Bob Gibson.

After watching Gibson strike out 12 men late in the season in the midst of a six-game winning streak, Smith reported back, "I don't see how this guy Gibson ever loses a game." New York had every reason to be concerned, he believed.

Four years later, Smith was with Detroit, charged with guiding what many considered the best talent in the American League. He'd taken over the Tigers after the 1966 season, following the sudden deaths of two managers, and inherited a team of young, promising position players, well-worn veterans, and a talented pitching staff that could never quite put things together.

How did Smith get the job? Many have speculated over the years that he was the economical choice. With his track record, he was lucky even to be considered. Yet others have said that, in fact, he was a perfect fit for the Tigers. This was a team that needed to be left alone. To Dan Ewald, who served as the Tigers' public relations director for 18 years, Smith was even-keeled and undramatic and brought stability to the team. This was a roster made up of both very young players — McLain, Horton, Lolich — and veterans who were desperate to win. A young manager prone to dramatics, or one who'd want to keep a tight grip on things, would not have been able to rein in this bunch, Ewald believed. Like the Cardinals' Red Schoendienst, Smith was comfortable stepping back and letting his players win games for themselves.

He had his own issues, however. Nicknamed "America's Guest" because he never turned down a cocktail, many thought of Smith as a functioning alcoholic. He didn't enforce curfews because he was often stumbling out of hotel bars himself late at night. Some saw him as the team's manager in name only. Relief pitcher Daryl Patterson always believed that, because of the team's talent, especially the pitching talent, "anybody could have managed that staff."

At times Smith could be comical. Once, during a game in 1969, Johnny Sain woke Smith from his nap to tell him that the starting pitcher might be in trouble and asked who he wanted to have warm up. Smith said to tell Tom Timmermann to get ready in the bullpen. Sain said he couldn't do that. When Smith asked why not, Sain reminded him that he'd sent Timmermann down to the minors just days before.

When Smith was alert and aware that he was a manager of a professional baseball club, he would try to reassert control, sometimes going too far. During a game in the 1968 season, with Joe Sparma pitching in the fourth inning, Smith inexplicably began to warm up Mickey Lolich, which didn't escape the notice of the starter.

With two on and one out, Smith pulled him though the team had a 1–0 lead. Afterwards, Sparma said that he didn't know if he could play for Smith anymore. Smith couldn't be bothered with his players' feelings. There was a game to win, and he was going to do it in his own way.

Needless to say, none of this sat well with Sain. The tension between Sain and Smith was already evident ahead of the ill-fated 1967 season.

Pitcher Mike Marshall could sense Sain's agitation as he watched his men taking batting practice, shagging fly balls.

"Can you tell me," Marshall asked, "what the point is to shagging balls in the outfield for forty minutes? How does that help us prepare for a game?"

Sain agreed with Marshall. He thought the pitchers would be better off sitting together and discussing pitching. But Sain was new to the team, and he didn't want to publicly clash with Smith.

"That's not what the manager wants us to be doing," he said. "He wants us all on the field shagging flies."

Because Smith would never get over his envy of Sain, who had arrived in Detroit with such fanfare, Smith would never come to trust him. It didn't help that the press invariably approached Sain, not Smith, during the 1967 pennant race. This wasn't Sain's fault, but Smith felt undermined from the start. The tension between the two emanating from Smith's passive-aggressiveness would ultimately make it impossible for them to work together.

It's customary for the pitching coach to be the one to walk out to the mound in the middle of the game if necessary, whisper something in the pitcher's ear, and maybe slap him on the ass as a way of settling his nerves. But in Detroit, it was Smith, not Sain, who made that walk. Sain preferred to watch quietly from the dugout. The pitcher already knew what was working and what wasn't, Sain believed. Whatever was going to go wrong would go wrong, and it could be discussed quietly afterwards. What was the point of making a spectacle? As *Detroit Free Press* sportswriter George Cantor observed in 1968, it was also Smith who'd walk out onto the field to congratulate the winning pitcher after the game. Cantor suggested that it wasn't "inconceivable" that Sain wouldn't return the following year.

Yet one thing Sain and Smith were in agreement about was how to treat McLain. Seven years earlier, Sain had witnessed the strain that Roger Maris was under as he fought to break Babe Ruth's single-season home run record. Now he watched McLain going through the same thing as the pressure to get 30 wins bore down on him. Both Sain and Smith thought it best to leave well enough alone.

Thus, McLain was allowed to speak out however he wished—especially about money, which over time became a topic he refused to leave alone. Early on he had said that hitters—Kaline, Norm Cash—were the ones who deserved to earn $100,000. Yet this deference now disappeared. At a certain point that summer, after every start, he never stopped boasting about earning $100,000 and about having pried a $67,000 pay raise from one of the most conservative, frugal franchises in baseball. By August, he was suggesting that if he won 30 games and that number didn't go up to *$200,000,* he might not be around the following season.

It was all out in the open now. The 30 wins. The salary to which he believed he was entitled. The Lear jet. There was no limit, it seemed, to McLain's aspirations, to his visions of grandeur.

And in 1968 no endorsement seemed too small for McLain, be it a product sold at K-Mart or a promotion for a clothing store in South Bend. Looking on, Carl Yastrzemski, the hero of the 1967 season, understood what Denny was facing and urged caution. Following Yaz's MVP season, there were late-night show appearances, free cars, and one banquet after another. There were airline commercials and endorsements for ice cream and condiments.

"Denny's got to be careful," he said. "It can swallow you up. I told him I'd compare endorsements with him so he'll know if they're giving him a fair shake. But it's so easy to overdo it. So very, very easy."

But Daryl Patterson felt that McLain simply couldn't help himself. It was his nature to be a big shot, to overreach if given the chance. He wasn't the sort to be content with merely being a great ballplayer. He could have been president of the United States, Patterson felt, but even then McLain would want to be president of the world.

McLain enjoyed fame and craved the power it gave him. But he was also forward-thinking. He understood fully even back then that he was trying to build a kind of brand for himself. In this, he was running on a parallel track with someone else, another brash, like-minded young athlete who was 500 miles away and spouted off about money as much as McLain himself did. This, of course, was Namath. Joe Willie. Broadway Joe. The 1965 AFL Rookie of the Year. The first quarterback to throw for

4,000 yards. During his career, Namath wore a fur coat on the sidelines and endorsed everything from Ovaltine to Coca-Cola to panty hose. He'd star on-screen with Ann-Margret. He was a fixture at nightclubs and could be spotted leaving his audacious apartment — with a mirrored bedroom ceiling and white llama rug — with beautiful women on his arm. He wasn't shy about leading a lifestyle that another generation of athletes might have kept well hidden from public view. If McLain hated the idea of being branded a playboy, Namath reveled in the image.

It's true that Namath was more handsome than McLain, and smoother in his delivery. That homey accent. The tan. Yet his suaveness doesn't entirely explain why he and McLain were perceived so differently. As McLain lobbied for $100,000, he was trapped in a sport whose owners didn't appreciate the changing times and didn't understand that they should be promoting their star players instead of trying to suppress them. It was different for Namath. At a time when the NFL and AFL fought over the best young players, AFL owners understood how important it was to draw college stars, no matter the cost. The AFL showcased innovation, which made the league cool in a way that Vince Lombardi's power sweep could never be.

Tigers owner John Fetzer or the Dodgers' Walter O'Malley or any other baseball owner would have been appalled by Namath's admission, "I wish I had been born rich. Oh, I know how to spend money. I really do. Boats, planes, cars, girls. I wish I could afford them all!" But those in charge of the AFL didn't flinch. Jets president Sonny Werblin had signed Namath to a total package of $427,000, understanding what the deal meant to his franchise and to the league itself.

"I believe in the star system," Werblin said at the time. "It's the only thing that sells tickets. It's what you put on the stage or playing field that draws people."

Meanwhile, Denny was the guy who would carry baseball forward into the next decade. No one believed this more than Sain, who pointed out that he himself and Warren Spahn, like Koufax, truly came into their own only after the age of 26. In 1968, McLain was only 24 and had already accomplished so much more. Sain believed there was much more to come.

Dick Tracewski, Koufax's roommate and close friend during his time with Los Angeles, saw Sandy in McLain too. Denny didn't have Sandy's fastball or his curve. No one did. But he was close. And McLain had both a slider and a changeup, which Koufax did not. Tracewski also believed that the arm angles McLain had developed would help prolong his career.

How did Denny stack up in terms of dedication, the quality that separates the average pitcher from the great one? As soon as the season started, Koufax lived baseball. He could keep his roommate Tracewski up until all hours talking about the game. On off days, Koufax would walk out to a corner of Crosley Field or Forbes Field to work with a catcher. In Los Angeles, Koufax would often invite Tracewski and his family over to his house. The kids could play in the pool, Koufax would tell him, but Tracewski should bring along a catcher's mitt.

"I've seen two Dennys in Detroit—last year's Denny and this year's Denny," Tracewski said in 1968. "This year he is a dedicated pitcher. His attitude is tremendous and it's spreading to other players. They love to play behind him."

But increasingly, McLain made it clear that something was wrong. By late July, he complained openly about how much his arm hurt, how it felt like a "thud." He could still pitch, but not without searing pain. His arm felt tired. It throbbed between starts. After his 25th win of the season, he announced that he'd torn a muscle in his shoulder and had to throw sidearm when he warmed up in the bullpen because the pain was too great.

McLain's self-diagnosis was overruled by the team doctor, who said that the real problem was that McLain's trapezius muscle was overdeveloped on his right side. The doctor explained that whenever McLain pitched, he dragged the shoulder muscle too far over and it hooked under the bones in his neck.

Whatever the case, as the innings amassed McLain began to take more and more cortisone. It wasn't unusual to find him in the training room, his right arm bulging from overuse. Dizzy Dean, the last man to win 30 games, warned that if the pain had become so unmanageable, McLain shouldn't pitch. In his single-minded fixation on a short-term goal, he risked jeopardizing his whole career. McLain relied too much on his arm, Dean said, and he didn't have the proper follow-through with his body.

Other pitchers had short-circuited their careers by making the same mistake. As George Cantor pointed out, Lefty Grove never pitched with the same authority after he won 31 games in 1931. And within three years of reaching his 31-12 mark in 1920, Jim Bagby had to leave baseball for good. McLain was risking everything for this one shot, this one season.

McLain understood what was at stake, but he couldn't stop. Not now. He was spent from all the innings he'd thrown, the demands on his time were overwhelming, and his marriage was increasingly strained. After his 29th win in Anaheim, McLain was just one game away from his goal since midseason. Once he reached it, he believed, he'd be able to chart a new future for himself and his family. He would get what he deserved.

14

A LOUSY PITCHER

HOW ABOUT A DODGER STADIUM hand for Bob
Gibson?"

These were the words that appeared on the electronic
scoreboard of Chavez Ravine on the evening of July 1, 1968. Less than a
month had passed since Don Drysdale "had done it" — eclipsing Walter
Johnson's scoreless-inning streak before a capacity crowd on the same
evening Bobby Kennedy was buried at Arlington National Cemetery.
Now Gibson had usurped the spotlight, recording 47⅔ straight scoreless innings.

After beating the Red Sox in the World Series, Gibson had emerged
as the league's best pitcher, a post left vacant for him by Sandy Koufax.
While Gibson would defer to the greatness of Juan Marichal and his arsenal of pitches and arm angles, those who'd watched Gibson perform
in October demurred.

That was because now they had proof. They had indisputable evidence of his ability to win and win when it mattered most. Before the
regular-season opener, Braves catcher Joe Torre tried to pin Gibson with
the shiny tin badge he believed Gibson deserved. Torre had studied all
the top-flight pitchers of the time, but watching the Series and seeing
Gibson's ball seemingly "hop over" the bats of the American League's

best hitters, Torre was blown away. Gibson, he said, "even struck me out while I was watching on television." No one could compare to him, Torre believed. No one.

Yet early in the season, the seemingly invincible Gibson had become something of an afterthought. By the end of May, he'd won only three games, having lost five. Some questioned whether he could measure up to the standard he'd set for himself the previous fall.

But by that July evening, Gibson had won six straight games, pitching complete-game shutouts in the last five. And here he was in Los Angeles, facing Drysdale himself—the man with whom he was so often compared—in the most anticipated match of the regular season. Just as they had done the night of Kennedy's funeral, the people of Los Angeles filled the stadium to capacity. They wanted to see if a once-insurmountable record could be toppled within a matter of weeks. They wanted to see if Gibson could make it happen.

Until that moment, Gibson had 30 shutouts on his résumé, but none against the Dodgers. He was a different pitcher now, though, or so it seemed. When he recorded two outs to begin the first inning, it looked like he would continue the streak, win his seventh straight game, keep the Cardinals well ahead of the Braves in first place, and make Drysdale's record moot.

But very quickly things began to unravel. With no one on, left fielder Len Gabrielson singled. Then, with catcher Tom Haller at bat, Julián Javier, the slight but reliable second baseman, watched the ball bounce up right in front of him so that he had to cover his face, allowing the ball to drop into right field. With Gabrielson at third, and holding an 0-1 advantage over right fielder Ron Fairly, Gibson unleashed one of the hardest pitches Fairly had ever seen. It was "screaming" as it reached the plate. It hit the dirt, sailing behind home plate, ricocheting off the foot of the home plate umpire, and hitting the screen.

At that moment, Gabrielson raced home and quite literally stomped on home plate, as if to prove to the 56,000 fans that he'd actually scored. He then raced into a welcoming Dodger dugout. Gibson meanwhile walked away from the mound, leering. With that, the crowd rose to their feet, politely acknowledging what Gibson had accomplished now that it was over. What should have been a dramatic and hard-fought contest had ended quickly on a dubious call. Had the scorer ruled it a passed ball by the catcher, Gibson's streak would have gone on. Instead, it was ruled a wild pitch and the run was charged to him — stopping his mark at 47⅔ innings, just 11 minutes and 20 pitches into his start.

Afterwards in the dugout, Gibson's catcher that evening, Johnny Edwards, who had done his best to block the ball, told Gibson, "I'm sorry, Hoot. I tried." Gibson shrugged off the apology and proceeded to finish the game. He didn't allow another Dodger to reach home plate. Only seven more batters would record hits. In the meantime, his teammates actually managed to score runs for him — five all told — and chased Drysdale from the contest. Gibson had won the game and beaten the man whose national reputation he envied, but he'd lost this particular shot at history.

The reticent Gibson did three television interviews before addressing the print reporters who choked the locker room. In the immediate aftermath, Gibson at first blamed Edwards. By his own account, he told reporters, "the fucker missed the ball." Translated by the *Los Angeles Times* for its family readership, Gibson's quote read, "It was the catcher's fault. He fouled up." The *St. Louis Post-Dispatch* recorded Gibson saying that Edwards "loused it up."

But Gibson quickly recanted. Shouldering the blame, he said it was a "a wild fastball. And it was my fault. I have no excuses." He said the ball sailed, and it was too tough for Edwards to handle. He'd simply lost control of his fastball, he said.

There have been some, writing in retrospect, who felt the call was incorrect — including Gibson. Gibson has maintained that had they been playing in another stadium, or had another scorer who wasn't influenced by hometown loyalties, the correct call would have been made and he would have easily eclipsed Drysdale. (Gibson's next start against San Francisco was a shutout.)

Why Tim McCarver, with whom Gibson had worked so well during his career, didn't start that night remained a question for many. It was a gut call, explained Red Schoendienst, since Edwards had caught the previous shutout Gibson had thrown — his fifth in a row. In the moments after the game, Edwards conceded his error, telling the press that it was a tough play, but one he should have made. Some 40 years later, however, he recalled things differently. It was a slider, not a fastball. And when the ball hit the dirt, Edwards believed it hit maybe two feet outside home plate. He had tried his best—diving after the ball to block it, but because it was thrown with such force, he couldn't do anything to stop it and keep Gabrielson from making it home. In his mind, there was never a question that it had been a wild pitch.

In the following game, at Candlestick Park, Edwards would catch Gibson again. This one was against Marichal, who had won 15 games by then. Up three runs with no one out in the sixth inning, Gibson allowed a single off Willie McCovey, a double off Jim Ray Hart, and then walked Dick Dietz. Edwards—whose two-run home run had helped give Gibson his three-run lead—had the natural impulse to walk out to the mound to "settle him down a bit."

"What the hell are you gonna tell me?" Gibson screamed. "I know what I'm doing wrong!" In fact he did. After Edwards returned to his place behind home plate, Gibson made the necessary adjustments, with spectacular results. With the Giants now all but assured of scoring at least one run, Gibson struck out Bobby Bonds with four pitches. Then Dave Marshall with four. Finally, he put an end to it all when he struck out Marichal himself on three. His arm aching, Gibson still finished the game—his sixth shutout of the season.

Shaking his head when asked what Gibson was throwing, Edwards could only say, "Unadulterated fire. That's what he threw."

Gibson would continue in this vein for the rest of the season. In August, after his ninth shutout, a 1–0 win against the Braves, Cardinals outfielder Bobby Tolan asked him, "Don't you ever get tired of shutting people out?" The fact of the matter was that Gibson had to throw shutouts in order to win. He was on his own. With each start, it became increasingly apparent that the Cardinals simply wouldn't hit.

Roger Angell would later call the Cardinals' hitting, or lack thereof, "starvation fare." What's worse was that the Cardinals, at least in the first two months as they struggled to pull away from teams like the Giants, couldn't win for *any* of their starters. This riled Gibson. Gibson would never call out his teammates during his own starts, said shortstop

Dal Maxvill, but when he wasn't pitching he'd grab helmets, bang them on the benches, and plead, "Let's go! The score's nothing-nothing. The pitcher's pitching his ass off, let's go!"

During this early dry spell, the usually chirpy clubhouse, so often filled with motivational chants and cheers led by Cepeda, fell quiet. When Gibson lost 1-0, in a 10-inning game, to Philadelphia — beaten by an RBI single by his friend Bill White when he threw a fastball at his knees — Tim McCarver followed Gibson into the training room in Connie Mack Stadium. McCarver tried to tell him how sorry he was and that he and the others knew that the "crappy hitting had gone on for too long."

"This is bullshit," Gibson said. "I'm tired of listening to these fucking excuses."

But what could he do? Throw shutouts. From June 2 through August 24, he won 15 straight games, with one no-decision. In each win, he pitched to completion. By mid-July, the Cardinals had done away with any doubts that they would repeat as National League champions as they opened up a 10-game lead. After Gibson's winning streak ended with Houston scoring two unearned runs in the ninth inning, Maxvill joked that whenever Gibson pitched it was "like having a night off."

It was inevitable that Gibson's relentlessness would cost him sooner or later. Early in May, after he pitched 12 innings and threw 179 pitches in a win against the Astros, you could hear him gasp as he tried to put on his coat. His arm throbbed. Seeing it "dropping" as the innings wore on, Edwards tried to tell Gibson that he should speak up, that they had plenty of people in the bullpen who were eager to pitch. Of course Gibson said nothing, keeping himself in it until the very last out.

Of his 34 starts that season, Gibson finished 28. But his aches never really abated. In September, he revealed to columnist Bob Broeg that before games he'd take an "Aspirin compound" to dull the pain.

"The arm hurts all the time," Gibson told Broeg. "A little or a lot, but I notice it most when I'm warming up. I feel it after releasing a pitch, but concentration on the job at hand seems to help."

No one could coax Gibson into walking off the mound that summer. In mid-July, Maxvill noticed Gibson trying to work over his right index finger, which was bleeding. He'd broken a nail, as he did each season on that particular finger, but this time the gash was deeper. Watching him wince, Maxvill tried to appeal to his sense of reason. There was still a season to play out, a pennant to win. And with their problems on offense, the team needed Gibson more than ever.

"Look, Gib," Maxvill told him, "it's none of my business and you're a raw-meat guy when staying in games, but how's the finger? It looks to me like it hurts more than it normally does. You don't have anything to prove to us. If it's hurting, get out. Why take the chance that it might put you out a couple of weeks?"

Gibson seemed to be considering Maxvill's advice, but instead of calling for a trainer or motioning to the dugout that it was time to exit, he spit on the wound, rubbed in some dirt from the pitching mound, and got back to business. *Case closed, Maxie. Get back to short.*

It was a story for the ages, highlighting Gibson's toughness and his stubbornness. A pitcher dealt with pain. He didn't leave a game at the sight of blood, even if it meant that he wouldn't make his next start. Gibson was a pitcher who believed in the present, who was focused on the task at hand. What happened afterwards was just that — *afterwards*.

Gibson knew that on any given night he was capable of shutting out any team in any ballpark, no matter how many innings or pitches it took. Tim McCarver would later talk about a midseason game when a batter began the inning with a triple. Uncharacteristically, the Cardinals had actually scored runs for Gibson, and McCarver counseled his friend that if the ball came to him, he should take the easy out — throw the ball to first and let the runner score. But Gibson would have none of it. He was going to go home with the ball if given the chance. That's when he really knew, McCarver said, that Gibson was on to something historic, and that Gibson knew it too.

By then, McCarver had caught Gibson for several years and had seen him pull off the spectacular. He'd seen Gibson win the 1964 pennant for the Cardinals in the final weeks of the season. He'd watched Gibson come back from injury in 1967 to quash the Red Sox's plans for "Lonborg and Champagne." But never before or since had he seen someone dominate the outside part of the plate like Gibson was now doing with right-handed hitters. His precision defied belief. You could take the width of two baseballs, McCarver said, mark that distance from the outside corner, and know that Gibson would hit that spot with near 100 percent accuracy.

Despite a delivery that looked wild and uncontrolled, Gibson knew precisely where the ball was going. It was always about one thing: the corner.

After Gibson beat the Astros 8–1 in the same game in which he treated his index finger with mud and spit, Rusty Staub said he thought the difference between the new Gibson and the old Gibson was his control. In previous years, Staub felt, if Gibson was behind in the count, he'd throw a fastball. You counted on it, waited for it. Now he was hitting the corners with curveballs and sliders.

McCarver thought so too. Gibson was finally throwing that slider to left-handed batters for strikes. Gibson would later explain that, in fact, he had two sliders. But his primary slider was a pitch he could throw to both left- and right-handed hitters. Gibson also threw at least two different kinds of fastballs, including a rising fastball that McCarver considered his best pitch. The combination of movement and speed was lethal. For left-handed hitters, it would stay on the inside part of the plate; for right-handed batters, it hung on the outside. Like his slider, it was a pitch that no one could hit.

His 20th win of the season, in early September, was against the Reds — a team stocked with young stars and just two years away from emerging as one of the most formidable offenses that baseball had ever seen. Pete Rose, the National League's leading hitter in 1968 with a .335 average, said afterwards that Gibson's fastballs were totally unpredictable. One fastball might come in straight at you. The next, he said, would sail. Another still would inexplicably move an inch so you couldn't reach it. Equally in awe, Rose's teammate Tommy Helms, the second baseman, believed he'd never seen a rising fastball like Gibson's.

But it wasn't just Gibson who was dominating the batters that season. The question on everyone's mind was: why can't anyone hit? Not since 1908 had the average number of runs in a game fallen so low. The combined batting average for both leagues fell to .237. No less than seven pitchers had ERAs under 2.00. There was Catfish Hunter's perfect game, but there were also four other no-hitters. Gibson and Drysdale and McLain were powerhouse pitchers, but their dominance only high-lighted a larger, and somewhat troubling, trend within the game.

Sandy Koufax, after watching the early pitching success in June, be-lieved it couldn't last for the entire year. Pitchers would always be ahead of the hitters, he said, at least early on in the season. Weather was one factor. So were the strong pitching arms coming out of spring, which would eventually exhaust themselves by August and September. By then, he thought, he would start seeing 12–10 scores. In 1968, though, those games never came.

"I'm not one to complain," Henry Aaron said, "but the umpires have changed the game. They aren't giving the batter a break on the strike zone. It's too big. And they've changed things people don't realize. Like throwing out the baseball. They just don't throw out black baseballs any-more, so when the ball comes in you can't see it and it freezes you. Then they say you can't step out of the batter's box. That takes something out of a hitter, too. People don't realize these things are happening but they can harm a hitter."

There was certainly something unsettling about it. After all, only seven years had passed since Roger Maris shot a ball into the deep cor-ner of right field at Yankee Stadium for his 61st home run — 22 more than his previous best. And only six years earlier, Koufax's teammate Tommy Davis drove in 153 batters, beating his career average by 95 runs. Baseball really was a different game.

Even the best hitters couldn't agree on why things had changed. Curt Flood blamed scheduling. Pete Rose faulted the ballparks. Willie Mays believed that the young pitchers he now faced came to the major leagues with a greater command of the mechanics of pitching. They understood how to change speed, and they were willing to throw a curveball or a slider when behind in the count. Don Drysdale believed that pitchers had become more studious in their craft, while the vast number of hit-ters had grown lazy and "stupid." Jim Fregosi likewise chalked up the hitting drought to better preparation. The best little league players were pitching from a young age and coming to the majors undaunted by the competition.

Some attributed the change to the raising of the pitcher's mound

from 10 to 15 inches after the record seasons posted by Mantle and Maris
and Davis. Baseball historian Gary Gillette suggested, however, that it
was another adjustment made by baseball commissioner Ford Frick that
gave pitchers a key advantage: the expansion of the strike zone in 1963.

Gillette felt that expanding the strike zone was an overreaction to
Roger Maris's home run in 1961 and Tommy Davis's spectacular 1962
season in which he not only drove in 153 runs but recorded 230 hits
while hitting .346 — leading the National League in all three categories.
With the expanded strike zone, the batter was "dead meat." Imagine trying to hit a 90-mile-an-hour fastball at your shoulders, never mind one
that came from Sandy Koufax or Don Drysdale, or for that matter a
slider sailing away from you that, because of the expanded zone, would
have been called for a strike.

And the elevated mound? Later Gibson would bemoan the loss of
those five extra inches, feeling that his game was hurt when the mound
was lowered back to 10 inches after the 1968 season. But in a sport whose
ballparks all had different dimensions — a home run in Detroit would
reach only the very edge of center field in Houston — it seems likely that
fluctuations in the height of the pitching mound were par for the course,
regardless of what was stated in the rulebook.

Sam McDowell believed, rulebook or not, that the hometown park —
or, for that matter, its groundskeeper — determined the pitcher's ultimate fate. His teammates Steve Hargan and Stan Williams wanted the
mound to be flat because they relied on sinkers and sliders and wanted
to be in a spot where they pitched around the knee. Like his teammate
Sonny Siebert, though, McDowell preferred the mound high, since his
best pitch was a fastball up and in toward the batter — a pitch that most
batters couldn't get their bat around quickly enough. Each time Mc-
Dowell stepped onto the mound at Cleveland's Municipal Stadium, he
knew that he was stepping onto *his* ground.

But as with everything baseball — and with all sport for that matter — race would play a part. Since Jackie Robinson integrated the National League in 1947, it had consistently drawn and come to rely upon
the best African American players — and hitters. At the same time, Gillette would later note, American League teams consistently buried their
best black players in their minor league systems, even through the mid-

1960s. Even as pitchers such as Gibson and Koufax, Maloney and Marichal, used the new zone to their advantage in one league, pitchers in the American League consistently faced inferior hitters with the same rules advantage in the other. How could anyone hit?

By the time of the 1968 All-Star Game — the first one held indoors, at the Astrodome — it was apparent that the pitchers would continue their dominance. The final score, like so many in 1968, was 1–0. It was nothing so dramatic as a home run or a steal of home that brought in the run, but a pedestrian double play at the top of the first inning in which the National League scored off Luis Tiant (who himself had pitched 42 consecutive scoreless innings and struck out 19 men in a single game that year). Denny McLain did his duty, arriving to pitch two innings between craps games at The Mirage, while Bob Gibson — held out of the game by his manager — helped his teammates warm up on the sidelines. At one point, National League pitchers retired 20 straight batters. Between the two teams, only eight batters managed hits. For writers like Dan Hafner, who described the affair as "dull" and "colorless," the All-Star Game served as the most urgent distress call to date that something needed to be done to help hitters.

With the pennant easily in hand — the Cardinals finished nine games ahead of San Francisco — Gibson ended his season in Houston in the usual way by then. Again he won 1–0, and again he pitched the game to its completion. It was his 22nd win against nine losses that season. He was the first player ever named back-to-back Player of the Month in the National League. He had thrown 13 shutouts, pitched over 300 innings, and finished 28 of his 34 starts. His ERA was 1.12, the fourth-lowest in history, and second only to Walter Johnson among pitchers who threw 300 innings or more.

The fact that Gibson won a mere 22 ball games and lost nine with those numbers was telling. As Gibson has said, had his team averaged four runs a game for him, he would have finished 31-2. Had they scored three, he'd have won 27 games, besting Marichal's 26 victories that season. As it stood, Gibson's record showed that a pitcher who gave up little more than one run a game could still lose nine games — another stark reminder that things were not as they should be.

Yet Gary Gillette believed that Gibson's greatness was exaggerated. He had a great year, and a great career — one worthy of the Hall of Fame. But as with Koufax, Gillette believed that the era itself, one in which pitchers with great fastballs and tremendous breaking pitches could thrive, partially generated that greatness. Gibson, for Gillette, would never rank as baseball's greatest pitcher. Nor would he rank among its top five. Two pitchers from a time nearly forgotten — Walter Johnson and Christy Mathewson — and two pitchers who came later — Greg Maddux and Roger Clemens — would belong on that list. For Gillette, Gibson was a terrific player. But he was also a terrific player on a terrific team — his reputation burnished by St. Louis's three World Series showings.

Even with his success in 1968, Gibson wouldn't soften, at least outwardly, and not to the press. When journalist Fred Katz arrived in St. Louis on opening day, he was hoping to write a piece that would capture the "wonderful camaraderie" of the Cardinals. He introduced himself to the star players, telling them that he'd be a presence in the locker room for a few days, trying to immerse himself in their world. No one seemed to have a problem with that. But when Katz approached Gibson to say hello, "there was no return smile, no sign of friendliness, only Gibson's wariness of strangers and new writers."

After the game, Katz was in the locker room with the players as they laughed and bantered with each other. Katz did what he was trained to do. He kept his distance while also trying to catch something — a line, an anecdote, a part of a scene — that he'd be able to use to illustrate his story. The players were fully aware of his presence and knew he was listening, but no one seemed to care. Suddenly Gibson started ranting about what he perceived as Katz's audacious eavesdropping. For Katz, it was Gibson "employing the old brushback."

By Gibson's own admission, he wanted to be unknowable, unreadable, a mystery to all — and he cultivated that image. Later, however, he would wonder if "the real pitcher that was me, had been devoured by the monster I created."

Lonnie Wheeler felt that Gibson, over time, had become a caricature of himself. Perhaps Gibson's signature scowl when he was pitching was not meant to be intimidating; maybe he was merely squinting to pick up the signs from the catcher, which was difficult for him without his

glasses. But he enjoyed the reaction to the scowl and used it, never trying to change it because it was both frightening and effective.

Race would continue to work against him, though not as had been
the case in Omaha. Because he was black, because of his demeanor,
Gibson seemed to the public the very embodiment of the black power
movement that had taken hold among Olympic athletes — even though
he never espoused those views and was largely silent on civil rights issues. In many ways, even though he'd come up in the era of Aaron and
Mays, Bill White and Frank Robinson, the better comparison remains
to DiMaggio or Williams. But because Gibson was a black athlete at a
time when black athletes spoke out against racial injustice, there were
those whose perceptions of him were colored by a racial agenda. Roger
Angell himself admitted to Gibson that when he watched him pitch, he
could never quite divorce the pitching from his race. Outfielder Jimmy
Wynn once described Gibson as a "mean black man." But Gibson believed his pitching was color-blind. And his 1969 Cardinals teammate
Mudcat Grant maintained that "Bob's anger ain't got nothing to do with
being black. That's him. That's him, that's all."

But however removed he might have felt from the unsettling outer
world of 1968, and however much he said he didn't give a fuck, Gibson would admit that something of the times broke through his facade.
After Robert Kennedy's death, he felt the same resentment that many
black Americans did. Kennedy was their candidate — not Eugene Mc-
Carthy or even Hubert Humphrey, the man who first pushed the Democratic Party to embrace integration. It was Kennedy who made the effort to travel into the heart of the urban ghetto, who was remembered
as being mobbed by black children as he drove in an open convertible
through the streets of Los Angeles. Gibson may have bristled at his depiction as a surly black athlete, but he couldn't completely dismiss the
fact that Kennedy's death meant something to him, that he pitched better angry, and that in the months following Kennedy's death "nobody
gave me any shit."

Lonnie Wheeler would interpret that sentiment as "incidental motivation," not the singular thing that drove him. Gibson never went looking for incentive or made a deliberate decision to turn events like Kennedy's death into motivation. But when they happened, they made him

angry. And Wheeler believed that his anger produced a mind-set that perhaps provided him with more than his usual measure of "competitive edginess." Gibson's intensity and focus were heightened that season, and his much talked about "game face" stayed on throughout the summer.

In 1967, and perhaps more so in 1968, Gibson seemed like a walking contradiction. He was a terrific teammate, an amiable guy, and hysterically funny. He was also moody, unforgiving, and impenetrable. Those who got to know him — including Angell and broadcaster Bob Costas — have said that once you got beneath the surface, the different facets of his personality made sense. Bob Addie, a sportswriter for the *Washington Post,* got a rare glimpse into Gibson's "fan mail," often written out of resentment and hate. Some of the people who wrote letters to him would never forgive Gibson for being black. The World Series games he won or the records he set didn't matter. He was, and would always be, a man of an inferior race.

"Why don't you and the other blackbirds on the Cardinals move to Africa where you belong?" one letter read. "If you and the other darkies can't read this because of your low mentality, get one of the white players to do it."

"I know I snap at reporters and they call me sullen and uncooperative," Gibson said. "It's a relief to go on the field. The pressure is here — in these letters — the day-to-day pressure of those people on the outside. There is no pressure in a baseball game. It's clean and competitive. There is honesty in performance."

In early July 1968, Dwight Chapin of the *Los Angeles Times* ran into Gibson at a Los Angeles hotel. This accidental encounter would produce the best glimpse into the Gibson of 1968 — perhaps better than his book written with Pepe. In their conversation, Chapin was struck by Gibson's openness and honesty. He found Gibson to be self-aware and more candid than any other professional athlete he had ever encountered. After the piece was finished and published, Chapin asked himself, *Why me?* Why hadn't he received the same treatment as Katz and all the other sportswriters who'd been snubbed by Gibson over the years? Perhaps, Chapin surmised, it was the circumstances of their meeting. It didn't take place in a locker room, and Chapin wasn't part of a gaggle of reporters swarming Gibson after a game. They were just two strangers in a room who naturally fell into conversation.

In Chapin's piece, Gibson opened up about how he felt moving into a white neighborhood, about his uneasiness when people treated him well, not because of who he was as a person, but because he was a baseball star. He talked at length about his troubles in the minor leagues — particularly in Columbus, Georgia — and expressed his frustration with the major corporations that were unwilling to let him endorse their products because of his race. Gibson said he admired the courage of those athletes who were prepared to boycott the Olympics, but he didn't agree with the claim that colleges and amateur sports had used black athletes for their own advantage, while giving them little in return.

That's all there was from Gibson that summer. There was no *Sports Illustrated* cover. *Time* didn't commission an artist to paint him in profile for its cover. A reporter from a large national publication wasn't assigned to shadow him on a road trip. *The Today Show* didn't invite him on to play guitar. Those honors and engagements were reserved for Denny McLain.

Nevertheless, as the regular season wound down and people looked forward to the fall, the comparisons between McLain and Gibson popped up with increasing frequency. Brent Musburger, then a newspaper columnist for the *Chicago American,* thought the two pitchers had a lot in common. He saw them both as dependable stoppers who could be counted on to snap a losing streak.

While St. Louis sportswriters and Cardinals officials said little about McLain, the Tigers organization wasn't so circumspect. Tigers vice president Rick Ferrell wasn't particularly impressed by Gibson. The closest comparison to him in the American League, he said, was Luis Tiant, whom they had seen and beaten. "Gibson," he added, "isn't much better." When asked how McLain and Gibson would fare in a matchup, Dick Tracewski said there was "no question" that it was "McLain all the way."

In late July, when McLain was pressed to predict how a game between the two might play out, he said, "If I give up a run, he'll win. If he gives up a run, I'll win. Really, it'll be one to nothing, two to one, something like that."

Gibson, not surprisingly, was more taciturn. It was the end of August, and a World Series between the Tigers and Cardinals was now inevitable. A reporter asked Gibson how he felt about pitching against McLain.

"The hell with McLain," he said. "We haven't won the pennant yet, and Detroit isn't in yet either."

Just days before St. Louis did win the pennant, Detroit columnist Joe Falls made the bold statement that McLain was "smoother, faster and, at this moment, a better pitcher than Bob Gibson." This was based on having seen Gibson in one game, a 5–4 victory that Gibson recorded for his 21st win of the season. Despite the win, Falls thought that Gibson was "forcing" his fastball and didn't intimidate any of the Dodgers hitters. Afterwards, when Falls asked Gibson about the World Series, it was clear that Gibson had had enough.

"The World Series!" Gibson said. "Who cares about the World Series? We're trying to win the goddamn pennant. That's all I care about. The hell with the World Series! I'll talk about that later."

Gibson must have known he'd crossed a line that time, and he apologized to Falls, something he was not known for doing. But Falls would write, "The man is a smoldering volcano, always on the verge of eruption. You don't really interview him. You argue with him. He challenges almost everything you ask him. It's that way on the mound, too. He challenges every batter he faces." Even so, Falls still saw him as beatable.

It had admittedly been an off night for Gibson, who'd cursed himself out in the locker room afterwards. Shoving his shoes into a duffel bag, he'd said, "Hell, I'm no good — I'm just a lousy pitcher." But Falls was too hasty in writing him off. It was the end of the season, and he had heard Gibson complain about his arm and watched him at his locker in pain, trying to regain whatever strength he had left. Gibson would be a new man. Nothing could have possibly prepared Falls or Detroit or Denny for the Gibson they'd see in October.

15

TALK TO ME

I N T H E E A R L Y M O R N I N G H O U R S of September 14, 1968, Denny McLain woke up on the couch of the split-level house that he and Sharyn had bought in the Detroit suburb of Beverly Hills. His three-year-old daughter Kristi was still asleep on his stomach. The biggest day of his life—a nationally televised Saturday afternoon game in which he was widely expected to record his 30th win—was ahead of him. He put Kristi to bed and tried—for a few hours at least—to find some measure of peace.

The makings of a celebration were all there. The house was full of family and old friends: his mother, whom he'd always resented for deny-ing him the chance to go to college; his brother Tom, whose own base-ball career was cut short by a car accident; and two Catholic priests. Later that morning one would offer up a single prayer, and Denny would ask for more than just one. He always wanted more.

He needed it. McLain had heard it for months now—the drumbeat of 30, of history in the making. He believed that an achievement like that would not only set his family up with the kind of life they were entitled to, but nullify all his previous failings, particularly at the end of 1967. He was now the golden boy. The one who could do no wrong.

As for his teammates, what could they do? Whatever their feelings about McLain's many absences — about his shady business dealings and late nights spent at questionable places, about the different rules he operated by — those feelings wouldn't bubble over until later. As long as he won his games, all they could do was shake their heads and go about their business. Al Kaline, who was in his 16th year with the Tigers that season, believed, like others, that this was a team on a mission. They'd let the prize get away from them in 1967, but now they were just a handful of games away from claiming it — and they knew that they couldn't get there without Denny.

When the press rushed the locker room in Tiger Stadium the day before, Mickey Lolich was waiting for them with a sign that read: ATTENTION SPORTSWRITERS DENNY MCLAIN'S LOCKER THIS WAY→.

This sign summed up the fragile relationship between the two players. As far as the world was concerned, McLain and Lolich couldn't have been more different. McLain's face — though tired and already creased with deep wrinkles, his teeth rotting from all the soda he drank — was still handsome. He still had a wry, wide-open smile and those arresting blue eyes. Lolich, with his roundish physique and protruding ears, didn't cut the same figure. He wasn't able to begin the season with the team because of his National Guard duties after King's death. And for a great deal of the year, while McLain performed as the stopper, Lolich struggled with his pitching and endured mistreatment from Smith, who, in his opinion, unfairly aimed his frustration at Lolich.

Despite his blue-collar appearance, Lolich was a boy who came out of the West. He developed his arm strength by throwing rocks at anything that ran or flew through the wide-open spaces of his hometown in Oregon, where his father worked as a parks director. Lolich, not McLain, was supposed to be the next big thing after he won 18 games in 1964 under the tutelage of Charlie Dressen. Dressen kept him from tipping his pitches, helped him adapt to a new windup, and encouraged him to throw his curveball when behind in the count. When Lolich beat the Yankees, he earned the praise of Mickey Mantle, who admired his ease and how effectively he kept the ball down.

By 1966, though, there were those who believed he'd never emerge as a consistent starter. The fans and pressmen never failed to mention his weight, his appearance, his inability to re-create what he had done against the Yankees in 1964. And now, as he watched the reporters and fans flocking to McLain, it appeared that despite nearly taking his team to the World Series the year before, he was all but forgotten.

There were those who still believed in him—namely Johnny Sain and his bullpen coach Hal Naragon. Neither could care less about his weight. And what did it matter how fast he could run so long as his arm was strong and able? Early in their time together, after Smith pulled him from a 1967 contest, Lolich was alone in the locker room when Sain approached him. Lolich didn't know Sain very well yet and expected that he'd tear into him about his performance. Instead, Sain asked Lolich, "Mickey, do you know that curveball you threw in the third inning?"

"Yes," Lolich said.

"Well now," Sain said in his folksy way, "that's what we're looking for. That was a great pitch."

And that was it. Lolich felt that perhaps he hadn't pitched a bad ball game after all. This was something Naragon had seen often when he and Sain were with the Twins—Sain's ability to lift a pitcher's spirits after a loss, to help him shake it off so he'd return to the field the next morning ready to work.

Naragon and Sain found much to like about Lolich when they began working with him their first spring together. Sain always preached about the importance of movement over speed. But Lolich had both—especially with his fastball. Lolich's fastball also had a natural sink to it —something Mantle picked up on in 1964 when he compared him to Whitey Ford.

In 1967, Sain and Naragon had watched him fight to get back on the winning ledger after that terrible stretch of 10 consecutive losses. At year's end, Sain felt that Lolich was the best pitcher in baseball, someone the team could really depend on, even though it was his teammate Earl Wilson who won 22 games. Especially in those final weeks of the season, the Tigers had turned to Lolich again and again, and he had come through for them. Even after McAuliffe's season-ending double play, Lolich stood out as someone the Tigers would be able to count on heading into the next year.

But for much of 1968, Lolich failed to deliver. In the days following King's assassination, when Detroit girded itself for another riot, Lolich was called back up for Guard duty again. During the season's opening days, he worked in the motor pool from 7:00 a.m. to 3:00 p.m. before going to Tiger Stadium to warm up in the bullpen. Instead of being the staff's steady hand, the second starter behind Wilson, he was the last Tiger starter to earn a win. His National Guard obligations kept him away from the mound for days at a time — including one nine-day stretch — so he'd resort to pitching to high school kids and a priest to try to stay in form.

When Lolich returned to the team, it was evident to everyone that he had lost his confidence and regressed back to the pitcher he was in 1966 and early 1967 — a talented pitcher who didn't believe in his own talent. Some fans accused Lolich of not trying, but his teammates knew that wasn't the problem. Lolich's catcher felt that he didn't think he was capable of making the "big pitches," even though the rest of the team knew otherwise. Even as a rookie in 1968, relief pitcher Jon Warden could see that Lolich was missing something — that conviction McLain had that every time he walked onto the field he was the very best damn pitcher in the league. As McLain began to win, Lolich withdrew into himself. His teammates and reporters could see Lolich's despair, and it was heartbreaking.

Eventually, in late July, Smith did the inevitable. He stripped Lolich of his starting spot. It had been nearly a month since Lolich had won a game, and he was exiled to the bullpen, along with fellow starter Joe Sparma, to work things out. Sain, who was often at odds with Smith when it came to pitcher-related decisions, believed this time that the move was the best thing for Lolich. Coming off a bad start, or a series of bad starts, Sain believed, had put the pitcher under tremendous pressure to make up for everything in the next go-round. It was a vicious spiral. Lolich needed to be out of the spotlight if he was going to regain his bearings and his confidence.

As it turned out, Sain's instincts were correct. In the bullpen, Lolich was spared the comparisons to McLain, and he was able to regain his focus. As a starter, Lolich said, giving up a run in the early innings meant little, since you knew you could count on your team to pick you up and even the score. But coming in from the bullpen, you knew that your team was often either tied or behind and that runners were already on base. Every pitch mattered, and there was no room for self-reflection or nerves. Lolich performed admirably under these conditions and even claimed, credibly or not, that he wouldn't mind staying in relief if that was how he could best help the team. Observing in Lolich a new resolve and concentration, Sain believed he'd returned to the pitcher he was the previous September. No one, certainly not Sain, believed that Lolich would stay in the bullpen for very long.

Lolich and McLain might have been perceived as total opposites, but they both sought adventure outside of the game. While McLain was obsessed with flying, Lolich drove no fewer than five motorcycles, climbed into racecars and hydroplanes for the thrill of it, and complained about the blandness of baseball. Also like McLain, Lolich, who would later promote Dixieland acts in pizza parlors in the era of rock 'n' roll, had musical aspirations that were oddly out of sync with the times.

"I've been called a kook, a flake, and crazy," Lolich said. "In baseball if you don't conform, if you don't do exactly what everybody else does, they say, 'He's screwy.' But that doesn't bother me. I just like to do what I feel like doing. I'm a fellow who likes to try all kinds of different things, challenging things. How else will I ever learn? How could I ever experience the thrill of racecar driving unless I get behind the wheel myself and drive?"

Despite their pitchers' many extracurricular interests, Sain and Naragon felt that both Lolich and McLain had strong work ethics, were open-minded, and shared a desire for self-betterment. Neither pitcher ever said that he didn't feel like throwing — the coaches wouldn't even have to ask — and both embraced the routine that Sain had set up for them. They saw the results, after all.

Yet both pitchers could cause problems for the man who had to catch them. Bill Freehan found that Lolich needed coddling and constant reassurance. That only added to the burden of coping with Lolich's left-handed delivery, which he'd learned after he hurt his right arm in a motorcycle accident. He would cock his left arm back behind his body — from the side his arm resembled an inverted V — and both hitter and catcher would have trouble anticipating his release point.

McLain posed different challenges. His windup, his leg kick, and his over-the-top delivery made him effective, but easy to anticipate. Both

Freehan and batters knew that his best pitches were his curveball and his high-rising fastball, as well as the controlled breaking ball he'd learned from Sain, and they could see the ball from the moment it left his hand. When he was behind in the count, both catcher and batter knew that he'd resort to throwing sidearm for strikes. And Freehan felt that his quick delivery, which his teammates appreciated because it kept them alert, was also the very thing that interfered with his focus. McLain needed to slow down. It was Freehan's job to make sure he did. More than a catcher, Freehan served as a babysitter for two unruly kids.

And even though McLain and Lolich had worked together amiably during spring training, that quickly changed once the real games began. In constant pain and believing he needed cortisone to keep his baseball career alive, McLain envied Lolich his "rubber" arm, his ability to pitch without pain. McLain knew that he could never return to that feeling of being able to throw with such ease. Lolich, for his part, grew tired of the attention McLain received as he kept winning, and he resented Denny's cavalier flouting of the rules that everyone else had to follow.

Lolich would later claim that he didn't hate Denny — not exactly. McLain had become the number-one pitcher and that was fine. What bothered him were the rules, the ones that everyone was supposed to follow and did — except for Denny. Lolich felt that McLain was forever "challenging management, flaunting it," until it proved to be too much.

Their mutual hostility was evident as the season progressed, but for the most part it never burst out into the open. There were those among the Tigers who believed that Lolich wished that he could be like McLain — outspoken, unreserved, unfiltered — but he just wasn't. With each headline, Lolich grew angrier and more resentful and eventually more determined. Jim Hawkins, who began covering the team in 1970, found their relationship unfortunate and petty. Daryl Patterson, a rookie in 1968, thought it was "comical as hell."

McLain believed that Lolich simply wanted to be the guy. It was jealousy, he felt. Yet he believed that Lolich had the best stuff — the best — that he'd ever seen. The two should have shared laughs with each other, been friends, McLain would lament. They should have been, he thought, Butch Cassidy and the Sundance Kid.

Instead, each seemed eager to push the other into the line of fire. Things finally did flare up publicly in the midseason of 1969, during the All-Star Game. McLain, by now a pilot, had flown Lolich and his wife to the game in Washington, D.C. Rain had delayed the contest by one day, and McLain would claim that he informed Lolich that he would need to leave right after he pitched, so that he could fly to Florida for prescheduled dental work to repair his teeth. Lolich, however, told one Detroit sportswriter that after McLain pitched in the fourth inning, he just announced that he was leaving. When Lolich asked McLain how he and his wife were supposed to get back to Detroit, McLain allegedly said, "That's tough. That's your problem."

"McLain doesn't think about his friends or teammates," Lolich told the reporter. "All he thinks about is himself. And look I want to see that in the paper, I have had enough of this stuff."

Sam McDowell would take Lolich's side. In the locker room following the game, he learned that McLain had showered and dressed, gotten on the airplane, and left his fellow pitcher behind. Cleveland's traveling secretary was left scrambling to help Lolich find a flight back to Detroit. McDowell thought it was the rudest thing he'd ever seen. But this wasn't a surprise to anyone. This incident, as much as anything, demonstrated who Denny was.

By the time Denny woke up for good on September 14, he was ready to perform. He retreated to the basement with his brother Tom. There was a song from his forthcoming album, called "Girl Talk," that he wanted his brother to hear. Chasing his breakfast with a soda, he spoke with the two priests who'd come up from Chicago. He fought on the phone with his agent in New York, then talked business with a man from Hammond. He played the organ alone for a bit, then finally headed out in his glistening new Cadillac — a gift from a local dealer. Tom dropped him off near the ballpark.

It must have been strange for him when he stepped out. No one noticed him or called out to him. While he might have expected the approach of miniskirted teenagers and their gruff fathers, slaps on the back, and assurances not to worry, instead he found silence and the anonymity of a mortal walking to Tiger Stadium — the crusty venue where he hated to pitch but which, during his meteoric existence there, he very much owned.

It was almost 12:30 when McLain walked into the locker room, which was buzzing with the welcome ruckus of cameramen and local beat reporters, dazed blokes who were unaccustomed to such fanfare for what was a regular-season game with a team that had all but won the pennant. He grabbed another Pepsi, hung up his clothes, and found, of all things, a six-leaf clover at the bottom of his locker. Walking out for batting practice, he flashed a wide smile to the catcher of the opposing team, the Oakland Athletics' Jim Pagliaroni, who was holding up a cardboard sign announcing that his own pitcher, Chuck Dobson, was going for no. 12 today. After McLain broke his bat, the Tigers outfielder Mickey Stanley — soon to become its serviceable starting shortstop — was quick to grab hold of it. He wanted to keep this particular piece of baseball history: the bat Denny McLain broke on the day he won his 30th.

"Hey, Denny," yelled A's outfielder Jim Gosger. "Send me one of your records."

"Call your manager," McLain said. "I want you in the lineup." (McLain then turned to the reporters capturing this exchange in their notebooks and said that he was only kidding, that Gosger actually hit him "pretty good.")

Turning to Chuck Dobson, McLain called out amiably, "Hey, 29, take a dive."

"I haven't had to lately," Dobson said. "It just comes naturally."

Back in the locker room, McLain fielded questions from reporters. Someone asked him about the *Life* profile that he hated and he was pressed for details on his breakfast. McLain told one reporter that he didn't care for people calling him McLain, that he was either Dennis or Denny or even Mr. McLain, but "none of this last name stuff." When a reporter asked where they could find him after the game — meaning after he won — McLain said, "You guys are presuming a lot, aren't you?"

At some point before the game, the beleaguered Tigers public relations man, Hal Middlesworth, told McLain that David Eisenhower and his fiancée Julie Nixon were in the stands and that he had to say hello to them. It was fitting that they'd be there. They had come off the campaign trail, standing in for Julie's father, who had emerged from the political wilderness to take his place as the Republican presidential nominee. They were a young couple whose shared beauty harkened back to an earlier America, a youth that a great many adults in 1968 so desperately wanted back. David, soon to enlist in the Navy, was a thin young man in a dark suit and striped tie, his hair cut short but not too short, with a toothy smile that made him seem like the very best fellow you'd meet while summering at Cape May. His bride-to-be, wearing a smart, sleeveless turtleneck, her hair pulled up high above her forehead, showed no anger, no displeasure with how the world now was—only pleasure in what it could be. In short, they were two happy people in an unhappy time, in love in a traditional way, their future together very certain.

After he warmed up, McLain went to greet them, accompanied by Mayo Smith. They were to be introduced by Tigers owner John Fetzer, the gray, thinly built man who would never understand the modern ballplayer but who would later be credited with doing the most to push baseball into the television age.

Before the game, at least outwardly, McLain showed no signs of stress. He didn't talk about Tommy Smothers, with whom he'd planned an hour-long television special and who was sitting in the stands. In his bullpen session with Naragon, he was just Denny, as loose as he'd been all season. It was only in the minutes before his start, in the quiet of the training room, that McLain betrayed some angst. Dizzy Dean himself, jowly and sporting a big white cowboy hat, had followed him in to see if he could be of assistance. McLain was full of "what ifs." What if he won this game and what if he actually earned $100,000? What would life be like? Of course, he first had to win.

As it happened, that would not prove easy. McLain toiled through the early innings, throwing 44 pitches before he even reached the fourth inning. He gave up not one but two home runs to Reggie Jackson. After Jackson hit his second, the entire Oakland dugout rose to their feet for a standing ovation. The A's were young and on the cusp of being the champion "Fighting A's" of the next decade. They weren't going to lie down for anyone. Lifted for a pinch hitter in the bottom of the ninth,

McLain left the game trailing 4–3. He needed two runs or else it was over . . . in front of everyone. The fans of Detroit. His mother. The millions watching on television.

And then, as his team had managed to do several times that season, they scored for him. It began with pinch hitter Al Kaline — the face of the franchise, who'd spent most of the season on the bench with an injured hand. On a 3-2 count from relief pitcher Diego Seguí, Kaline drew a walk, then ran hard into third as Mickey Stanley singled up the middle.

And now Denny could feel it. The whole stadium could as well. At the very least, it appeared that he wouldn't lose the game. Everything was going his way, as it had all season. How else could you explain the A's Danny Carter, one of the league's best defensive first basemen, misfielding a ball hit meekly halfway up the first-base line by outfielder Jim Northrup after Mickey Stanley had singled, moving Kaline to third? Amazingly, Carter threw it wide of the plate, so that his catcher, Dave Duncan, was forced to leap for the ball with his arm outstretched as it sailed past, allowing Kaline to run in beneath him. Kaline stumbled and rolled over home, reaching back for the plate to make sure he was safe. How could this game not be tied?

Kaline had already made up his mind before Northrup's weak grounder that if he saw a high-bouncing ball, he would break for home, and that, when Carter fielded it, he would bump Duncan, knocking the ball loose. Of course, with Carter's throw, he didn't have to.

Willie Horton was up next. As it happened, at that moment fans John Kujawaski of Detroit and Wayne Jones of Roseville brandished a 20-foot-long banner reading, HIT THAT BALL, WILLIE! When asked afterwards if he'd had a plan, Horton said he had only one thought at that moment — hit the ball as hard as he could and "run like hell."

Watching from the dugout, McLain for once was quiet. He'd wrapped a towel around his head and paced as the A's brought everyone in — including the outfielders — so that they could make a play at home. That decision would prove costly. When Horton did hit the ball as hard as he could, it sailed over the head of left fielder Jim Gosger, who would have caught the ball cleanly had he been playing at normal depth. Watching the ball from third, Stanley stepped slightly off the bag, then retreated slightly, before clapping his hands and dashing for home.

At that point Sharyn McLain, who'd put up with so much all season, lost her composure. Like Denny, she was rarely out of the spotlight. She had arrived at Tiger Stadium wearing an off-white Jonathan Logan wool knit outfit with a red silk scarf, matching heels, and a red tote bag that held toys and snacks for her daughter. She was on her feet watching the end of the game, gripping the guardrail, and when Stanley came in for the winning run, she began to cry—whether from happiness or relief wasn't clear. She grabbed her daughter, who'd been running down the aisle, and smothered her with hugs and kisses. The strain of the 30 wins had been like a balloon, she said—something that hung over her family every day. Finally the air had been let out of it.

In only his second year broadcasting Tigers games on television, Larry Osterman had already seen a lot. In 1967 he witnessed two no-hitters—one pitched by Joe Horlen in Chicago, the other by Steve Barber in Baltimore. At the time, he had thought, *What are the chances of getting to see one no-hitter, much less two?* But this was something else. Looking down from the broadcast booth, he saw Dizzy Dean's hat and the crush of people surrounding McLain. And Denny's radiant grin, which broadcast to everyone at the park that he had done it.

Once again the "Last-Lick" Tigers had come back after facing a deficit in the seventh inning. McLain had won with seven of those comebacks, and it's for this reason that baseball historian Gary Gillette and many others have called into question McLain's 1968 accomplishments. It wasn't so much McLain's brilliant pitching that brought him 30 wins, Gillette said—others surpassed him in that regard—as the fact that the Tigers simply "beat the hell out of the opposition." That season they proved the harshest against teams facing Denny McLain.

Afterwards, surrounded by his teammates, Denny told Sandy Koufax, who was covering the game for NBC, how grateful he felt for what his team had done. "Oh, Sandy, it's the greatest bunch of ballplayers I've ever played with. I've been saying that for five years. [He hadn't.] They've just been fantastic. They've been making clubs beat themselves and [that's] exactly what happened here today."

Dean put him in a bear hug, and then Fetzer came up to congratulate him. Later, after most fans had left the park and McLain was enjoying the moment with his teammates in the locker room, he could still hear the noise from outside. It was the sound of 10,000 people chanting, "We want Denny! We want Denny!" Hal Middlesworth implored him, "You've got to come outside, Denny. Those people will never go home unless you go out to see them."

Walking through the tunnel and onto the field, the chanting getting louder, McLain surveyed the fans he'd castigated only months before. "Look at this, will ya?" he said. "Look at those people. I can't believe it." Speaking to the press later, he was anything but humble. He blamed one of the home runs he gave up to Jackson on the layout of Tiger Stadium. As for his salary demands, he told the reporters that he didn't give a damn what the Tigers general manager thought. He deserved everything he'd asked for.

"I hope they announce my $100,000 salary soon," McLain said.

The following morning, A's executive vice president and consultant Joe DiMaggio sat with a reporter as he ate breakfast in a Detroit hotel. Two years had passed since Gay Talese wrote about DiMaggio's silent season, about his days spent quietly watching pretty girls from his restaurant near the Wharf in San Francisco, about his secluded nights among a small cadre of friends who had very little to do with baseball. He'd been coaxed back into the game, upon the team's arrival in Oakland, by A's owner Charlie Finley. The man who as a player had treasured his solitude and who, in retirement, had become a quiet figure — distrustful even — was open when he talked about his feelings about McLain. Yet where one might have expected harsh words for the pitcher and his camera-hugging ways, DiMaggio saw only a bright future for him — one that went beyond baseball.

"McLain has a great plus for himself," DiMaggio said. "He is a master at the organ role. He can go into nightclubs in Las Vegas, Miami Beach, Chicago . . . and give a great act. People who wouldn't pay a nickel to see McLain, who wouldn't give a penny for his autograph, will love him at the organ."

When McLain arrived at the clubhouse that afternoon, it had all the atmosphere of a brunch following a night of wedding revelry — silent and polite, the room was deeply subdued. No one had expected him to show up that day, but as with everything, who could predict what Denny would do? Kaline, smoking a cigar, watched as McLain walked in with a member of the Smothers brothers' television staff. When Stanley, who'd scored the winning run the day before, asked if he could have McLain's glove, McLain first offered it up for $1,000 and then said he'd sell the ball he used to the highest bidder and donate it to Catholic Charities. The mail waiting for him included a telegram from vice president and Democratic presidential nominee Hubert Humphrey. Congratulating him, Humphrey signed off as "Your teammate — Hubert H. Humphrey."

"Hell no," McLain said when asked if he was campaigning for Humphrey. "I'm not even a Democrat, I'm not a Republican either. I'm for [comedian] Pat Paulsen. If Pat can get a few more votes, he'll win this thing."

With a listless crowd expected at Tiger Stadium that day — the parking lot was empty and the visiting reporters all but gone — Mickey Lolich was on his own again. The day before, on Denny's big day, Detroit's Croatian Hall had celebrated Mickey Lolich Day, an event that drew some 500 people. And today, for the first time in his major league career, Lolich was pitching in front of his parents, who'd flown in from Oregon. His 13–0 shutout was his eighth win in his last ten decisions. It was the first time his parents had seen him win on the major league level, and it was the first game his daughter Kimberly had attended all season.

"Maybe if I win a couple more I can get booked on *Ed Sullivan* and ride my motorcycle," he said ruefully.

With all the hoopla surrounding Denny and his 30 wins, what few people noticed was that McLain's arm was getting weaker as the season progressed and Lolich was actually outperforming him with each successive start. But this was Denny's town.

Reggie Jackson, who was inconsolable after Saturday's game, was one of the few willing to question McLain's supremacy. When he heard Dizzy Dean suggest that McLain had taken something off those two home run pitches — one a changeup hit into the lower stands, the other a curve blasted into the upper stands — Jackson was angry. Did that also apply to his 26 other home runs that season?

While he called McLain a fine pitcher, Jackson pointed out that he was "not Mr. Gibson." Everyone would learn that soon enough. For the moment, though, McLain—who'd landed a second *Sports Illustrated* cover—believed that he was capable of anything. It was up to someone else to prove him wrong.

16

OLD MEN

J ACKIE ROBINSON WAS WAITING. It was the early afternoon of August 28, 1968, on the eve of the Democratic National Convention, and Robinson found himself with Elgin Baylor sitting in Hubert Humphrey's hotel suite in Chicago. In a matter of hours, against the backdrop of the Chicago police force exerting brute control through billy clubs, Humphrey would clinch his party's nomination for the presidency of the United States.

But for now, Humphrey was running late. Understandably, he had a lot to do. Meetings with advisers. Consults with speechwriters. By the time he sat down to lunch with Robinson and Baylor, it was past 1:30, and even then, as the three shared sandwiches and conversation, one could sense Humphrey's attention flickering, drifting toward the television and the campaign coverage on the convention floor.

Republicans would later claim Robinson as their own. But Humphrey and Robinson had a history together, stretching back to a difficult primary campaign in Wisconsin eight years before. That was before Robinson had thrown his lot in with Nixon. Looking back on the 1960 race, most people remember the images of Jackie and Dick together, but just months earlier Robinson was stumping for Humphrey in Wisconsin in an effort to defeat the corrupt Kennedy machine, as he saw it.

Moreover, Robinson believed in Humphrey. Humphrey had had the courage to deliver a speech at the 1948 Democratic National Convention that called on his party to take a stand against segregation, and this at a time when the Dixiecrats still controlled a great deal of the party. It was a speech that would help outline the principles of liberalism from that point on. And it was something Robinson would never forget.

Robinson, who first met Humphrey in 1959, never saw him waver in these principles, and took time away from his job at Chock Full o'Nuts to campaign with him for the nomination. After Humphrey's defeat in the 1960 Democratic campaign, he wrote to Robinson, "You are a national hero in the truest sense of the word, and I am one of your fans. I believe in you.

"It is always difficult to lose," he would go on, "but sometimes there is a victory in defeat. I am sure that the remaining Democratic candidates are taking a firmer stand on the vital issues of our day. I know that we have educated them in the field of human rights. What is more, our campaign efforts caused people to think — to think on the big issues and not just about personality and looks." Of course he was speaking of the Kennedys.

By 1968, Robinson was no longer at the height of his political power, but Humphrey still believed he could help the campaign. As Robert Kennedy and Eugene McCarthy went head to head in the state primaries, Humphrey sought out Robinson, who at the time was still under the employ of Nelson Rockefeller. Robinson had not lost faith in Humphrey, but he was nothing if not loyal. Writing to the vice president in the first days of May, he said he felt honored by Humphrey's request, but that Rockefeller's "desires dictate my actions."

Nearly four months later, however, Robinson was in Chicago at Humphrey's side. Humphrey told Robinson and Baylor that he had reached out to Rockefeller, even proposed the idea of a coalition government as a way of keeping the country out of Nixon's grisly grasp.

"Nixon has made a calculated decision," he said as the three ate their cheese sandwiches. "This law-and-order issue [Nixon's "tough on crime" initiative] is subdued racism. They made it an issue and we're going to challenge them."

For Robinson, this seat at the table had come at a high price. Though many dismissed his role within the Rockefeller administration, it had been Robinson dispatched by Rockefeller the summer before to quell the Buffalo riots. It was Robinson who stood with Rockefeller as he tried to implement broad civil rights measures. In so doing, Robinson opened himself up to vicious attacks from young, militant blacks. Called an "Uncle Tom" and "House Nigger," Robinson fired back, defending not only his own views but those of his friend the governor. He'd seen firsthand how Rockefeller responded to his disapproving peers within the Republican Party, how he stood firm in his opposition to the conservative tack laid out by Barry Goldwater. Rockefeller, Robinson believed, was someone who followed up on things, someone he could trust.

So when Rockefeller announced his presidential bid late in the campaign, after initially saying he wouldn't run, Robinson welcomed him into his home, where some 70 members of the National Newspaper Publishers Association had gathered. Robinson spoke briefly about his son's experiences in Vietnam and then talked about Nixon, whose election, he now believed, would be deeply detrimental to the Negro cause.

After Nixon won the Republican nomination, Robinson believed that the GOP had told the black man to "go to hell." After Nixon's ascent, he would resign his place within the Rockefeller administration, albeit with the faint hope that he would one day return to the fold. In the meantime, he marshaled whatever political capital he still had left to help Humphrey. None of his fellow Rockefeller Republicans would follow his lead. Some, for whom party allegiance trumped all else, found his actions reprehensible. He became a pariah.

Robinson was a man without a party—but not without a candidate to support. Rachel always felt that it was the opportunities he'd had to actually sit and speak with Humphrey outside a campaign event that drew Jack to him. He saw courage in Humphrey, the very same trait that had driven Robinson himself through sports and in the life that came after. There was a personal connection between them, one that went beyond brief conversations at assembly halls. With his country in peril, Robinson felt that Humphrey was the man he could trust.

In Rachel's view, it was a lack of such a connection that would always separate her husband from Robert Kennedy. Even as the vast majority of African Americans supported Kennedy, just as they'd supported his

brother eight years earlier, Robinson and Bobby would remain near ene-
mies. As his brother's political enforcer, Bobby had gone after Robinson
over his role in the Wisconsin Democratic primary, calling Robinson a
paid ringer for Humphrey, which he was not. Going further, Kennedy
accused Robinson of being anti-union in his role as a Chock Full o'Nuts
executive, which led Robinson to declare that Bobby wouldn't "hesitate
to use lies, innuendoes and personal attacks on those who disagree with
him to get his candidate into the White House."

There were moments, of course, when the two men might have
reached a détente. Robinson appreciated a good deal of what Bobby
sought to do as attorney general. He had acted to protect the marchers
in Birmingham and those who risked their lives as Freedom Riders. He
had helped place civil rights on JFK's domestic agenda. Robinson admired Bobby's courage and his willingness to act. Whatever ill will remained from the 1960 presidential campaign should have been put to
rest. But Bobby's decision, after his brother's assassination, to run for
the Senate in New York, where he defeated the Republican incumbent
Kenneth Keating, a man Robinson cared for deeply, only reignited their
mutual distrust.

As Kennedy's stature rose among African Americans, Robinson continued to believe that the shimmering persona masked the true man. In
an unfortunately timed column — he had filed it earlier but it appeared
in the *New York Amsterdam News* three days after Bobby was shot —
Robinson wrote that Kennedy had done a terrific job of "brainwashing"
a great many people and that he found it difficult to understand "how
they can allow the glamour of the John F. Kennedy name to blind them
to record.

"The record will show some commendable contributions Bobby
made as head of Justice under his brother," Robinson wrote. "It will
show also some damning things. It will show how Bobby upheld the
appointment of segregationist judges in the South. It will show how he
urged the Freedom Movement to 'cool off' at times when the Movement
needed the moral support of all sincere men. It will show that Bobby's
Justice Department persecuted the Martin Luther King forces in Albany,
Georgia . . . Hubert Humphrey is no Bobby-come-lately to the cause."

Following the assassination, Robinson apologized for the timing, but he would not apologize for the sentiments expressed, unpopular as they might have been with the many civil rights leaders who supported Kennedy.

"I do not believe a man is a man to apologize for having voiced that which he sees as the truth," he wrote. "I brought it up to say that, regardless of my differences with those who idolized the late Senator Kennedy, I knew at all times that he was a brilliant man, that he made some important contributions to racial progress in America and that he deserved better — as any man does — than to be gunned down because someone disagreed with him or hated him or what he stood for."

Now Robinson had come to Chicago to lend support to the candidate whose consistency he admired. How he even managed to do it seemed remarkable, given everything he'd endured that year. In May, Robinson had lost his mother, the one who had moved her family west from Georgia to Pasadena. He'd suffered a heart attack that prevented him from making one last stand against Nixon at the Republican convention in Miami. A few days before he shared sandwiches with Humphrey, Jackie Jr. was again at the center of things. This time it was more than a skirmish. Jackie Jr. had been arrested for allegedly pointing a gun at a police officer in Stamford, where he was found with a 19-year-old named Janet Wallace; police had arrested her for "loitering for the purposes of prostitution" and charged Jackie Jr. with using "females for immoral purposes." More than a mere addict, he was now a criminal in the truest sense, a man whose life — like those of so many he went to war with — had gone terribly wrong.

And yet it didn't stop his father from making this last stand. In the aftermath of the Republican convention and his risky repudiation of the Republican Party, Robinson formally endorsed Humphrey at the Freedom National Bank in Harlem, which he'd helped found and which would stand for decades after his death. Accompanying Humphrey was a young aide named Norman Sherman, who'd first worked for Humphrey as a senator and then followed him to the vice president's office, where he helped work on the space program. Now he watched Humphrey with Robinson and Joe Louis, two men once seen as American icons, as people whose words had mattered in helping shape the lives of African Americans but whose importance was fading daily.

The crowd outside on 125th Street, which years before would have clamored to see Robinson, was indifferent at best. As his official biographer recounted, there were those who cheered for him, but many did not; they seemed to have no memory of all that he'd risked and accomplished. One man yelled, at the sight of Robinson, "Uncle Tom!"

Sherman didn't go inside the bank but remained outside with the press. While Humphrey and Robinson spoke, he saw a man accost Louis. He was short and militant, wearing something resembling a dashiki. He barely reached Louis's chin. But that didn't stop the man from screaming at Louis, once the heavyweight champion and hero to the world. Sherman thought Louis might punch him, but he didn't. Instead, Louis remained calm, saying nothing, then watched the man walk off, his arms waving, still shouting.

Later, when putting together his autobiography, Robinson would say that he could neither sing the National Anthem nor salute the flag. Rachel hated that he said that. She knew that he would come off as bitter, as someone who hated his country. But he still loved his country, the one he'd served in both wartime and peace. Now, looking out onto a beleaguered landscape, he wondered what part he could still play in reclaiming it.

Seven years. That was all it took for the black-and-white era of Mantle and Maris — of a Yankee dynasty that seemed like it could go on forever — to crumble. That happened thanks in no small part to the pitching of Bob Gibson. But it was the two Yankees hitters who, in going after Babe Ruth's single-season home run record, ultimately forced this course correction that ushered in the Year of the Pitcher. Now their time was up.

Maris, at least, found peace when his Yankees run came to an end. It's been documented again and again how much he disliked New York, how his silent manner wasn't a good fit for the city or its sportswriters, who were used to more gregarious types like Billy Martin and Whitey Ford, Mantle and Yogi Berra. Columnists like Jimmy Cannon seemed to delight in skewering Maris, criticizing his overall attitude as well as his baseball aptitude. He was selfish in their stories. Joyless. In 1962, Cannon castigated Maris for not breaking Ruth's record in 154 games and christened him "The Whiner."

Over the course of four years, Maris's home run count dropped from 61 to eight in 1965. What the Yankees kept quiet was that he'd irreparably injured his hand. Surgery followed, but Maris would never regain his strength. He couldn't cope with any kind of fastball. He had to hope for off-speed pitches, which were becoming increasingly rare.

By the end of 1966, baseball had become an albatross for Maris, and he wanted out. When he agreed to the Yankees' request to hold off announcing his retirement until the start of spring training in 1967, they promptly traded him within days to the Cardinals. St. Louis still had the tight nucleus of their 1964 world championship team and didn't know what to expect from him. From being a malcontent, however, or someone who expected others to come to him, he turned out to be the one reaching out. He was the man introducing himself to the fellas, and within days everything the Cardinal players had heard and read about Maris was put aside. Almost instantly, he became one of them. He joined them for beers. He ate shrimp with them at an oyster bar in St. Petersburg during spring training. He joked easily with his teammates and got along with the sympathetic St. Louis press. And though stripped of his power, McCarver felt that Maris was not only still an excellent hitter but also faster and a better fielder than anyone believed.

It was evident to Dick Schofield, who briefly shared an apartment with Maris and Clete Boyer when they played in New York, that Maris was a different, more relaxed person with the Cardinals. In 1968, as members of the Cardinals, both Schofield and Maris were now living in an apartment complex out by the St. Louis airport, and Maris had actually taken the step of bringing his family along, which he never did while playing for the Yankees. Schofield saw a man who seemed comfortable in his surroundings, though his interest in playing the game was waning.

"There's a big difference being on a ball club where you don't always have people on your tail. All the players in the National League were just great," Maris said. "I had never played in the league before. But they made me feel right at home. In the American League, except at Kansas City, people were all over you."

Even so, he was ready to move on. "I want to get out of baseball," he said. "I don't feel I'm doing the wrong thing. I've had my share of fun.

When I started, I set 10 years in the big leagues as my goal. Well, I've sur-passed that by two. Now I'm ready to stay home for a change."

He'd intended for the 1967 season, during which he helped the Car-dinals win the pennant, to be his last. But at the Cardinals' pennant cel-ebration in Philadelphia, Maris joked that he would stay, even take a pay cut, if only Busch would bestow on him a lucrative Budweiser dis-tributorship. That winter he got what he asked for — a distributorship in Gainesville, Florida, which Maris's brother Rudy would run until Maris's time in baseball was up.

Busch reportedly discussed beer franchises with many players. But as the Major League Baseball Players Association gained in influence and Busch's friendly if paternalistic demeanor turned more combative, no one else from the 1967 or 1968 teams would get that chance. Not even Bob Gibson, though he and Busch had spoken about it and Gib-son had prepared himself for a similar retirement bonus. Gibson would forever believe that because of his involvement with the 1972 players' strike, Busch would never revisit the issue or give him the same oppor-tunity he gave Maris.

This treatment would continue to gnaw at Gibson's lifelong friend Rodney Wead. Maris had barely played for the Cardinals and then been rewarded for two brief, unspectacular seasons. Gibson would have killed for such a chance. Wead had seen a slew of "roughneck guys" get-ting endorsements while real financial rewards, including the beer dis-tributorship Gibson desperately wanted, eluded his friend. Hell, Wead thought, look at Mickey Mantle and everything he'd earned outside the game while being "drunk every day."

Mantle, progressively struggling with alcohol, had hung on with the Yankees. Often in debilitating pain from a series of searing injuries to both of his knees, every at-bat seemed a struggle for him. The great cen-ter fielder of his time now struggled to play first base.

Even Marvin Miller could see how badly things had deteriorated for Mantle. Miller had happened to be in the locker room after a meeting with the Yankees, and as he watched Mantle getting ready, in great ag-ony, before a spring training game, he came to fully understand the extent of the man's pain. Here was Mantle being left unattended, without a trainer in sight. The entire locker room had emptied out, and here he was alone. How, Miller thought, could they treat anyone — especially someone the caliber of Mantle — like this?

Unlike Maris, Mantle had largely kept quiet about his intentions to retire. Though everyone knew he wouldn't appear again as an active player for the Yankees in 1969, the Yankees player representative, pitcher Steve Hamilton, convinced Mantle to hold off on making an official announcement until the spring. Having successfully negotiated their first collective bargaining agreement in 1968, the players had gotten a taste of their own power. At stake was a proper pension plan. When the executive board player representatives met with Miller in San Francisco before the 1969 season, and with players awaiting their proposed contracts from the clubs, Miller told them, "I would be derelict if I didn't point out to you that signing a player contract at this point in time is giving up your strength. For many of you, the pension plan will eventually pay you more money in your lifetime than you're gonna earn as a player. And to give up your bargaining power to negotiate an appropriate pension so that you can get a salary this coming year would be penny wise and pound foolish."

After a brief recess, the player reps returned to their hotel rooms to call their teammates to ask them for two things: (1) their support for a policy of not signing player contracts until the pension plan agreement was in place, and (2) permission to use players' names — especially star players' names — as a way to demonstrate to the media that the Players Association had the full support of the ballplayers, even those who were earning the big-time salaries. When the meeting reconvened, Miller found near-unanimous support. None of the stars had said, "Don't use my name." That fear was gone.

Yet when it came time for the Yankees rep to speak, Hamilton asked to pass, saying that he wanted to go last. When his turn finally came, Hamilton reported, in his delightfully drawn-out way, that he had spoken to each of his teammates and everyone had agreed — save one.

Most believed that the lone holdout was Mantle. But Hamilton told the group that Mantle had said, "Steve, I've just about made up my mind that I'm really not gonna play anymore so I'm not gonna sign a contract."

"Have you told the club this, that you intend to retire?" Hamilton asked.

"No."

"Have you told any newspaper man?"

"No."

"Have you told anybody?"

"Yeah," Mantle said. "I've discussed it with my wife."

"Okay," Hamilton said. "Do me a favor. Let us use your name as someone who's not going to sign his contract next year and don't mention to anybody that you've made the decision to retire."

"Will this help the players and the union?" Mantle asked.

"Definitely."

"You've got it," Mantle told him.

But even with Mantle keeping quiet about his retirement plans, everyone knew. Denny McLain certainly knew when he faced Mantle in a near-empty stadium on a gray September 19, 1968. It had rained heavily the day before, and the Tigers had already won the American League pennant. Mantle needed one home run to pass Jimmie Foxx for third on the all-time list, behind Babe Ruth and Willie Mays. In August, Mantle had told a reporter from Detroit that all he wanted was one, just one more home run. For his entire career, he said, he'd been chasing someone. "If I hit one more, they can chase me." There were 9,000 people in the stands. In the years to come, thousands of others would claim they had been there too.

Looking at Mantle, McLain saw his hobbled hero, whom he knew he would be facing for the very last time. Every child of the 1950s loved Mantle, yet McLain felt a special kinship with him. Like McLain, in his heyday Mantle had lived flamboyantly and recklessly, seemingly without thought for the consequences, chased by premonitions of early death. For both men, the day of reckoning would come.

In the seventh inning, with the scant crowd standing in ovation and the Tigers leading 6–1 with no one on base, McLain called his catcher, the backup Jim Price, to the mound.

As they had done throughout the season, the Tigers had scored for

McLain — this time with six runs. McLain had gotten his 30th win. His team had won the pennant. When Price got out to the mound, McLain said, "I want Mantle to hit one."

"Whaddya mean?"

"Let's just let him hit one," McLain said. "Look. I'm going to throw a pitch, and I want him to hit a home run. He needs one more to move up on the all-time home-run list."

"You're kidding, right?" said Price.

"Jesus Christ, Price, he can't hit a six-run homer!"

"Okay, how am I supposed to tell him?"

"All you gotta do is say, 'Be ready, Mick.'"

Price delivered the message, but Mantle took the first two pitches for strikes. At that moment, McLain wondered if it was worth it after all. He could simply strike him out — that would have been easy at that point in Mantle's career. But after two meekly thrown fastballs down the middle, Mantle asked Price if McLain was going to throw more of the same. Price went back out to the mound. When he returned, he assured Mantle that yes, McLain would throw that way again. When Mantle fouled off the next pitch, an exasperated McLain yelled out, "Mickey, where do you want the fucking ball?"

McLain signaled with his hand precisely where the pitch would go — this time on the inside part of the plate. And this time things went according to plan. McLain served up the pitch Mantle asked for, where he wanted it. The ball sailed into the upper deck. When he crossed home plate, Mantle yelled, "Thank you!" (When Joe Pepitone demanded the same VIP treatment, McLain promptly knocked him down.)

This was vintage McLain. And as with his other hijinks that season, no one really faulted him for what he'd done. Not Ray Lane or Larry Osterman sitting in the broadcast booth. Not Jerry Green, who was writing for the *Detroit News*. Not the fans. And not his fellow Tigers players, who whooped and shouted and clapped as if it had been a game-winning hit by one of their own. Only Dick Tracewski would later feel it wasn't the right thing to do. (Gibson too was predictably put off. Long after his retirement, Gibson would write that he would have sooner dropped his pants on the mound than do something like that. Showing respect to Mantle would have meant pitching to him as if he were still the player he once was, maybe even adding some power so as to "blow his ass away, if I could.")

Though this moment wasn't officially the end for Maris or for Mantle, in many ways it felt like the death knell for an era. The Yankees, the standard by which all other baseball teams were measured, were dead. And the great Mickey Mantle had had to rely on the pity of the league's most charismatic goofball to break a record.

None of this was of much consequence to the Tigers. Two days before, they'd won the American League championship. After trailing in the seventh inning, a clutch RBI at the bottom of the ninth by Don Wert, the team's weakest hitter, brought in the winning run — setting off chaos in the stands.

"Let's listen to the bedlam," Tigers radio announcer Ernie Harwell said. Fans flooded the field as the public-address announcer called for calm and "hippies" tore up the sod. Policemen guarded home plate. Inside the Tigers clubhouse, the celebration wasn't any more restrained. Players threw one another into the whirlpool. No one escaped the shaving cream. As Larry Osterman and Ray Lane interviewed the players one by one, Denny positioned himself on-screen for nearly the entire telecast. When he wasn't looking straight at the camera, he could be seen standing to the side struggling with a bottle of champagne, hoping to spray the lens, but to no avail.

Johnny Sain, meanwhile, was nowhere to be found. "We're trying to get John Sain to come," television announcer George Kell told the audience. "But John won't come. John's lost in the crowd."

At one point, McLain sat down at Mayo Smith's desk and put his feet up, as if he owned the place. He told the baseball writers that, if he had his way, he'd install a Hammond organ there. Again he brought up the subject of a $100,000 salary, saying it wouldn't be nearly enough to take on the manager's job.

"This guy was fabulous," Smith said. "But this wasn't a one-man team. You didn't win pennants that way."

"Gentlemen," McLain said to the press. "I want to say right now that Mayo Smith will pitch the first game of the World Series."

When a photographer suggested that Smith "get behind Denny," Smith replied, "I'm always behind him."

Dick Tracewski had seen pennant celebrations before in Los Angeles, but none like this. Perhaps it was intense because of how long it had been since Detroit won the pennant — the last time was in 1945. The carousing spilled out of the clubhouse and lasted late into the evening. The *Detroit News* writer Jerry Green somehow managed to get into the A. C. Lindell, a Detroit sports bar, where he counted no fewer than 20 Tigers players in attendance. Pitcher Fred Lasher threw up in the back of Al Kaline's car. McLain woke up in the back of a limo in Dearborn next to a woman he didn't know, his memory a blur.

Throughout the city, there was celebratory destruction. The Tigers had had a terrific season and finished what they'd started the year before. In the process, myths were born that would endure for decades, as best epitomized by the team's well-meaning owner, John Fetzer, who told Smith, "You may not have only won a pennant — you may have just saved the city of Detroit, too."

The Tigers did set an all-time attendance record in 1968. And yes, the black and white citizenry had come together in support of the team. But the accomplishments of a professional baseball team could never truly mend the cavernous rift between blacks and whites in Detroit, built on decades of bad feelings. To claim otherwise would have been delusional. George Wallace, the segregationist governor of Alabama, still drew large crowds across Michigan as he embarked on his presidential campaign while the Tigers played on. Twelfth Street, the epicenter of the 1967 riots, was still in shambles. The pennant could neither stop white flight out of Detroit nor tamp down the growing sense that the city, once the epitome of the urban dream, could not conquer its inner demons.

Afterwards, William Serrin, in the Detroit *Free Press,* wondered, "What makes whites seek out blacks and pummel them and shake their hands? Why, 13 months after the costliest riot in American history, did blacks and whites love each other without reservation?"

"Temporarily you had a truce," psychiatrist Paul Lowinger told him. "It's a good feeling while it lasts; it's just like church. The thing is, they don't take it home. But it feels awfully good while people are doing it; and it proves human beings have the capacity for love."

However, he added, "I refuse to be optimistic about it. If it takes a pennant or a World Series to do it, God help us, we're that bad off. A pennant happens only every 23 years in Detroit."

For Al Kaline, it was his first pennant since he arrived in the Detroit clubhouse as an 18-year-old, having bypassed the minor leagues, so thin he was forced to borrow a batboy's uniform, so young that it fit him well. Toothy, with a wide boyish smile that he never really lost, Kaline had grown up in the industrial section of Baltimore. His father had worked in a broom factory, his mother at a distillery. From the time Kaline was 15, the Tigers scout Ed Katalinas — the same man who brought McLain on board — had watched him, waiting for the day he would graduate from high school. When he finally did in 1953, Katalinas quickly signed him.

"How can you avoid superlatives about a boy who at eighteen went direct from high school to the majors," a writer for the *Saturday Evening Post* wrote in 1955, "who won a regular job at nineteen, and who this year, at twenty, has jumped the upper brackets of the American League in every important phase of hitting?"

It all came too quickly. At age 20, he won the American League batting title — becoming the youngest player to do so. *The Sporting News* in 1957 printed a photo of him alongside Joe DiMaggio, implying that Kaline was the second coming. Kaline was going to have a golden future. And then he didn't. He played on mediocre, if not terrible teams. The injuries came early and often. He injured his knee, tore ligaments in his ankle, and shattered his cheekbone. He broke his collarbone and tore cartilage in his ribs. In 1967 he injured his hand, not by making a spectacular play, but by slamming his bat against the bat rack in frustration. Though Campbell denied ever seriously considering trading him, it's a fact that Kaline nearly ended up with the Minnesota Twins in a trade that would have brought Jim Kaat to Detroit.

"If I was the general manager I'd seriously think about trading Al Kaline this year," Kaline said before the 1967 season, "particularly if the ballclub is hurting for an infielder and relief pitching after spring training."

That never happened, but Kaline continued to suffer. In 1968, Oakland pitcher Lew Krausse struck him on the right forearm, fracturing the ulnar bone. He missed 60 games that season. Like Gibson in 1967,

Kaline watched his team win the pennant without him. He wanted to be out there, but there was nothing he could do. Jim Northrup had done a spectacular job filling in for him in right field. Yet Kaline still felt anxious, hoping to play at least some part in the World Series to come. He was getting older and didn't know if he'd ever have another chance.

Even so, just hours before the Tigers clinched the pennant, Kaline went to Smith and told him that Willie Horton and Mickey Stanley and Jim Northrup deserved to stay in their starting spots for the Series. He had waited all this time, but they had earned this. He had not. Kaline couldn't see how Smith could put any of the outfielders on the bench.

Smith, who knew what they would be up against facing Gibson, said perhaps Kaline could try his hand at third base. Instead, when Horton was injured late in the year, Kaline moved back to right field and started to hit again. This led Smith, never one for innovation, to make a decision that still seems absurd. Instead of putting Kaline at third, he decided to move his stellar center fielder Mickey Stanley to shortstop.

"What do you think?" Smith asked Kaline and some other veterans when he informed them of the move. They told him that Stanley was their best athlete and if anyone could do it, he could. Kaline felt that Smith, never known for daring or innovation, was making the most daring move a manager ever made.

Stanley started at shortstop in the final six games of the regular season and played with understandable shakiness. In his first game against Baltimore, he committed two errors, but followed with two terrific plays. He was nervous and, despite the spoken support of his teammates, felt as if he was messing with their World Series winnings. Yet when they returned home to Detroit, Stanley felt a shift in feelings among his teammates. Maybe he really could do the job, and do it well. Maybe this move really did give them the best chance against Gibson.

The Cardinals, who had won their second consecutive NL pennant that season, were watching these maneuvers from afar. They were heavy favorites, in spite of their hitting. And the Tigers' 11th-hour shake-up smelled like desperation. They were so terrified of Gibson, it seemed, that they were willing to try anything in order to score runs.

All of the Tigers' adjustments would now be tested. The matchup between Gibson and McLain, spoken about since midseason, was fi-

nally here. In this World Series between two Rust Belt cities set along
the water—the last before the advent of the Eastern and Western Divisions and play-offs—the country would learn much about risk and
consequences, about falling down, about patriotism, and about how
much celebrity yearnings could carry a person when seen by millions.
And one team would understand what it meant to stare straight into the
darkened, withering face of a living god.

17

TROUBLE

IN ITS OCTOBER 14, 1968, issue, *Newsweek* reprinted a cartoon from *The New Yorker* that had appeared the year before. Drawn by William Hamilton, it shows a father, balding and slightly stooped, with a baseball and glove in his hands and a look of entreaty on his face. His grown son stands before him in a sport coat, his hands shoved into his pockets, his hair shaggy and unkempt. His body language and expression are scornful and condescending.

"No, Dad," the son says derisively in the caption, "I *don't* want to go out and toss the old pill around."

It's a heartbreaking little scene. The father is so earnest in his short-sleeve Oxford, and no doubt bewildered by his son's indifference. Is this the same kid who was always eager to play catch? The son sees the ball and glove as emblems of the past; they hold no interest for him.

This cartoon appeared on the same page as a column written by Pete Axthelm and entitled "The Great National Bore." It was a broad indictment of baseball and its anachronistic ways. Axthelm decried the game's movement away from urban (read: black) neighborhoods. He called out Commissioner William Eckert as a "bumbling," overwhelmed figurehead who was incapable of leading baseball into the future. Axthelm argued that, though baseball's leadership refused to believe it, other sports were increasingly capturing the attention of the American public. The problem, he wrote, was that the game had locked out the very men who could bring innovation to the game, freethinkers like Bill Veeck and Lakers owner Jack Kent Cooke.

Axthelm wrote that baseball's problem was "that it is the national pastime, while football and basketball can lay more legitimate claims to be national *sports*. And in America in 1968, how many people are still seeking slow-paced, relatively undemanding ways to merely pass the time?"

Baseball, he said, was "out of step with modern living. Most potential sports fans now live in an urban, well-educated society; for better or for worse, they demand fast action, some mental challenges and a measure of violence in sports entertainment. Football, basketball and hockey provide these elements, while baseball crawls along at its dreary pace."

Axthelm wasn't alone in his beliefs. More and more, others were coming to the same conclusion — that baseball was limping along toward its own demise. In a piece called "Will Baseball Have a Future?" journalist Bill Furlong pointed out that per-game attendance had fallen 13.5 percent in 1968. And he served up a damning critique of baseball's place in modern America: "For suddenly — in the 1960s — social cachet meant nothing. Gentility meant nothing. The values of the past meant nothing. All that mattered was violence. And reality. And the struggle of the individual against his environment — in most cases, against the smothering intentions of The Establishment. So baseball committed the cardinal sin — it became irrelevant."

Still others believed that baseball's problem was not systemic but rather had to do with the play itself. Those like Johnny Sain, who thought nothing was more thrilling than a 1–0 contest, were in the minority. Most writers and fans yearned for the kind of explosive offense associated with the days of Babe Ruth. Different ideas were floated for counteracting pitcher dominance. Dick Young suggested expanding the distance between the mound and the plate to 65 feet. Players from Henry Aaron to Rod Carew to Pete Rose made suggestions ranging from lowering the mound and shrinking the strike zone to limiting the number of pitchers a club could carry.

And then there was Bill Veeck, the legendary promoter and innovator. In a 1951 publicity stunt meant to boost attendance for his American League ball club in St. Louis, Veeck had signed a little person to bat in a major league game. As the owner of the Cleveland Indians, Veeck began the first steps toward the integration of the American League by signing Larry Doby in 1947. He set the skies of Chicago's South Side ablaze with fireworks shooting from his scoreboard with every White Sox home run. And it had been Veeck who pushed to plant ivy on the outfield walls of Wrigley Field.

Of course Veeck had something to say about the state of baseball in 1968. On the one hand, he predicted that baseball would just "gradually disappear" one day. But he also had some suggestions for bringing the game up to date in the short term. He said that baseball had to cut the cord of its hazy connections to the past. In most years, he argued, the World Series wasn't even a contest between the two best teams. It pitted against each other the two best teams from two separate associations that had been set up in another era. In addition to reducing the schedule to 142 games, Veeck suggested totally restructuring the two leagues based on geography in order to reduce player fatigue and making what he called the "Pay TV" model a priority.

William Eckert was certainly not the man to lead the charge into the next decade. At a time when baseball needed an autonomous, forward-thinking leader, someone with a vision for how to package the game for television and stay relevant, it was stuck with a commissioner who was ignorant of the importance of the medium and often beholden to the wishes of nearsighted owners.

Following the 1968 season, certain changes were eventually instituted. The height of the mound was lowered from 15 inches to 10 inches and standardized across the major leagues. The strike zone was reduced. After much consternation, both the National and American Leagues agreed to expand by two teams each (news of a Montreal franchise led several U.S. congressmen to condemn the move in the House of Representatives) and to adopt a new divisional play-off system that would create four pennant races instead of the old two.

It wasn't easy to get to this point. By the middle of the summer, American League owners had embraced the idea of a divisional system, but the National League believed that they could continue to operate as before. National League owners planned to go forward with their own expansion plans with one pennant winner. Of all people, it was John Fetzer —the man who seemed to show so little interest in the daily operations of his own club—who understood how impractical this was.

Fetzer argued that baseball should act as one corporation, with two divisions. Rather than having the American and National Leagues at odds with each other, the governing forces could act as a group. A partnership, he believed, would benefit them far more than rival, competing forces.

Moreover, the Tigers owner believed that divisional play would be a step forward, especially in light of expansion. Otherwise, as he pointed out, the fans wouldn't have the slightest interest in any teams besides the top three or four and the rest of the teams, with no pennant or World Series prospects, would simply slog through their seasons. It simply didn't seem fair, he said, to ask "ownership in 12 cities to put up millions of dollars and not be able to salvage something out of baseball other than one winning a pennant."

Fetzer also understood better than most of his peers that baseball was losing the demographic battle. If the sport was going to survive, it needed to embrace change. "If we refuse to make our game attractive to the young people of this country, baseball is going to be a dying sport," Fetzer said. "There are nearly 200 million people in this nation, and half are 25 or younger. When you get statistics that indicate the older you are, the more you enjoy baseball . . . well, there's a message we had better not ignore."

The way forward was anything but clear. But as someone who had amassed his fortune through broadcasting, Fetzer knew how important television would be. In the early 1960s, he'd proposed a prime-time weekly baseball telecast, not unlike the spectacle the NFL would eventually put on the air in 1970 with *Monday Night Football*. He wanted a weekly event that went beyond the Saturday afternoon *Game of the Week*. Baseball, he believed, had the potential to greatly expand its reach, even as football was expanding its domain.

There was a time when NFL commissioner Pete Rozelle would open a bottle of champagne the day after the conclusion of the World Series to mark the moment when America's pastime had ended and his season could truly begin. Yet at the conclusion of the 1967 Super Bowl, no one could deny that a great change was underfoot. Rozelle's National Football League and its rival, the American Football League of Al Davis and Joe Namath and Hank Stram, had grasped how to use television to grow their sport. As the two leagues prepared to merge, football would set the course that all sports would follow. In 1970, more Americans watched the Super Bowl than had seen Neil Armstrong walk on the moon.

Even a young Gerald Early, who would go on to be one of the main voices in Ken Burns's exhaustive documentary on baseball, felt that football was simply more exciting, more modern. He saw it working better on television. It had more drama — though the game seemed counterintuitive for the times. At the very same moment when the country had turned against a real war, it had fallen in love with brutish combat and on-field fighting.

Early, for his part, liked when things didn't work in football. The busted plays. The missed blocking assignments. And the desperate need to come up with something, anything, at a moment's notice once all the regimentation and planning that went into just one play came undone gave the sport, he felt, an improvisational quality that baseball could never match — at least not on TV.

Nor did baseball have — despite the brilliance of Bob Gibson's slider and Denny McLain's showboating — players like handsome, smooth-talking Joe Namath, whose celebrity transcended football. An effortless showman, Namath had appeared on the cover of *Sports Illustrated*, the lights of Broadway behind him, before he'd even played a single game. Those lights would stay on him from then on.

It would all come together for football in early 1969 when Namath, having led his team to the AFL championship, squared off against the Baltimore Colts in Super Bowl III. The heavily favored Baltimore team found themselves outplayed in dramatic fashion by the Jets. Though that game was played in 1969, Early considered it one of the great cultural turning points of 1968. For a certain generation, Early felt, watching that game would change everything.

NBC — the same network that muddled through its baseball telecasts, which were filled with dead air — somehow knew what to do with the game of football. It was television at its best. The shots of the Jets shifting formations. New York coach Weeb Eubank on the sidelines wearing a suit and white socks. The cameras cutting to close-ups of players' faces. Matt Snell running for a first down and taking oxygen on the sidelines. Namath releasing, then watching the flight of the ball. The players walking back to the huddle, the linemen with their hands on their hips. It made you feel like more than just a spectator — it made you feel like you were part of the game. And TV made it possible.

How could baseball compete? In a bound brochure sent out to advertisers before the start of the 1969 season, NBC declared that the coming year was shaping up to be a "real winner for Major League Baseball": it was going to be a "Year of Innovations." There were new managers with new teams and new markets. But first, there was one last World Series to play between the winners of the final true pennant, one last championship round between the very best of the American and National Leagues. One last October.

18

SEVENTEEN

H ERE THEY WERE. It was 10:17 in the morning on October 1, the day before the World Series was to start in St. Louis, and Denny McLain and Bob Gibson stood in front of the Cardinals dugout at Busch Stadium, shaking hands and exchanging pleasantries. McLain had walked through the tunnel, up the steps of the visiting dugout, and across the field, journalists close on his heels. This was it, the moment the press had been anticipating since midseason.

Bob Gibson waited for him inside the first-base dugout.

"I'm Denny McLain," Denny said. "It's a pleasure to meet you."

"Thanks," Gibson replied. "I'm Bob Gibson."

After they shook hands, McLain told him, "I've heard a lot about you. I read your book. It's very good."

Almost immediately, members of a television crew — presumably NBC, the network broadcasting the games — put a microphone around McLain's neck asking him to test it out.

"One-two-three-four," McLain said.

Feeling unusually playful — especially around an opponent — Gibson jumped in and said, "Five-six-seven-eight."

Then the producer asked McLain to say something else. Rarely at a loss for words, McLain asked what he should talk about. Gibson smirked. He could say anything, replied the producer. Denny only had to say it "just a little louder."

"One-two-three-four," McLain repeated, and Gibson followed suit once more with, "Five-six-seven-eight."

It was a rare light moment that season. Sandy Koufax, who was a network broadcaster that day, asked Gibson, "A lot has been made of this meeting. Tell me, is this a grudge match between you guys?"

"No," Gibson said. "It's not a grudge match. This is the first time I've ever met Denny. I don't know anything about him. He's a nice guy."

McLain gamely agreed, but of course he'd made earlier comments that suggested otherwise. In Baltimore, on the day he failed to win his 32nd game of the season (only his second loss on the road), he said he finally had heard enough about St. Louis, about their talent and dominant pitching, about how they would roll over the Tigers in the Series.

"If somebody tells me about how great they are, I'll be sick," he said. "I'm just sick of hearing about how we don't belong on the same field with them. It's one thing to go into the World Series as the underdog and another thing to be ridiculed. Listen, I don't just want to beat those guys, I want to demolish them.

"I don't see how pitching in St. Louis gives such a big advantage to Bob Gibson," McLain continued. "Look, I'm 17-1 on the road. And when I give up a home run, it goes out on the power alley, not down the foul line. Busch Stadium is just the kind of park I like to pitch in." (McLain actually lost two games away from home.)

McLain's comments were not a secret to Gibson. As soon as he made them, they were tacked to a bulletin board in the Cardinals' locker room. Gibson, for his part, had two totems: a taped sign above his locker proclaiming, I'M NOT PREJUDICED, I HATE EVERYBODY, and a stuffed tiger attached with its own message: A TIGER'S A 500-POUND PUSSY.

For all their competitive zeal, the two had grown wary of talking publicly about their matchup. But it was all the press could talk about. It was an irresistible story. You could argue that Luis Tiant had a better season than McLain, but unfortunately played for a terrible team. Or that Mickey Lolich, once he returned to his rightful place in the rotation, had pitched better than McLain in the last weeks of the season. But the front pages had gone to press. The 31-game winner versus the man with the 1.12 ERA. One black. One white. This was the story.

Of the millions looking forward to McLain versus Gibson, those in the know favored Gibson from the start. Holding court at the Chase-Plaza Hotel before the Series, Dizzy Dean said that Detroit's right-handed power hitters, specifically Willie Horton, would have a terrible time with Gibson. Bob Feller shared this sentiment. Koufax thought Gibson would eat McLain alive.

Roger Maris warned his teammates, especially the left-handed hitters, that they would have the most trouble against Lolich — who had been ignored by the national press all year long as McLain basked in the spotlight. Dean felt the same way, as did former Cardinal Ken Boyer, who thought Lolich was better suited to go up against the Cardinals' ace. Another warning came from Astros executive John Mullen: the Cardinals, he said, would have to "wake up to beat this Detroit club. They're going to have to do a lot of things right."

In the days leading up to the Series, Johnny Sain looked at the match-ups and compared them to the 1966 World Series, when the Orioles swept the Dodgers. Like the Tigers, Baltimore featured terrific young pitchers — namely Jim Palmer and Dave McNally. Since July, the entire Tigers staff had an ERA of 2.70. The Cardinals hitters didn't scare Sain. He was sure that his young pitchers — his trio of McLain, Lolich, and Earl Wilson — could take them.

For months now, McLain had lived large, pitched on no sleep, done whatever he wanted. The Series didn't change that. Hours after his meeting with Gibson, one could see McLain playing the organ at the Gashouse Lounge of the Sheraton-Jefferson Hotel on the eve of the Series. He'd come into the bar with his teammates and their wives, and when someone recognized him, he was talked into playing a few numbers. He pounded out "Money Is the Name," "Laura," "One of These Days," and "Restless Wind." At one point, center fielder Jim Northrup stood up, making up words to accompany a ballad, and then announced, "We're even going to play a few tunes for Bob Gibson."

The revelry would continue late into the evening and then repeat itself the following night. Roger Angell, *The New Yorker*'s baseball correspondent, was there, sitting at a table with Sharyn McLain and her parents, Lou and Della Boudreau. It was an awkward spot to be in, watching the couple's son-in-law act so irresponsibly the night before a game in which millions of people expected him to perform at his best. Finally, five minutes before midnight, McLain told the crowd it was time to leave.

"I might not beat Gibson tomorrow," McLain said, "but I sure as hell can beat him playing the organ."

None of this sat well with many in the organization, including Tigers broadcaster Ray Lane. This was McLain telling them that he'd won 31 games and he could do whatever he wished. Perhaps, Lane felt, this was how McLain stayed loose, but still, for Lane, as for many others, it was all too public.

McLain didn't see the harm. They were all out with their wives. They were having a good time, and they would play baseball the following day.

"How much better can life get?" he asked himself.

Larry Osterman felt a sharp shiver when he heard it. He wasn't on air that day, but he and his wife had gone to St. Louis to watch the first two games of the Series and were sitting with members of the Tigers' front office. When Bob Gibson, who had been warming up in the right-field bullpen, finally walked out onto the infield, the cheering from the crowd of over 54,000 was like nothing Osterman had ever heard before. It was electric and worshipful. Here was the second coming.

Gibson hadn't bothered reading the scouting report on the Tigers, so confident was he in his pitching. The Tigers had read up on Gibson, though, and understood that in order to hit him, they would have to be aggressive and chase his fastball, no matter the speed. What the reports couldn't tell them, however, was just how effective his slider was—or how he would use his curveball, despite disparaging it, in critical spots, leaving the entire Tigers' lineup at a loss.

Predictably, things got off to a rough start for the Tigers. Their first batter was Dick McAuliffe. Even with his bat tilted at a 45-degree angle and his body nearly perpendicular to Gibson, he couldn't handle Gibson's fastball on the inside corner. He swung and missed. Two batters later, Al Kaline found himself lunging at a slider near the center of the plate for his third strike.

The next inning, Gibson began working on Norm Cash — a pull hitter and the only Tigers starter with actual World Series experience — by throwing pitches out of the strike zone, all of them low, before striking him out on a high fastball. He teased Willie Horton, throwing him a breaking ball for a strike, followed by another, before striking him out with a curveball that dropped in the traditional 12-6 motion. He struck out Jim Northrup with his secondary slider, which broke over the plate. In two innings, Gibson had struck out five of the six men he faced.

Watching from the dugout, Johnny Sain was confused. Was Gibson throwing a curveball or a slider? The two pitches seemed indistinguishable to him. All he knew was that he was watching a master at work. Dick Tracewski would later describe Gibson's breaking pitch as a "swerve," a combination of a curveball and a slider that Gibson delivered with the same sort of movement as his fastball, and with just as much speed.

No one understood Gibson's mechanics better than Gibson himself. Following the game, he said that 20 percent of the breaking pitches he threw were sliders and another 10 percent were curves. McCarver believed that four of the five Tiger hits came off Gibson's sliders, and only one came off a fastball. And despite Gibson's performance, the catcher believed that he had seen his friend — without the world watching — pitch better.

Kaline's at-bat in the fourth was more of the same. Gibson began with four straight breaking pitches, then followed with three fastballs. With the count even, Gibson let a fastball slip off his fingertips so that it went straight over Kaline's head, forcing him to the ground. Upright once more, Kaline struck out looking as the pitch hit the outside corner — the eighth strikeout of the game.

The only hint of trouble for Gibson came in the sixth inning. With one out, McAuliffe had singled off Gibson's first pitch, a fastball. After Gibson struck out Mickey Stanley, Kaline doubled off another slider. When McCarver came to the mound, Gibson asked who was the next batter after Norm Cash, who was coming up. McCarver told him it didn't matter, and he was right. Cash, who admitted that his teammates were perhaps trying to overpower Gibson, struck out on a pitch high and away. No Cardinal infielder had to make a play on a ball hit to him in the whole game. Not one.

Before the game, Eugene McCarthy, the man whose success in the Democratic primary in New Hampshire had forced a sitting president to forgo seeking reelection, predicted that the contest between Gibson and McLain "could be like the general election. They might go on and on to no decision and the result would have to be decided by the House of Representatives."

McCarthy had stuffed his campaign speeches with sports analogies, but his quest for the presidency was over. He was in St. Louis on assignment as a special correspondent covering the Series for *Life* magazine, along with longtime *Life* writer Loudon Wainwright. A fine baseball and hockey player in his day, McCarthy let Wainwright keep score as he quietly looked on. Nearby, David Eisenhower, sitting with his wife-to-be Julie Nixon, was screaming for the Tigers to do something, anything. Frank Sinatra, wearing a suit and tie, told NBC's Tony Kubek that he expected the Cardinals to win the Series in five.

Angell, for his part, couldn't take his eyes off Gibson. Here was a pitcher who was both impressive and frightening, someone who looked as if he were pitching from 55 inches away. Sitting with the St. Louis fans, the *Detroit Free Press* columnist Bob Talbert predicted that the Cardinals would most definitely take the Series in four. The fans around him began talking about how many more championships they would win after this one, because it was apparent that this Series was over.

McLain was understandably tired, and not only from the night before. He had pitched on three games' rest for most of the season, led the league in starts with 41—completing 28 of them—and thrown 336 innings. The pain in his arm was constant and unbearable. He would need another cortisone shot and take greenies to begin the game, and by the third inning he was visibly suffering. Examining the faces of the two men, Harry Caray—the St. Louis announcer calling the contest with NBC's Curt Gowdy—said that Gibson looked like a young 32, while McLain's pained expression gave him the appearance of an old 24.

Before the start of the Series, there had been a question of whether a National League home plate umpire—in this case, Tom Gorman— would permit McLain the high strike, which was more commonly called in the American League. From the start, though, the Cardinals hitters had made up their minds to stay away from his rising fastball and see what happened. When one Tigers pitcher complained that McLain had gotten that call all season, Cardinals manager Red Schoendienst countered that McLain's high pitches in this game weren't a strike in any league, much less the majors.

McLain could sense something was wrong even while warming up in the bullpen. But he was confident that once the game began, he'd regain his form. Nothing had gone wrong for him all season, no matter what he did. He could handle this.

But while Gibson showed unworldly control, McLain struggled. When he tried to locate the ball up and away from hitters, it would come in high and close to them. When he tried the opposite, the ball would drop down on him. Although he fell behind early in his counts in the first two innings, he pitched like the crafty burglar Tommy John believed him to be. And for two innings, it looked like he might pull it out. In the first inning, he hung a curveball to Roger Maris, who hit it hard to right field. It was a moment reminiscent of Maris's record-breaking home run in 1961 — but this time it didn't go over the outfield wall. This time Kaline caught it. The next inning, McLain again hung a curveball, this one to McCarver on the very first pitch, allowing McCarver to sprint all the way to third with only one man out. By now McLain was working out his right arm, trying to loosen it. With the first run standing on third, McLain fell behind 2-0 with the next two batters, but each time he recovered. He forced Mike Shannon to swing on a high fastball for a third strike, and then, after throwing a number of high fastballs to shortstop Julián Javier, he froze him with a curveball for strike three. Maybe McLain *had* worked things out.

In the fourth, however, the Cardinals' plan fell into place. McLain walked Roger Maris on four straight pitches, then threw two more balls to Orlando Cepeda before recording his first strike of the inning. Again it appeared that McLain would get out of trouble. He threw Cepeda nothing but fastballs, reached a full count, and then forced the 1967 MVP to pop up. Then came McCarver, who walked after McLain again threw four straight pitches out of the strike zone, all of them high. With two men on base, Shannon didn't strike out but instead singled on a 2-2 count, and Willie Horton fumbled the ball, allowing one man to score and the two trailing him to reach scoring position. Javier, who was up next, didn't work the count with McLain, but brought in the third run of the inning on the first pitch he saw. It was a slider, which McLain didn't want to throw, but he needed a strike. Javier was waiting for it.

McLain was finished, pulled for a pinch hitter after pitching a scoreless fifth. And he was mad. He had allowed only three hits, and Horton's error had cost him dearly. Smith, he felt, had given up on him far too early, even though it was evident to everyone that he couldn't go on much longer. The Tigers were desperate now, down three runs and with little chance of coming back.

After the game, McLain sat in the locker room, his hat hanging off the top of his head. No, he didn't have any issues with the National League strike zone. Yes, he was stunned when he was pulled from the game. He admitted to having terrible control, but he still felt hurt over being pulled. Asked if his next meeting with Gibson in Game 4 would be any different, McLain said, "Yeah. I'm going to win."

But McLain wasn't the story that afternoon. Detroit relief pitcher Jon Warden swore he could hear it even from the bullpen — that terrifying pop of the ball slamming against McCarver's glove. Though Gibson had relied heavily on his breaking ball that day — the slider, the curve, the "swerve" — he threw it with the same force as his fastball and was capable of placing it where it was unhittable.

Walking back out to the mound in the ninth inning, Gibson had no idea he was one strikeout away from tying Sandy Koufax's World Series strikeout record of 15. By then, Lou Brock had extended the Cardinals lead to 4–0 with a home run against reliever Pat Dobson. Gibson just wanted to finish the game, shut out the Tigers, and exit the field.

With one man on, Kaline — the man Smith had gambled on for more offense — had a chance to make something happen. This time Gibson threw according to the scouting report — beginning with a fastball, then following through by throwing Kaline one breaking pitch after another. Kaline did his best, but finally he struck out like everyone else — the 15th of the afternoon. Walking back to the dugout, Kaline, his back to Gibson, heard the roar of the crowd and knew those cheers were not meant for him. McCarver, peering at the giant scoreboard announcing Gibson's feat, didn't know if he should tell Gibson what was happening. Would he want to know?

Gibson, who was accustomed to pitching quickly, grew angry. They were two outs away, and McCarver wouldn't return to his crouch behind the plate. He called for McCarver to throw the ball back to him so they could finish the game, but McCarver just pointed to the outfield, to the scoreboard that told everyone that Gibson's 15 strikeouts had matched Koufax. Gibson looked back for a moment and then got the ball from McCarver.

Norm Cash was next. He'd struck out twice in his previous at-bats, but this time he was determined to stay with Gibson. He fouled off a series of pitches before, alas, succumbing once again — to a slider on the inside part of the plate. Today it didn't matter where Gibson placed the ball. Cash swung and missed for strikeout number 16.

Again, Gibson glanced back at the scoreboard and then called for the ball. Before the game, he'd been asked how he felt about a student demonstration by members of the Students for a Democratic Society, and he had said he didn't give a fuck. He had a ball game to pitch. Now it was time to finish it.

One of the best power hitters in the American League in 1968, Willie Horton quickly found himself down by two strikes. In his final pitch to Horton, Gibson again threw a slider on the inside corner, though McCarver had positioned himself on the outside part of the plate. Horton thought it was a ball, but he couldn't have reached it anyway. History would remember Horton flinching, and McCarver would say he heard him grunt — something Horton would deny. Regardless, when Tom Gorman signaled a third strike, the game was mercifully over. Watching from the on-deck circle, Jim Northrup felt relieved. *Better you than me*, he thought.

Afterwards, Eddie Matthews tried to steady a demoralized bunch. It was just another game, he told them. It wasn't their fault — Gibson would have beaten anybody that afternoon. But now they knew how he pitched and what he might throw. They were professionals and had to make adjustments.

Publicly, though, the Tigers didn't disguise their awe. Cash compared Gibson to Superman. Kaline surmised that Gibson might pitch even better in the shadows cast by Tiger Stadium in Game 4. Angell, for his part, was taken aback by how little pleasure Gibson seemed to derive from it all. There didn't seem to be a palpable lightening of his mood or a let-up in his intensity. When he responded to a reporter's question about his performance that day by flatly declaring, "I'm never surprised by anything I do," Roger Angell felt an unusual unease seep across the room. Angell, just beginning his life as the game's great literary luminary, had never heard black players speak the way Gibson did. Gibson, he could see now, was his own man.

Meanwhile, Phil Pepe, who was between newspaper jobs at the time, had agreed to write a column about the Series in Gibson's name that would appear in the *Daily News* in New York, as well as in papers in St. Louis, Detroit, Omaha, and Philadelphia. Before the other reporters showed up in the clubhouse after the game, Gibson told Pepe, "I've got something I'm not gonna give them. I'll save it for us."

There was only one thing to save. Gibson had withheld from the other sportswriters the fact that he'd received a phone call from the vice president, Democratic presidential candidate Hubert Humphrey, McCarthy's once-rival. Humphrey had watched the game on television and then called to congratulate Gibson, telling him, "I'm with you all the way."

Pepe wrote up the column, which landed on the front page of the *Daily News* with the bold-faced headline: "Bob Fans 17, Blanks Tigers: The Day I Broke Koufax's Record." Gibson's image, glower and all, was splashed across the page. Pepe felt that the column resuscitated his career. He would work for the *Daily News* for nearly 20 years.

Pepe believed that, with this game, Gibson had finally found the respect that had eluded him nationally all season. He could see that Gibson felt he deserved as much as McLain, if not more, for what he'd done all season — *Today Show* or not. Again, it was an issue of pride — not that Gibson said that out loud. But he'd gotten to face the kid who won 31 games, and he'd won with ease.

That evening Denny was back doing what Denny always did — sitting in the same hotel lounge where he'd played the organ the night before, responding to the tug of a packed room, one that wanted him to repeat his performance on the organ. In truth, he hadn't pitched badly. He just hadn't been Gibson. And he hadn't been McLain either. He'd been average.

"Mr. Gibson was super today," McLain said when the audience asked him to sing. "I don't even feel bad about getting beat. He pitched one helluva ball game. I can't sing and I don't pitch too well, either."

He didn't believe that, of course. But the rest of the country thought this was it — the Tigers had been exposed and were likely to fall in five games, if not four. A Cardinals repeat seemed inevitable.

This opinion was also held by Gerald Early, who would later settle in St. Louis but at this moment was just a young man watching on television. Kaline. Horton. Cash. Who cared? They all seemed helpless against the Cardinals, and more important, against Gibson. Little did he know.

19

MUDDERS

B EFORE THE FOURTH GAME of the World Series, Jackie Robinson boarded a jet in Washington, D.C., with his political ally Hubert H. Humphrey. Robinson's faith in himself had been badly shaken that year, but he had forced himself into the fray once more. Richard Nixon, his onetime friend, seemed ready to take the presidency. And damn if he wasn't going to do everything he could to stop him.

Headed to a baseball game in which he had no rooting interest, Robinson sounded off to reporters about a Republican plan he'd gotten wind of to sabotage the results of the coming election. Whether he'd previously cleared his remarks with Humphrey was uncertain. Robinson claimed to have knowledge of a GOP plan to dispatch armed "militants" to the Negro ghettos, where they would go door to door dissuading residents from stepping behind a voting curtain in November. This intelligence purportedly came from a friend who had attended a strategy session of Republican leaders in New York. The idea, according to the friend, was to sequester blacks in their homes, preventing them from having a say in what happened in the last general election of the 1960s.

Robinson was angry. In desperation, he had reached out to his former employer, Nelson Rockefeller. This supposed plan to suppress the vote ran counter to everything they had fought for; it was not worthy of the Republican Party they believed in. Robinson was upset with Rockefeller for giving up the fight, for abandoning the party's founding ideals and embracing segregationists. He told Rockefeller he was sharing the "same bed" with Nixon and Strom Thurmond, along with the old South. He felt the same way about New York mayor John Lindsay and Senator Jacob Javits, both liberal Republicans. And he scolded the young Michigan congressman John Conyers, who wasn't doing enough, Robinson felt, to help Humphrey as Wallace's and Nixon's popularity surged in his state. "John," he said, "ought to know what's happening."

Baseball hadn't been part of Robinson's life for several years now, but Humphrey felt that he needed Robinson there beside him. So Robinson obliged. If he could do or say anything to change the course of the race, he'd do it—even if it meant going to a baseball game. With the pain in his legs, he could no longer sit as he once had. Rachel could see that he no longer enjoyed the game that owed him everything. But there was something bigger at stake: it was up to him, he felt, to stop a Nixon presidency.

Two more games had been played since Humphrey called up Bob Gibson to congratulate him after he'd struck out Willie Horton in Game 1. In the Series' second game, the Tigers' bats, previously muzzled by Gibson, started hitting again against a helpless Nelson Briles and three relievers (including a young Steve Carlton), winning 8–1. Their starter, Mickey Lolich, proved himself the pitcher Maris and Dean and Boyer had warned the Cardinals about, pitching a complete game while allowing a single run in the sixth. He also hit a 360-foot home run, the first of his career.

But whatever lessons the Tigers took away from their win seemed to leave them once the teams returned for their three games in Detroit. Tim McCarver and Orlando Cepeda each hit home runs in Game 3 as the Tigers cycled through five different pitchers in a 7–3 defeat. Afterwards, a dejected Al Kaline, who was having a fine Series and homered in the game, said, "I think we're in bad shape if we lose Sunday's game. We've got to think we can beat Gibson."

In one cartoon printed in the *Detroit Free Press,* Gibson is shown in full Superman costume, much as McLain had been, and a St. Louis ball cap, standing with his hands on his hips and gazing calmly into the distance. The caption reads, "Let's hope that the phone booths around Tiger Stadium are too crowded to be used as a dressing room for the mild mannered." Beside him is a miniature tiger, tugging at his costume and pleading, "OK Gibson, come off it, give Denny back his uniform!" Heroic imagery aside, the hope remained that Game 4 would be a kind of do-over — that this time McLain and Gibson would be more evenly matched, as once predicted, that the game would be breathtakingly close, decided by a single run.

Desperate to alleviate the pain in his arm, McLain had been taking "X-ray" treatments in addition to the cortisone shots, but everything proved ineffective. Going into this fourth game, with his team down two games to one, he would have to do his best to get through it and hope that his teammates would give him a lead to hold on to.

"If you get to Gibson you'll break their spirit," Willie Horton said before Game 4. "Everywhere you went in St. Louis, all you heard is Gibson, Gibson, Gibson. Like there's nobody else on the team. I think that if we can beat him once — even if it's a 1–0 game — that we can knock them off. Just beat him any way we can. I don't even want to talk about what happened the first time we saw him. I know I was nervous waiting to go up the first time in that game. Maybe it will be different this time."

Desperation had sunk in. With over 28 million homes tuning in, rain had forced a 37-minute weather delay before the game even began. This still was the World Series, still the pinnacle of American sports, and there was no way anyone would call the game and prevent the second attempt at a Gibson-McLain duel from taking place.

Finally, the game started, even as it kept raining. Perhaps the umpires should have just called it after McLain threw his second pitch in the top of the first. This was his rising fastball, the one the Cardinals had avoided when they faced him the first time, but now Lou Brock swung at it, sending the ball into the bleachers for a home run. Then, with no one on and a slow roller hit by Maris, McLain, the best-fielding pitcher on the team, dropped the ball while trying to cover first base.

Tigers broadcaster George Kell, who'd watched McLain all season, remarked that Denny wasn't throwing as hard as he was capable of. He couldn't. All year he'd thrown his curveball and fastball from a three-quarter-sidearm position while ahead in the count. It was his out pitch. But now he was doing it early and often. He allowed McCarver to single, and when he did throw a sidearm pitch that Mike Shannon hit meekly into the infield, Mickey Stanley cut in front of the second baseman to get it, but his throw wasn't in time. That play allowed McCarver to score, and by the end of the inning McLain and the Tigers were already behind by two runs.

As it began to rain harder, McLain decided to throw nothing but off-speed pitches. He seemed desperate. In the third inning, Curt Flood swung at the first pitch, a curve sailing away from him that he hit into center field for a single. With one out and the rain coming down harder than it had all day, McCarver also swung at the first pitch — launching it between center fielder Jim Northrup and left fielder Willie Horton. When Horton fumbled the ball on the warning track, Flood had already scored and McCarver had his second triple of the Series. The spectators in the stands had their umbrellas open. Mike Shannon then doubled, driving in McCarver for the fourth run of the game.

Finally, Mayo Smith came out to speak to his pitcher. The skies had grown ominous, and the rain now pounded the field. Smith, McLain, and catcher Bill Freehan stood there for a long time, trying to decide what to do. Though McLain recorded another out, it was becoming impossible to play. After McLain walked Javier — the last batter he faced — in the third, all six members of the umpire crew sprinted onto the field to consult with each other. They then ordered another delay. This one would go on for 74 minutes. The game would continue, but McLain was done. He told Smith he wanted to be pulled. His right shoulder felt terrible.

McLain had never been a mudder. But his arm had felt terrible even before the first pitch. He did what he had to do, believing that you had to take your turn and if "you get the shit kicked out of you, you get the shit kicked out of you."

Probably the game should have been called at that point. It was clear that was what the umpires wanted to do. Arguably, play shouldn't have even been started, given the forecast that afternoon. But Commissioner Eckert, consistent with his track record of poor decision-making, took the matter into his own hands and insisted that the game go forward.

Bob Hope quipped in his monologue after the Series, "I didn't realize how hard it was raining until I noticed Flipper playing shortstop." *Zing!* And "the only guy who felt at home was Curt Flood."

Meanwhile, during the rain delay, Gibson continued to brood, eating ice cream, waiting to pitch again and get this damn thing over with. The night before, he'd been pranked in his hotel room. Someone claimed to have a telegram for him, and people were giggling and banging on his door for half an hour. Later he got a phone call asking for Denny McLain. They were trying to rattle him. But when had Bob Gibson ever been rattled?

Gibson wasn't the pitcher he'd been in Game 1. That was clear. In the second inning, with one out, he actually allowed two runners to reach base — walking Horton on four straight pitches and giving up a line drive to right field to an aging Eddie Matthews. But he struck out Bill Freehan, who fouled off pitch after pitch before Gibson caught him looking with a fastball. And then he retired McLain — the Tigers' last hope to score — on a foul ball that Cepeda leaped up to catch. It was over.

When play finally resumed, it resembled less a baseball game than a Marx Brothers romp. One team, determined not to get to the fifth inning — at which point the game would be considered official — was trying to stall, while the other was trying to hurry things along so they could lock in a 3–1 advantage. Twice the Cardinals ran to get themselves tagged out. The weak-kneed Orlando Cepeda tried to steal to end the fourth inning, and then in the fifth Julián Javier began a halfhearted dash for second while the pitcher still held the ball in his hand. All the while, the Cardinals continued to add on. Leading off the fourth, Gibson hit a home run off a hanging curveball to deep center field, and Brock followed with a triple, scoring on a Maris groundout. By the end of the fourth, the Cardinals led 6–0.

The Tigers fans prayed for a rainout as the players dawdled and tried to delay play. During the fourth, Norm Cash, who was playing first base, walked to the mound to "chat" with his pitcher, Daryl Patterson, when he had nothing to tell him. When Gibson took the mound in the bottom of the inning, the sky was black. Willie Horton, who wasn't shy about taking his time at the plate under normal circumstances, was absorbed in knocking the mud from his spikes. He stepped out of the batter's box several times, ran to the dugout to look for a towel, stomped loudly on the dugout steps trying to clean those shoes. Gibson turned away, his hands on his hips. He was about to blow his top. But the dismal conditions would get to him too. The grounds crew had covered the mound with sand, but Gibson would struggle with footing — seeming to slip off the mound at times. You could see his breath as the temperature began to drop. In later innings, Gibson himself began to stomp the ground, trying to get the muck off his cleats.

But even in these conditions, Gibson was still Gibson. After the rain delay, he'd somehow found a way to loosen up his arm and throw his seventh straight complete World Series game, striking out ten batters. Bob Hope would joke that "you have to hand it to Gibson — it's not easy to strike out ten men while treading water." Gibson's pitching coach, Billy Muffett, marveled, "It's unbelievable that a guy can pitch so hard four hours after he first warms up. That showed his stamina and desire at their best."

The accolades piled up. Yet despite Gibson's authoritative performance, it was Brock whom everyone was talking about. It was Brock who'd led off Game 4 with the home run, galvanizing the Cardinals, and who'd contributed a double and a triple in the first four games of the Series. It was Brock who'd irked more than one Tigers player in Game 2 when he stole a base — twice — when his team was down five runs. Now, with the Cardinals leading by nine runs in Game 4, it was Brock, standing on second base after having doubled, who understood that one more steal — his seventh — would match two separate World Series marks. As *Newsday* writer Joe Donnelly wrote at the time, Brock was spectacular — tying his own record of seven steals in a single World Series and matching Eddie Collins's all-time mark of total Series swipes. Sure, it was bad form to steal when your team was so far ahead, but Brock wasn't one to abide by unwritten rules.

Before Brock's dash toward third, Bill Freehan stood up and tried to stare him down. The catcher took off his mask, expressing his anger and frustration out loud. But Freehan knew that Brock would do whatever he pleased, regardless of the vitriol coming his way. Crouched once more, Freehan was helpless as Brock took off for third on a slow-moving curveball. He felt he had a chance for the record — something Kaline himself admitted he would have done — and damn if he wouldn't try to take it.

The Tigers were exasperated. Apart from their offensive rally in Game 2, St. Louis had outplayed and outpitched them in three of the four games. Their defense was terrible. McLain, their stopper all season, had lost two games and possibly wouldn't pitch again if the Series went on. They'd fought so hard to come from behind in the late innings of the regular season. Had they finally reached the end?

Throughout the game, Jackie Robinson looked dispassionately out onto the field. He was willing to sit there, through the rain delay, watching a game that had become basically unwatchable. But by the seventh inning, with the Cardinals well ahead and his legs throbbing, he turned to Humphrey and told him he had to go.

"I'm not as hardy as you are," Robinson said. The game had strained Robinson to his absolute limits. Game 5 would take the Tigers to theirs.

20

ANTHEMS

A DAY AFTER BOB GIBSON once again put his team in position to win the World Series, he stood with his teammates in Tiger Stadium. He didn't want a replay of last year, when he'd pitched the Cardinals to a 3–1 lead only to have to come back in Game 7 to beat Boston. Now they could end things today and return to St. Louis as back-to-back World Series champions, and possibly the team of the decade.

But what was this? Before Game 5 could begin, Gibson listened to the worst thing he'd ever heard in his life (though he's also said he "sort of liked it"). It was the soft, personalized version of the National Anthem, *our* National Anthem, a song he'd heard countless times before countless sports contests. Only this time something was different. Very different. The anthem's cadence was a personal one, not militaristic or haughty — a sweet, nearly melodious translation of a song inexplicably tied with baseball ever since it was played without warning during the seventh-inning stretch in Game 7 of the 1918 World Series. "The Star-Spangled Banner" had become intertwined with not only baseball but all sports. Today it was sung by a man whom America had given so much to — José Feliciano. Now, in his own way, he was trying to give something back.

That was one way listeners could choose to hear José Feliciano's approach to the National Anthem as he sat with a small band at his back, his seeing eye dog at his side (Feliciano had lost his eyesight at birth), and his words wafted over the loudspeakers through the warm air of the stadium and millions of televisions and radios across the country. After all, he was an immigrant success story: born in Puerto Rico, Feliciano had grown up in Spanish Harlem. He'd made a name for himself with his Latinized rendition of "Light My Fire" by the Doors, and he was the first Latin artist to cross over to the U.S. pop charts. He had arrived. But now Feliciano would feel the wrath of the nation he loved.

It all came about by accident, really. Tigers announcer Ernie Harwell, who loved music and wrote songs on the side for most of his life, was asked to put together the pregame performers for the Series by Tigers general manager Jim Campbell. Harwell settled on Margaret Whiting, the Detroit-born actress and singer, for Game 3, followed by Marvin Gaye and Feliciano. Feliciano was an afterthought — and the only performer without a true Detroit connection.

When Campbell saw the list of performers, he wasn't concerned about Whiting, whose career stretched back to the 1940s, or Feliciano. He was worried about Gaye. An ex-marine and straitlaced, conservative type, Campbell had no appreciation for the new Motown sound, despite its Detroit roots, and wouldn't stand for any kind of frippery in his stadium. He instructed Harwell to tell Gaye to stick to the traditional version of the song.

It wasn't until 1983, at the NBA All-Star Game in Los Angeles, that Gaye would give us the greatest, most all-time original performance of the anthem. But at Tiger Stadium in 1968, Gaye did as he was told. He sang it "straight" before Game 4 — to the disappointment of Feliciano, who wanted to deliver a more personal interpretation of the anthem when his turn came.

There were those who enjoyed it — even loved it — including Marvin Miller, George Vecsey, and Phil Pepe, all of whom found Feliciano's rendition wonderful. But Michigan governor George Romney said he was "disappointed," suggesting that Feliciano had somehow desecrated a sacred song. Both NBC and the local affiliate in Detroit were besieged with phone calls and telegrams from across the country. A group of Vietnam veterans recovering in a VA hospital in Houston wrote an outraged letter to *The Sporting News:* "Some of us have seen people die in Vietnam, soldiers singing parts of the National Anthem as they gave their lives for our country. Then to be in a hospital with injuries and illnesses we got in service and to hear the Anthem sung in such a dishonorable way! If some of us had been in the color guard, we would have walked off the field. This was a disgrace to patriotism, to men in the service and to baseball."

Marvin Miller believed the boos and negative reactions to Feliciano's version of the anthem merely reflected his experience in Detroit. By the time he had arrived at the stadium, he was already shaken. He and his wife Theresa, along with the union's general counsel Richard Moss and his wife, had taken a taxi from their hotel. As they were chatting among themselves, their white taxi driver spotted a lone black man crossing the street.

"There's one of them!" the driver said, breaking up their conversation.

"What?" Miller said, thinking the driver was pointing out a dangerous figure for them to watch out for. Instead, the man began ranting about "niggers," claiming they had destroyed his city and had no business being there to begin with. He used the terrible word again and again, perhaps seeking out a sympathetic ear among his all-white passengers, whom he believed might understand his anger and hate. They did not. As far as Miller could see, this was not a city on the mend from the racial conflicts of the previous summer, but a place still suffused with resentment and fear.

Jim Campbell, who prized uniformity and tradition above all else, fumed. He nearly fired Harwell over the mishap. In the end the voice of the team for so many remained, but Tigers broadcasters Ray Lane and Larry Osterman felt a coolness set in between the two men that never really went away.

"If anybody's responsible, it's me," Harwell said in response to all the uproar. Going further, he defended Feliciano by saying, "A lot of people feel it must be sung very formally and staid. But I think a guy's got a right to put his own feeling into a song. There was nothing desecrating about it."

The Tigers players were just as divided. Reliever John Hiller was appalled. As he would do for the rest of his life, he believed in tradition. It was the National Anthem, and there was just one way, Hiller believed, to sing it. Willie Horton, though, thought that by shaking things up, Feliciano had actually brought the Tigers good luck. And Al Kaline recalled that after the initial shock wore off, some players on the team had said, "Well, it might be our rally song."

Aesthetic considerations aside, Feliciano's rendition had thrown off Mickey Lolich's pregame routine. So far he'd been Detroit's only winning pitcher in the Series, beating the Cardinals in St. Louis in Game 2. Usually the singing of the anthem gave Lolich 10 to 12 minutes to prepare in the bullpen — to loosen his arm, to mull over Sain's advice — but this time, because of the length of the song, before he knew it the umpires were telling him it was time to go. He wasn't ready.

Up first was Lou Brock. He was now batting .500 with eight hits in 16 plate appearances. Like Boston in 1967, Detroit made the mistake of seeing Brock as solely a great base stealer, underestimating him as a hitter. It was his terrific power at the plate that often got him on base, where he'd use his speed to take an extra base. He was, as Tigers pitcher Jon Warden put it, "a little shit."

Brock hammered Lolich's pitch into the right-field corner for a double. It was his fifth extra-base hit of the World Series and the eighth time he'd been on base in two games. In fact, right then Brock might have broken the two stolen base records he'd tied the day before had Curt Flood not hit a bloop single, scoring him from second.

Lolich seemed unnerved by Flood, who danced back and forth from first base. Again and again he checked on the Cardinals center fielder before throwing an actual pitch to Orlando Cepeda. It didn't matter. With the count 2-2, Flood took off. Tigers catcher Bill Freehan, hitless through four games, made a terrible throw that forced second baseman Dick McAuliffe to fully extend himself as Flood slid in cleanly. Flood had done his job in rattling Lolich. Now it was Cepeda's turn.

Having worked a 3-2 count, Cepeda got a pitch that no hitter could miss — a fastball right down the center of the plate. When Cepeda hit it, all left fielder Willie Horton could do was watch the ball sail overhead and into the outfield stands. Flood's RBI single had given St. Louis their first run of the game. Cepeda's home run gave them a 3–0 lead. At this point, Tigers manager Mayo Smith sent two relievers — Don McMahon and Fred Lasher — to warm up in the bullpen. But he wouldn't need them. Lolich managed to retire the next two batters and keep his team in it.

In the bottom of the fourth inning, with the Tigers still trailing by three runs, Cardinals starter Nelson Briles faced the top of the Tigers' batting order. Mickey Stanley, the center-fielder-turned-shortstop, hit a pitch on the far outside part of the plate, driving it far into the right-field corner. Right fielder Ron Davis lost track of it as it bounded around the outfield grass. By the time the play was over, Stanley was on third. Norm Cash brought him home with a long sacrifice fly.

Up next was Willie Horton, who had struggled both offensively and defensively in this postseason, despite a fine spring and summer. He too hammered a ball into deep right field, but rather than stay at second, he kept going. Though he was never especially fast — Charlie Dressen had tried repeatedly to get him to lose weight — Horton insisted on trying to take three. As he slid head first, the throw came into third. Had it been two inches to the right, he would have been out. But it wasn't. With Briles visibly unnerved, Steve Carlton began to warm up in the bullpen.

Then came the hop off the bat of Jim Northrup. It looked like a routine ground ball when it came toward second baseman Julián Javier. Without warning, though, the ball jumped up on him and he froze. All Javier could do was leap up for it, but the ball only grazed the tip of his glove before falling into the outfield. It wasn't his fault. And you couldn't blame Briles. But it was still an RBI single that brought home the second run of the game for the Tigers.

Cardinals manager Red Schoendienst believed that the hop changed the course of the game, though it's been largely forgotten because of what later happened in the top of the fifth. With one out, Lolich once more faced Brock, who had singled again in the third. Only a year before, Brock had lamented his lack of fame and endorsements, grumbling, "No one knows my name." After coming to the Cardinals in the middle of the 1964 season, he figured that he'd be a recognizable figure, a well-rounded ballplayer who could do more than just run, and someone who deserved the endorsements that seemed to elude most black players. And so far in this Series, no one — not McLain or Lolich or Earl Wilson or any of the relievers Smith had used — could stop him. If the Series had ended that afternoon, it's a sure bet that Brock would have been named Most Valuable Player.

With his team up by only one run and with one out in the inning, Brock crushed a fastball from Lolich into right-center field. Broadcaster Curt Gowdy wondered out loud, "How can a guy get any hotter?"

But the play that followed would color the way people perceived Brock for the rest of his Hall of Fame career. Second baseman Javier was up to bat and seemed to redeem himself for his play in the field with a single hit deep into left field, where Willie Horton was waiting. Earlier in the Series, Horton had expressed his displeasure at being lifted for a defensive replacement late in ball games. Now he set himself up for the play of his life. Having fielded the ball, he fired it home, where Freehan — whom Horton had known since they were 13 — was waiting. It was a play he had prepped for some time. In the scouting report and the film the Tigers had received, one could see that Brock had a tendency to "drift" from third base to home. He wouldn't slow down per se, but there was a break in his stride, allowing for a play at the plate.

It all happened in a series of freeze frames. Brock hesitating as he goes from second to third, looking back not once but twice to see if the shortstop has snared the ball and then checking to see where it has landed. Freehan calling off the cutoff man, third baseman Don Wert, so the ball can come straight to the plate. Brock drifting far off the baseline and then coming home, with Freehan blocking the plate. Horton's perfect throw, coming in chest-high at the precise moment Brock takes his final step toward home plate. Freehan spinning around with the catch and tagging Brock, who then makes a second run at the plate, and Freehan retagging him. After some deliberation, umpire Doug Harvey calling Brock out — enraging Brock and the entire Cardinals bench.

"If you tagged me the first time why did you tag me the second time?" Brock asked Freehan.

Freehan shot back: "If you thought you touched home plate the first time, why'd you come back to touch it a second time?"

Pointing to Brock's spike marks on the ground, Freehan showed that they were a good two and a half inches away from home plate. Brock came in standing up, and Freehan was able to block him, preventing him from getting a foot on home plate. From the vantage point of many on both benches, had Brock slid, he might very well have scored and extended the St. Louis lead.

They were still up by one run, but there were some Cardinals who began to feel uneasy about what had just happened, including pitcher Dick Hughes. That was it for him, he would say later, the turning point we look for in sports. Any umpire would have followed the unwritten rule in the game — that when in doubt on a close play like that, if the runner slides, you call him safe. But when Brock didn't do that, everything changed.

Roger Angell felt that he'd seen a pivotal point in a movie. From then on, he believed the Tigers were going to win. And talking to those around him in the press box, it seemed that everyone else now felt the same way.

Still, Brock believed that he was safe and that he'd scored. He maintained that because Freehan had blocked the plate, there was no way for him to slide in safely without getting tagged. He wasn't trying to run Freehan over by coming in standing up, he said. He was trying to sneak by him.

But a forlorn Schoendienst said of his star, "If he slides, he makes it easy."

Brock's Series-changing non-slide would forever inspire second-guessing. Tim McCarver believed that not sliding had given Brock his best chance to score given where Freehan had set up. Brock *had* to come in standing up. Horton had made the throw of his life. If Brock had slid, Freehan would have stopped him. No one could block the plate better. And no one, he believed, with the possible exception of Willie Mays, would have come into home plate and jolted a catcher with more force than the Cardinals' left fielder.

Sometimes we remember only the signature moment, losing sight of what happened afterwards. When Carlton Fisk waved his home run fair in Game 6 of the 1975 World Series, the Red Sox didn't follow through with a win against the Big Red Machine the following night. When the ball got past Bill Buckner in the extra innings of the 1986 Series, the score was already tied, and then the Red Sox blew a three-run lead in the next game to allow the Mets to take the championship. Similarly, Brock failed to slide in the fifth inning, not the ninth. The Cardinals were still leading, albeit by only one run. And they were up three games to one overall. There was no reason to think this might be the most pivotal play of the Series.

But Lolich, who suddenly seemed to have a new lease, was finally able to prove himself. After throwing a terrible curveball to Cepeda in the first, Lolich went after him with nothing but fastballs in the at-bats that followed. He began mixing up off-speed pitches with fastballs on the inside to left-handed hitters that they couldn't catch up to. Against the right-handed Ron Davis, he threw three fastballs, all out of the strike zone, before striking him out on a high pitch that was far from a strike. Facing Brock again in the top of the seventh, Lolich worked him low and away and then up and in before Brock finally lined the ball hard — only to have Dick McAuliffe rob him of a single. Lolich showed no drop in velocity from the second inning on. Afterwards, Orlando Cepeda, amazed by Lolich's stamina, wondered why he didn't win 20 games every year. Many in Detroit wondered the same thing. All his life Lolich had felt like a secondary figure — to Kaline, and especially to Denny. Perhaps his day had finally come.

Lolich had done his part, but would it be enough? In the bottom of the sixth, the Tigers couldn't score after loading the bases. Then came the seventh. Standing in the on-deck circle, watching his teammate Don Wert at bat, Lolich kept looking back into the dugout to see who Mayo Smith would send up to pinch-hit for him. But no one stood up. In the late innings of a close game that might decide the championship, Smith refrained from pulling his weak-hitting pitcher. Later Smith said that if Wert had gotten a hit, he would have sent someone in to bat for Lolich. As it was, with one out in the seventh, he left Gates Brown, the American League's best pinch hitter, sitting on the bench.

No one could quite believe what was happening. From his post at shortstop, Dal Maxvill kept looking to see who was going to hit. Mayo had to pull Lolich, right? At one run down in the seventh and with Briles losing steam? This is when a manager makes a move.

But Kaline wasn't surprised. Neither he nor the rest of the team ever knew what Smith was going to do. For them, their manager was in his own orbit. Lolich was pitching superbly. Why not keep him in and see if the rest of the team could come back, as they had done so often that year?

With that, Lolich took his place at the plate. Working the count to 2-1, Lolich hit what seemed to be a pop fly into right field. Ron Davis dove for it, but ultimately couldn't come up with the ball. Smith's gamble had paid off. Cardinals pitching coach Billy Muffett finally made the march to the mound and pulled Briles for the reliever Joe Hoerner to face Dick McAuliffe, who singled. The team's best hitters now gave Detroit a chance.

Forty times during the regular season the Tigers had rallied to win after trailing in the seventh inning. In their three postseason losses so far, they'd failed to get close. They were due. With two men on, Stanley worked the full count before Hoerner walked him to load the bases. Next up was Kaline. He had waited 16 years for this moment. Standing on third base, Lolich wanted to score of course. But he especially wanted Kaline to be the one to drive him home. Everyone did.

Kaline just wanted to do his job. He didn't care about a home run. He knew he couldn't hit it up the middle and into a double play. On a fastball on the outside corner, he singled into center field, driving in the tying and go-ahead runs. Standing on first, he looked relieved, but he didn't smile or clap. He just stared at the next hitter, Norm Cash, who would also single to add on another run. By the end of the seventh, the Tigers led 5–3, and a confident Lolich was prepared to pitch his team through the final two innings.

With two men on and two outs in the ninth, Lolich faced Lou Brock again. Despite his base-running faux pas, Brock had three hits in this game and was still St. Louis's most dangerous hitter. If anyone could rally the Cardinals, he could. But something had changed. Instead of his usual firepower, Brock meekly hit a ground ball to Lolich. Game over.

In the press box, an exasperated George Vecsey now fumed. In coming to the *New York Times,* he had believed — falsely — that he would be traveling to Mexico City to cover the Olympics. Instead, he was the secondary storywriter for the World Series. It had been a long summer for him — one in which he had questioned his vocation and what it meant, not only for himself but for a world whose center could no longer hold.

And while he loved St. Louis and the Chase Hotel and the bars on Euclid Avenue, he had a young family at home and was desperate to return to them. Instead, he was scrambling to find some transport south.

Afterwards, as NBC's Tony Kubek began to interview Mickey Lolich, Governor Romney — the man whose presidential ambitions had all but ended with misunderstood comments he made over the Vietnam War the previous year — came running over and vigorously shook Lolich's hand up and down, as if loosening up his arm.

"That's terrific, Mickey!" Romney said. "You're the hero of Tigertown!"

But who would pitch next? Kaline didn't think Denny's arm or Earl Wilson's leg would permit either to pitch again. He guessed that Smith would start Joe Sparma to begin Game 6 and empty his bullpen to force a Game 7, then pitch Lolich on short rest. Lolich envisioned a scenario in which Wilson might take the next game, leaving McLain to start the finale, which he could finish should Denny's arm begin to give way again.

As for McLain, who just the day before had announced that he was done for the Series, he now tried to backpedal. "There are a lot of things you can do about pain as a professional athlete to get ready for a game," he said.

When asked if he meant another shot of cortisone, he replied, "I didn't say that."

The Tigers had persevered, but they desperately wanted to get to Game 7, as the Red Sox had done the year before. And as with their predecessors, winning Game 6 would now mean facing *that* man again. For his part, Kaline, for whom Smith had risked everything by putting him in the lineup, wanted one more chance against Gibson.

21

SLIPPING

BEFORE THE FINAL GAME of the World Series in St. Louis on October 10, Bill Freehan sought out Johnny Sain. The talk around the clubhouse was that Sain was on his way out, no matter the outcome of Game 7. As had happened when he was with the Yankees and Minnesota, Sain had become a polarizing force. He'd earned the respect and deep allegiance of his pitching staff, but he'd managed to rile the people in charge. His departure, many believed, was now a given: he would walk out the doors of the Detroit clubhouse no matter the outcome, never to return. As was his way, he would return to Arkansas until he got a call from another desperate team seeking out the man who could change — truly change — the fortunes of its pitching staff. Detroit and Sain appeared to be over.

Fearing this, Freehan wanted to catch him before he was gone. "John," Freehan told him, "maybe I won't get a chance to say goodbye to you after the World Series, so I want you to know I've learned more baseball from you than anyone else."

He meant it. Like most pitching coaches, Sain knew a lot about the mechanics of pitching and had valuable insights about developing a pitcher's arm and training it to do something that physiologically arms aren't designed to do. Where Sain stood out, though, Freehan felt, was in his ability to zero in on an individual pitcher's strengths and weaknesses, mental and physical. He didn't try to mold his pitchers in the image of one of the past greats. He saw no reason to compare them to Whitey Ford or Mudcat Grant or Warren Spahn. They were Denny McLain and Mickey Lolich and Earl Wilson. They were his guys. For all the press attention Sain attracted at times, his instinct was always to step back and let the spotlight remain on his staff.

Sain had taught Freehan how to make things seem fun for his pitchers and how to make the man with the ball feel as if he was in control and could do anything he wished. Moreover, Sain had taught Freehan that a pitcher's job was done just *before* he grew tired. He wanted the pitcher to leave the game still believing in himself, without the self-doubt that comes with failure.

As Jim Kaat had so daringly put it upon Sain's hasty, ill-fated exit from the Twins, Freehan later said that should he ever become a manager (years after his retirement, Freehan served as the University of Michigan head baseball coach, then as a catching instructor with Detroit), he would call Sain on the very same day he got the job to "talk to him all day about human insight."

It's no surprise that Sain's coaching style proved incompatible with Mayo Smith's and that the two eventually reached an impasse. Jim Bouton found that out a year later when, desperate to leave the short-lived expansion Seattle Pilots, he expressed a desire to pitch for Sain again. His mentor and friend told him there was "no chance" that would ever take place.

"We've got four pitchers now who've all pitched less than ten innings this year," Said told him. "That Mayo Smith is not a very good man to pitch for. The last guy to pitch a good game is his man, and he overuses him and neglects everybody else. There are three or four pitchers on this club he doesn't even talk to."

After Game 5, Smith was at a loss about how to proceed. His team had played admirably, but now they needed to win two more games and two of his best pitchers — McLain and Wilson — were hurt. When asked directly about what he could do, Smith said he could possibly start Wilson, but when McLain then walked by and winked, Smith knew — just knew — whom he'd start in Game 6.

"How's your arm?" Smith had asked McLain, twice a loser to the greater Gibson.

"I can pitch anytime you want me to," McLain told him.

McLain said that he fully expected to pitch again in the Series. His shoulder problems persisted, but he felt fine at the moment. A stunned press corps didn't know what to make of Denny's pronouncement. What had changed? they asked him.

Nothing, he said. He claimed that his earlier statement about not being able to pitch again was just a joke meant to mislead a particular reporter and trick him into filing a fake story. George Cantor, who was a young reporter for the *Free Press* at the time, would claim that what McLain actually said was that he was trying to "get back at one of the Detroit writers—the little, curly-haired Jew cocksucker." Cantor, who believed that he was the reporter in question, even though he wasn't Jewish, was prepared to write off the whole incident as Denny being Denny. But his colleague Joe Falls wasn't as forgiving. McLain had gone too far.

A confrontation ensued in the Tiger Stadium clubhouse. McLain denied having used an ethnic slur, though Falls and Cantor had heard it from a reliable source, and he refused to apologize for something he claimed he hadn't said. Falls, a large, burly man who showed no fear of any player, no matter how tight his hold on the public imagination, wouldn't let him off the hook. Tempers flared, and it looked like they might come to blows. Cantor feared that, should punches be thrown, McLain would hurt his hand and the World Series would be lost—and it would be their fault. A number of Tigers players came rushing to separate the two men. When Smith heard what was happening, he came out of his office to try to diffuse the situation. According to Cantor, Smith summoned the two writers for a private talk.

"Boys," he said, "I'm going to tell you something my daddy back in Missouri told me a long time ago. Never get into a pissing match with a skunk."

Upon arriving at the Sheraton-Jefferson Hotel in St. Louis the evening before Game 6, McLain for once did the responsible thing and retired to his room.

Smith had kept secret his decision about which pitcher would start until hours before the start of Game 6. McLain, having taken another cortisone shot, would now get his third chance. This wasn't quite the redemption he might have hoped for. That would have been pitching against Gibson again in Game 7. But it was enough.

Jim Northrup, who'd been moved to center field for the Series, had a perfect vantage point from which to evaluate McLain's performance that day. In the first two games, he was dropping down too much, using his sidearm motion in a way he hadn't all season. Northrup could see that McLain wasn't relying on his two strengths — his overhand fastball and his curveball. He was hurting. It would be Northrup, more than anyone else, who made sure that McLain didn't have to strain himself or exit early, as he'd done in his first two postseason outings.

The Tigers scored their first five runs against St. Louis starter Ray Washburn. The last four came when Northrup, facing reliever Larry Jaster, hit the lone grand slam of the Series, driving in the Tigers Washburn had left on base. Soon Schoendienst made another move, replacing Jaster with Ron Willis. But it wasn't enough. The Tigers recorded a 10-run third inning, tying a 39-year World Series mark. This early lead allowed McLain to find his groove again. The Cardinals used seven different pitchers in their 13-1 loss, while McLain, returning to his overhand motion, held the Cardinals to one run and nine hits while throwing a complete game.

"Now that we win a game 13-1," McLain said afterwards, "I suppose you writers will say anyone could have won the game. Maybe so, but I'm just glad it was me. I didn't feel I had a thing to prove. I want to thank all the guys on the club. I wish I could take everyone in with me for salary negotiations."

In thinking about who might pitch against Gibson in Game 7, Smith for once didn't have to worry about McLain. He could start Pat Dobson, the weak link in the Tigers rotation, or the ailing Earl Wilson. But in the middle innings of Game 6, with the win locked in, Smith settled on Lolich.

Smith had used pitchers on two days' rest before. He'd used McLain on short rest at times during the regular season. But this was the World Series, and the Tigers had scored only one run against Gibson in two games. When Smith asked Lolich if he could pitch, Lolich reminded him that he'd only had two days' rest, but Smith persisted. He was going on a hunch, one of a series of successful, daring hunches that had marked his maneuvers late in the season and in the World Series.

"Do you think you can pitch five?" Smith asked Lolich.

"Yeah," Lolich said. "I guess so."

One of Lolich's most vocal supporters was Sain. His reasons had nothing to do with Lolich's arm, Sain said, and everything to do with his mental toughness. By the time of the game, Sain believed, Lolich would have convinced himself that he was pitching on three days' rest, not two. Moreover, with the exception of the first inning of Game 5, he'd handled the Cardinals as well as Maris had predicted.

"He'll come right back," Sain said. "I'm sure of it."

The Cardinals had been in this position before. They'd squandered a two-game lead in the 1967 Series, allowing Boston to come back and force that final game against Gibson. In a deciding game, when everything was on the line, he could be counted on to be unbeatable.

That's been the theory passed down through the decades — that because they felt they knew they had Gibson in the Series finale, the Cardinals might have eased off in Game 6. McCarver believed that having Gibson in this spot was ultimately the team's great strength but also its undoing. Still, as Dal Maxvill, who went hitless in the Series, later said: "You go out there and there's 50,000 people in the ballpark and another 80 million watching on TV, and you're not gonna try your best? Gimme a break. Come on, that's not true."

Looking back to Game 5, Johnny Edwards would feel that something had changed with that game, with that play at home. The Cardinals should have won the championship then, and they certainly weren't planning on losing Game 6. An intangible shift had taken place. Al Kaline felt it before Game 7. It was a collective loss of confidence. Now, more than ever, the Cardinals clung to the arm of one man.

As he looked forward to the matchup, Roger Angell couldn't help but feel that the game had all the trappings of cinema. Gibson was heroic, athletic, striking in his appearance. Lolich looked somehow baggy, his throwing motion odd. Gerald Early just believed that the "fat guy" — Lolich — couldn't possibly win.

Despite having willed their way back into contention, the Tigers had their own doubts. Dick Tracewski felt a shared unease, the sense that their chances against Gibson were simply "not good. Not good." Even Mayo Smith sought to temper expectations before the game, telling his team, "This guy is not Superman. He's beatable. But even if we don't win, we've had a helluva year."

Norm Cash, who'd provided comic relief throughout, shot back, "Mayo, I don't know about him not being Superman. He's dressing in a phone booth over there."

From the early innings of Game 7, Gibson appeared to be in top form. He mixed and matched speeds and placement, changing the batter's eye level. As in the first game of the Series, he threw a lot of breaking balls. In the first inning, he threw a large curveball that caught the outside corner and caught Kaline looking for a strikeout. He struck Kaline out again in the fourth, this time with a fastball placed in the same spot. The hardest-hit ball — he'd allowed only an infield single through five innings — was hit deep into center, where Curt Flood caught it standing on the warning track.

But Gibson would be the first to admit that he was working without his best stuff that afternoon. Even after recording the game's first out, second baseman Dick McAuliffe told his teammates that Gibson wasn't the same pitcher they'd faced earlier in the Series. Watching from the bullpen, Daryl Patterson — unlike many of his teammates — claimed that he could tell that Gibson was getting worn down. He looked tired, Patterson thought, and his speed and location weren't nearly as crisp as they'd been in Games 1 and 4. As the game progressed, Patterson began to think the unthinkable: "We're gonna get him."

Unlike Gibson's opponent in the first two games of the 1967 Series, Mickey Lolich proved to be his equal. Jim Kaat believed that Lolich's true weapon was his three-quarter delivery, which made it nearly impossible for hitters to see the ball until it was right on top of them. Because he was able to hide the ball so well, Lolich relied heavily on his breaking ball, which broke late and was especially effective against left-handed hitters.

Even pitching on short rest worked to Lolich's advantage that day. He noticed in the bullpen that his fastball didn't have its usual velocity. But because he threw a sinkerball, less velocity meant that the ball would be heavier. How heavy a pitch was had nothing to do with weight — the ball was about five ounces when it left Lolich's hand and still the same weight when it hit the catcher's glove. But a "heavier" sinker would continue to dip through the strike zone. Thanks to Lolich's skill — and an assist from gravity — the pitch would hit the catcher's glove with a surprising amount of force. To a hitter, this "heavier" sinker would be a lot tougher to handle than a faster, straighter pitch. Unless the batter hit a sinker on the bat's sweet spot — which is only a one- or two-inch square — he wasn't going to make solid contact. As Jim Lonborg would explain, "To pitch on two days' rest actually meant you had a better sinker most of the time. You just had to get it there."

Lolich noticed the change early on. On normal rest, his ball would sink three to four inches, but now it was sinking as low as eight. Moreover, Lolich saw that the Cardinals hitters, who had struggled all season, were willing to swing at his sinker, which often fell below the strike zone. He wasn't striking people out, but he was forcing them to hit the ball near the ground, taking away their power. In the second inning, with a runner on first, he got Roger Maris to hit a sinker that ended with a double play. Maxvill came next and chopped a ball to third base on the same pitch to end the inning. In the fourth, Lolich used his sinker to jam Flood on the inside part of the plate, forcing him to hit a one-hopper to the shortstop. At one point, seven straight Cardinals batters hit the ball into the infield for outs.

In the bottom of the sixth, Lolich again faced Brock. He'd given up three straight hits to him in Game 5, two for extra bases. If the Cardinals were going to break out and score runs for Gibson, Brock was likely to be the catalyst. On the second pitch, Brock lined a ball past Stanley into left field for a single. Concerned, Freehan approached the mound to speak with his pitcher.

"You all right?" asked Freehan. "Anything I can do for you?"

"Yeah," Lolich replied. "Can you get me a couple of hamburgers between innings?"

Standing on first base, Brock studied Lolich, then started walking away from the base — taking a lead that, by Norm Cash's estimate, was a good 20 feet off the bag. It was a cocky move, a Brock move, and this time he had gone too far. Cash yelled for Lolich to throw over. Brock had already taken off for second base, and Cash was able to relay to Stanley, who tagged him out. Why Brock had decided to take a big lead in a game like this was anybody's guess.

With two outs, Lolich gave up another single, this time to Curt Flood. He'd thrown a sinker that jumped in on Flood's hands. Flood grounded to Stanley, but still managed to reach base. Flood wasn't nearly as fast or as brazen as Brock, but it was apparent to everyone that he was running. Again the Tigers were ready. In perhaps one of the more comical sequences in World Series history, Flood stranded himself between first and second. Lolich threw to Cash, who threw to second baseman Dick McAuliffe, who threw back to Cash, who threw back to Lolich, who lobbed the ball to Stanley, who finally tagged Flood out as he tumbled to the ground. With two plays, the Cardinals had run themselves out of the inning and quite possibly the Series.

However, what happened next in the top of the seventh overshadowed all of this. Gibson had managed to keep the Tigers scoreless through six, which meant that over the course of three World Series starts, he'd allowed only one run in 24 innings. And it looked like he could continue like this forever. He began the inning by striking out Stanley as the shortstop tried but failed to check his swing on a breaking ball. Then Kaline hit a two-hopper to Shannon. First baseman Norm Cash was up next. He worked a full count, then muscled a single to right field. Horton followed with another single past Maxvill. At this point, McCarver did what he seldom dared to do: he went to talk to Gibson on the mound.

Gibson was admittedly exhausted. The breaking pitches that had served him so well were beginning to hang. With the following hitter, Jim Northrup — who'd homered for the lone run against Gibson in Game 5 and who'd hit a grand slam the day before — Gibson tried throwing a fastball away to prevent him from pulling the ball. Undeterred, Northrup hit it to deep center field.

Most considered Flood the game's most reliable center fielder. But at this particular moment, he had no chance. With a sea of 50,000 white shirts in the stands, seeing the ball off the bat on a sunny afternoon was a challenge for even the most gifted defensive players. It had also rained heavily the day before, soaking the field and creating muddy spots on the turf. As with Brock, Flood's legacy would change on a single play.

Watching Flood from behind the plate, McCarver had a clear view of Flood's right foot getting caught in the mud as he attempted to turn back and make the catch. Suddenly he saw Flood racing back toward the outfield fence as two Tigers crossed the plate and Northrup came into third with a triple. He'd seen Flood recover on similar balls hundreds of times, but the field had made this one unplayable.

Looking back from shortstop, Maxvill believed it was a matter of approach. Had Flood taken a different angle on the ball, he would have caught up to it and ended the inning, and the scoreless game would have continued. After the game was finished, Maxvill never felt so badly for anyone in his life.

Everyone seemed to have his own take on whether the ball would have been catchable even in perfect conditions. Sitting in the upper deck on the first-base side, Tigers broadcaster Ray Lane figured that Flood would make a play on the ball even after his misjudgment, that his speed and instincts would allow him to recover. Cardinals pitcher Larry Jaster thought that the ball was more difficult to judge because it was a line drive rather than a fly ball. Flood had a split second to decide whether to go in or go back. He simply made the wrong choice.

Others — mostly Tigers — maintained that there was no way Flood, as good as he was, could have caught the ball, regardless of field conditions. As Fred Lasher and Daryl Patterson and Dick Tracewski saw it, the ball was just hit too hard. Maybe it wouldn't have been a triple if not for Flood's misstep, but they all believed that it would have been a base hit. Watching from the upper deck on the third-base side, broadcaster Larry Osterman had a perfect view of the play. Turning to the person sitting next to him, he said, "That's the ball game right there."

As it turned out, Osterman was right. The Tigers would score once more in the seventh — on a ball that Brock misplayed in left field — and again in the top of the ninth. With their limping offense, the Cardinals just couldn't catch up. That play would trail Flood for the rest of his life. His widow, the actress Judy Pace Flood, watched him play it over and over again in his head as if on a loop. He wanted it to stop — but it never did.

In the dugout after the three-run seventh, Flood tried apologizing to Gibson, but Gibson wasn't having it. He didn't fault Flood, and he would consistently defend him over the years. Gibson had walked out to center field himself before the game, and he saw firsthand what trouble an outfielder would have trying to pick out the ball. He initially thought Flood would catch Northrup's drive, but if Flood of all people couldn't make a play on it, then no one could. "It was just circumstances," Gibson felt. "You know. Shit happens."

A couple of hours after the game, Rodney Wead, along with some of the Gibson contingent, waited in the stadium to see his friend. Knowing him as he did, Wead believed that Gibson would be frazzled, "torn to bits" about how things had played out. Since boyhood, Wead had seen Gibson become the man he was that day—someone who lingered over losses and was unable to accept failure. Instead, he found acceptance in Gibson.

"Damn," Gibson said. "When I saw Curt turn, all I could do was look back and say, 'Oh no!'"

He'd been outpitched. And thank God it hadn't been by McLain. He simply couldn't forgive Denny for the statements he had made about wanting to destroy the Cardinals, not just beat them. Those were the kind of words that stayed with him, comments made in haste that he could never forgive, because he was Bob Gibson.

What followed that play was inevitable. The Tigers added another run off Gibson, and after Lolich gave up one run in the ninth, with two outs, McCarver popped up to Freehan. Series over. *Fini.* Freehan rushed toward Lolich and hoisted him into the air, and the usual celebration ensued. Pitchers sprinted out from the bullpen to the infield. The Tigers rushed into the visiting locking room, where champagne, the commissioner, and a trophy awaited them. Mayo Smith's every move suddenly seemed brilliant. He'd switched a center fielder to shortstop. He didn't pinch-hit for his pitcher when down in the fifth game. He started Lolich on two days' rest. Had any one of those decisions gone the other way, baseball would remember him as a fool. Now, for some, he was seen as bold, even fearless.

For Lolich, the win was a vindication. He'd been the whipping boy all season, but with his postseason performance, he'd proven himself equal to or even better than McLain. And he had a World Series Most Valuable Player Award to prove it. Some on the team — especially pitcher Fred Lasher — would smile about that fact forever. Lolich had won three games in the Series and showed up McLain. He'd finally done it — proving Sain right while emerging from Denny's shadow.

Even McLain didn't seem to be terribly put out. In the Tigers' locker room after the game, McLain grabbed one bottle of champagne after another, shaking them up and spraying them without mercy. For a man who'd set himself apart from the team, he was with them now.

The Cardinals, understandably, were numb. They'd come into the Series as heavy favorites, only to have everything unravel for them in a way no one could have guessed. The best base runner of his time made two grave, game-costing mistakes. The great center fielder of his era misjudged a ball when it mattered most. And the superhuman Bob Gibson proved to be mortal after all.

In Detroit, meanwhile, everything came to a standstill. After the final out, thousands of people came running out of office buildings. By one estimate, a crowd of 150,000 congregated on the streets to celebrate the championship. Broadcaster Ernie Harwell described it as the "biggest spontaneous celebration in peacetime American history."

The party continued into the evening and spilled onto the runways of Detroit Metro, the city's main airport. According to one police account, 25,000 people gathered to greet the plane the team had chartered from St. Louis. They toppled fences, ran across runways, and forced flight cancellations. But they were waiting at the wrong place. Officials had redirected the Tigers' flight to a small suburban airport, where a much smaller crowd of 400 had gathered. Among them were George Romney and Detroit mayor Jerome Cavanagh. The Tigers had played a terrific World Series, silenced their critics, and finished what they had started the season before. And now they were home. The season had ended. Baseball as we'd known it would change from that moment. It was time to move on.

22

AFTER THE FALL

T HIS WAS HIS TIME. On the evening of October 12, 1968, Denny McLain, whose arm had weakened but whose tireless yearning and seemingly limitless ambition had not, was again at the center of things. Of course, he'd had his chances to shine brightly and failed twice against Gibson. But he'd earned some measure of redemption in Game 6 when the Tigers scored an insurmountable number of runs for him, forcing a Game 7. McLain had done his part when finally asked. It was now time to get his.

On this night, the blended wool uniform of his day job was nowhere in sight. Instead, with millions of Americans looking on, he sat at that hulking, tanklike Hammond organ wearing a blue tuxedo, with the rest of his quartet standing off in the background. There was a great deal of seriousness to him as he pounded forcefully on the organ, like a musician with something to prove. Occasionally he peered to his left and then to his right with a wry smile. For a man whose life would forever be weighted by hubris or fear or both, he at last seemed happy.

After he'd finished playing his chosen song, "The Girl from Ipanema," the show's host, Ed Sullivan, let out a "yes in-dee-dee!" But Sullivan's excitement came off as both feigned and stiff, the meek cry of a man whose importance had faded. It had been a little more than four years since those four fine young men, still clean-shaven and mop-headed, wearing suits, had stepped onto the tarmac of JFK airport in New York—the new gateway for millions who would come to this country and change it for the better—so that they might stand on Ed Sullivan's stage before millions, introducing themselves to America and, in the process, the world.

Now Sullivan was left with McLain—twice a loser for a world championship team. He had other people on his roster—Sugar Ray Robinson. the Beach Boys. Pearl Bailey. Jim Henson's Muppets with Mickey Lolich (whom McLain managed to accidentally insult on his first night during his two-week gig playing the organ at The Riviera) and Babe Ruth's widow watching from the stands. There was an astronaut and Richard Pryor who, being restrained in his tone and language for this show, was stripped of the very thing that made him a comic for the ages.

All of it seemed random, like the taped Bob Hope special that aired around the same time. But this was worse. The young Beatles' appearance on his stage in 1964, albeit in black-and-white, had meant something, something real and tangible. That had been a stand-alone, singular moment for what was not yet a fully fragmented America. The parents watching the Beatles on *The Ed Sullivan Show* knew that something was altogether different. So too did their newly empowered teens. And Sullivan, who helped shepherd a young Elvis Presley to stardom, must have known that with that performance, he was now at his unmatched height as the cross-generational emperor of television. He was the man who had both made careers and ended them. He was simply unmatched in his day.

Ed Sullivan may not have mattered anymore, but for McLain his show remained a living, vibrant thing—something he could aspire to, a showcase that would secure his life after baseball. Soon after McLain finished his song, Sullivan introduced another musician, an Omaha, Nebraska, native who was then "batting .450" on the "gee-tar." As Sullivan turned back to the stage, the viewer could see Gibson emerge in a light brown, double-breasted suit that ran nearly to his neck, barely revealing his tie and yellow dress shirt. McLain and Gibson shook hands. Then Bob picked up the electronic guitar that someone had placed close to McLain during the breakaway.

When McLain suggested that they play something "easy," the now-soft-spoken Gibson, the one who appeared on *Gentle Ben,* said, "You go ahead and I'll catch up."

Together they played something clearly rehearsed—a small, seemingly original, untitled ballad hastily put together and memorable only because of the two men who performed it. With Gibson alongside him, McLain played the organ more gently than he had when he was alone on the center stage, while his counterpart stared at his instrument as he played, looking up at the camera for only a few seconds at a time. In the background, the colors fluctuated unnaturally—a backdrop meant for another scene, for other performers who had earned that backdrop. Finally, and mercifully, McLain finished the number with a *bump-buma-bump* progression. Applause followed. And with that they were done.

After the 1968 World Series, Gibson would later lament, things would never be the same again. He was right. The owners, who had watched attendance fall precipitously, were finally ready to admit that there was something to this football business. And that perhaps they had miscalculated with the changes they instituted after Maris's and Mantle's home run rampage during the 1961 season. Changes were needed. As Rick Hummel, who would later cover Gibson for the *St. Louis Post-Dispatch,* put it, he liked great pitching as much as anyone else—just not every night.

The following spring you could see McLain working with Sain to adjust his mechanics on the lowered mound. What Sain stressed to Denny was the importance of positioning following the ball's release. Legs, balance, your position *after* your delivery—that was what Sain believed would sustain pitchers now. For McLain, the lowered mound combined with his shorter frame on the mound led him to overtax his arm. No longer driving with his legs, he started forcing pitches with a strained motion that ultimately severed his tendons.

For Gibson, the changes to the strike zone were equally unsettling. Because his bread and butter was his slider rather than the arm-killing 12-6 curveball that McLain depended on, the mound posed less of a problem. But with the new rules, Gibson found he couldn't rely on the high strike anymore. Previously the uppermost strike call could reach as high as the armpit, and Gibson had counted on it, but that call would no longer be available to him.

Other dramatic changes would follow. The start of free agency after the 1976 season would allow starters to command a premium, and pitchers would become hyperspecialized. Now there would be middle relievers, left-handed and right-handed specialists, and ninth-inning closers. With the need to protect arms because of how much they cost a ball club, a "Year of the Pitcher" would never happen again. And never again would we see starters regularly finishing their starts and even going beyond the ninth inning in extra-inning games. (Jack Morris's superb 10-inning performance to win the deciding game of the 1991 World Series is the exception.)

This last change was especially disheartening to Johnny Sain. Two decades later, in the mid-1980s, Sain was coaching the Atlanta Braves, the only team in the majors that hadn't recorded a complete game. In an 11-inning game against the Cubs at Wrigley Field, Atlanta went through three pitchers, including the starter, who was relieved after six. Gibson would have refused to leave the mound.

Among all the other changes that were afoot in baseball, the Cardinals team that Gibson had known and loved in the 1960s would soon be dissolved. Before the 1968 World Series, the Cardinals were the highest-paid team in baseball history and had failed to pay dividends for their owner. Beginning in the spring of 1969, when Orlando Cepeda was traded for Joe Torre, Gibson would see the team coming apart.

It would only spiral from there. No one had the kind of year they needed to in 1969 — not with the Mets, led by a remarkable young pitching staff, playing as they did. After the season, Busch and general manager Bing Devine made history with the trade that became a watershed moment in baseball and in all of professional sports when they deal Tim McCarver and Curt Flood and two others to the Phillies.

We know the rest. Flood had no interest in playing for Philadelr and wrote to then commissioner Bowie Kuhn in December. Th Philadelphia had offered Flood compensation on par with the very best players, Flood told Kuhn that he had no intention of r to the team. He wanted to play, but he wanted to play for a c′

choosing and wished to consider offers from other teams. He was not, as he wrote to Kuhn, "a piece of property to be bought and sold irrespective of my wishes."

With these words, Flood took the thankless first step in challenging baseball's reserve clause and unshackling the next generation of players from their indentured servitude. His case went before the U.S. Second Circuit Court of Appeals and then the Supreme Court. Not a single Cardinal player — or *any* active player — attended his first trial in New York. Even Gibson felt he couldn't risk it. Only Hank Greenberg, Jackie Robinson, and Bill Veeck testified on his behalf. Flood would lose his lawsuit and fail in his appeal in a 5–3 decision by the Supreme Court in 1972.

In the meantime, in the aftermath of that spectacular 1968 World Series, both the Cardinals and the Tigers lost their footing. The camaraderie and spunk that defined the Cardinals' clubhouse in 1968 would disappear. There was no excitement, even after they won games. Gibson admitted as much to a visiting reporter in 1971.

"You would have thought I'd just lost," Gibson said after a 4–2 win in 1971. "There's no spirit at all. It's like, 'Well, we got the work done; let's try it again — see if we can get this one over with.' The everyday enthusiasm we had three years ago isn't here. We would *lose* a ballgame and come in and cheer damn near as hard as if we had won the game, trying to pep everyone up."

The Tigers were still intact as a team and had the talent to reach another World Series, but they didn't have the right manager to push them toward it, and perhaps they didn't have the drive. Even though they won 90 games in 1969, they couldn't catch the all-powerful Orioles, who won 109. They finished in second place in the newly created American League Eastern Division. Al Kaline believed that the 1968 Tigers built around its minor league system and by then, "we used it all up." Even general manager Jim Campbell, who had shaped and groomed the team champions and saw them as *his* boys, admitted that he probably held on to certain players longer than he should have.

Regret. That was what Willie Horton felt. Regret over championships that might have been. Mayo Smith's hands-off approach wasn't what the team needed in 1969. Their now division rival Baltimore would go on to win three straight American League pennants, winning one World Series. Under another manager, Horton believed they would have been capable of at least one more title.

But they would have needed McLain. For most of the 1968 season, Denny wouldn't stop talking about making $100,000 — a figure no Tigers player had ever reached. McLain wanted it, expected it. Whatever missteps he made, he was the face of the franchise, and he believed the team should pay him whatever that was worth. When it came time to negotiate, Campbell offered him $60,000 for his efforts. When McLain threatened to walk out, Campbell told him that for every minute he didn't sign, the club's offer would decrease by $1,000. In the end, McLain would earn $65,000 for the forthcoming season.

And the usual trouble was brewing. McLain seemed incapable of reining in his reckless impulses. Following the 1968 Series, the rookie Jon Warden got a call from McLain inviting him to his house. When Warden arrived, McLain ushered him into his office.

"What are you gonna do with your World Series check?" McLain asked.

"I don't know," Warden said. "That's a lot of money, man." Warden had grown up on a farm in southwest Ohio. His mother had stared at the check when it came. It would take her a whole year to make that kind of money. Warden got it without pitching in a single Series game.

"I've got this paint company," McLain said. "I've got Ford, Chrysler, GM. I've got all of them. We're gonna make a ton."

McLain rattled off the names of veteran players who'd invested with him, players who, Warden assumed, understood something about business and knew how to manage their money. Yet driving home, Warden could only think of his mother and how much the check would mean to his family. How could he just hand it over to McLain?

Yet McLain was determined to build his paint business. He rented offices in Southfield, Michigan, and hired people to help him run things. On television, during the pregame and postgame telecasts, he seemed more interested in talking up the company he'd built than in discussing the game he'd just pitched. Once, while on a trip to the West Coast, McLain directed broadcaster Ray Lane to look out on the Golden Gate Bridge, boasting to Lane and fellow broadcaster Ernie Harwell that "just yesterday, my paint company landed the contract to paint that entire bridge." Speaking about this and all his various ventures, he would admit to his stupidity.

"I kept pouring my money into it," he said. "but I didn't know what I was doing."

All the while he continued to pitch much like he did in 1968. He won 24 games and lost only nine in 1969, earning his second consecutive Cy Young, though he shared this one with Baltimore's Mike Cuellar. But the Tigers were struggling, and his teammates chafed at McLain's constant flaunting of the rules. Things he'd gotten away with the previous season when the team was winning—flying his own plane, showing up late to the ballpark, skipping team meetings—were no longer so readily tolerated.

But the tension between McLain and his teammates paled in comparison to the untenable contempt between Smith and Johnny Sain. Even though he'd grown close to owner John Fetzer, Sain didn't win any friends in management when he supported the Players Association's pension battle with owners before the season. Campbell and Smith didn't agree with Sain when he insisted that they bring 11 pitchers north —but somehow Sain got his way. Had the Tigers gotten off to a strong start against the Orioles, Sain's quirks could have been tolerated. As it was, despite superb starts from both Lolich and McLain, the rest of the team couldn't rise to the occasion.

Smith and Sain had never gotten along. Smith was steamed that Sain wanted his pitchers to train separately from the rest of the team. He routinely ignored Sain's advice and kept him out of the loop with regard to management decisions. After more than two seasons together, the men were barely on speaking terms. Everything finally came to a head when the team sold Dick Radatz to the Expos in 1969, which Sain learned about secondhand.

That was it. In a breach of clubhouse confidentiality, Sain told a reporter about his difficulties with Smith: "If my advice isn't used and there are no results from what I'm doing, then it's time to leave." Upon hearing this, in August, Campbell decided he'd had enough. Once again, Sain had found a way out.

There were no public letters of support this time, but McLain spoke his mind as always, telling the press, "I won over 60 games pitching for Sain. He did an awful lot for me. How can you give someone like that his outright release?" Lolich was more hesitant initially, fearing repercussions from the club, but he acknowledged Sain on his radio show, expressing his gratitude for Sain's faith in him. "John Sain has had quite an influence on my life," he said.

For Sain, it wasn't exactly a triumphant homecoming. Back in Arkansas, his marriage was all but finished, strained by the itinerant lifestyle that kept him away from his wife and four kids for months at a time. His exasperated wife said she was "tickled to death" that he was fired because "Goodness knows I need him here." Soon they would divorce, and the settlement would force Sain into bankruptcy.

The lone positive was that Sain wasn't around to deal with the fallout from McLain's February 1970 *Sports Illustrated* cover. It was the same cover image of McLain as in July 1968, when the story was about his pursuit of 30 wins. This time, however, the headlines against a black background were "Denny McLain and the Mob" and "Baseball's Big Scandal." All the rumors were true, the magazine said. It accused him of running a bookmaking operation. It said that mobsters had stomped on his foot. His actions were not only reckless but criminal.

Commissioner Bowie Kuhn summoned McLain to New York. After weighing the accusations against him, Kuhn announced on April 1, 1970, that McLain had been duped and that he was never truly a partner in the bookmaking operation. He gave McLain a three-month suspension, which most viewed as light considering the charges he faced.

The players merely shook their heads. By now, Jim Hawkins, just beginning his career as a sportswriter in Detroit, believed that they knew they had to distance themselves from McLain — for the sake of their own lives and careers. McLain's relationship with the press had only gotten worse, but perhaps because Hawkins was a new face, McLain decided to open up to him. There was no history or acrimony yet, as with the established writers at the *Free Press* and the *News*. In secret, Hawkins went to McLain's house, where they spent the afternoon together. McLain wanted his story out, but there remained that need, that craving to be out in the public.

For the rest of the team, McLain had become an afterthought. He was gone. And they had begun to go on without him. In fact, rookie Elliott Maddox was amazed when he watched the more veteran players joke about it. It seemed entirely plausible, and hilarious, that McLain had been duped by mobsters. It fell to the usually taciturn Jim Campbell to stand up for McLain, at least publicly. McLain was going through a hard time, Campbell said, and the Tigers weren't going to abandon him now.

Three months to the day after his suspension began, Denny once again took the mound at Tiger Stadium. To Hawkins, that game had all the excitement of opening day, if not a postseason game. There was a capacity crowd and a sense that anything was possible. In the press box, the writers had placed their bets as to how long McLain would last. Because of the crush of reporters, they couldn't divide up the pool into entire innings, but had to break it up into thirds. Hawkins put his money on 5⅓ innings, which earned him the cash.

In many ways, that was McLain's last great moment in Detroit, a final reminder of what he had meant. On August 28, McLain pulled a locker room stunt that earned him another suspension. Maddox would contend that it wasn't even McLain's idea. The main instigators were Norm Cash and Jim Northrup, who not only came up with the prank but brought McLain ice water in a Tupperware-type tub from the trainer's room. Several players egged him on.

The first target was Jim Hawkins. As he came into the locker room, one Tiger teammate called Hawkins over to sit down with him. The young writer had no idea that McLain was behind him, ready to dump a bucket of water over his head. After it happened, McLain immediately grabbed a large floor fan and started patting at Hawkins's sports coat, trying to dry it. It wasn't malicious, it was a joke, Hawkins said, and he took it as such.

But Watson Spoelstra — McLain's second target and someone McLain had feuded with during his early years in Detroit — didn't take it so well. Later in the press box, Hawkins got a call from Jim Campbell, who asked, "Did McLain dump water on you?"

"Yes."

"But why didn't you tell me?"

"Because it was none of your fucking business."

"Well, I'm making it my fucking business!" Campbell screamed, slamming the phone down. He suspended McLain for the second time that season. A third and final suspension was handed down before McLain could even make it back. The circumstances are murky, but ostensibly involved McLain carrying a gun onto an airplane or flashing it in a restaurant. Maddox has always felt that there was no gun, that Jim Campbell had simply had enough. And McLain and Hawkins both contended that backup catcher Jim Price had something to do with it. Whatever the case, Kuhn again summoned McLain to New York and suspended him for a third time, ending his season.

"I want to be traded," McLain groused. "I just don't want to play for Jim Campbell. It's not the city of Detroit, it's not Mayo Smith, it's not John Fetzer . . . it's just that one man."

On the second day after McLain came back from his first suspension, Campbell called McLain into his office. He had told the still-young man that if he did one thing wrong, he would suspend him. For McLain, that was it. How, he said, could a person possibly play for a man "when you know if you spit in the wrong way, he's going to knock you off the stool?" McLain believed that Campbell was merely trying to show off his toughness in what had been a tough season. But, McLain said, "if he thinks he's had it tough, he should check with me."

It was over. For real this time. Campbell was intent on getting rid of McLain, but that would be no small feat. He needed a taker. And who would want McLain not only after his multiple suspensions but also after 1970, when Detroit finished 79-83 (after which the Tigers fired Smith), their first losing season in seven years?

Enter Bob Short, owner of the Washington Senators, one of baseball's worst teams. He had either the audacity or the stupidity to offer two pitchers and two position players for McLain, Maddox, Don Wert, and Norm McRae, despite the strong misgivings of manager Ted Williams.

Campbell could relax now. Right after the trade, he threw out his antacids. He knew McLain was finished. Everyone knew it. Only Short couldn't see it. He remembered the McLain of 1968. He complained to Campbell repeatedly during the 1970 season, "You're depreciating *my* ballplayer. Keep him there in Detroit and he's worth nothing." He would have given anything to get McLain, so he did.

When McLain arrived at spring training in 1971, noticeably over-weight, among his teammates was Curt Flood. After the trial, Flood had taken a year off from baseball, but now he was back. With his case headed to the Supreme Court, how could he bring himself to return to the game he'd likened to a plantation system? Well, money. And how could any owner employ a player who was suing baseball? Short had a failing franchise on his hands, and he needed stars, no matter what distractions they might bring.

Short's gamble wouldn't pay off. The cover of a spring 1971 issue of *SPORT* introducing the three men who would come to define the team's waning days in Washington should have been a clear signal to how badly this would turn out. All of them are grimacing, unsmiling, by order of the cameraman. Williams, the greatest hitter who ever lived, grimly stares down while Flood crosses his arms. And there is Denny, his hat pulled up above his head, his face aged, his slightly opened mouth revealing seemingly still-damaged teeth. The three men seem not just old but on the precipice of something terrible.

Which they were. Although Flood had spent only one season away from baseball, he just couldn't hit. Nor could he do the very thing he was best known for—play center field. He was also already a full-on alcoholic. After being lifted as a defensive replacement and playing in just 13 games, Flood told the team via telegram that his layoff time away from the game was simply too much to overcome. After that, he quite literally disappeared.

Not that Flood could have made much of a difference. The team lost 96 games. At times Maddox and Ted Williams had to be separated in the dugout. Williams, who loathed the very idea of McLain on his team, accused McLain and Maddox of undermining his authority. And the 225-pound McLain, supposedly the team's ace, started 32 games but won only 10, leading the league in losses.

Elliott Maddox, who had grown close with McLain, could see how badly Denny hurt. He needed to go on the disabled list, but did not. Had he taken a couple of months off, Maddox felt, Denny might have saved his career. Instead, he kept on pitching.

And using cortisone. McLain had resorted to using a private doctor for treatment, something he kept secret from Williams and the rest of the team. McLain would say again and again, "My arm is killing me," while sitting with Maddox on the bench.

"My arm is gonna fall off," McLain told him more than once that year. "God, I wish I could throw a curve, but I can't. My arm would just stop if I tried to throw it."

Before the 1969 All-Star Game in Washington, Bob Gibson finally met Jackie Robinson. According to Gibson, they were both standing in line to meet, of all people, Spiro Agnew and Richard Nixon before a banquet at the White House. They agreed later that it wasn't worth the effort.

Agnew's presence on the 1968 Republican ticket was what finally convinced Robinson to support Humphrey. As early as January 1969, Robinson had gone to the White House with black leaders, seeking an audience with Nixon, only to be rebuffed. Nixon had earned Robinson's trust, calling him an ally and friend, when it was expedient, but then cast him aside when he was no longer useful.

And yet Robinson's relationship with Nixon wasn't entirely over. Robinson did return to the Nixon fold in 1972, helping to raise $150,000 at a benefit sponsored by the Black Committee to Reelect the President. The decisive issue here was Robinson's conviction that the United States should stay the course in Vietnam. Though it had nearly ruined his namesake and oldest son, he would never waver in his support for the war.

And despite the snubs from Nixon, Robinson continued to press the president on issues of race. After Nixon was first elected, Robinson wrote to him, "Mr. President, Black people cannot afford racial conflict; White people cannot afford one. And it's a fact that American people cannot afford one. If we are to survive as a nation, we must do it together. Black people will work for one America if we are given hope."

Though Robinson should have been ready to give up the fight by 1968, and let others lead the way, he simply couldn't. Even in his diminished physical state, Robinson stepped in to help save a white man from certain death at the hands of black militants from Harlem. He started a construction company and helped put Charles Rangel in Congress. He confronted Nixon on busing and took it upon himself to find new leadership for the Freedom National Bank. He was accosted by a white New

York City policeman in the lobby of the Apollo Theater for no other reason than that he was black.

Still, Robinson wasn't too worn down to take to task one of his closest allies, Governor Nelson Rockefeller, for his disastrous handling of the 1971 Attica prison riots and a slowdown in the civil rights progress that Rockefeller had championed. He wrote to Rockefeller, he said, with deep regret, since he was "just confused and discouraged and feel a good friend has let me down."

"Times have changed, Jackie," Rockefeller replied, "and it would be easier for me if I in fact had 'lost the sensitivity and understanding' that you felt I had. It would be a lot easier for me emotionally. I can only say to my old friend that they haven't changed — but conditions have changed.

"All I can say," Rockefeller went on, "is that I am doing my best in a very difficult period and I hope in time you will understand this. I hope we can sit down together and talk it over sometime soon. Just let me know if you want to."

Times had gotten only worse for Robinson. It was a difficult period in Robinson's personal life as well and the final heartbreak was still ahead. By 1972, Jackie Jr. had finally found sobriety and a calling — as an advocate for individuals struggling with drug addiction. But this hopeful new stage in his life was short-lived. On June 17, 1972, he lost control of his car on the Merritt Parkway in Connecticut, crashed into an embankment, and was killed.

When his daughter Sharon looked at her father after Jackie's death, she saw a man adrift. He was alone, submerged by physical and emotional darkness. A man who once had an unassailable mission had totally lost. If 1968 had taken a great deal out of him, 1972 had brought upon him a terrible denouement.

"First Mr. Rickey and my mother, and then your brother," he said to her. "Now I wonder if I am losing my wife."

After Jackie Jr.'s death, Robinson's onetime ghostwriter, William Branch, drove out to Connecticut to see him. Branch hadn't called to say he was coming. When he knocked, Robinson came out of the house and stared straight at him, but he was nearly blind.

"Yes," Robinson said.

"Jackie," Branch said. "It's me. Bill Branch."

"Bill," he said, "Come on in."

The two sat talking for a couple of hours, renewing their friendship. Rachel made sandwiches for them and brought them something to drink. Robinson told Branch that he was going to Cincinnati for a World Series game between the Oakland Athletics and the Reds. Major League Baseball was honoring him on the 25th anniversary of his first appearance with the Dodgers. There was a rumor that Nixon would present him with a trophy. Robinson joked to Branch that Rachel had threatened not to attend if Nixon actually made an appearance (he didn't). Robinson told Branch he'd reach out to him after the ceremony. They'd catch up. That call never came.

For Jackie, this was his family's "last hurrah." They were all together in the soulless confines of Riverfront Stadium. Not that Robinson cared about the aesthetics. He just didn't want to be there. Baseball had given him so much, but it had also exacted a huge toll. And while he'd witnessed African American players flooding into the sport, he had yet to see them hold positions of power and become the next Branch Rickeys or Charlie Dressens.

But Kuhn had promised him that they were working on the problem, so Robinson came. Standing among the players in their garish new uniforms, who were about to play a game on artificial turf, Robinson seemed like a visitor from another time.

"I am extremely proud and pleased to be here this afternoon," he said, "but must admit I'm going to be tremendously more pleased and more proud when I look at that third base coaching line one day and see a black face managing in baseball."

He never got the chance. Robinson died nine days later. And thus these remarks remain as his last defiant words, challenging baseball to do the right thing, to keep working toward racial equality. Of course there would be other black stars, men who would make fortunes from the game. And there would be other players—like Jim Bunning—who would find ways to parlay their name recognition into positions of political power. But Jackie Robinson would be the last person to come out of baseball who truly believed that he could help change the world and would relentlessly and selflessly pursue that goal.

When he died on October 24, there was a public outpouring of grief. The service at Riverside Church was attended by 2,500 people. They mourned the baseball player, the barrier-breaker. And they honored the man he had become after his baseball career was over — the fearless warrior for American citizens, both black and white.

In 1970, after he'd parted ways with the Tigers, Sain stared into the unknown. There were no new suitors knocking on his door, desperate for his coaching services. By now he had alienated four clubs, clashing with managers who couldn't appreciate his genius and lacked the self-confidence to leave him alone to do his job. Other teams saw this clubhouse tension and stayed away. So Sain took a job as a roving minor league instructor with the Angels. He couldn't have been happy going into it, but traveling through those Western minor league towns, working with pitchers of all levels who were willing to buy into his beliefs, replenished him in a way he could have never imagined.

That fall, Sain was back as a major league pitching coach, this time for the White Sox, working under Chuck Tanner, who had taken over the team in the waning days of the season. What made all the difference in their working relationship was that Sain hadn't been forced on Tanner. The two had met while Tanner was managing in the Angels' minor league system. And they actually liked each other.

So when Chicago plucked Tanner, he wanted Sain with him. For the first time since those early days with Ralph Houk, a manager had actually chosen Sain to teach his pitching staff. Because Tanner wasn't threatened by Sain — and didn't fear, as other managers had, that Sain was trying to undermine his control — he left him alone.

Sain was finally free to do as he pleased. Free to train his pitchers separately from the rest of the club. Free to implement new ideas. He helped Jim Kaat, let go by the Twins, refine his form and set him on the path to winning 20 and then 21 games. Stan Bahnsen, once the Yankees' young hope and the 1968 Rookie of the Year, had fallen on hard times. That ended when Sain helped him win 21 games in 1972. Perhaps Sain's most remarkable project, however, was a onetime reliever named Wilbur Wood, who, during a four-year stretch beginning in 1971, won 20 or more games a year.

Sain's personal life found new life as well. He had been living in a camper near Midway Airport. When he met Mary Ann Zaremba in July 1972, she was 35 years old and already a widow. After a whirlwind courtship, Sain proposed and they were married on August 24. It didn't seem like the sort of relationship that could last. There was the age difference, as well as Sain's all-consuming dedication to his work. Against tall odds, the two would stay married for the rest of Sain's life.

From a distance, Sain kept an eye on McLain's career. It can't be said that Denny — the youngest pitcher ever to win 100 games — didn't try after that debilitating, demoralizing 1971 season with the Washington Senators. After being traded to the Oakland Athletics, he started only five games for them before being banished to the minors. But then he rose from the depths, landing back in the major leagues with the Braves. Some 50,000 people came to see his debut as an Atlanta Brave at Fulton County Stadium.

"This time Denny, you've got a whole city in the palm of your hand," wrote Furman Bisher. "Yea, the whole South, if you can stand the diet and accent and the weather. Be our guest. Be nuts. But win. This time, Denny, don't blow it."

He wasn't even 30. Pitchers had come back from arm problems before. But while McLain had managed through moxie and medication in the past, he wouldn't last with the Braves. After just eight starts and a 6.50 ERA, they released him during spring training in March 1973, and stints with two other minor league teams lasted only a few weeks. McLain had always been looking for a life after baseball. Now he finally had it.

"I'm proud to say Denny McLain is a good friend of mine," Sain said at the time. "And, I don't mind saying he was the greatest competitor I've ever seen in baseball. They made a lot to-do about his comings and goings. But all I know was that he was always ready to pitch when it was his turn. What more can you ask?

"I always thought he took a lot of bum raps on the suspension thing,"

Sain said. "He always had an eye out for a buck and maybe he did invest some money without checking it out first. Maybe he wasn't smart . . . A guy like that, well . . . other people just wait for him to stumble and get his face in the mud so they can walk on his back.

"What a shame . . . what a damned shame," Sain concluded. "What a career he had, but what a short one."

Yes, Gibson's 1.12 ERA will never be matched. And 1968 was the pinnacle of his career. But the Gibson after 1968 remained a true force to contend with. Just as people tend to forget McLain's second straight Cy Young in 1969, they overlook how much Gibson accomplished in the years after his last World Series game. They forget that he followed 1968 with two terrific seasons, in spite of the changed rules. His no-hitter against Pittsburgh in 1971 is merely a footnote.

In 1970 Gibson was on his way to winning 23 games and another Cy Young Award. Sparky Anderson, who at the time was managing the Cincinnati Reds — perhaps the best-hitting team of the decade and forever remembered as "The Machine" — had just watched Gibson strike out 15 of his hitters. In no way did he think Gibson was finished.

"Nobody better ever say that Gibson is over the hill," Anderson said. "He's still got to be the best pitcher in baseball."

Still, there is no escaping the indignities of age. In an effort to jumpstart the Cardinals' offense in 1969, Gibson tried to steal as often as he could when he reached first base. As a result, he jammed his knee. His arthritic elbow got worse. Then, in 1973 in Shea Stadium, as he attempted to pivot while fielding a ball, he tore his right knee. He fell to the ground with such force that family and friends of Joe Torre who were sitting in the stands thought Gibson had suffered a heart attack. Clearly, this wasn't 1964.

Gibson also admitted that the rage that had long driven him on the mound was beginning to subside. In 1972 he would confess: "When I go out to pitch, I'm angry. I have contempt for the other team. But I'm 36 now and not quite as mad as I used to be. Success hasn't changed me. It's that I'm older. You don't fight as much when you're older. It's easier to live with things now."

Even so, the Cardinals continued to look to him when it counted.

He started in the final game of the 1974 season against the Montreal Expos, when the Cardinals had a mathematical chance to capture their first Eastern Division title. Gibson had been here before. He'd clinched two pennants for the Cardinals and won the seventh game of the World Series for them twice.

As the game progressed, however, Cardinals manager Red Schoendienst could see that something was wrong. Gibson was clearly struggling. In the past, he'd been able to work his way out of it. But not this time. With a man on in the eighth inning and a 2–1 lead against the Expos' Mike Jorgensen, Gibson couldn't deliver. This time the ball didn't just sail over the head of his center fielder. It sailed beyond the outfield wall — costing the Cardinals their chance at the National League pennant.

"Maybe I should have walked Jorgensen," Schoendienst said afterwards. "But I wasn't about to take out Gibby. He'd won too many big ones for me."

Gibson's baseball career should have ended right there. But before the 1975 season he announced that he would return for one more year. At one point the highest-paid pitcher in the history of baseball, earning $150,000, Gibson was now willing to take a $10,000 pay cut to keep playing ball. He admitted that he no longer had the same level of concentration he once did, but he said he'd do his best to help the Cardinals for one last year. At the press conference, general manager Bing Devine sat beside Gibson looking somewhat forlorn — as if he had a premonition of how it would all end.

Gibson started only 14 games and went 3-10 in 1975. He certainly didn't expect to end his career in the bullpen. His final game would be against the Chicago Cubs in September. Red brought him in in the sixth inning of a tied game. First Gibson let the Cubs go ahead by one run. Then, with the bases loaded, a middling pinch hitter named Pete LaCock hit a fastball, *Bob Gibson's fastball,* over the right-field wall. Gibson finished the inning, but he wouldn't finish out the rest of the season. As he told everyone, if he couldn't get out Pete LaCock, well, fuck it.

After the game, Gibson met up with Rodney Wead, then living in Chicago. Wead had been with him, at least in spirit, at every moment since Gibson first ventured out of North Omaha, seeking to escape the ghetto. Now, over dinner at one of their favorite restaurants on Wacker Drive, what Wead saw was despair. Not about baseball — baseball was over. Gibson was still upset over his divorce, Wead said. He now had to revise his plan for the rest of his life.

Five years earlier, Gibson had envisioned a different kind of ending for himself. Perhaps, he said, he'd act like he was planning to walk a batter intentionally. But then, as the batter leaned over the plate, *his* plate, expecting four balls away, Gibson would plunk him instead.

"I'm going to find a guy like Cincinnati's Bernie Carbo," Gibson said. "The kind of guy who's next up and won't stay in the on-deck circle, but keeps meandering off behind the plate to see what you're throwing. I'm going to plunk him with a pitch, too, while he's back there giving a look."

In St. Louis, the Cardinals honored Gibson for his 17 years of service, 251 wins, and 3,117 strikeouts. Gussie Busch, who had once discussed a Budweiser dealership with Gibson, gave him a motor home. As someone drove him around the stadium in a convertible, an organist played "Try to Remember" and "Auld Lang Syne."

Five years after Gibson retired, Roger Angell came out to Omaha to interview him for a *New Yorker* profile, perhaps one of Angell's finest pieces in his fine career. Gibson, following his divorce from his first wife Charlene, had remarried, in an interracial union with a white woman named Wendy Nelson that, Rodney Wead believed, would keep Gibson from settling in what he felt was an intolerant St. Louis. But in Omaha he had begun to enjoy all the spoils of a post-baseball life. He'd opened up a restaurant and served as chairman of the board of a bank he helped found. But none of these business ventures would occupy him for long. The Gibson whom Angell encountered seemed dissatisfied, if not slightly bored. Although he had turned down an initial job offer with the Cardinals, Angell was struck by how eager Gibson now was to somehow return to baseball. He missed it.

Gibson confided to Angell that he was worried about his place in baseball history. He was concerned that the Hall of Fame wouldn't be open to him, or that the process would drag on for years because he'd been so unkind to the press — and because he had married outside his race. But his fears proved unfounded. In 1981, he made it in on the first ballot, having received 84 percent of the vote. He got 337 votes, compared to Don Drysdale's 243 and Juan Marichal's 233. Neither Drysdale nor Marichal would reach the Hall that year.

The same year Gibson was inducted, he joined Joe Torre, then manager of the Mets, on his coaching staff. When he first retired, Gibson had tried working as a commentator for ABC's baseball broadcasts, with disastrous results. Working for Torre, though, would be a real job in baseball. The question was, what exactly was Gibson's job description?

As Torre famously explained: "It's not like adding a second pitching coach. Rube [Walker] is still our pitching coach. But like myself, Rube is a former catcher. We just felt that perhaps the pitchers can relate more to one of their own — a former pitcher.

"Rube is a fine settling influence on the pitchers and they have great respect for him," he continued. "But he can carry them just so far. Maybe Gibby can carry them the rest of the way. Maybe he can light a fire in some of them."

He lasted just one season in New York. In 1982, Torre and Gibson were coaching in Atlanta, where Torre landed after being fired by the Mets. Torre installed Gibson as a full pitching coach. It was a post that Johnny Sain had held briefly during the 1977 season. Now Gibson was tasked with helping a talented team reach the play-offs for the first time since 1969.

There was initial success. But despite the Braves winning the National League's Western Division — owner Ted Turner seriously contemplated having Gibson return from retirement to pitch the deciding game — Gibson wasn't cut out for the job. He fought openly with his former teammate Dal Maxvill, who was now the third-base coach. But more to the point, he didn't have it in him to be a teacher. He lacked patience.

He also clashed with Sain, who had been working with minor league pitchers in the system for the last five years and whose teaching methods ran counter to what Gibson was telling his pitchers in the majors. Gibson stressed the importance of lifting weights and running in the off-season, of being aggressive in order to get ahead of the hitter. When Sain's pitchers came up from the minors, they felt they had to unlearn what Sain had taught them. Gibson had no use for Sain's ideas, many of which he deemed bizarre.

About one young pitcher, Rick Mahler, Gibson groused, "He pitches backward, like Sain teaches him. He pitches ball one, ball two and then goes after the batter. You can't do that."

Sain played nice and advised his staff to take the coaching advice à la carte — to pick and choose what they thought they could use. Sain had coached many pitchers who threw hard — including McLain. He felt that Gibson ignored the very principles of movement that had been critical to his own success. Sure, his fastball had been terrific. But it was that slider that had had so many hitters helplessly lunging at the ball.

"What's aggressiveness?" Sain said. "You can be aggressive through a change of speed. What are you going to do, try to overpower every batter? You take away the element of surprise if you do that. I was released four times when I was in Class D ball because I didn't have velocity. But in the end I made it to the majors, and I did it by throwing breaking balls and off-speed pitches."

Torre and Gibson would last just three seasons with the Braves. When Turner fired Torre and his staff after the 1984 season, it was Sain who replaced Gibson. Yet even Sain couldn't change the fortunes of a substandard staff. This was a world away from McLain and Lolich, not to mention Wilbur Wood. When Sain was dismissed in the spring of 1987, pitcher Rick Mahler said, "It's kind of bad to see Johnny go out. He's probably done more for me in my career than anyone else. But I think Johnny was getting to the point where he was good at talking about pitching, but there were a lot of things he didn't want to do."

Sain was a thinker and innovator, but he was also a survivor. He had weathered an interminable minor league career to emerge as one of the best pitchers of baseball's postwar era. And he never lost his baseball intelligence. Even after he was fired in 1987, he continued to scout with the Braves, and he was even called up by general manager Bobby Cox to see if he couldn't fix whatever ailed a onetime disciple Larry McWilliams.

In real retirement by 1993, Sain was once standing in a bookstore near his home in Oak Brook, Illinois. He was 76 years old. Somewhat sheepishly, he revealed the book in his hand — Machiavelli's *The Prince*. Sain claimed he was buying it for a friend.

"I was trying to explain some of Machiavelli's concepts," Sain said, "especially the parts on cunning, but I just figured it might be easy to get him one of the books and let him read it for himself."

For the next nine years, Sain would continue to update his theories while traveling all over with Mary Ann. He read widely. What mattered most was to keep moving forward, to approach life with an open mind.

"I think the biggest thing anyone should realize is that if you're afraid to fail, you'll never truly succeed," Sain said, just as he had told so many pitchers on so many different teams. "And if you can think, you can succeed."

Even after his debilitating stroke in 2002, Sain did his best to redefine himself. With Mary Ann at his side, he struggled through therapy. He had to teach himself again how to speak, to read, to shave. He had to learn to live a new life.

"Hey John," Chuck Tanner — the manager with whom he'd lasted the longest — told him during this difficult period, "we're in the fifth inning and it's a nine-inning game."

Sain hung on as long as he could. When he died in 2006, there was a rush to celebrate his playing career and his pairing with Warren Spahn. But his greatest legacy, arguably, was his work with pitchers. Could the Yankees and Twins and Tigers have won pennants without him? Maybe. But could anyone else have pried the kind of performances that he did from players as diverse as Jim Bouton and Mudcat Grant, Denny McLain and Mickey Lolich, Wilbur Wood and Whitey Ford? Probably not. Modern-day coaches like Leo Mazzone of the Braves cite his influence and look to him as a guide. How did he do it? How was he able to change the lives of so many men long after his own playing days were over? Sain was never one to dwell in the past. All that mattered was the now.

"I just wish that everything that came to me at such a young age had come later," Denny McLain said. "I didn't know what to do with it then, how to handle it. I took it out and burned it in the street. I acted like it would never end, and it does. Regardless of who you are, it does."

McLain was speaking in 1983. His dreams of achieving fame and glory through music, of rising above the ordinary ranks of has-been athletes, had come to naught. He wasn't able to build a brand for himself the way Joe Namath and others had. He could see the money that was out there to be earned in the era of free agency. But he showed terrible judgment—both in his business dealings (including that bookmaking scheme) and in pinning such high hopes on his musical career.

The players who came after could rely on the counsel of agents and corporate sponsors, whose job it is to protect their players' interests and keep them rich. McLain had no such guidance. But even if he'd had an agent, it's not hard to imagine that he would have found a way to sabotage it all. That seemed to be his fate. After he left Atlanta and the major leagues, his career over at the age of 29, he made one misstep after another. He took a job as a general manager of a minor league team in Memphis, only to leave it bankrupt. (He claimed that it had already been in financial trouble.) There was a projection television venture, an investment in walk-in medical clinics, a failed investment in a shopping mall. Then things took a turn toward the criminal.

By the time McLain entered Courtroom 3 in the U.S. courthouse in Tampa in April 1985, his weight had ballooned, by some accounts, to nearly 300 pounds. He had filed for bankruptcy twice. He'd just been in custody for five weeks following his conviction on racketeering, extortion, conspiracy, and drug trafficking charges. The first trial after his arrest in 1984 had ended in a mistrial. But this time he'd lost his case. While working as a loan officer, federal authorities said, he'd begun a bookmaking operation, loaning money at obscene rates, making the debt essentially unpayable. When one borrower couldn't pay, McLain and his associates had threatened to cut off his ears and threatened another borrower's wife and children. To top it all off, a jury had convicted him of possessing three kilograms of cocaine with the intention of distributing even more.

During sentencing, his lawyer argued that McLain was a "patsy" in all of this. But in handing down her 23-year prison sentence, federal judge Elizabeth A. Kovachevich told McLain, "Perhaps your greatest gullibility is that you don't admit to yourself your own guilt."

Just 29 months later, however, McLain was free again after his conviction was overturned on technical matters. Out of prison, he briefly ran a minor league hockey team and signed autographs for money. In anticipation of another trial, McLain pleaded guilty to reduced charges in 1988 and was handed a 12-year sentence, but this time he was given probation with time served.

He tried to get his life back on track. He returned to Detroit. He was still a beloved figure there, and soon he was playing the organ again for paying gigs. He worked as a radio talk-show host and paired up with Eli Zaret to do a television show. He had returned to a place of lucrative prominence in Detroit, where he could exist forever.

In 1978 a fire at his home in Lakeland destroyed everything, including all his baseball awards. But what completely derailed his second act and sent him on another downward spiral was a much graver personal tragedy. In 1992, his daughter Kristin was killed in a car accident involving a tractor-trailer. At that time McLain was reportedly earning $400,000 from his radio show and a sports show on television — four times what he'd once demanded from Jim Campbell — but his daughter's death unsettled him, unleashing old demons.

His broadcast partner and friend Eli Zaret could do nothing. McLain had put his life back together — he was a star again, someone who could talk about politics and family, who could engage listeners without talking about sports at all, whose show had great ratings — but with Kristin's death, none of it mattered.

McLain soon returned to his old habits. In 1993, McLain and a partner purchased Peet Packing, a small-town meatpacking plant with a long history. Almost immediately, $3 million went missing from the company's pension fund. The company filed for bankruptcy two years later. All signs pointed to the two men, who faced conspiracy, money laundering, mail fraud, and embezzlement charges. When a jury convicted Denny in 1996, there was no escape hatch this time, no chance of a mistrial. It would be 2004 before he got out of prison again.

There would be no third act. Or would it be fourth? After he was released, he lived in a halfway house while working at a 7-Eleven. Sharyn McLain, his long-suffering wife, had filed for divorce not long after he started his prison term. But McLain believed that if anyone could forgive him, it would be her. Eventually they remarried and settled back into life in suburban Detroit. In 2013, doctors diagnosed Sharyn with Parkinson's disease. Afterwards, McLain, who often used a wheelchair to get around, underwent bariatric surgery and lost 162 pounds. By the time of his remarriage, he'd begun paying restitution — some $25,000 a year — to the 100 people who once worked for him at Peet Packing. He started a small scrap iron business, tried his hand at radio again. He wrote a third autobiography, *I Told You I Wasn't Perfect,* in which he attacked nearly every teammate from Al Kaline to Mickey Lolich and every sportswriter who'd once worked in Detroit. His mother was to blame for his upbringing, he said. His father had been abusive. Nothing, in short, was actually his fault. All along, he'd meant well. Either he'd been misled or misunderstood.

But he remains someone people still want to approach, to be close to. As Zaret has found, when McLain shows up at public events, there are still those who are willing to overlook everything because of that one year, those 31 wins. They love him. Amazingly, Zaret believes, there are some people whom he didn't defraud or steal from who will "compartmentalize his true character" because of what he once meant.

For all his prickly reclusiveness and his combative relations with the press — his angst about being underappreciated or forgotten — it's Bob Gibson, after all, who has stood out above his peers and remains the great avatar of his era. Of all his peers who helped make 1968 such an unforgettable, unrepeatable year, he's the one we remember. McLain, much as the old cartoon depicted him, rode that rocket — until he crashed. Thanks to his hubris and penchant for self-destruction, the racy headlines have supplanted our memories of his baseball career. But Gibson, distant and unapproachable, has only risen in stature. In retirement, he has finally earned the recognition that eluded him as a player. As Gerald Early would note, his reputation exceeds that of any of his peers, with the possible exception of Koufax. He's become a cultural icon, one who stands for competitiveness, for winning when it matters most.

Gibson's reticence, though, remains curious. There's always been a contradictory pull — a desire for recognition and affirmation despite the aloof attitude. As his other ventures fell away, he gravitated back to baseball. There were the coaching stints under Torre in New York and Atlanta, and even for the Cardinals briefly in 1995. He hosted a radio call-in show for the Cardinals' flagship station for a number of years and spent one season with ESPN. He worked as a special adviser to the president of the American League. As of this writing, both he and Lou Brock serve as special advisers to the Cardinals—the kind of post often given out by major league teams to their retired stars. They come to spring training, donning new versions of their old uniforms.

Not everyone remembers or even knows how special they are. The *St. Louis Post-Dispatch*'s Rick Hummel always feels a measure of happiness when he sees current players actually engage Gibson, who doesn't volunteer much but will speak for hours with any player who approaches him. Watching him in camp, Hummel often feels for both Gibson and Brock. They have much to offer, but someone has to ask them first.

A few years after Angell interviewed Gibson for *The New Yorker,* he stepped into a crowded elevator for a World Series game. After one stop, the elevator emptied out. Angell stayed on, looking straight ahead, when he heard a familiar voice behind him.

"How quickly they forget."

Turning around, Angell saw that it was Bob Gibson. Here was the man who could have done anything he wanted, pursued any sport of his choosing, but chose baseball. What Gibson didn't understand was that, by doing that, he'd ensured that he would never fade from memory. No one would ever forget.

EPILOGUE

RESCHEDULING DENNY MCLAIN.

These were the words that greeted me upon entering a huge warehouse in the City of Industry, a bleak industrial suburb of Los Angeles. I had come here in May 2012 expecting to see both Denny McLain and Bob Gibson, who were scheduled to sign bats and balls and photographs together as part of what I assumed would be a large baseball card show.

Even though it was a staged event and unlikely to generate an anecdote for my book, I decided to fly out for it from my home in Brooklyn. After all, it was at a similar event at the Holiday Inn O'Hare in 1987, at the height of the baseball memorabilia market, that McLain, at the moment free from jail, ran into Johnny Sain for the first time in a decade. Sain had been released from his coaching duties for the Braves and didn't have a stable of young pitchers to mentor. He was there with his second wife, Mary Ann, whom McLain had never met.

"Johnny," McLain said, rising from his table. "Great to see you."

"Mary Ann," Sain said, "this is Denny McLain. My last 31-game winner."

And with that, it was as if no time had passed between them. McLain was still the stallion, and Sain was still trying to tame him. For a few minutes, they spoke about the past. They remembered that game against Boston in 1968 when McLain, on sheer guts, struck out, in succession, Cleon Jones, Carl Yastrzemski, and Hawk Harrelson. It was then that McLain had really known that winning 30 games was within reach.

The last time the two had seen each other was when Sain was working with pitchers from the Atlanta Braves' minor league team in Richmond and he needed help. He brought one of his pupils to meet with the one person he thought he could learn from: Denny McLain. McLain told the young man that his success as a pitcher depended entirely on what he did when behind in the count — 2-0, 3-1, 3-2. Sain told this pupil that it was "as good a description of pitching as I've ever heard."

The three chatted for a few more minutes, and then Sain told McLain that he and Mary Ann were headed back home to Oak Brook.

"I really appreciate you coming over," Denny said as the two men shook hands. "Stay out of trouble."

Sain and Mary Ann left with a signed photograph from McLain — whose autograph, at that time, was selling for $4. It was only later that Sain noticed the inscription.

"It's nice to see you John," McLain had written. "And don't forget I made a star out of you."

By 2012, when I went to California, Sain was long dead. As were Curt Flood, Don Drysdale, Mickey Mantle, and Mayo Smith. Jim Northrup, whose grand slam in Game 6 sealed McLain's only win in the Series, had died the year before. Bill Freehan, whose historic block at home plate against Lou Brock changed the course of the Series, was alive but suffering from Alzheimer's disease.

And by now, my faith in what the game meant to the nation during 1968 had been undermined — especially when it came to Detroit. As I would find out very soon, there was little support for the idea that the Tigers calmed racial tensions in the city. Even the supposed "happy riot" and celebration that followed the Series win would prove to be a myth — right from the start.

"I hope this town is happy," a Detroit policeman said after the last out of Game 7. "And I hope that Detroit never wins another World Series." On the job for 20 hours, he was exhausted. He and his force were helpless to stop the looting of downtown department stores. They couldn't rein in the amped-up crowd.

One store owner said, "This has had a very destructive effect on Detroit. It was unbelievable to see so many police on the streets and still have looting and damage like the downtown merchants suffered."

Yet nothing could stop the mythologizing. Detroit was a city reborn, all thanks to the Tigers' victory. At least that was the widely embraced story line. After the championship, Governor George Romney wrote to Tigers owner John Fetzer: "The deepest meaning of this victory extends beyond Tiger Stadium and beyond the sports pages, radio broadcasts, and the telecasts that have consumed our attention for several months.

"This championship occurred when all of us in Detroit and Michigan needed a great lift," Romney wrote. "At a time of unusual tensions, when many good men lost their perspective toward others, the Tigers set an example of what human relations should be."

Auto executive Henry Ford II told Fetzer, "Your fighting, winning team is the best tonic Detroit could have." And Willie Horton, who was from Detroit, proudly proclaimed, "I believe that the 1968 Tigers were put here by God to heal this city."

And so on. We want to believe that the sports we play and watch are more than just games. We want to endow them with a greater meaning, with a moral weight, to somehow justify our obsession. The joy of the game doesn't seem to be enough. Baseball is especially susceptible to this outpouring of nostalgia because of our belief that the sport, in crossing generations, somehow reflects a simpler age, even though we all know that our American story has never been simple.

Dick Tracewski acknowledged that the Tigers' success may have eased racial tensions in 1968, but the idea that he and his teammates were playing with that particular goal in mind is "strictly a myth."

"We weren't in tune with the social ramifications of the riot or anything like that," he said. "I'm sure that people were taken with the Tigers, with the way we played, the way we came back. But certainly nobody in the clubhouse ever thought about it or talked about it. Once the season starts, all you do is look forward to the next game. And that was it."

The fact is that baseball's impact on society is minimal. It certainly didn't stop the rising tide of racial hatred in Detroit. George Wallace found great support there during his presidential runs in 1968 and in 1972. Though Wallace's campaign fizzled in 1968, four years later Wallace actually *won* the Michigan Democratic primary, taking every white ward in Detroit, with his greatest backing coming from the last white enclaves in the city's Northwest and Northeast sections. Coleman Young, Detroit's African American mayor from 1974 to 1994, rose to power in a shifting racial and economic landscape and held onto it for decades in large part by capitalizing on antiwhite sentiment in a majority black city. This was not a city on the mend.

"The stuff about it pulling the city together is a white person's view, really," said baseball historian and author Gary Gillette. "Detroit never came back together — period. If you want to say that the '68 Tigers were popular, that after the Tigers won the World Series there were black people and white people dancing in the streets? Sure. If you want to say that they brought the city together on a superficial level? Yeah. Did that stop white flight? No. Did that stop all sorts of racial violence in the city? No. Did that stop all the ugliness in mayoral elections that came after, when the race card was played? No. Did that stop the largely racial war between Detroit and the suburbs? It seems to me that's something white people say to assuage their conscience. Like that one magical team, for one special summer, could change things."

As of this writing, going into the 2017 season, the Tigers are one of the most competitive teams in baseball. Since 2006, they've won two American League pennants, and during one stretch they won four straight division titles. In 2013, third baseman Miguel Cabrera became the first player since Frank Robinson to win the Triple Crown. Pitcher Justin Verlander is one of the best pitchers in the American League. The Tigers *should* be a source of great civic pride for Detroit. But the fact is that the Tigers cannot help Detroit — and some have argued that they've helped make things worse.

As Joe Drape chronicled in the *New York Times,* a divide has grown between the people who actually live in Detroit and the players and white suburban fans who come to Comerica Park — the edifice that replaced Tiger Stadium in 2000 to the tune of $300 million, more than $100 million of which came from taxpayers — and leave as soon as the last pitch is thrown. The Tigers have done little to revitalize their city, which struggles to pay its employees and provide basic services to its citizens.

Still, traveling to California in 2012 would give me a chance to see the two men whose matchup the country had waited for with such anticipation 44 years before. So I went. Parking my rented Ford Focus in a spot reserved for customers and workers at an aluminum and glass factory, I walked into what seemed to be a large weekly flea market rather than a baseball card show. Near the entrance, a "Magic: The Gathering" tournament had just begun, and I was stopped in my tracks by a sign an-

nouncing that, due to a family emergency, McLain would not be attending. The dream matchup was not to be.

What was I expecting? Certainly not a cordial conversation between
the two men, given what they'd said about each other in the past. I didn't
even expect McLain, with whom I'd spent two days driving around the
previous November, to remember me. Once during that trip he'd left me
sitting at a restaurant where he'd agreed to pick me up only an hour before. A few months later, when I emailed him about contact phone numbers for other players, he replied, "Who is this?"

No, in truth I was there for Gibson. For over a year, other people
— including Rodney Wead and St. Louis sportswriter Rick Hummel —
had approached him on my behalf. I'd corresponded with his business
manager, Dick Zitzman, to no avail. The Cardinals were no help. I tried
reaching out to him myself. I tracked down every reporter I knew who'd
spent any time with Gibson. Each one told me the same thing: he's impossible to reach, but if you do get to him, he's a tough but insightful guy.

The closest I had come was the previous October in St. Louis. I was
waiting for Rodney Wead at a restaurant in the city's West End when his
car pulled up. From a distance, Wead stuck out his long hand, waving
for me to come over, and I stood and waited for a few minutes until he
finished talking on the phone. Then he got out slowly, shaking his head,
a towering man in a red tracksuit.

"Man, that was Gibson," he said. "That man does not shut up."

"Except to me," I said.

We laughed about that. Over breakfast we talked about those early
days in Omaha. About Gibson's brother Josh. About the tormented letters Gibson sent Wead from Columbus, Georgia, when he was in the minor leagues. About the racism they'd both encountered over the years,
even as Gibson became a superstar. How St. Louis never really embraced
his friend as one of its own.

Toward the end of our conversation, Wead shook his head and said,
"He's been very good to me, and I guess I in turn. I wish he was more
open sometimes, you know, but that's Gibson."

I've often found an underlying sadness in those who once played
professional sports. The plight of the professional athlete is that, even as

he ages, other people's memories of him are fixed in time. They refuse to move with him, never wavering from their reminiscences of him as a very young man whose career would most certainly end at the same time in life as their own careers and lives would be taking off. The former athlete is forever being asked to relive those days when he was 26 or 27, to replenish our collective memory. It's awful. Yet there are many former athletes who oblige, who are willing to spend the time reliving those days for us. Bob Gibson simply isn't one of them.

"But you have to play along with it," said Eli Zaret, McLain's friend and ghostwriter. "Because if you revile the fans for being who they are, then you're pissing on your own profession. I ran into a lot of guys like that over the years. Bill Laimbeer in basketball is a perfect example — enjoyed a wonderful career thanks to the irrational behavior of the fanatics and yet had no respect for the fans. He thought they were a bunch of idiots to even care about it. Well, you can't have it both ways. So I can see where Gibson's angst would come from. If you really felt that Solly Hemus was racist and you thought it was disgusting playing for the people in the organization, do you really want to talk about it 40 years later? I don't know."

Walking into the event space where the signing was supposed to take place, I was immediately struck by the total absence of sentiment. The days of the great autograph and baseball card shows that I had known as a young man were clearly over. I had expected to see a large, over-the-top display of McLain and Gibson, but they were barely represented in the memorabilia for sale. There was a booth selling lanyards with the logos of all 32 NFL teams and a table selling autographs at a discount — $7 for hockey legends, $20 for baseball and football players. Off to the side was a booth with photographs and magazines — including the 1970 *Sports Illustrated* with McLain's mug on the cover and the headline "Baseball's Big Scandal." I paid a man $69 for a ticket to have Gibson sign my baseball. (It was $99 to have him sign a bat or a jersey. A McLain-autographed ball fetched $20.)

There were fewer than 100 people in line when Gibson finally emerged and took a seat at a metal folding table. I suppose in some ways I fancied myself as Gay Talese coming to San Francisco to see Joe

DiMaggio, the private man finally relenting to the writer's plea. Yet this was not the pier of San Francisco. There were no Sicilian fishermen who protected DiMaggio as one of their own, no pretty young girl snapping pictures as both they and the stoic baseball hero looked on. Whatever happened here — in this industrial labyrinth east of Los Angeles — would not lead to the greatest magazine story of all time.

Lining up behind a man holding a replica of Gibson's jersey, I patiently waited. Dick Zitzman took each ticket and passed it down to Gibson, who would quickly sign an item and say a few words about the weather or the Cardinals before moving on to the next ticket-holder.

At last it was my turn. I handed the ball to Gibson. He was 76 years old, and up close he looked tired, his face coarse. He had aged more gracefully than his peers, however, and looked even more muscular now than the wiry pitcher who used to fly off the left side of the mound. The Nehru jacket was gone. So was the gold medallion. His hair was nearly all gray now, but at least he had all of it.

In addition to the ball, I had brought along a sealed letter. It was nearly identical to several letters I had been trying to get to Gibson for the past several months. In it I explained that I hadn't meant to ambush him, that I wanted to speak to him because I considered this book part of the historical record and I wanted to get things exactly right.

But now that I was actually in front of Gibson, I suddenly found myself stammering. I don't usually lose my head around famous and powerful people. But Gibson was different. Several years ago, a motorist named Miguel Sanchez allegedly cut Gibson off in traffic in Omaha. Ten miles later, at a gas station along Interstate 80, he found himself in a fistfight with Gibson. Both men were initially cited, but neither was charged. In the end, no criminal action was taken — police said they couldn't determine who started the fight — but it served as a reminder of one thing: cross Bob Gibson at your own peril.

"Mr. Gibson," I said, having given him my ball and holding my letter out to him, "Rodney Wead probably told you about me."

"Can you speak up?" Gibson said.

"I'm a journalist from New York writing a book about the 1968 World Series," I said, trying to hand off my envelope. Gibson stared straight at me then, and suddenly there was a commotion among the event's organizers. They surrounded him, wanting to know who I was and why I was there.

"He's a journalist doing some sort of story," Gibson said.

"I just wanted to give him this letter," I explained, putting it down on the table.

"We don't even know if we even want that," one man said. Then a large man with a crew cut escorted me off to the left, where I was to wait until people cleared out so I could talk to the agent.

After a little while, he led me to the opposite end of the table, where Dick Zitzman studied my envelope for a moment and finally said, "I've seen your name before."

"Oh," I said. "Are you Dick Zitzman?"

"I am," he said.

"Look," I explained, "I just wanted to get the letter in front of him."

"I'll let you know," he said before turning his attention to the few people left in line.

Of course I never heard from him again, or from Gibson for that matter. But afterwards, I stood off to the side watching as the remaining ticket-holders handed Gibson their items. At exactly 11:43, Gibson got up. He moved to a table behind a large black curtain. Over the course of the next half-hour, a dozen or so latecomers arrived and were led by a staff member behind the curtain, where Gibson continued to sit.

Finally, at 12:30, a heavyset man with a white goatee looked around and yelled out, "Last call for Gibson ticket-holders!" There were none.

When I could no longer see Gibson in silhouette behind that curtain, I began to walk away. Nearby a far larger crowd was gathering for one-time Dodger catcher Paul Lo Duca. As I stood there in front of a sign advertising upcoming appearances — Fernando Valenzuela, Magic Johnson — I heard someone ask, "Is he coming on the 28th?"

I looked at the boy. He was no more than 12, and he and his friends were walking through the hall with their bikes. They'd probably never even heard of Gibson or McLain.

"Who?" I said.

"Matt Kemp," he replied, referring to the young outfielder then playing for the Dodgers.

"I guess so," I said.

With that, he and his friends began to wander through the 65,000-foot space whose owners had deemed it the "largest and best" collection of vendors for collectibles. Walking through the miscegenated displays of wrestling figurines and Transformers, past the comic book stalls and booths and people selling collectible pins, I realized that all *this* told the current story of America today — not baseball. That year, in 2012, only 12.6 million people bothered to watch the World Series. The game of Gibson and McLain, Sain and Drysdale seemed very much in the past.

Dispirited, I walked back to my rental car, mentally preparing myself for Los Angeles traffic. Dropping my reporter's notebooks in the passenger seat, I suddenly realized I'd forgotten something: the baseball I'd paid Gibson to sign for me. While taking notes and haggling for overpriced comics, I'd simply left it behind. Running back, I made my way through the same stalls, looking for where I might have dropped it. I even explained what happened to the men running the autograph session. They were sympathetic and offered to sell me one of the balls Gibson had signed for them.

I declined the offer. As I drove back to Los Angeles, I realized I'd have to tell the young man to whom I'd promised the autographed ball what had happened. I'd have to tell him that the baseball was gone. I'd have to tell him Bob Gibson was gone.

ACKNOWLEDGMENTS

The idea for this book came over a discussion on a warm, optimistic evening in Washington, D.C. It was based on a simple premise that somehow, in the midst of a season of darkness, baseball had calmed a nation. It was an idealistic notion, and one I was ready to buy into. I was wrong.

Almost from the start of my research, I began to encounter complexities and nuances I could have never imagined would arise with a book devoted to sports. In the reporting and writing, I needed — and got — invaluable assistance from people across the country as I tried to answer questions in order to write with authority and produce an intellectually honest book. Any factual errors or omissions are my own.

I'm terribly grateful to all the people, listed in the bibliography, who agreed to take time out of their lives and speak to me on the record, but some are worth special mention here. Rodney Wead and Lonnie Wheeler deserve my undying thanks for helping me understand the mysterious figure that is Bob Gibson. Rachel Robinson, Roger Angell, and the late Marvin Miller helped provide context and clarity in looking back to a most difficult time.

I am equally indebted for the help provided by relative strangers. Bill Dow and Marvin Steele opened up doors and assisted greatly in my reporting, as did Mark Pattison and Dave Raglin from the Mayo Smith Society and Rick Thompson with the Detroit Tigers. Tim Wiles and Freddie Berowski at the A. Bartlett Giamatti Research Center of the National Baseball Hall of Fame and Museum gave me much-needed assistance and bolstered my sanity during my extended period of work there in 2011. Both have since left the organization, but I am forever indebted for their help and expertise to a novice researcher. Ron Simon, Curator of Television and Radio at the Paley Center for Media, was generous with both his time and his help in finding valuable video for me to watch. Ezra Edelman, Brad Snyder, Robert Lipsyte, Harvey Araton,

Gary Gillette, Michael MacCambridge, Al Eisele, Jud Branam, and George Vecsey were beyond generous in their counsel and insight. The Creighton University Athletic Department, Minnesota Historical Society, and Nebraska Historical Society all gave me unexpected and much-needed assistance as well.

There was the baseball itself. I needed to see what actually took place. In that regard, I owe special thanks to both Nick Trotta and Louis Baracelli of MLB Productions for helping me obtain invaluable footage from the 1968 World Series as well as other audiovisual materials. Joshua Rogol spent hours breaking down that grainy World Series film, play by play, pitch by pitch. It was a difficult task, but one that he performed heroically.

I got much-needed help on the ground level. Caroline Jones, my editorial assistant, not only did research and transcribed audio but proved to be a worthy sounding board throughout. Julia Livshin spent months on the initial edit of an unwieldy, sprawling manuscript and turned it into something of which we could both be proud. I cannot say enough about the exhausting work Lori Azim did in helping me deliver the finished product in its very last stages.

No one believed that Jackie Robinson would become a character, much less a central figure, in this work. When he did, David McMahon and Sarah Burns from Florentine Films were generous in sharing their time and knowledge as I tried, in my own way, to bring his postbaseball life to the page. It's an honor to be associated with their wonderful documentary of a complicated man and American hero.

In this area, I cannot begin to ever repay both Jonathan Eig and Michael Long. Jonathan offered logistical and emotional assistance. Michael, time and again, lent a hand in understanding and documenting Jackie Robinson's later years.

I also owe a debt to those who literally let me into their homes. Tim Tucker opened his house in St. Louis without ever having met me. My relatives, Ravi and Rajya Adibhatla, gave me a room so I might pursue my reporting in Michigan. Near the completion of my research, the Chirra family in Los Angeles did the same.

Throughout, friends and colleagues helped me in one fashion or another. I've often said I would never be able to accomplish anything without help from the extended *New York Observer* diaspora. This was no exception. Andrew Rice, Terry Golway, Jim Windolf, Devin Leonard, Lisa Chase, James Kaplan, Alexandra Jacobs, Frank DiGiacomo, Jay Stowe, Tom McGeveran, Josh Benson, Andrew Goldman, Felix Gillette, Peter Stevenson, George Gurley, and Jason Gay all helped with either editorial or emotional guidance during challenging times. So too did my former editors at *The Atlantic,* Cullen Murphy and Scott Stossel, as well as my great teacher and friend Richard Ford. This also extends to former colleagues, including Clara Jeffery, David Plotz, Denise Martin, and Jon Birger.

Of course, such counsel and support also came from elsewhere. I've been fortunate to have support and guidance from lifelong friends Charlie Michael and Subha Xavier, Ephraim and Erik Zimmerman, Kara Roggenkamp, John Nimis, Megan Bernstein, and Joe and Clare Squance as well as others from Oxford, Ohio, David Hirsch and Ellen Beurk foremost among them. I don't think I could feed myself, much less write a book, without Peter Kafka, Cindy Lobel, Stephanie Auwerter, Chad Anderson, and Ryan and Carrie Nelson. My surrogate parents—Ben Joravsky and Pamela Fox, Rick Nelson and Gary and Suzi Graham— were always there in my corner when I had to retreat to it.

I cannot begin to express the debt I owe to those who have been with me from the beginning, ever since this book started to take shape in Washington, including, among others, Bruce Falconer, Tammy Tuck, Jeff and Gillian McClelland, Ryan Farney, Brian and Annie Marie Shaw, Amanda Jonas, Josh Freedom DuLac, and Steve and Beth Hodgin. And I am deeply thankful to those who had to put up with me as I toiled in New York, namely, Jennifer Saba, Ken Li, Edmund Lee, Michael Learmonth, Scott Wells, Jane Moore, Nisha Gopalan, Joachim Carels and Becca Krauss, Lee Fennimore, Tanja Shub and David Simbandumwe, Russell Pearlman, and Andrea Faville Pearlman.

I would not have been able to physically write this book without the Brooklyn Writers' Space at the now-defunct Room 58. Not only did it provide the facilities to work, but I grew to count on the advice I received there from others who have written books—like David Berreby, Mark Yarm, and Hernán Iglesias-Illa—on how to see something so large through to its end.

It's fair to say that there would be no book without my agent, Howard Yoon. Outside of his great professional expertise and guidance, Howard has been a great friend to both me and the book. He oversaw nearly every aspect of the book from its conception to completion. He and the rest of the staff at the Ross Yoon Agency are without parallel.

I have to thank my terrific editor at Houghton Mifflin Harcourt, Susan Canavan, for believing in the book's premise and for her undying patience throughout the process. When we first spoke about it, I told her I thought I could finish the book in 13 months. She told me that was "highly unrealistic." She was right.

I could have asked for no greater moral, and often financial, support than the support provided by my family. My cousin Tejaswini Ganti (along with her husband Vipul Agrawal) provided not only food and shelter and support but access to all the research tools that New York University has to offer. My father, Rama Rao Pappu, perhaps the most patient, supportive man one would ever meet, was the most thoughtful, reassuring backer I needed during often stressful times. My sister Suguna and her family — her husband Ravi Durvasula and my two nieces, Maya and Samsara Durvasula — never lost faith that I could do it. Their belief became my own.

In writing this book, I could never imagine that it would find its way to print without three of the greatest influences in my life. I would never have gone forward with the idea had I not had the blessing of the late Peter W. Kaplan, whom I relied on constantly for editorial and emotional guidance. Likewise, the late David Carr and his family helped ground me in the real world during what could often be a lonely time. It's very rare to have even one great professional mentor in one's life. I had two.

And finally, a word for my mother, Surya Kantham Pappu, who referred to this as my "Cincinnati Reds Book" before her death. Her tenacity and work ethic were unmatched, even as she struggled to hold on in the last days of her life. I hope that I was able to bring those same values to this work. In writing about men like Denny McLain and Don Drysdale and Bob Gibson, I often wondered how they would match up against my mother's toughness. The answer was always simple: they wouldn't.

NOTES

Author Note

All descriptions of pitches and scenes from the 1968 World Series came from hours of study and charting by Joshua Rogol, as well as my own personal observations, unless noted otherwise.

Prologue: Hope

page

ix *In October 1968*: Jerry Green, *Year of the Tiger: The Diary of Detroit's World Champions* (New York: Coward-McCann, 1969), 221–222.

Paired at the end after absurd: The Bob Hope Show, season 19, episode 2, NBC, October 14, 1968.

who had seemed like a "tot": Museum of Broadcasting, ed., *Bob Hope: A Half-Century on Radio and Television* (exhibition catalog) (New York: Museum of Broadcasting, 1986), 26.

x *No one, McCarver would later joke*: Tim McCarver, interview by author, January 7, 2012.

xi *Years later McLain would speak*: Denny McLain, interview by author, November 16, 2011.

xii *"I can't imagine what else can happen to us this year"*: Arnold Rampersad, *Jackie Robinson: A Biography* (New York: Alfred A. Knopf, 1997), 429.

xiii *"Baseball has sold itself as a civic monument"*: Bill Veeck with Ed Linn, *Veeck — As in Wreck: The Autobiography of Bill Veeck* (New York: Putnam, 1962; reprint, Chicago: University of Chicago Press, 2001), 104.

xiv *That wasn't the word one would use: The Bob Hope Show,* October 14, 1968.

Gibson hadn't been able to stomach McLain's harsh words: Bob Gibson with Lonnie Wheeler, *Stranger to the Game: The Autobiography of Bob Gibson* (New York: Penguin Books, 1994), 197–198.

xv *McLain's yard looked like a car lot*: Denny McLain, interview by author, November 17, 2011.

1. Silent Film

1 *Now he is home: Baseball Classics: 1948 World Series, Cleveland Indians vs. Boston Braves* (Naperville, IL: Rare Sportsfilms, 1988).

2 *As he told the great baseball writer Roger Kahn*: Roger Kahn, *The Head Game: Baseball Seen from the Pitcher's Mound* (New York: Harcourt, 2000), 185.

"If I hadn't changed": Bill Surface, "Johnny Sain Teaches the Power of Positive Pitching," *New York Times Magazine,* April 20, 1969.

the Boston Red Sox signed Sain: Rich Westcott, *Masters of the Diamond: Interviews with Players Who Began Their Careers More Than 50 Years Ago* (Jefferson, NC: McFarland & Co., 1994), 111.

In 1942, with his pitching staff depleted: Pat Jordan, "In a World of Windmills," *Sports Illustrated,* May 8, 1972.

3 *According to him, he left dents in buildings:* Kahn, *The Head Game,* 186.

"*saw the light*": Surface, "Johnny Sain Teaches," 69.

Here was the Babe: Jim O'Donnell, "Mind over Batter," *Chicago Tribune,* October 10, 1993.

"*cutting off two of my fingers*": Ibid.

4 *Cy Young called him "wonderful":* Westcott, *Masters of the Diamond,* 107–116.

6 *Jim Kaat, who immediately took to Sain:* Jim Kaat, interview by author, June 22, 2012.

to deliver an "out pitch": Rick Talley, "The Man Who Manufactures 20 Game Winners," *Sports Today,* August 1972.

He was free: Jordan, "In a World of Windmills."

7 "*very glad when this baseball is over*": Arnold Rampersad, *Jackie Robinson: A Biography* (New York: Ballantine, 1997), 310.

8 "*hard to remember what my life was like just a brief year ago*": Ibid., 319.

"*I was tempted to take advantages*": Ibid., 317.

just a year before Evers was murdered: The Curious Case of Curt Flood, produced by Ross Greenburg and Rick Bernstein, written by Aaron Cohen (New York: HBO Sports, 2011).

"*There are those, black and white, who have challenged*": Martin Luther King Jr., "Address to the Southern Christian Leadership Conference Hall of Fame Dinner in Honor of Jackie Robinson," read on behalf of King by Reverend Wyatt Tee Walker, New York City, July 20, 1962.

9 "*not much of a writer*": William Branch, interview by author, February 23, 2012.

10 *The enduring image of her husband:* Rachel Robinson, interview by author, January 26, 2012.

Robinson remained angry: Rampersad, *Jackie Robinson,* 344–345.

When Robinson refused to appear in a photograph: Belford Lawson, interview by Ronald Grele, January 11, 1966, Digital ID JFKOH-BVL-01, John F. Kennedy Oral History Collections, John F. Kennedy Library, Boston.

Time and again, Kennedy tried to change Robinson's opinion: Jackie Robinson, "Jackie Robinson," *New York Post,* June 3, 1960.

in spite of efforts by men like Connecticut governor Chester Bowles: Jackie Robinson, "Jackie Robinson," *New York Post,* July 6, 1960.

"*Senator Kennedy is not fit to be President*": Rampersad, *Jackie Robinson,* 344.

11 "*time has arrived in America*": Hubert H. Humphrey Jr., address before the 1948 Democratic National Convention, Philadelphia, PA, July 14, 1948, available at *American Rhetoric,* www.americanrhetoric.com/speeches/huberthumphey1948dnc.html (accessed January 13, 2017).

"*He thinks calling Martin would be 'grandstanding'*": William Safire, "View from the Grandstand," *New York Times,* April 13, 1987.

12 *He could count on men like Bill White:* Brad Snyder, *A Well-Paid Slave: Curt Flood's Fight for Free Agency in Professional Sports* (New York: Penguin Group, 2006), 159.

found him disinterested: Rachel Robinson, interview by author, January 26, 2012.

gave the young man "holy hell": George Vecsey, interview by author, March 2, 2012.

13 "*certain truths about human relations*": Jackie Robinson, *Baseball Has Done It,* edited by Charles Dexter (Philadelphia: Lippincott, 1964; reprint, Brooklyn, NY: IG Publishing, 2005), 22.

2. Lost Fathers

15 *that a better life and a new start await somewhere else:* Dennis Mihelich, interview by author, May 17, 2012.

It was the packinghouses: Rodney Wead, interview by author, October 10, 2011.

Hopkins, one of the founding fathers: David McCullough, "The Course of Human Events," 2003 Jefferson Lecture in the Humanities.

16 *"I was fatherless":* Bob Gibson with Phil Pepe, *From Ghetto to Glory: The Story of Bob Gibson* (New York: Popular Library, 1968), 5.

"Good. Please don't kill me": Gibson and Wheeler, *Stranger to the Game,* 12.

seemed haunted by what they witnessed there: Ibid., 10.

he noticed that Josh always had a book in his hands: Rodney Wead, interview by author, October 10, 2011.

To him, Josh was simply "everything": Ibid.

17 *Josh had run up against his own limits:* Gibson and Wheeler, *Stranger to the Game,* 15.

But Wheeler felt that there was: Lonnie Wheeler, interview by author, November 26, 2011.

18 *His mother — with whom he had a fraught relationship:* Denny McLain with Eli Zaret, *I Told You I Wasn't Perfect* (Chicago: Triumph Books, 2007), 20.

he heard it from the neighbors: Eliot Asinof, "'I Snap Back Real Quick,'" *SPORT,* June 1970.

though he would later recant that account: McLain and Zaret, *I Told You I Wasn't Perfect,* 20–21.

Afterwards, when they told Tom: Denny McLain, interview by author, November 16, 2011.

"You're going to grow up to be somebody": McLain and Zaret, *I Told You I Wasn't Perfect,* 16.

19 *McLain did his best to portray:* Ibid., 14–15.

He felt insecure — both "emotionally and financially": Asinof, "'I Snap Back Real Quick.'"

but Wead would remember: Rodney Wead, interview by author, October 10, 2011.

because he was black: Gibson and Wheeler, *Stranger to the Game,* 21–22.

His former teammate Jim Morrison: Leo Adam Biga, "My Brother's Keeper: The Competitive Drive MLB Hall of Fame Pitcher Bob Gibson's Older Brother, Josh, Instilled in Him," *Leo Adam Biga's My Inside Stories* (blog), April 30, 2010, https://leoadambiga .com/2010/04/30/my-brothers-keeper-the-competitive-drive-mlb-hall-of-fame-pitcher -bob-gibsons-older-brother-josh-instilled-in-him/ (accessed January 13, 2017).

20 *That game taught him something:* Gibson and Wheeler, *Stranger to the Game,* 22–23.

"fulfilled our quota of Negroes": Ibid., 23–24.

Wead felt that Josh took the rejection harder: Rodney Wead, interview by author, October 10, 2011.

21 *They wanted to win:* Phil Hersh, "Life in the Halls of Shame," *Chicago Tribune,* July 12, 1985.

"this is a once-in-a-lifetime opportunity": Denny McLain, interview by author, November 16, 2011.

McLain knew that his mother didn't care: Ibid.

22 *"Why didn't you sign with me?":* Ibid.

23 *"curse in private":* Gibson and Wheeler, *Stranger to the Game,* 35–36.

One was Gibson. The other was Larry Bird: Bill Fitch, interview by author, January 16, 2012.

"there's Dynamite there if you roll it the wrong way": Ibid.

in towns as far-flung as Crofton, Nebraska, and Chamberlain, South Dakota: Gibson and Wheeler, *Stranger to the Game,* 38–39.

24 *since he could outrun any man on the team:* Bill Fitch, interview by author, January 16, 2012.

though he never believed he would be a star: Tom Nemitz, "Number 45: Bob Gibson," *White & Blue Review* (blog), October 6, 2010, http://whiteandbluereview.com/?p=8432.

placing a newspaper there: Bill Fitch, interview by author, January 16, 2012.

a scout named Frank Fahey wrote out an evaluation card: Frank Fahey evaluation card, "Scouting Report Folder, Selected Hall of Fame Members," Giamatti Research Center, Baseball Hall of Fame, Cooperstown, NY.

the Yankees said he wasn't worthy: Gibson and Wheeler, *Stranger to the Game,* 42.

But Fitch said that Gibson got plenty: Bill Fitch, interview by author, January 16, 2012.

25 *"If you come to Cincinnati":* Ibid.

3. Rising

26 *"We're going to the big leagues":* Jim Hawkins, *Al Kaline: The Biography of a Tigers Icon* (Chicago: Triumph Books, 2010), 163.

but Horton admired it even then: Willie Horton, interview by author, March 22, 2012.

then hit it from 60 feet, six inches away: Ibid.

27 *a place that seemed to him wholly apart from modern American life:* McLain and Zaret, *I Told You I Wasn't Perfect,* 24.

the need to advance beyond the raw materials he'd come with: Ibid., 28.

"He thought he was king of everything": David Wolf, "Tiger on the Keys and the Mound," *Life,* September 13, 1968.

28 *to serve as fodder for other teams:* McLain and Zaret, *I Told You I Wasn't Perfect,* 32.

"You throw pretty hard": Denny McLain, interview by author, November 16, 2011.

"all you're going to do is worry": Eric Kinkopf, "McLain's Wife Endures Life Full of Worries," *Syracuse Herald American,* September 6, 1987.

29 *just weeks after they first began dating:* McLain and Zaret, *I Told You I Wasn't Perfect,* 31–32.

"I don't want a quitter": Denny McLain, interview by author, November 16, 2011.

"she keeps me in line": Asinof, "'I Snap Back Real Quick.'"

kept a careful eye on McLain in Clinton: Denny McLain, interview by author, November 16, 2011.

30 *he was doing just fine:* David Halberstam, *October 1964* (New York: Villard, 1994), 103.

throwing what he called "soft strikes": Gibson and Wheeler, *Stranger to the Game,* 43–44.

31 *He would not learn the vile, racist meaning of this slur:* Ibid., 45.

"It wasn't something that you talked about": Greenburg and Bernstein, *The Curious Case of Curt Flood.*

He was at a loss: Rodney Wead, interview by author, October 10, 2011.

or any of the Cardinals who were black: Gibson and Wheeler, *Stranger to the Game,* 48.

32 *"I felt like a nigger":* Greenburg and Bernstein, *The Curious Case of Curt Flood.*

"Hey, this is unbelievable": Jim Maloney, interview by author, February 29, 2012.

33 *through a physical, dehumanizing divide:* Ibid.

hoped that one day he could return: Peter Golenbock, *The Spirit of St. Louis: A History of the St. Louis Cardinals and Browns* (New York: HarperCollins, 2000), 432.

without considering Gibson's input: Halberstam, *October 1964,* 109.

walk away from the sport altogether: Golenbock, *Spirit of St. Louis,* 435.

calling him either a "black son of a bitch" or "black bastard": Halberstam, *October 1964,* 109.

34 *treated as men rather than 12-year-olds:* George Vecsey, interview by author, March 2, 2012.

he threw "everything at the same speed": Golenbock, *Spirit of St. Louis,* 434.

a brooding, dark, intimidating figure: Mel Nelson, interview by author, October 28, 2011.

35 *Busch, who initially saw owning the team merely as a marketing tool for Anheuser-Busch:* Golenbock, *Spirit of St. Louis,* 405.

36 *didn't make any fundamental changes to Gibson's delivery:* Lonnie Wheeler, interview by author, November 26, 2011.

Keane could also be critical and demanding: Gibson and Wheeler, *Stranger to the Game,* 71.

"much less played with one": Ibid., 60.

something McCarver could never imagine a black man doing: Each man had a different memory of the bold move. Gibson remembered offering to lick his teammate's ice cream (ibid., 60), while McCarver remembered it as a sip of orange soda (Halberstam, *October 1964*, 220–221).

called him out as either a "little cannibal" or a "nigger": Halberstam, *October 1964*, 276.

Gibson recalled getting "right up in McCarver's face": Gibson and Wheeler, *Stranger to the Game*, 60.

37 *"What the hell are you doing out here"*: Halberstam, *October 1964*, 276.

"Don't come out here": *Studio 42 with Bob Costas*, season 1, episode 2, MLB Network, June 15, 2009.

led one teammate to call him a "positive tyrant": Jerry Izenberg, "The Indispensable Cardinal," *SPORT*, November 1967.

"because it's his ball game": Bob Broeg, "McCarver: The Pip Who Won't Be 'Wally Pipped,'" *St. Louis Post-Dispatch*, March 5, 1968.

38 *a variety of motions at their disposal*: Jim Kaat, interview by author, June 22, 2012.

"knock the bat out of your hand": Dick Groat, interview by author, January 19, 2012.

said changed the game forever: Kahn, *The Head Game*, 157.

the Hall of Famer shrieked after finding out who he was: Gibson and Wheeler, *Stranger to the Game*, 56.

39 *Marichal finally "broke"*: Al Stump, "'Always They Want More, More, More,'" *Saturday Evening Post*, July 29, 1967.

though he would later deny the remark: "Marichal Steaming over Mag Piece — 'I Never Said That,'" *The Sporting News*, August 5, 1963.

40 *He relished it, his friend Lonnie Wheeler felt*: Lonnie Wheeler, interview by author, November 26, 2011.

Torre insisted that Gibson throw a pitch: Halberstam, *October 1964*, 269.

41 *As Gibson wrote, the 1964 Cardinals*: Gibson and Wheeler, *Stranger to the Game*, 82–83.

While Vecsey enjoyed speaking: George Vecsey, interview by author, March 2, 2012.

42 *"I've gotta get out of here"*: Ibid.

43 *the throw beat the hustling Pepitone*: *Studio 42 with Bob Costas*, June 15, 2009.

deliver it with all the grace: Marvin Miller, interview by author, July 26, 2011.

"You can't say enough about Gibson," Keane told reporters: Gibson and Wheeler, *Stranger to the Game*, 101–102.

44 *"Hoot, you're on your way"*: Ibid., 102.

the modern athlete personified: Gerald Early, interview by author, October 9, 2011.

a symbol of a new breed: Arnold Hano, "Bob Gibson: Symbol of a New Breed," *SPORT*, May 1968.

45 *trying to regain his confidence and vigor*: Arthur Daley, "Sports of the Times: Boudreau's Son-in-Law," *New York Times*, April 17, 1966.

a team that stressed the use of the overhand curveball: Ibid.

46 *the manager would tell him that he would win*: Denny McLain, interview by author, November 16, 2011.

Leggett wrote about his signature drink — Pepsi-Cola: William Leggett, "Here Come the Young Turks," *Sports Illustrated*, July 11, 1966.

47 *"I guess maybe all the notoriety affects your personal life"*: Ibid.

"God strike me down if I said those things": Joe Falls, "Only Denny Knows for Sure," *SPORT*, October 1968.

screamed at him, belittling him and demanding a retraction: Ibid.

called the Tigers a "country club team": Mark Mulvoy, "Dizzy Dream for Jet-Set Denny," *Sports Illustrated*, July 29, 1968.

48 *"With all the managerial problems we've had"*: McLain and Zaret, *I Told You I Wasn't Perfect*, 60.

Later, when the press voted him Tiger of the Year: Ibid., 54.

Willie Horton believed: Hawkins and Kaline, *The Biography of a Tigers Icon,* 163.

his unhittable arm had been rendered unliftable: McLain and Zaret, *I Told You I Wasn't Perfect,* 52.

shot him up first with Xylocaine to "deaden" his shoulder: Ibid., 52.

"Fuck the Gipper": Denny McLain, interview by author, November 16, 2011.

49 *he simply didn't have it in him to go on:* Pat Jordan, "The Trials of Jim Maloney," *SPORT,* November 1969.

"Listen, if a guy's arm is sore": Ibid.

"smart people are awfully smart in their own living rooms": Bob Sudyk, "Can 'the Next Koufax' Finally Make It?" *SPORT,* April 1967.

50 *"Don't worry. It happens to me every time":* Marvin Miller, interview by author, July 26, 2011.

That sense of insecurity led McLain's teammate John Hiller: John Hiller, interview by author, May 17, 2012.

He could see McLain growing addicted to it: Mike Marshall, interview by author, November 2, 2011.

51 *He believed that the Tigers had his best interests in mind:* Denny McLain, interview by author, November 16, 2011.

the world "wants winners and results": Bill Surface, "Johnny Sain Teaches the Power of Positive Pitching," *New York Times Magazine,* April 20, 1969.

4. Testimony of Pilots

52 *"organization I've been looking for":* Milton Richman, "Johnny Sain Appreciates Support from Jim Kaat," *Dispatch* (Lexington, NC), March 8, 1967.

Sain was told that Smith was a gentleman: Jordan, "In a World of Windmills."

53 *McLain referred to the man from Arkansas as "Mr. Sain":* Watson Spoelstra, "Bengals Will Make Things Hot for Orioles, Mayo Promises," *The Sporting News,* January 28, 1967.

Detroit writer Joe Falls foresaw: Joe Falls, "Turmoil on the Tigers — Does It Still Exist?" *SPORT,* June 1967.

54 *he was putting far more into the team than the rest:* Jordan, "In a World of Windmills."

"the best pitching coach ever": Ibid.

"I tell him how I'm gonna use the pitchers and he does it": Ibid.

He was happy in the company of his pitchers: Mary Sain, interview by author, February 29, 2012.

55 *"he has been both a starter and reliever":* Max Nichols, "Twins Go High to Grab Sain — Top-Drawer Tutor for Hurlers," *The Sporting News,* October 31, 1964.

"I don't want to appear as a superman": Ibid.

loved pitchers who could throw deep into ball games: Jim Kaat, interview by author, June 22, 2012.

56 *"The idea is to stimulate the imagination":* Talley, "The Man Who Manufactures 20 Game Winners."

"it'll rust out before it'll wear out": Jim Kaat, interview by author, June 22, 2012.

Sabathia said, "I'd love doing that": Ibid.

57 *considered a castoff when the Indians traded him:* Ibid.

sending their children to a small, impoverished, segregated school: Jim "Mudcat" Grant, Tom Sabellico, and Pat O'Brien, *The Black Aces: Baseball's Only African American Twenty-Game Winners* (Farmingdale, NY: Avetine Press, 2007), 9.

"Don't be no fool": Jim "Mudcat" Grant, interview by author, September 14, 2011.

He felt that it was the wisdom of these words: Ibid.

58 *"How in the hell did y'all do it"*: Ibid.

"I want you to run like you just stole two watermelons": Grant, Sabellico, and O'Brien, *The Black Aces*, 221.

"This land is not so free; I can't go to Mississippi": Jim Thielman, *Cool of the Evening: The 1965 Minnesota Twins* (Minneapolis: Kirk House Publishers, 2005), 42.

"I can't go to Mississippi and sit at a lunch counter": Grant, Sabellico, and O'Brien, *The Black Aces*, 219.

59 *"we're going to hang you from the nearest tree"*: Ibid.

opting to dispatch Wilks to the minors instead: Thielman, *Cool of the Evening*, 42.

Grant endeared himself to both black and white fans: Jim "Mudcat" Grant, interview by author, September 14, 2011.

60 *What separated Sain from other coaches*: Ibid.

"Now don't complain": Ibid.

led Yankees third baseman Clete Boyer to joke: Thielman, *Cool of the Evening*, 46.

61 *Sain felt he couldn't really talk to Mele*: Jordan, "In a World of Windmills."

a mental lapse by reliever Jerry Fosnow: Marshall Smith, "The Twins' Miracle Coach," *Life*, September 10, 1965.

"It isn't that all-fired easy": Ibid.

"they're more likely to come for advice if I'm right there": Joe Gergen, "White Sox Are Feeling Sain's Pulse," *Newsday*, August 12, 1971.

62 *"But money isn't that important to me"*: Richman, "Johnny Sain Appreciates Support."

he had to pull over to the side of the road: Jim Kaat, interview by author, June 22, 2012.

Sain would be his very first hire: Richman, "Johnny Sain Appreciates Support."

"like the Green Bay Packers allowing Vince Lombardi to quit": "Scorecard: Kaat's Meow," *Sports Illustrated*, October 17, 1966.

63 *"If Johnny Sain told me to ram my arm into a wall"*: Richman, "Johnny Sain Appreciates Support."

anxious when they first arrived in Lakeland: Hal Naragon, interview by author, August 3, 2011.

"cautious preparation": Surface, "Johnny Sain Teaches the Power of Positive Pitching."

Sain rotated his arm fully 360 degrees several times a day: Daryl Patterson, interview by author, July 7, 2011.

64 *"the pitcher throws, and the catcher catches"*: Arnold Hano, "Bill Freehan: Tough Leader of the Tigers," *SPORT*, August 1968.

"You've got the uniform on. Yesterday's gone": John Hiller, interview by author, May 17, 2012.

Sain was never afraid to approach Marshall: Mike Marshall, interview by author, November 2, 2011.

65 *an understanding of situational pitching*: Fred Lasher, interview by author, September 9, 2011.

But Sain and Naragon thought highly: Hal Naragon, interview by author, August 3, 2011.

For McLain, he said, it took a year: William B. Mead, *Two Spectacular Seasons: 1930: The Year the Hitters Ran Wild, 1968: The Year the Pitchers Took Revenge* (New York: Macmillan, 1990), 140.

"We're really close, we're really close": Denny McLain, interview by author, November 16, 2011.

"throw that fucking pitch": Ibid.

66 *Sain helped refine*: Hal Naragon, interview by author, August 3, 2011.

Sain helped McLain study for his own pilot exams: Kahn, *The Head Game*, 200.

to trigger an "automatic physical reaction": Jordan, "In a World of Windmills."

5. The Break

67 *"That was fun. That was really fun"*: Dal Maxvill, interview by author, October 8, 2011.
 Larry Jaster — who had been sent home: Larry Jaster, interview by author, July 10, 2011.

68 *"Nobody can escape the tensions of 1967"*: George Vecsey, "Violence in Baseball," *SPORT,* October 1967.
 That, Gibson believed, should have been enough: Gibson and Wheeler, *Stranger to the Game,* 134.
 with something along the lines of "Fuck you": Dal Maxvill, interview by author, October 8, 2011.

69 *"probably one of the best fights"*: Johnny Edwards, interview by author, November 12, 2011.
 McCarver said had a history with Cepeda: Tim McCarver, interview by author, January 7, 2012.
 McCarver later said he'd never seen anything quite like it: Ibid.
 Behind home plate, Edwards tangled: Johnny Edwards, interview by author, November 12, 2011.
 A policeman stuck his billy club: Jim Maloney, interview by author, February 29, 2012.
 Gibson, who jammed his finger in the midst of the brawl: Neal Russo, "'Boxing' Makes Debut at Bish in Brawl Game," *St. Louis Post-Dispatch,* July 5, 1967.

70 *"he didn't want to knock people down"*: Dick Groat, interview by author, January 19, 2012.
 "affected me as much as anybody's I've ever known": Gibson and Pepe, *From Ghetto to Glory,* 109.
 "the worst year I ever had in my life": Dick Groat, interview by author, January 19, 2012.

71 *guidelines for maintaining good posture:* Gibson and Wheeler, *Stranger to the Game,* 107.
 while touring spring training camps: Marvin Miller, interview by author, July 26, 2011.

72 *"There'll be some things"*: Ibid.
 a genuine sense among players that they belonged together: Dick Hughes, interview by author, May 9, 2011.

73 *he played guitar in a team band:* Ibid.
 with the fierceness that fires the best of teams: Gerald Early, interview by author, October 9, 2011.
 "Our skins might be lighter": Stump, "'Always They Want More, More, More.'"
 Marichal would quickly deny most of the reporting in the piece: Bob Stevens, "Marichal Steaming over Mag Piece — 'I Never Said That,'" *The Sporting News,* August 5, 1963.
 even banned Spanish music in the locker room: Orlando Cepeda with Herb Fagen, *Baby Bull: From Hardball to Hard Time and Back* (Dallas: Taylor Publishing, 1998), 75.
 "You can't make most Negro and Spanish players": James S. Hirsch, *Willie Mays: The Life, the Legend* (New York: Scribner, 2010), 418.

74 *the article had irrevocably damaged his standing as a ballplayer:* "Cepeda Sues Look — $1 Million," *San Francisco Chronicle,* May 24, 1963.
 he was considered damaged goods: Bob Hunter, "How the Cards Got Cepeda," *San Francisco Examiner,* August 12, 1967.
 "Finally," Brock continued: Leonard Shecter, "Orlando Cepeda: Why He Had to Come Back," *SPORT,* October 1967.
 their era had passed all too quickly: Gay Talese, "The Silent Season of a Hero," *Esquire,* July 1966.

75 *Maris, out of spite:* Golenbock, *The Spirit of St. Louis,* 479.
 Maxvill, among others, had pressed Shannon to resist: Dal Maxvill, interview by author, October 8, 2011.
 "It's been fun since I've been here": Fred Katz, "Life with the Cardinals," *SPORT,* July 1968.

"We have speed and power": Cepeda and Fagen, *Baby Bull*, 133.

76 *Gibson firmly said, "We're waiting"*: Shecter, "Orlando Cepeda."
structures erected primarily for football: Gary Gillette, interview by author, January 14, 2012.
But to walk into something so big: Dal Maxvill, interview by author, October 8, 2011.

77 *That was enough*: Dick Hughes, interview by author, May 9, 2011.
When Marvin Miller, now charged: Marvin Miller, interview by author, July 26, 2011.
It was too big: Tim McCarver, interview by author, January 7, 2012.
The second Busch Stadium: Gibson and Pepe, *From Ghetto to Glory*, 98.

78 *Some reward, Gibson felt*: Gibson and Wheeler, *Stranger to the Game*, 105.
the police, who would routinely pull him over: Ibid.
George Vecsey would later cringe: George Vecsey, interview by author, March 2, 2012.
"We don't allow niggers": Gibson and Wheeler, *Stranger to the Game*, 105.
Once, he was told he couldn't drink a Coca-Cola in a local bar: Ibid.
With one home, the family endured: Ibid., 123.
Perhaps more insidious: Rodney Wead, interview by author, October 10, 2011.

79 *expecting the ball to sail away from them*: Gibson and Wheeler, *Stranger to the Game*, 111.
"maybe even bends back a little like a screwball": Ibid.
From then on, he'd occasionally overthrow it on purpose: Ibid., 111–112.
Stiffening his wrist eventually helped make the slider unhittable: Gibson and Pepe, *From Ghetto to Glory*, 134–137.
Gibson knew how to control the outside corner against right-handed hitters: Roger Angell, *Once More Around the Park: A Baseball Reader* (New York: Ballantine Books, 1991), 127.
how to break up a hitter's internal rhythm: Ibid., 128.
"mean and loose": Ibid.

80 *he wanted to remain that mysterious figure*: Rodney Wead, interview by author, October 10, 2011.
It wasn't a line drive: Tim McCarver, interview by author, January 7, 2012.
screaming like a banshee through the pitching mound: Golenbock, *The Spirit of St. Louis*, 482.
his slider, by now his best pitch: Gibson and Pepe, *From Ghetto to Glory*, 163.

81 *That might have happened had the ball come two inches further*: Ibid.
"I'm fine," the grounded Gibson said: Dal Maxvill, interview by author, October 8, 2011.
The trainer sprayed the spot with ethyl chloride: Gibson and Pepe, *From Ghetto to Glory*, 166.
Maxvill could only hope: Dal Maxvill, interview by author, October 8, 2011.
he'd seen this season as a way to earn more income: Ibid., 167–168.

82 *In a rare moment of self-pity, he asked himself*: Hano, "Bob Gibson: Symbol of a New Breed."
While he recuperated, he'd still be able to throw: Ed Wilks, "Redbird Notes: Gibson Willing Even if Leg Wasn't," *St. Louis Post-Dispatch*, July 17, 1967.
When Wead traveled from Omaha: Rodney Wead, interview by author, October 10, 2011.
the funniest damn thing he'd ever seen: Tim McCarver, interview by author, January 7, 2012.
"Get out of the clubhouse!": Doug Feldman, *El Birdos: The 1967 and 1968 St. Louis Cardinals* (Jefferson, NC: McFarland & Co., 2007), 135.
He hung a sign around his neck: "Worth a Thousand Words?" (caption), *St. Louis Post-Dispatch*, August 11, 1967.

83 *Instead, the pitcher opened up to him*: Terry Dickson, "No-Nonsense Pitcher: Bob Gibson Likes People, but Wants Privacy, Too," *St. Louis Post-Dispatch*, September 24, 1967.
"But the message came through": Ibid.
"The only time I've felt": Neal Russo, "Gibby Makes Winning Return," *St. Louis Post-Dispatch*, September 8, 1967.

84 *"I was never surprised at anything Bob did"*: Tim McCarver, interview by author, January 7, 2012.

6. Into the City of Ashes

85 *a yacht that had been docked at a private club*: Dick Tracewski, interview by author, March 2, 2012; Al Kaline, interview by author, March 20, 2012.

a metropolis came undone: Dick Tracewski, interview by author, March 2, 2012.

86 *Now everything was gone*: Ibid.

87 *"of all the accomplishments in the recent history"*: Sidney Fine, *Violence in the Model City: The Cavanagh Administration, Race Relations, and the Detroit Riot of 1967* (East Lansing: Michigan State University Press, 2007), 33.

In May 1967, the Detroit News: "Amid Racial Troubles: A Significant Gain" (editorial), *Detroit News*, May 6, 1967.

"Big Cities," he concluded: Jerome Aumente, "Can the Cities Survive?" *Detroit News*, April 30, 1969.

"Detroit has been the model of intelligence": Fine, *Violence in the Model City*, 1.

The New York Times *lamented that Detroit*: Ibid., 32.

The city's murder rate had grown precipitously through the decade: Ibid., 415.

by 1967 Detroit was really past its prime: Thomas J. Sugrue, *The Origins of the Urban Crisis: Race and Inequality in Postwar Detroit* (Princeton, NJ: Princeton University Press, 1996), 19.

What she discovered was a base inequity: Mary Ann Weston, interview by author, November 11, 2011.

88 *At some point, a bottle was thrown*: Ibid.

Holding a bullhorn, he pleaded: Susan Holmes, "Negro Leaders Plead for 'a Safe City,'" *Detroit Free Press*, July 24, 1967.

"We're with you": Ibid.

Cavanagh asked Governor George Romney: Fine, *Violence in the Model City*, 172.

blamed the Republican governor for his incompetence in action: President Lyndon B. Johnson, "Address After Ordering Federal Troops to Detroit, Michigan" (July 24, 1967)," available at: millercenter.org/president/speeches/detail/4039 (accessed August 7, 2013).

89 *2,509 stores had been looted, burned, or otherwise destroyed*: Fine, *Violence in the Model City*, 291.

In his first autobiography: Gibson and Pepe, *From Ghetto to Glory*, 149–150.

Serrin, who was born in Saginaw: William Serrin, interview by author, June 25, 2012.

90 *some 77 percent of black residents*: Fine, *Violence in the Model City*, 179.

as 11-year-old boys brazenly looted stores: Ibid., 177.

No longer a beacon: Karen Rothmyer, *Winning Pulitzers: The Stories Behind Some of the Best News Coverage of Our Time* (New York: Columbia University Press, 1991), 130.

Barbra Stanton, whose brilliant reporting: Fine, *Violence in the Model City*, 462–463.

91 *Ray Lane, who saw the smoke beyond left field*: Ray Lane, interview by author, January 27, 2012.

After he left the stadium: Ibid.

"For Detroit, seven runs, twelve hits, no errors": George Cantor, *The Tigers of '68: Baseball's Last Real Champions* (Dallas, TX: Taylor Publishing, 1997), 45.

waxing lyrical about a sailing trip he'd taken: Joe Falls, "Who Says Sailing's a Sport for Sissies?" *Detroit Free Press*, July 25, 1967.

His publisher, he wrote, "told me that I wasn't to write": Joe Falls, "How Important Are Sports?" *The Sporting News*, September 7, 1968.

That evening Denny McLain returned to his home: Denny McLain, interview by author, November 6, 2011.

92 *Lolich planned on barbecuing some ribs:* George Cantor, "Lolich Loses 10th in a Row: But Tigers Win 'Cap,'" *Detroit Free Press,* July 24, 1967.

In truth, it wasn't until he arrived home: Cantor, *The Tigers of '68,* 6.

"I'd rather get shelled by line drives any day than by bullets": Whitey Sawyer, "Lolich Prefers Shelling on Mound to Riot Duty," *Detroit News,* July 29, 1967.

93 *"Willie Horton was the single greatest reason":* "1968: The Year of the Pitcher" (episode 4), *Baseball's Seasons,* MLB Network, January 28, 2009.

George Cantor said that when Horton joined the Tigers: A City on Fire: The Story of the '68 Detroit Tigers, written by Armen Keteyian and Jeff Sarokin (New York: HBO Films, 2002).

Decades later he would still hear them: Willie Horton, interview by author, March 22, 2012.

"I've never lived in Detroit": Watson Spoelstra, "The Story on Sain: Not Mad at Twins," *Detroit News,* April 14, 1967.

"Would you trade the Detroit staff ": Ibid.

94 *"I'm going to build myself up":* Watson Spoelstra, "Wilson to Lead Cheers for McLain in Opener," *Detroit News,* April 11, 1967.

younger players pitted against more seasoned ones: George Cantor, "Tiger Players Hold Private Meeting . . . Still Lose 7th in Row," *Detroit Free Press,* July 18, 1967.

"I think we're ready to make our move": Post-Dispatch Wire Services, "McLain Shoulders Detroit Load," *St. Louis Post-Dispatch,* July 28, 1967.

kicked his locker in frustration: McLain and Zaret, *I Told You I Wasn't Perfect,* 74.

95 *"I don't know if anyone will believe it":* George Cantor, "McLain Injured; Out for Season?" *Detroit Free Press,* September 21, 1967.

was it an injured ankle or dislocated toes?: Green, *Year of the Tiger,* 15.

provided "none of them falls off a sofa": Joe Falls, "Only Denny Knows for Sure," *SPORT,* October 1968.

What was evident to him, though: Larry Osterman, interview by author, November 12, 2011.

96 *crushed and dislocated McLain's toes:* Morton Sharnik, "Downfall of a Hero," *Sports Illustrated,* February 23, 1970.

along with a Pepsi executive, Edwin Shober: McLain and Zaret, *I Told You I Wasn't Perfect,* 68.

at the time of the $46,000 claim: Mark Amour, "Denny McLain," last revised July 1, 2015, available at: *Society for American Baseball Research,* http://sabr.org/bioproj/person /6bddedd4 (accessed January 20, 2017).

"Hey, look, Denny, if it's the truth, that's a great story": Eli Zaret, interview by author, March 30, 2012.

An embarrassing, dubious accident: Denny McLain, interview by author, November 6, 2011.

McLain was certainly distracted: McLain and Zaret, *I Told You I Wasn't Perfect,* 73.

"How about coming out and kicking some field goals": Joe Falls, "Denny Doesn't Get Kicks on Sidelines," *Detroit Free Press,* September 29, 1967.

97 *forced to return a Mercury Cougar:* Pete Waldmeir, "Lolich Celebrates Again with the Help of Gladding," *Detroit News,* September 5, 1967.

Sain didn't want him to try anything new: George Cantor and Joe Falls, "Now He's Relaxing and Winning: 'I Was Trying Too Hard' — Lolich," *Detroit Free Press,* September 10, 1967.

With Detroit's World Series hopes again lifted: John Peterson, "City's Pennant Stake a Cool $6 Million," *Detroit News,* September 8, 1967.

98 *Soon after, Mudcat demanded a trade:* "Five for the Flag," *Sports Illustrated,* August 7, 1967.

The racial tensions could only grow worse from there: Bill Furlong, "The Feuding Twins: Inside a Team in Turmoil," *SPORT,* April 1968.

99 *who were once again caught ill prepared by a riot:* Joe Dowdall, "Fans Rip Apart Tiger Stadium," *Detroit Free Press,* October 3, 1967.

    He talked of the agony and "unparalleled despair": William Serrin, "Tiger Fans Had Fun Up Until Last Out of Season," *Detroit Free Press,* October 2, 1967.

100 *McLain, for his part, felt helpless:* Denny McLain, interview by author, November 6, 2011.

    "Watch out for him next year": Jim Kaat, interview by author, June 22, 2012.

7. A Black Man Wins in Boston

101 *The governor had believed, perhaps naively:* Maurice Carroll, "Buffalo Still Tense; Patrol Is Resumed: Buffalo Is Still Tense as Police Restore Patrols in Ghetto," *New York Times,* July 1, 1967.

    an out-of-touch emissary for an out-of-touch governor: Frank Besag, *The Anatomy of a Riot: Buffalo, 1967* (Buffalo, NY: University of Buffalo Press, 1967), 116.

    the angry young crowd he'd met with at the YMCA that summer: Carroll, "Buffalo Still Tense."

102 *"is one of the most bigoted guys in organized baseball":* Jackie Robinson, *First Class Citizenship: The Civil Rights Letters of Jackie Robinson,* edited by Michael G. Long (New York: Henry Holt and Co., 2007), 258.

    Upon hearing about Robinson's comments: Ibid.

    "I am sorry but in my opinion Yawkey": Ibid.

    try out at Fenway Park with the grumbling Red Sox: Howard Bryant, *Shut Out: A Story of Race and Baseball in Boston* (New York: Routledge, 2002), 23–33.

    Jewish Boston politician Isadore "Izzy" Muchnick: Ibid., 24.

    given the chance to sign not only Robinson: Hirsch, *Willie Mays,* 62.

103 *"Truth speaks for itself":* Jackie Robinson, *Beyond Home Plate: Jackie Robinson on Life After Baseball,* edited by Michael G. Long (Syracuse, NY: Syracuse University Press, 2013), 9.

    to see the Chairman live: Sam Jones, interview by author, January 12, 2012.

104 *Gibson and his teammates had wanted the Twins to prevail:* Neal Russo, "Redbirds Rooted Against Bosox," *St. Louis Post-Dispatch,* October 2, 1967.

    Reportedly no hotel in Boston proper: "Cardinals Unwelcome Guests in Boston," *Springfield Daily News,* October 3, 1967.

    hundreds of Sox fans chanting "Welcome No. 2": Neal Russo, "Boston 'Welcomes' Birds: Red Sees Cards in 6 or 7 Games," *St. Louis Post-Dispatch,* October 3, 1967.

    There, holding court with Boston reporters: *Springfield Daily News,* "Cardinals Unwelcome Guests in Boston."

    That evening before the first game: Pete Golenbock, *The Spirit of St. Louis: A History of the St. Louis Cardinals and Browns* (New York: HarperCollins, 2001), 487; Gibson and Wheeler, *Stranger to the Game,* 141–142.

    Pitcher Nelson Briles was the lone white person: Golenbock, *The Spirit of St. Louis,* 487.

    Celtics stars K. C. Jones: Ibid.

105 *Embry and K.C. might have played in Boston:* Sam Jones, interview by author, January 12, 2012.

    Russell described the city as a "flea market": Bryant, *Shut Out,* 58.

    He had proudly marched on Washington: Ibid., 81.

    a view not shared by Jackie Robinson: Bob Sales, "Robinson Renews Yawkey Bigot Rap," *Boston Globe,* October 25, 1967.

106 *How could he fail to make an impact:* Studio 42 with Bob Costas, June 15, 2009.

    The newspaper called for a new park to be built: "Start the Stadium Now" (editorial), *Boston Globe,* October 3, 1967.

"I hope the Legislature will act as soon as this World Series is over": "Stadium in Time for '70 Series Promised by Turnpike Boss," *Boston Globe,* October 9, 1968.

107 *They knew that he'd broken his leg:* Jim Lonborg, interview by author, April 23, 2012.
    To fall behind was to stay behind: Ibid.
    "Gibson threw hard": Ed Wilks, "Yaz Gets His Licks Too Late," *St. Louis Post-Dispatch,* October 5, 1967.

108 *A tall, dreamy-looking bachelor:* Al Hirshberg, "How Gentleman Jim Lonborg Became a Pitcher," *SPORT,* October 1967.
    In an era when it was unheard of for athletes to pose: "Dressed Right for Sport: Jim Lonborg," *SPORT,* March 1968.
    The relationship seemed absolutely perfect: Jim Lonborg, interview by author, April 23, 2012.
    Many, including manager Dick Williams: Hirshberg, "Gentleman Jim Lonborg."

109 *never "to give a batter a break":* Ibid.
    Williams believed that Lonborg had turned the corner: Ibid.
    However, it was Sandy Koufax: Jim Lonborg, interview by author, April 23, 2012.
    "Have you ever thought about": Ibid.

110 *"perfect moments":* Jim Lonborg, interview by author, April 23, 2012.
    Gibson had "honestly" felt: Bob Sales, "Just Another Game — Gibson," *Boston Globe,* October 12, 1967.

111 *That same evening, when* Boston Globe *writer Will McDonough:* Will McDonough, "Lonborg Admits He's a Little Scared," *Boston Globe,* October 12, 1967.
    At the park the following day: Jim Lonborg, interview by author, April 23, 2012.
    Lonborg had hoped for two things: Ibid.
    Gibson would later admit: Gibson and Pepe, *From Ghetto to Glory,* 186.

112 *After the eighth:* Francis Rosa, "Gibson Couldn't Pitch Another Inning," *Boston Globe,* October 13, 1967.
    Gibson's breakfast of scrambled eggs: Ed Wilks, "Gibson's Breakfast Is Lost in Shuffle," *St. Louis Post-Dispatch,* October 12, 1967.
    But like Gibson, he was hot-tempered: Rick Hummel, interview by author, August 30, 2011.
    They enjoyed one another's company: Ibid.

113 *Gibson was "blasé about his job":* Bob Sales, "Gibson 'Tired Before It Started,'" *Boston Globe,* October 9, 1967.
    Of course, nothing could rattle Bob Gibson: Gibson and Wheeler, *Stranger to the Game,* 147.
    Cardinal players chanting in unison: "1967: The Impossible Dream" (episode 11), *Baseball's Seasons,* MLB Network, January 13, 2010.
    drinking, not spilling, champagne: Studio 42 with Bob Costas, June 15, 2009.
    Les McCann play jazz piano: Gibson and Wheeler, *Stranger to the Game,* 146.
    Now McCann entered the locker room: Gibson and Pepe, *From Ghetto to Glory,* 190.
    he retold the story of his Red Sox tryout: Sales, "Robinson Renews Yawkey Bigot Rap."

114 *"I don't think in a country such as ours":* Ibid.

8. Winter of Recriminations

115 *a handsome wooden plaque listing the pennant standings:* Dan Ewald, interview by author, January 16, 2012.
    trade Denny McLain: Jerry Green, "Deals That Fell Through Put Tigers in Flag Drive," *Battle Creek Enquirer & News,* August 25, 1968.

116 *Thus, Campbell was stuck with a headache:* Ibid.
    Inexplicably, Campbell had made plans: Hal Naragon, interview by author, August 3, 2011.
    Broadcaster Larry Osterman said: Larry Osterman, interview by author, November 12, 2011.

particularly after the death of Horton's parents: Willie Horton, interview by author, March 22, 2012.

When Bazooka held a bubble gum: Jim Hawkins, "No Bubble-Blowing for Tigers," *The Sporting News,* September 13, 1975.

In the early 1990s, when the team's new management: Ernie Harwell with Tom Keegan, *Ernie Harwell: My 60 Years in Baseball* (Chicago: Triumph Books, 2002), 20.

117 Detroit News *writer Jerry Green saw Campbell:* Jerry Green, interview by author, May 9, 2011.

Once, in a caustic contract negotiation: Dan Ewald, *John Fetzer: On a Handshake: The Times and Triumphs of a Tiger Owner* (Champagne, IL: Sycamore Publishing, 1997), 21.

The phone call Maddox expected: Elliott Maddox, interview with author, February 4, 2012.

"It's my club": Marvin Miller, interview by author, July 26, 2011.

118 *A lone motorboat glides:* "Batter Up," *Gentle Ben* (season 1, episode 21), directed by George Cahan, CBS, February 4, 1968.

119 *Sitting with Mark on the bleachers:* Ibid.

120 *No, the real Gibson was the one:* Hano, "Bob Gibson: Symbol of a New Breed."

The Sporting News, *a St. Louis institution, had long tired:* Bob Broeg, "Gibby Irked by Editorial Criticism," *St. Louis Post-Dispatch,* February 28, 1968.

"I wasn't particularly touched": Hano, "Symbol of a New Breed."

121 *This was the man the sportswriter Phil Pepe met:* Phil Pepe, interview by author, December 8, 2012.

Pepe wasn't the first choice of anyone: Ibid.

John Eric Lake disappeared: Denise, "Missing Man: John Eric Lake — NY — 12/10/1967 file," Missing/Located Persons, East: DC, DE, MD, NJ, NY, and PA, *Project Jason Forum* (original website, no longer active, accessed June 16, 2012), available at: https://projectjason.org /forums/topic/305-missing-man-john-eric-lake-ny-12101967/#comment-2430   (accessed January 23, 2017). See also Eric Lake, interview by author, June 28, 2012.

122 *Lake's drinking had gotten out of hand:* Eric Lake, "The John Lake Story," *John Lake* (blog), available at: www.johnlake.com (accessed December 12, 2012); Eric Lake, interview by author, June 28, 2012.

The dissolution of his marriage and financial troubles: Denise, "Missing Man: John Eric Lake — NY — 12/10/1967 file"; Eric Lake, interview by author, June 28, 2012.

In an account Sandra gave to a private detective: Lake, "The John Lake Story"; Eric Lake, interview by author, June 28, 2012.

When Pepe first met with Gibson in Manhattan: Phil Pepe, interview by author, December 8, 2012.

123 *"Tell that guy it's my book":* Ibid.

felt that he became *Bob Gibson:* Ibid.

Gibson said that he felt "unburdened": Gibson and Wheeler, *Stranger to the Game,* 181.

Pepe considered it a "trailblazer": Phil Pepe, interview by author, December 8, 2012.

Gibson wasn't in position to be himself yet: Lonnie Wheeler, interview by author, November 26, 2011.

As he wrote with the help of his new ghostwriter: Jackie Robinson, "Mixed Emotions over Boycott of Olympics," *New York Amsterdam News,* December 16, 1967.

124 *"Maybe we, as Negro athletes":* Ibid.

In the green room for half an hour: Harry Edwards, interview by author, February 23, 2012.

125 *To Edwards, who understood the conditions:* Ibid.

By mid-December 1967, the OPHR: Amy Bass, *Not the Triumph but the Struggle: The 1968 Olympics and the Making of the Black Athlete* (Minneapolis: University of Minnesota Press, 2002), 135.

with the pledged support of a number of athletes: Jules Boykoff, "Jules Boykoff: John Carlos, Tommy Smith, and the Political Olympics," *Verso* (blog), October 17, 2016, available at: http://www.versobooks.com/blogs/2885-jules-boykoff-john-carlos-tommie-smith-and -the-political-olympics (accessed November 11, 2016).

126 *Later, Gibson, in a forthright interview with* Los Angeles Times: Dwight Chapin, "Bob Gibson: Black Man Nobody Wanted — Until He Was a Hero," *Los Angeles Times,* July 5, 1968.
In February 1968, he stepped forward: Robert Lipsyte, "Politics and Protest," *New York Times,* February 10, 1968.
"When I was an athlete": Ibid.
After all, Jesse Owens: Bass, *Not the Triumph,* 93.

127 *a poster of Black Panther Huey Newton: Episode 2 of Jackie Robinson,* directed by Ken Burns, Sarah Burns, and David McMahon for Florentine Films, PBS, April 11, 2016.
a young basketball star who — unknown to Robinson — had hit her: Arnold Rampersad, *Jackie Robinson: A Biography* (New York: Ballantine, 1998), 427–428.
But young Chip: Chip Logan, interview by author, February 13, 2012.
Robinson was visibly shaken: Rampersad, *Jackie Robinson,* 423.

128 *see in his son his own failure as a father:* Ibid.
"God is testing me": Rachel Robinson with Lee Daniels, *Jackie Robinson: An Intimate Portrait* (New York: Harry N. Abrams, 1996), 201.
Rachel believed that Jackie Jr. had been born too soon: Ibid.
Jackie Robinson's namesake had done unthinkable, unspeakable things: Rampersad, *Jackie Robinson,* 422–425.
because it was part of the image he wanted to project: Ibid., 424.

129 *The political and public life, she felt:* Rachel Robinson, interview by author, January 26, 2012.
great stature in spite of family tragedy and deteriorating health: Gerald McLaughlin, interview by author, February 2, 2012.
They spoke for nearly an hour: Ibid.

9. The Silent Spring

130 *In one retelling, he hadn't seen the ball:* Jeffrey Denberg, "With or Without Money, Agee Is a Rich Man," *SPORT,* March 1970.
couldn't move out of the way quickly enough: Joseph Durso, "Agee Hurt as Mets Bow," *New York Times,* March 10, 1968.
But suddenly, at Al Lang Field: Ibid.

131 *see Gibson plunking "him good":* Johnny Edwards, interview by author, November 12, 2011.
But Edwards knew what he'd heard: Ibid.
Ed Charles had warned Agee: George Vecsey, "Sports of the Times: Amazing Mets Lose Their Leadoff Man," *New York Times,* January 23, 2001.
outfielder Cleon Jones told his Mets teammate: Ron Swoboda, interview by author, February 27, 2012.
he would once again feel that dread: Ibid.
Agee's closed-in stance: Gibson and Wheeler, *Stranger to the Game,* 182.

132 *"Indiscriminately hitting men is a form of pouting":* Hano, "Bob Gibson: Symbol of a New Breed."
breaking the young man's left scapula: Gibson and Wheeler, *Stranger to the Game,* 76.
Late in Gibson's career, after his first marriage was over: Studio 42 with Bob Costas, June 15, 2009.
During his rookie season with the Braves: Dusty Baker, "Dusty Baker on Unwritten Rules of Baseball and Hitting Behind Hank Aaron," interview by Dan Patrick, *The Dan Patrick Show,* DirectTV Sports Group, May 17, 2012, text available (audio no longer available)

at: www.danpatrick.com/2012/05/17/dusty-baker-on-unwritten-rules-of-baseball-and-hit ting-behind-hank-aaron/ (accessed October 24, 2013).

"Hoot, why'd you hit that young kid": Ibid.

Despite everything Gibson had done: George Vecsey, interview by author, March 2, 2012.

Even Phil Pepe, his hardworking first ghostwriter: Phil Pepe, interview by author, December 8, 2012.

133 *One magazine in its baseball preview issue:* Editors, "Baseball '68," *SPORT,* May 1968.

134 *"Why can't these motherfuckers hit?":* George Vecsey, interview by author, March 2, 2012.

There was something about it: Ibid.

This was the environment that rookie: Jon Warden, interview by author, May 2, 2011.

135 *Then one day Sain quietly told him:* Ibid.

That's not to say that Sain didn't understand: Ibid.

But Sain did believe in the importance of training: Ibid.

136 *sporting orange hair and had traded in his thick glasses for contacts:* Cantor, *The Tigers of '68,* 17.

He'd spent the off-season in bowling alleys: McLain and Zaret, *I Told You I Wasn't Perfect,* 83.

What Tigers broadcaster Ray Lane discovered: Ray Lane, interview by author, January 27, 2012.

Jerry Green, then a football beat writer: Jerry Green, interview by author, May 9, 2011.

137 *"I've seen the Promised Land":* Martin Luther King Jr., "I've Been to the Mountaintop," speech delivered at Mason Temple, Memphis, TN, April 3, 1968, available at: American Rhetoric, http://www.americanrhetoric.com/speeches/mlkivebeentothemountaintop.htm.

That evening in St. Petersburg: Tim McCarver, interview by author, January 7, 2012.

By Gibson's own account, he and King had crossed paths: Gibson and Wheeler, *Stranger to the Game,* 184.

he couldn't possibly understand what he felt as a black man: Ibid.

integration could change people: Ibid.

In Houston, Jim Kaat was riding in a car: Jim Kaat, interview by author, June 22, 2012.

138 *After King's assassination, Marvin Miller fielded:* Marvin Miller, interview by author, July 26, 2011.

Gibson and his teammates opposed a regular start: Gibson and Wheeler, *Stranger to the Game,* 184.

Clemente and King had spent time together: Mead, *Two Spectacular Seasons,* 122.

139 *It was in this atmosphere of angst:* George Vecsey, interview by author, March 2, 2012.

dedicate one of his victories from Sen. Eugene McCarthy: Stan Isaacs, "This Time Sen. Mc-Carthy Won't Be Shut Out," *Newsday,* October 4, 1968.

"I need to work out": George Vecsey, interview by author, March 2, 2012.

In the silence of the stadium: Ibid.

he'd never felt prouder to be a Negro: Rampersad, *Jackie Robinson,* 379.

Robinson and King were openly at odds over Vietnam: Robinson, *First Class Citizenship,* 255–257.

140 *In a telegram, he had implored Kennedy:* Ibid., 173.

When the Robinsons arrived at the Logans': Lee Murphy, interview by author, February 14, 2012.

The Robinsons had just come from visiting Jackie Jr.: Rampersad, *Jackie Robinson,* 427.

Murphy could feel the vast undercurrent of fear: Lee Murphy, interview by author, February 14, 2012.

For Rachel, as for so many others: Rachel Robinson, interview by author, January 26, 2012.

At the time of King's assassination, almost one-third: Feldman, *El Birdos,* 227.

141 *When he first joined the Guard in 1962:* Pete Richert, interview by author, February 7, 2012.

Red Schoendienst spoke glowingly: Bob Broeg, "McCarver: The Pip Who Won't Be 'Wally Pipped,'" *St. Louis Post-Dispatch,* March 5, 1968.

Richert had by now gotten used to juggling: Pete Richert, interview by author, February 7, 2012.

Like everyone else, Richert was scared: Ibid.

winter ball in Nicaragua or Venezuela: Jim Kaat, interview by author, June 22, 2012.

142 *when the Cubs arrived in Cincinnati:* Mead, *Two Spectacular Seasons,* 122.

embarrassed to be a white man playing baseball: Jim Kaat, interview by author, June 22, 2012.

Senators relief pitcher Dave Baldwin felt: Dave Baldwin, email interview by author, February 20, 2012.

Sam McDowell felt that there wasn't a single person: Sam McDowell, interview by author, March 3, 2012.

10. 8:45

143 *"It was 8:45 on Saturday":* Dwight Chapin, "Drysdale Passes Umpire's Test for 'Greasy Kid Stuff,'" *Los Angeles Times,* June 9, 1968.

In Chapin's wonderful portrait: Ibid.

not the "string of pearls": Don Drysdale, with Bob Verdi, *Once a Bum, Always a Dodger: My Life in Baseball from Brooklyn to Los Angeles* (New York: St. Martin's Press, 1990), 151.

144 *who stood that night in the runway:* William Leggett, "The Season of the Zero Hero," *Sports Illustrated,* June 17, 1968.

Drysdale would prove more violent: Jane Leavy, *Sandy Koufax: A Lefty's Legacy* (New York: HarperCollins: 2002), 179.

The next time Brock was up: Ibid.

145 *Maglie's lessons were simple and tough:* Drysdale and Verdi, *Once a Bum,* 58.

"Unless you get used to looking at this guy": Melvin Durslag, "L.A.'s Fiery Strike-Out Artist," *Saturday Evening Post,* July 1, 1961.

maintained that Stan Williams—not Drysdale—was the meanest: Lonnie Wheeler, interview by author, November 26, 2011.

146 *With his arm behind him, Drysdale would hook his wrist:* Dick Tracewski, interview by author, March 2, 2012.

At the Los Angeles Memorial Coliseum: Durslag, "L.A.'s Fiery Strike-Out Artist."

Watching this, Fresco Thompson: Ibid.

Not long after he arrived in California, he met Ginger: "The Drysdales in Showbiz," *Los Angeles Herald Examiner,* September 9, 1963.

147 *Chapin felt that Drysdale was not only cooperative:* Dwight Chapin, interview by author, March 26, 2013.

the likes of Donna Reed and Tippi Hedren: Lynn Lilliston, "Celebrity Moms and Moppets on Parade: Charity Fashions," *Los Angeles Times,* February 20, 1968.

If there was any doubt about his focus: John Wiebusch, "'Villainous' Big D Really a Good Guy," *Los Angeles Times,* April 2, 1968.

"I've had it. I couldn't throw another pitch": Dan Hafner, "Drysdale Beats Astros—And It's 1–0 Again," *Los Angeles Times,* May 19, 1968.

He rarely brought it up when he spoke: Nancy Fieux, interview with author, March 4, 2012.

As a matter of superstition: Ibid.

Drysdale had already matched Luis Tiant's: Dwight Chapin, "Doc White Pulls for Drysdale to Break His Shutout Mark: White's Record," *Los Angeles Times,* June 4, 1968.

148 *It was late in the morning on May 31:* Dwight Chapin, "Franks Disputes Record, Calls Umpire Gutless: Franks Protests," *Los Angeles Times,* June 1, 1968.

Over 46,000 people: Nancy Fieux, interview by author, March 4, 2012.

Before the start, Minnesota senator Eugene McCarthy: Dan Hafner, "Drysdale Sets Record! Fifth Shutout in Row: Unusual Ruling Enables Big D to Survive Hectic Ninth as Dodgers Top Giants," *Los Angeles Times,* June 1, 1968.

149 *For most of the evening, Drysdale had used his slider:* Mead, *Two Spectacular Seasons,* 158.

Drysdale, who threw 150 pitches: Chapin, "Franks Disputes Record."

When Dietz passed away in 2005: Associated Press, "Dick Dietz, 63, Who Didn't Try to Avoid a Drysdale Pitch, Dies," *New York Times,* June 30, 2005.

Walking into the clubhouse after the game: Chapin, "Franks Disputes Record."

Drysdale's catcher, Jeff Torborg: Hafner, "Drysdale Sets Record!"

Meanwhile, Chapin and other writers waited: Dwight Chapin, interview by author, March 26, 2013.

When the Giants finally allowed them in: Chapin, "Franks Disputes Record."

spit tobacco juice on Chapin's shoes: Dwight Chapin, interview by author, March 26, 2013.

150 *"It was the worst call I've ever seen":* Chapin, "Franks Disputes Record."

That day Drysdale woke at noon: Dwight Chapin, "Drysdale Admits He Was More Nervous Than Against Giants," *Los Angeles Times,* June 5, 1968.

Drysdale was "simply unbeatable": Ibid.

It was after midnight: Dorothy Townsend, "Crumpled Page May Hold Last Kennedy Writing," *Los Angeles Times,* June 8, 1968.

151 *"I want to first express my high regard for Don Drysdale":* United Press International, "A Moment of Victory, Then the Dream Died," *Los Angeles Times,* March 5, 1968.

Drysdale heard it all transpire: Steve Rushin, "The Season of High Heat," *Sports Illustrated,* July 9, 1993.

The two would sometimes spend time together in Los Angeles: Scott Howard-Cooper, "The Year of the Pitcher: 1968: Big Stars Were Drysdale, Gibson, McLain; Seven Had ERAs Below 2.00," *Los Angeles Times,* July 10, 1988.

At that same moment of collective shock: Mudcat Grant, interview by author, September 14, 2011.

152 *And it was through JFK:* Ibid.

Grant and Savage had seen Bobby: Ibid.

Nothing at that moment seemed probable: Ibid.

Before Don Drysdale's next start on June 8: Scott Howard-Cooper, "The Year of the Pitcher: 1968: Big Stars Were Drysdale, Gibson, McLain; Seven Had ERAs Below 2.00," *Los Angeles Times,* July 10, 1988.

Drysdale had spent the day as millions of Americans had: Al Goldfarb, "Don Drysdale: What Does He Do for an Encore?" *Complete Sports,* May 1969.

153 *The cheers were deafening:* Leggett, "The Season of the Zero Hero."

"It was bound to happen sooner or later": Dwight Chapin, "Boyer Carefully Handles Slow Hopper for Record: Boyer Handles Record," *Los Angeles Times,* June 9, 1968.

The following year he went on the disabled list: Associated Press, "Medication Doesn't Work — Big D May Quit," *San Bernardino Sun-Telegram,* August 10, 1969.

11. Out There

155 *"You guys are wrong":* "45-Minute Delay: Reds Balk at Starting," *St. Louis Post-Dispatch,* June 9, 1968.

156 *Following the assassination, Tim McCarver:* Post-Dispatch Wire Services, "Cards Oppose Playing Sunday," *St. Louis Post-Dispatch,* June 7, 1968.

By majority vote, the Cardinals had decided: Neal Russo, "Cards, Reds Still Hope Not to Play Sunday," *St. Louis Post-Dispatch,* June 8, 1968.

Pappas struggled, tussled with teammates: Associated Press, "Pappas-Nuxhall Feud Boils," *Utica Daily Press,* February 22, 1967.

157 *Dick Wagner insisted that the club:* Russo, "Cards, Reds Still Hope."

As afternoon turned to evening: Jim Ferguson, "Pappas Resigns as Player Rep," *Dayton Daily News,* June 10, 1968.

Howsam said the team had consulted with Eckert: St. Louis Post-Dispatch, "45-Minute De-lay."

158 *Pappas did his best to assure his teammates:* Ibid.

they voted at least twice not to play: Milt Pappas, interview by author, September 15, 2011.

When he got back to his clubhouse: Ibid.

The turn of events had been mainly instigated by Bristol: Ferguson, "Pappas Resigns."

He asked for nine fellows: St. Louis Post-Dispatch, "45-Minute Delay."

Maloney would later say he'd been penciled in: Jim Maloney, interview by author, February 29, 2012.

Maloney felt an obligation to play: Ibid.

159 *"If nine guys go out there and play, then we'll all go":* Ferguson, "Pappas Resigns."

Pappas understandably felt drained and underappreciated: Milt Pappas, interview by au-thor, September 15, 2011.

"Our position is that we had scheduled this game": Ferguson, "Pappas Resigns."

on Friday, June 7, the San Francisco Giants had released their own passive-aggressive state-ment: George Vecsey, "Giants Yield to Mets and Postpone Today's Game Out of Respect for Kennedy," *New York Times,* June 8, 1968.

160 *The Mets had voted twice not to play:* Joe Donnelly, "Mets Vote, Reject Giants Game: Action Backed," *Newsday,* June 7, 1968.

When Hodges conveyed their final decision: Vecsey, "Giants Yield to Mets."

Unlike Bristol and Howsam, however, M. Donald Grant: Donnelly, "Mets Vote, Reject Gi-ants."

As the Mets' player representative, Ed Kranepool, said: Vecsey, "Giants Yield to Mets."

while Hodges spoke about taking time to pray: Mort Zachter, *Gil Hodges: A Hall of Fame Life* (Lincoln: University of Nebraska Press, 2015), 289.

some Mets players walked through Haight-Ashbury: Ron Swoboda, interview by author, February 27, 2012.

George Vecsey and some other sportswriters: George Vecsey, interview by author, March 2, 2012.

161 *And that's what they got:* Ibid.

Like the Reds, the Houston Astros: Russo, "Cards, Reds Still Hope."

In the end, 23 of the Astros played: Milton Gross, "The Ballplayers' Drive for Indepen-dence," *SPORT,* August 1969.

Neither would Pirates infielder Maury Wills: Tim Wendel, *Summer of '68: The Season That Changed Baseball, and America, Forever* (Boston: Da Capo Press, 2013), 46.

all three were fined: Gross, "The Ballplayers' Drive."

Catching flak for his decision, Spec Richardson: Red Smith, "Week-End of Shame in World of Sports," *Boston Globe,* June 10, 1968.

162 *"The refusal of the Mets to play":* Ibid.

Kennedy aide Frank Mankiewicz wrote telegrams: Arthur Daley, "Sports of the Times: Compounding a Felony," *New York Times,* June 12, 1968.

"These players are not acting so they can go on a picnic": Marvin Miller, interview by author, July 26, 2011.

Following Jim Lonborg's 22-win 1967 season: Jim Lonborg, interview by author, April 23, 2012.

163 *Oscar Robertson and Bill Russell, Vince Lombardi:* Robert Lipsyte, "Sports of the Times: The Teammates," *New York Times,* June 8, 1968.
      "National Sportsmen for Kennedy": Ibid.
      "We want a voice in schedule-making": Hano, "Bill Freehan: Tough Leader of the Tigers."

164 *Marvin Miller could sense:* Marvin Miller, interview by author, July 26, 2011.
      Sam McDowell, whose father had worked as a steelworker: Sam McDowell, interview by author, March 3, 2012.
      The Yankees were just as relentless: Jim Bouton, interview by author, February 21, 2012.
      Dal Maxvill, who would later take his turn as a player representative: Dal Maxvill, interview by author, October 8, 2011.
      Jim Lonborg immediately felt a new strength: Jim Lonborg, interview by author, April 23, 2012.

165 *Deemed the "Unknown Solider":* Arthur Daley, "Sports of the Times: Mental Blanks," *New York Times,* June 11, 1968.
      Speaking in his own defense: St. Louis Post-Dispatch, "45-Minute Delay."
      Gussie Busch, the Cardinals' overlord: August A. Busch Jr., "A Statement by August A. Busch, Jr., President, St. Louis Cardinals to Cardinal Players, St. Petersburg, Florida, March 22, 1969."
      This was apparent in 1970 when Steve Carlton: Red Smith, "Gussie's Crying in His Beer," *Philadelphia Inquirer,* March 16, 1970.

166 *Irish politician protecting his ward:* Marvin Miller, interview by author, July 26, 2011.
      Cronin said to Miller, "You know, young man": Ibid.
      But it is true that the following December, 150 players: Charles Maher, "Top Stars Back Threatened Baseball Strike," *Los Angeles Times,* December 5, 1968.
      the MLBPA negotiated its first collective bargaining agreement: Mark Armour and Dan Levitt, "A History of the MLBPA's Collective Bargaining Agreement: Part 1," *The Hardball Times,* November 7, 2016, available at: http://www.hardballtimes.com/a-history-of-the-mlbpa-collective-bargaining-agreement-part-1/# (accessed November 26, 2016).
      The agreement also called for a "study committee": United Press International, "Players Ask New Look at 'Reserve,'" *St. Louis Post-Dispatch,* July 31, 1967.

167 *In a roundtable discussion late in 1969:* The Editors of SPORT, "Simpson, McLain, Unseld, and Orr Sound Off on Sports in the '70s," *SPORT,* December 1969.
      In just a few years with the Players' Association: Marvin Miller, interview by author, July 26, 2011.

168 *"You're underestimating us":* Ibid.

12. Unclenched Fists

169 *In the summer of 1970:* The Editors of SPORT, "Time Out with the Editors: Athletes and Protest," *SPORT,* July 1970.
      Clemente would have told them: Mead, *Two Spectacular Seasons,* 195–196.
      But by the same measure: Ibid., 194.

170 *When Cleveland relief pitcher Billy Rohr:* Bob Sudyk, "Tiger Fans Slug It Out," *Cleveland Press,* June 8, 1968.
      "Baseball's function is not to lead crusades": Robinson, *Baseball Has Done It,* 109.

171 *Kareem Abdul-Jabbar:* Bass, *Not the Triumph,* 187.
      "It's certainly regrettable we have to take this stand": Robert Lipsyte, "Sports of the Times: The Spirit of the Olympics," *New York Times,* August 1, 1968.

172 *Afterwards, under tremendous pressure:* Richard Hoffer, *Something in the Air: American Passion and Defiance in the 1968 Mexico City Olympics* (New York: Simon & Schuster, 2009), 67.

Jesse Owens — the greatest Olympian of all: Dave Zirin, "The Explosive 1968 Olympics," *International Socialist Review,* September–October 2008.

173 *yet Jackie Robinson, whose brother Mack was a teammate:* Lou House, host, episode 20, *Black Journal,* National Educational Television, January 1970, accessed through the Museum of Television and Radio, New York.

But now Robinson called the sprinters' protest: Ibid.

A Birmingham native, Mays chose not to take part: Bass, *Not the Triumph but the Struggle,* 202.

For journalist Robert Lipsyte, the difference lay: Robert Lipsyte, interview by author, March 2, 2012.

174 *But in 1968, as Bouton's time with the Yankees:* Jim Bouton, interview by author, February 21, 2012.

Six days before the start: Jim Bouton, "A Mission in Mexico City," *SPORT,* August 1969.

He had one main task: Ibid.

175 *Bouton didn't think he was risking much:* Jim Bouton, interview by author, February 21, 2012.

with his flashes of insolence and activism: Ibid.

After all, with roughly one-third of all players: Mead, *Two Spectacular Seasons,* 138.

176 *When the sportswriter Arnold Hano profiled Bill Freehan:* Hano, "Bill Freehan: Tough Leader of the Tigers."

When pitcher Dave Baldwin, early in his career: Dave Baldwin, email interview by author, February 20, 2012.

By 1970, George Vecsey, now covering the Yankees: George Vecsey, interview by author, March 2, 2012.

177 *As 1968 wore on, Vecsey grew increasingly restless:* Ibid.

And that was that: Ibid.

As an undergraduate at the University of Michigan: Elliott Maddox, interview by author, February 4, 2012.

178 *Later, when Maddox joined the Mets:* Ibid.

He was black and had attended college at Michigan: Ibid.

Harry Edwards of all people: Harry Edwards, interview by author, February 23, 2012.

179 *Like Edwards, cultural critic Gerald Early was willing to forgive:* Gerald Early, interview by author, October 9, 2011.

"an angry quip": Lonnie Wheeler, interview by author, November 26, 2011.

He was eloquent about the need for "open housing": Hano, "Bob Gibson: Symbol of a New Breed."

180 *Yet there were things that perhaps he should have left unsaid:* Ibid.

13. President of the World

181 *What would it take — how many wins:* Surface, "Johnny Sain Teaches the Power of Positive Pitching."

"Anything you can conceive or believe": Ibid.

The newspaper strike by the Free Press *and* Detroit News: Mary Ann Weston, interview by author, November 11, 2011.

182 *But Denny was proving impossible to talk to:* Mary Ann Weston, "Our Tigers Are Charmers," *Detroit Free Press,* August 24, 1968.

As they traveled on the Tigers' team bus: Mary Ann Weston, interview by author, November 11, 2011; Bill Freehan, *Behind the Mask: An Inside Baseball Diary,* edited by Steve Gelman and Dick Schaap (New York: World Publishing Co., 1970), 41–42.

and ultimately in her story: Mary Ann Weston, "Tigers Ogle Short Skirts — But Keep Chivalry Alive," *Detroit Free Press,* August 26, 1968.

McLain would put her off: Mary Ann Weston, interview by author, November 11, 2011.

When Tom Loomis from the Toledo Blade: Green, *Year of the Tiger,* 84.

When a blown call cost him a no-hitter: Ibid., 98.

183 *In his 25th win, with no outs in the sixth:* Ibid., 155.

Once during the 1968 season, Sain and his pitching staff: Falls, "Only Denny Knows for Sure."

184 *"the biggest front-running fans":* Green, *Year of the Tiger,* 42.

McLain even blamed them for the Tigers' collapse: Ibid.

quickly telling Tom Loomis to clarify: Ibid., 43.

"Why the fuck did you say this?": Denny McLain, interview by author, November 16, 2011.

only to be roundly booed: Green, *Year of the Tiger,* 49–50.

McLain's wife found a smoke bomb: Denny McLain, interview by author, November 16, 2011.

Another time, after a win: Green, *Year of the Tiger,* 39.

"I get an ovation when I warm up": David Wolf, "Tiger on the Keys and the Mound," *Life,* September 13, 1968.

185 *Broadcaster Paul Carey believed:* Paul Carey, interview by author, January 23, 2012.

His fastball came in one of three ways: Denny McLain, "'30 Wins? It's Going to Be Tough' — McLain," *Detroit Free Press,* August 11, 1968.

With his sidearm delivery: Ibid.

Sam McDowell, whose promising career: Sam McDowell, interview by author, March 3, 2012.

"Control is God-given": Joseph Kane, "Baseball: Tiger Untamed," *Time,* September 13, 1968.

186 *Late in 1968, however, one reporter noted that Sain:* George Cantor, "Unsung Tiger Hero: Sain" (editorial), *Detroit Free Press,* September 5, 1968.

when to throw a rising fastball instead of a sinking one: Mulvoy, "Dizzy Dream for Jet-Set Denny."

his movements as graceful as a ballet dancer's: Falls, "Only Denny Knows for Sure."

As spring turned to summer and McLain's star shone brighter: McLain and Zaret, *I Told You I Wasn't Perfect,* 89.

"You can't satisfy everybody no matter what you do": Watson Spoelstra, "No. 24 for McLain Keeps Tigers Hot," *Detroit News,* August 13, 1968.

"Aw, why try to kid about it anymore?": Joe Falls, "'Sure, I'm Shooting for 30,'" *Detroit Free Press,* August 13, 1968.

is portrayed as Superman: Dick Mayer, "Would You Believe 35 Wins?" (cartoon), *Detroit Free Press,* August 18, 1968.

187 *McLain in an astronaut suit:* Dick Mayer, "25 and Still Counting" (cartoon), *Detroit Free Press,* August 20, 1968.

"Denny is their boy, their hero of the hour": Joe Falls, "The 'Other Side' of Tiger Denny," *Detroit Free Press,* September 3, 1968.

He had little regard for the truth: Larry Osterman, interview by author, November 12, 2011.

McLain claimed that the Detroit newspaper strike actually helped: Green, *Year of the Tiger,* 133.

He felt that the writer unfairly portrayed him as an undisciplined playboy: Watson Spoelstra, "Picture Story Burns Denny," *Detroit News,* September 11, 1968.

"Hey Honey, how'd you like to fuck a five-game loser?": Cantor, *The Tigers of '68,* 108.

188 *He also spoke openly about his plans to use baseball:* Mulvoy, "Dizzy Dream for Jet-Set Denny."

he unabashedly expressed his desire for a Lear jet: Kane, "Baseball: Tiger Untamed."

"I'm a mercenary": Ibid.

Nothing, he said, made him happier than sitting in front of a keyboard: Denny McLain, interview by author, November 16, 2011.

"a pain in the ass": Dave Dexter, *Playback: A Newsman–Record Producer's Hits and Misses from the Thirties to the Seventies* (New York: Billboard Publications, 1976), 202.

Of the 60,000 records Capitol eventually issued: Ibid., 203.

189 *he wasn't the guy with the guitar or the mike:* Mead, *Two Spectacular Seasons,* 137.

"Denny says he's an organist first and a baseball player second": Freehan, *Behind the Mask,* 56.

McLain stayed at the craps table: Mulvoy, "Dizzy Dream for Jet-Set Denny."

this incident was emblematic of McLain's incredible run of luck: McLain and Zaret, *I Told You I Wasn't Perfect,* 90.

Freehan believed that McLain could "turn on his valve": Freehan, *Behind the Mask,* 32.

190 *No team, he believed, played better with a lead:* Denny McLain, interview by author, November 16, 2011.

As the time dwindled away before the start of one game in Cleveland: Dick Tracewski, interview by author, March 2, 2012.

Dick Tracewski could no longer count the number of times: Ibid.

As a rookie, Jon Warden tried to pay: Jon Warden, interview by author, May 2, 2011.

Relief pitcher John Hiller saw McLain as a loner: John Hiller, interview by author, May 17, 2012.

Paul Carey often found Denny alone: Paul Carey, interview by author, January 23, 2012.

191 *"Denny was Denny":* Tom Matchick, interview by author, September 13, 2011.

Curfew had long passed: Ray Lane, interview by author, January 27, 2012.

After watching Gibson strike out 12 men: Neal Russo, "Doubters Climb on Gibson Bandwagon," *The Sporting News,* October 31, 1964.

192 *Smith was even-keeled and undramatic:* Dan Ewald, interview by author, January 16, 2012.

Relief pitcher Daryl Patterson always believed: Daryl Patterson, interview by author, July 7, 2011.

Once, during a game in 1969, Johnny Sain woke Smith from his nap: Tom Matchick, interview by author, September 13, 2011.

During a game in the 1968 season, with Joe Sparma pitching: Cantor, *The Tigers of '68,* 96–97.

193 *"what the point is to shagging balls in the outfield":* Mike Marshall, interview by author, November 2, 2011.

The tension between the two: Jordan, "In a World of Windmills."

it was also Smith who'd walk out onto the field: Cantor, "Unsung Tiger Hero: Sain."

194 *Early on he had said that hitters—Kaline, Norm Cash:* Green, *Year of the Tiger,* 113.

At a certain point that summer, after every start: Ibid., 146.

"Denny's got to be careful": Joe Falls, "Yaz Gives Denny Words of Advice," *Detroit Free Press,* August 18, 1968.

But Daryl Patterson felt that McLain simply couldn't help himself: Daryl Patterson, interview by author, July 7, 2011.

he was trying to build a kind of brand for himself: Denny McLain, interview by author, November 16, 2011.

195 *Namath's admission, "I wish I had been born rich":* John Devaney, "Joe Namath's Good Days and Bad," *SPORT,* November 1967.

"I believe in the star system": Robert H. Boyle, "Show-Biz Sonny and His Quest for Stars," *Sports Illustrated,* July 19, 1965.

No one believed this more than Sain: Pete Waldmeir, "Poise and a Strong Right Arm Carrying McLain to the Heights," *Detroit News,* August 17, 1968.

196 *Dick Tracewski, Koufax's roommate and close friend:* Joe Falls, "Who's Best—Koufax or Denny?" *Detroit Free Press,* August 14, 1968.

As soon as the season started, Koufax lived baseball: Ibid.

By late July, he complained openly: Green, *Year of the Tiger,* 138.

he announced that he'd torn a muscle in his shoulder: United Press International, "McLain Has Torn Shoulder Muscle," *Pittsburgh Press,* August 20, 1968.

McLain's self-diagnosis was overruled by the team doctor: "McLain: 'No Torn Muscle,'" *Detroit Free Press,* August 21, 1968.

McLain began to take more and more cortisone: George Cantor, "Pain or No, Denny's Eye on No. 30," *Detroit Free Press,* September 10, 1968.

197 *McLain was risking everything for this one shot:* Ibid.

14. A Lousy Pitcher

198 *"How about a Dodger Stadium hand":* Neal Russo, "A Wild Pitch by Gibson—And That Snaps the Streak," *The Sporting News,* July 13, 1968.

While Gibson would defer to the greatness of Juan Marichal: Bob Gibson and Reggie Jackson with Lonnie Wheeler, *Sixty Feet, Six Inches: A Hall of Fame Pitcher and a Hall of Fame Hitter Talk About How the Game Is Played* (New York: Doubleday, 2009), 29.

but watching the Series and seeing Gibson's ball seemingly "hop over": Neal Russo, "Braves' 1st Worry: Gibby," *St. Louis Post-Dispatch,* April 9, 1968.

199 *It was "screaming":* Dan Hafner, "Wild Pitch Ends Gibson's Bid in First Inning: Cardinal Star Goes on to 5–1 Win over L.A.," *Los Angeles Times,* July 2, 1968.

200 *Afterwards in the dugout:* Ed Wilks, "Gibson Glad to Win, 5–1, Jokes About Wild Pitch," *St. Louis Post-Dispatch,* July 2, 1968.

"the fucker missed the ball": Gibson and Wheeler, *Stranger to the Game,* 189.

Translated by the Los Angeles Times *for its family readership:* Dwight Chapin, "History Not on Bob Gibson's Side," *Los Angeles Times,* July 2, 1968.

Edwards "loused it up": Russo, "A Wild Pitch by Gibson."

But Gibson quickly recanted: Chapin, "History Not on Bob Gibson's Side."

Gibson has maintained that had they been playing: Gibson and Wheeler, *Stranger to the Game,* 189.

fifth in a row: Russo, "A Wild Pitch by Gibson."

In the moments after the game, Edwards conceded his error: Chapin, "History Not on Bob Gibson's Side."

201 *Some 40 years later, however, he recalled things differently:* Johnny Edwards, interview by author, November 12, 2011.

Edwards—whose two-run home run: Ibid.

"What the hell are you gonna tell me?": Ibid.

"Unadulterated fire. That's what he threw": Ed Wilks, "Gibson's 6th Shutout Tops Giants," *St. Louis Post-Dispatch,* July 7, 1968.

"Don't you ever get tired of shutting people out?": Neal Russo, "Gibson Policy: No Walks and No Runs," *St. Louis Post-Dispatch,* August 10, 1968.

"starvation fare": Angell, *Once More Around the Park,* 141.

Gibson would never call out his teammates: Dal Maxvill, interview by author, October 8, 2011.

202 *When Gibson lost 1–0, in a 10-inning game, to Philadelphia:* Gibson and Wheeler, *Stranger to the Game,* 186.

whenever Gibson pitched it was "like having a night off": Neal Russo, "Redbirds Get Well at Bat for Gibson," *St. Louis Post-Dispatch*, August 29, 1968.

Early in May, after he pitched 12 innings: Neal Russo, "Cards Share Ribs, Javier Hogs RBIs," *St. Louis Post-Dispatch*, May 2, 1968.

But his aches never really abated: Bob Broeg, "Marichal — as Well as Luck — Continues to Elude Gibby," *St. Louis Post-Dispatch*, September 9, 1968.

No one could coax Gibson into walking off the mound: Ed Wilks, "Gibson Shrugs Off Raw Finger to Win, 8–1," *St. Louis Post-Dispatch*, July 13, 1968.

203 *Tim McCarver would later talk about a midseason game*: Tim McCarver, interview by author, January 13, 2012.

You could take the width of two baseballs: Studio 42 with Bob Costas, June 15, 2009.

204 *After Gibson beat the Astros 8–1*: Wilks, "Gibson Shrugs Off Raw Finger."

Gibson was finally throwing that slider: Studio 42 with Bob Costas, June 15, 2009.

Gibson also threw at least two different kinds of fastballs: Gibson and Wheeler, *Stranger to the Game*, 153.

a rising fastball that McCarver considered his best pitch: Golenbock, *The Spirit of St. Louis*, 496.

Like his slider, it was a pitch that no one could hit: Ibid.

His 20th win of the season: Neal Russo, "Javier's Blast Lets Gibby Reach No. 20," *St. Louis Post-Dispatch*, September 3, 1968.

205 *Sandy Koufax, after watching the early pitching success*: Jack Stevenson, "Koufax Says Hitters Will Catch Up Without Rule Changes," *Los Angeles Times*, June 2, 1968.

"I'm not one to complain," Henry Aaron said: Lou Prato, "The Shrinking Hitter: Baseball Stars Tell What Went Wrong in '68," *SPORT*, January 1969.

Curt Flood blamed scheduling: Ibid.

Willie Mays believed that the young pitchers he now faced: Dick Young, "How I'd Shake Up Baseball," *SPORT*, November 1968.

Don Drysdale believed that pitchers had become more studious: Neal Russo, "Bat Night? Schoendienst Looks for One," *St. Louis Post-Dispatch*, May 24, 1968.

Jim Fergosi likewise chalked up the hitting drought to better preparation: Prato, "The Shrinking Hitter."

206 *Gillette felt that expanding the strike zone*: Gary Gillette, interview by author, January 14, 2012.

Sam McDowell believed, rulebook or not: Sam McDowell, interview by author, March 3, 2012.

American League teams consistently buried their best black players: Gary Gillette, interview by author, January 14, 2012.

207 *For writers like Dan Hafner, who described the affair as "dull" and "colorless"*: Dan Hafner, "Pitchers Turn All-Star Classic into a Farce: National League Chalks Up 6th Straight Victory," *Los Angeles Times*, June 10, 1968.

As Gibson has said, had his team averaged four runs a game: Gibson and Wheeler, *Stranger to the Game*, 195.

208 *Gibson's greatness was exaggerated*: Gary Gillette, interview by author, January 14, 2012.

When journalist Fred Katz arrived in St. Louis on opening day: Fred Katz, "Bob Gibson: A Man Who Challenges You in Every Way," *SPORT*, July 1971.

By Gibson's own admission, he wanted to be unknowable: Gibson and Wheeler, *Stranger to the Game*, 164.

Gibson, over time, had become a caricature of himself: Lonnie Wheeler, interview by author, November 26, 2011.

209 *he could never quite divorce the pitching from his race*: Angell, *Once More Around the Park*, 149.

Outfielder Jimmy Wynn once described Gibson as a "mean black man": Baseball's Seasons, "1968: The Year of the Pitcher" (episode 4), MLB Network, January 28, 2009.

But Gibson believed his pitching was color-blind: Gibson and Wheeler, *Stranger to the Game,* 165.

"Bob's anger ain't got nothing to do with being black": Mudcat Grant, interview by author, September 14, 2011.

Gibson may have bristled at his depiction as a surly black athlete: Gibson and Wheeler, *Stranger to the Game,* 188.

"incidental motivation," not the singular thing that drove him: Lonnie Wheeler, interview by author, November 26, 2011.

210 *"Why don't you and the other blackbirds on the Cardinals":* Mead, *Two Spectacular Seasons,* 149.

This accidental encounter would produce the best glimpse: Dwight Chapin, interview by author, March 26, 2013.

211 *In Chapin's piece, Gibson opened up about how he felt:* Chapin, "Bob Gibson: Black Man Nobody Wanted."

He saw them both as dependable stoppers: Brent Musburger, "Denny McLain Has 100 Grand Ideas for 1969," *Chicago American,* August 16, 1968.

Tigers vice president Rick Ferrell wasn't particularly impressed: George Cantor, "Secret's Out! Tigers Are Spying on Cardinals," *Detroit Free Press,* September 1, 1968.

When asked how McLain and Gibson would fare in a matchup: Falls, "Who's Best — Koufax or Denny?"

"If I give up a run, he'll win": Green, *Year of the Tiger,* 136.

212 *"The hell with McLain":* Ibid., 158.

Just days before St. Louis did win the pennant: Joe Falls, "Why I'll Take Denny over Gibson," *Detroit Free Press,* September 13, 1968.

Gibson must have known he'd crossed a line: Ibid.

But Falls was too hasty in writing him off: Ibid.

15. Talk to Me

213 *In the early morning hours of September 14, 1968:* David Condon, "The Day Denny McLain Pitched His $100,000 Game," *Chicago Tribune Magazine,* October 27, 1968.

Later that morning one would offer up a single prayer: Tom Fox, "The Day Denny McLain Won No. 30," *SPORT,* December 1968.

214 *this was a team on a mission:* Al Kaline, interview by author, March 20, 2012.

Mickey Lolich was waiting for them with a sign: Green, *Year of the Tiger,* 189.

Lolich, with his roundish physique: Cantor, *The Tigers of '68,* 190.

Despite his blue-collar appearance: Dan Holmes, "Mickey Lolich," Baseball Biography Project, Society for American Baseball Research, available at: http://sabr.org/bioproj /person/070f71e4 (accessed March 6, 2014).

215 *There were those who still believed in him:* Hal Naragon, interview by author, August 3, 2011.

Sain felt that Lolich was the best pitcher: Green, *Year of the Tiger,* 147.

But for much of 1968, Lolich failed to deliver: Cantor, *The Tigers of '68,* 21.

216 *His National Guard obligations kept him away:* Green, *Year of the Tiger,* 37; Wendel, *Summer of '68,* 12.

Lolich's catcher felt that he didn't think he was capable: Ibid., 58.

Even as a rookie in 1968: Jon Warden, interview by author, May 2, 2011.

Eventually, in late July, Smith did the inevitable: George Cantor, "Bullpen 'Siberia' to Lolich, Sparma," *Detroit Free Press,* August 15, 1968.

217 *Observing in Lolich a new resolve:* Green, *Year of the Tiger,* 148.

    they both sought adventure outside of the game: Tom Fox, "No. 2 Pitchers Drive Motorcycles . . . ," *SPORT,* February 1970.

    complained about the blandness of baseball: Pete Waldmeir, "Oh, You're Some Crazy Guy, Mickey Lolich," *Detroit News,* September 12, 1968.

    had musical aspirations that were oddly out of sync with the times: Fox, "No. 2 Pitchers Drive Motorcycles . . ."

    both Lolich and McLain had strong work ethics: Hal Naragon, interview by author, August 3, 2011.

    Bill Freehan found that Lolich needed coddling: Hano, "Bill Freehan: Tough Leader of the Tigers."

    McLain posed different challenges: Ibid.

218 *In constant pain and believing he needed cortisone:* Denny McLain, interview by author, November 16, 2011.

    Lolich felt that McLain was forever "challenging management, flaunting it": Cantor, *The Tigers of '68,* 188.

    Jim Hawkins, who began covering the team in 1970: Jim Hawkins, interview by author, February 7, 2012.

    "comical as hell": Daryl Patterson, interview by author, July 7, 2011.

    McLain believed that Lolich simply wanted to be the guy: Denny McLain, interview by author, November 16, 2011.

    The two should have shared laughs with one another: Denny McLain, interview by author, November 16, 2011.

219 *Lolich, however, told one Detroit sportswriter:* Fox, "No. 2 Pitchers Drive Motorcycles . . ."

    "McLain doesn't think about his friends or teammates": Associated Press, "Latest Feud: Lolich Blasts McLain," *Cleveland Plain Dealer,* July 25, 1969.

    Sam McDowell would take Lolich's side: Sam McDowell, interview by author, March 3, 2012.

    By the time Denny woke up for good on September 14: Fox, "The Day Denny McLain Won No. 30"; Alfred Wright, "Golden 30 for Show Biz Denny," *Sports Illustrated,* September 23, 1968.

    It must have been strange for him when he stepped out: Ibid.

220 *It was almost 12:30 when McLain walked into the locker room:* Joe Falls, "Step-by-Step to History," *Detroit Free Press,* September 15, 1968.

    "Hey, Denny," yelled A's outfielder Jim Gosger: Fox, "The Day Denny McLain Won No. 30."

    Someone asked him about the Life *profile:* Pete Waldmeir, "Denny Wraps It Up in Style During and After the Game," *Detroit News,* September 15, 1968.

    he was pressed for details on his breakfast: Fox, "The Day Denny McLain Won No. 30."

    "You guys are presuming a lot, aren't you?": Wright, "Golden 30 for Show Biz Denny."

    At some point before the game: Fox, "The Day Denny McLain Won No. 30."

221 *After he warmed up, McLain went to greet them: The Year of the Tiger '68: Official Detroit Tiger Film* (release date unavailable), narrated by Ernie Harwell, coordinated by Burton Sohigian Advertising, Inc., and produced by Associated Film Contractors, Inc., as a special project for the National Bank of Detroit.

    In his bullpen session with Naragon: Hal Naragon, interview by author, August 3, 2011.

    Dizzy Dean himself, jowly and sporting a big white cowboy hat: Green, *Year of the Tiger,* 192.

222 *And now Denny could feel it:* Watson Spoelstra, "Tiger Rally Gives McLain No. 30," *Detroit News,* September 15, 1968.

    Kaline had already made up his mind: Watson Spoelstra, "Kaline's Gamble Pays Off," *Detroit News,* September 15, 1968.

20-foot-long banner reading: Lee Winfrey, "It Just Had to Be Willie," *Detroit Free Press,* September 15, 1968.

When asked afterwards if he'd had a plan: George Cantor, "Just 'Hit It and Run Like Hell,'" *Detroit Free Press,* September 15, 1968.

223 *At that point Sharyn McLain:* Linda LaMarre, "Mrs. Denny Misty-Eyed," *Detroit News,* September 15, 1968.

She had arrived at Tiger Stadium: Detroit News.

In only his second year broadcasting Tigers games on television: Larry Osterman, interview by author, November 12, 2011.

called into question McLain's 1968 accomplishments: Gary Gillette, interview by author, January 14, 2012.

Denny told Sandy Koufax, who was covering the game for NBC: The Year of the Tiger '68: Official Detroit Tiger Film.

224 *Dean put him in a bear hug:* Ibid.

Later, after most fans had left the park: Joe Falls, "Golden 30 Stuns Even Denny," *Detroit Free Press,* September 15, 1968.

Speaking to the press later, he was anything but humble: Waldmeir, "Denny Wraps It Up in Style."

"I hope they announce my $100,000 salary": Condon, "The Day Denny McLain Pitched His $100,000 Game."

The following morning, A's executive vice president and consultant Joe DiMaggio sat with a reporter: Ibid.

When McLain arrived at the clubhouse the next afternoon: Fox, "The Day Denny McLain Won No. 30."

225 *With a listless crowd expected at Tiger Stadium that day:* Jack Berry, "'My Best Game of the Year' — Lolich," *Detroit Free Press,* September 16, 1968.

226 *While he called McLain a fine pitcher:* Larry Middlemas, "A's Slugger Fumes," *Detroit News,* September 15, 1968.

16. Old Men

227 *Jackie Robinson was waiting:* Theodore H. White, *The Making of the President 1968* (New York: Atheneum, 1969; reprint, New York: Harper Perennial Political Classics, 2010), 340.

It was the early afternoon of August 28, 1968: Hubert H. Humphrey, diary entry, August 28, 1968, Hubert H. Humphrey diary, Hubert H. Humphrey Papers, Minnesota Historical Society, St. Paul.

But for now, Humphrey was running late: Ibid.

By the time he sat down to lunch with Robinson: White, *The Making of the President 1968,* 340.

228 *"You are a national hero in the truest sense":* Hubert H. Humphrey, letter to Jackie Robinson, July 1, 1960, Hubert H. Humphrey Papers.

Writing to the vice president in the first days of May: Jackie Robinson, letter to Hubert H. Humphrey, May 3, 1968, Hubert H. Humphrey Papers.

Nearly four months later, however, Robinson was in Chicago: White, *The Making of the President 1968,* 340–341.

229 *"Uncle Tom":* Jackie Robinson, "I Must Live with Myself," *New York Amsterdam News,* January 20, 1968.

"House Nigger": Jackie Robinson, "Gov. Rockefeller," *New York Amsterdam News,* January 13, 1968.

Robinson spoke briefly about his son's experiences in Vietnam: "Host to Rockefeller: Jack Roosevelt Robinson," *New York Times,* June 24, 1968.

then talked about Nixon: Rampersad, *Jackie Robinson,* 429.

GOP had told the black man to "go to hell": Jackie Robinson, "Note to GOP: Go to Hell," *New York Amsterdam News,* August 17, 1968.

In the meantime, he marshaled: Rampersad, *Jackie Robinson,* 431–432.

Rachel always felt that it was the opportunities he'd had: Rachel Robinson, interview by author, January 26, 2012.

In Rachel's view, it was a lack of such a connection: Ibid.

Even as the vast majority of African Americans supported Kennedy: Rampersad, *Jackie Robinson,* 344.

230 *Going further, Kennedy accused Robinson of being anti-union:* Ibid., 347.

But Bobby's decision, after his brother's assassination: Jackie Robinson, "Seeing Through the Kennedy Glamour," *New York Amsterdam News,* September 9, 1964.

As Kennedy's stature rose among African Americans: Jackie Robinson, "We Must Look at the Record," *New York Amsterdam News,* June 8, 1968.

231 *"I do not believe a man is a man to apologize":* Jackie Robinson, "Regarding the Late Senator Kennedy," *New York Amsterdam News,* June 22, 1968.

A few days before he shared sandwiches: Associated Press, "Jack Robinson Jr. Is Held on Morals and Gun Charge," *New York Times,* August 25, 1968.

232 *there were those who cheered for him:* Rampersad, *Jackie Robinson,* 431.

Sherman didn't go inside the bank: Norman Sherman, email interview by author, May 22, 2012.

Robinson would say that he could neither sing: Jackie Robinson, as told to Alfred Duckett, *I Never Had It Made: An Autobiography of Jackie Robinson* (New York: Putnam, 1972; reprint, New York: HarperCollins, 1995), 12.

Rachel hated that he said that: Rachel Robinson, interview by author, January 26, 2012.

In 1962, Cannon castigated Maris: Jimmy Cannon, "Maris . . . 'The Whiner' . . . a Threat to Yank Pennant," *New York Post,* March 21, 1962.

233 *What the Yankees kept quiet:* Ed Wilks, "Pity and Pride in Maris's Farewell," *St. Louis Post-Dispatch,* October 11, 1968.

By the end of 1966, baseball had become an albatross: Golenbock, *The Spirit of St. Louis,* 479.

he turned out to be the one reaching out: Dal Maxvill, interview by author, October 8, 2011.

though stripped of his power, McCarver felt: Tim McCarver, interview by author, January 7, 2012.

who briefly shared an apartment with Maris and Clete Boyer: Dick Schofield, interview by author, October 17, 2011.

"There's a big difference being on a ball club": Bob Sales, "St. Louis Cured Blues for Maris," *Boston Globe,* September 25, 1968.

234 *But at the Cardinals' pennant celebration in Philadelphia:* Neal Russo, "Maris Will Return, Beer Deal Indicates," *St. Louis Post-Dispatch,* November 3, 1967.

Busch reportedly discussed beer franchises with many players: Gibson and Wheeler, *Stranger to the Game,* 234.

This treatment would continue to gnaw: Rodney Wead, interview by author, October 10, 2011.

Even Marvin Miller could see how badly things: Marvin Miller, interview by author, July 26, 2011.

235 *Though everyone knew he wouldn't appear again as an active player:* Ibid.

Yet when it came time for the Yankees rep to speak: Ibid.

236 *For his entire career, he said, he'd been chasing someone:* Joe Falls, "Stanley a 'Little Nervous,'" *Detroit Free Press,* August 24, 1968.

Looking at Mantle, McLain saw his hobbled hero: Denny McLain, interview by author, November 16, 2011.

237 *"I want Mantle to hit one":* McLain and Zaret, *I Told You I Wasn't Perfect,* 111–113.

no one really faulted him for what he'd done. Not Ray Lane: Ray Lane, interview by author, January 27, 2012.

or Larry Osterman sitting in the broadcast booth: Larry Osterman, interview by author, November 12, 2011.

Not Jerry Green, who was writing for the Detroit News: Jerry Green, interview by author, May 9, 2011.

Only Dick Tracewski would later feel it wasn't the right thing: Dick Tracewski, interview by author, March 2, 2012.

he would have sooner dropped his pants on the mound: Gibson and Wheeler, *Stranger to the Game,* 200.

238 *"Let's listen to the bedlam":* The Year of the Tiger '68: Official Detroit Tiger Film.

"hippies" tore up the sod: Phil Corner, "A Tiger Riot in Happytown," *Detroit News,* September 18, 1968.

Denny positioned himself on-screen: "1968 Detroit Tigers Win the Pennant, Part 1 of 3," WJBK broadcast of Tigers' pennant celebration, Detroit, September 17, 1968, available at: https://www.youtube.com/watch?v=p8PJpCkuU9s (accessed April 1, 2014).

"We're trying to get John Sain to come": "1968 Detroit Tigers Win the Pennant, Part 3 of 3," WJBK broadcast of Tigers' pennant celebration, Detroit, September 17, 1968, available at: https://www.youtube.com/watch?v=89p2G8RQQLY (accessed April 1, 2014).

At one point, McLain sat down at Mayo Smith's desk: Green, *Year of the Tiger,* 206–207.

"This guy was fabulous": Pete Waldmeir, "In the Midst of a Hullabaloo, Sparma Is an Island of Emotion," *Detroit News,* September 18, 1968.

239 *Dick Tracewski had seen pennant celebrations before:* Dick Tracewski, interview by author, March 2, 2012.

Green somehow managed to get into the A. C. Lindell: Jerry Green, interview by author, May 9, 2011.

Pitcher Fred Lasher threw up: Fred Lasher, interview by author, September 9, 2011.

McLain woke up in the back of a limo: McLain and Zaret, *I Told You I Wasn't Perfect,* 110.

as best epitomized by the team's well-meaning owner: Nancy Kool, "Enlightenment and the Oldest Tiger," *Monthly Detroit,* April 1981.

George Wallace, the segregationist governor of Alabama: Sugrue, *The Origins of the Urban Crisis,* 265.

"What makes whites seek out blacks and pummel them": William Serrin, "In the Wake of a Pennant, Color Blindness Prevails," *Detroit Free Press,* September 19, 1968.

240 *"How can you avoid superlatives about a boy:* H. C. Butler, "The Tigers' Million-Dollar Kid," *Saturday Evening Post,* September 3, 1955.

Kaline was the second coming: Hal Middlesworth, "Can Kaline Fill Bill as 'Another DiMag'?" *The Sporting News,* September 25, 1957.

Kaline nearly ended up with the Minnesota Twins: Joe Falls, "Turmoil on the Tigers—Does It Still Exist?" *SPORT,* June 1967.

Kaline continued to suffer: Al Kaline, interview by author, March 20, 2012.

241 *Even so, just hours before the Tigers clinched the pennant:* Joe Falls, "'Don't Play Me,' Kaline Tells Mayo," *Detroit Free Press,* September 19, 1968.

Smith, who knew what they would be up against: Green, *Year of the Tiger,* 212.

"What do you think?" Smith asked: Al Kaline, interview by author, March 20, 2012.

Stanley started at shortstop: Joe Falls, "With Stanley, It's No Gamble," *SPORT,* March 1969.

17. Trouble

243 *In its October 14, 1968, issue, Newsweek reprinted:* Pete Axthelm, "The Great National Bore," *Newsweek,* October 14, 1968.

This cartoon appeared on the same page as a column: Ibid.

244 *per-game attendance had fallen 13.5 percent in 1968:* Bill Furlong, "Will Baseball Have a Future?" *SPORT,* May 1969.

expanding the distance between the mound and the plate: Dick Young, "How I'd Shake Up Baseball," *SPORT,* November 1968.

Players from Henry Aaron to Rod Carew to Pete Rose: Lou Prato, "The Shrinking Hitter: Baseball Stars Tell What Went Wrong in '68," *SPORT,* January 1969.

245 *Veeck who pushed to plant ivy:* Paul Dickson, "Diamond in the Ivy," Baseball Hall of Fame, available at: http://baseballhall.org/discover/Wrigley-field-ivy (accessed January 26, 2017).

he predicted that baseball would just "gradually disappear": Axthelm, "The Great National Bore."

But he also had some suggestions for bringing the game up to date: Bill Veeck, "My Plan to Remodel the Majors," *SPORT,* May 1968.

246 *Of all people, it was John Fetzer:* C. C. Johnson Spink, "Fetzer Raps Disunity in Majors," *The Sporting News,* June 15, 1968.

It simply didn't seem fair, he said: Ibid.

In the early 1960s, he'd proposed a prime-time weekly: Clifford Kachline, "'Broadcasting' Says Sponsors Will Rush to Back Fetzer Plan," *The Sporting News,* October 19, 1963.

There was a time when NFL commissioner Pete Rozelle: Michael MacCambridge, *America's Game: The Epic Story of How Pro Football Captured a Nation* (New York: Anchor Books, 2004), 192.

247 *In 1970, more Americans watched the Super Bowl:* Ibid., 274.

football was simply more exciting: Gerald Early, interview by author, October 9, 2011.

Though that game was played in 1969: Ibid.

It was television at its best: Super Bowl III, NBC, January 12, 1969.

248 *In a bound brochure sent out to advertisers:* NBC, "It's a New Ballgame" (brochure), date unknown, A. Bartlett Giamatti Research Center, National Baseball Hall of Fame and Museum, Cooperstown, NY.

18. Seventeen

249 *It was 10:17 in the morning on October 1:* Green, *Year of the Tiger,* 214.

Bob Gibson waited for him inside: Joe Falls, "'Hello, Denny. I'm Bob Gibson,'" *Detroit Free Press,* October 2, 1968.

250 *"If somebody tells me about how great they are, I'll be sick":* George Cantor, "Denny Blasts Cards, Fails to Win 32," *Detroit Free Press,* September 24, 1968.

Gibson, for his part, had two totems: Steve Rushin, "The Season of High Heat," *Sports Illustrated,* July 9, 1993.

251 *Holding court at the Chase-Plaza Hotel:* Neal Russo, "Diz—Gibby Can't Be Beat," *St. Louis Post-Dispatch,* October 1, 1968.

Bob Feller shared this sentiment: Bob Broeg, "Hall of Famer Gibson: Memorable Intensity," *The Sporting News,* January 31, 1981.

Roger Maris warned his teammates: Tim McCarver, interview by author, January 7, 2012.

former Cardinal Ken Boyer, who thought Lolich: Russo, "Diz—Gibby Can't Be Beat."

Astros executive John Mullen: the Cardinals: Ibid.

In the days leading up to the Series, Johnny Sain: Watson Spoelstra, "Tigers' Pitching Staff Could Silence Cardinal Bats," *Detroit News,* September 29, 1968.

Hours after his meeting with Gibson: "Night Before Series Opener," *Boston Globe,* October 3, 1968.

He'd come into the bar with his teammates: Green, *Year of the Tiger,* 217.

He pounded out "Money Is the Name": *Boston Globe,* "Night Before Series Opener."

252 *sitting at a table with Sharyn McLain and her parents:* Roger Angell, interview by author, May 4, 2011.

five minutes before midnight: "Denny Does Cinderella Act," *Detroit News,* October 2, 1968.

None of this sat well with many in the organization: Ray Lane, interview by author, January 27, 2012.

McLain didn't see the harm: Denny McLain, interview by author, November 17, 2011.

Larry Osterman felt a sharp shiver: Larry Osterman, interview by author, November 12, 2011.

Gibson hadn't bothered reading the scouting report: Phil Pepe, interview by author, December 8, 2012.

The Tigers had read up on Gibson: Studio 42 with Bob Costas, June 15, 2009.

253 *Gibson had struck out five of the six men:* Game 1, *1968 World Series,* NBC, October 2, 1968.

Watching from the dugout, Johnny Sain was confused: Cliff Keane, "Gibson Awes Tigers 4–0," *Boston Globe,* October 3, 1968.

Gibson's breaking pitch as a "swerve": Dick Tracewski, interview by author, March 2, 2012.

20 percent of the breaking pitches: Larry Middlemas, "Denny's Blast Needles Cards," *Detroit News,* October 3, 1968.

four of the five Tiger hits came off Gibson's sliders: Jerry Green, "'He Has Had Better Stuff' — McCarver," *Detroit News,* October 3, 1968.

Gibson asked who was the next batter: Jack Herman, "Gibson 'Surprised' Tigers with Breaking Ball," *St. Louis Globe-Democrat,* October 3, 1968.

Cash, who admitted that his teammates: Ray Fitzgerald, "Tigers Tried to Overpower Gibson — Cash," *Boston Globe,* October 3, 1968.

254 *Before the game, Eugene McCarthy:* Stan Isaacs, "This Time Sen. McCarthy Won't Be Shut Out," *Newsday,* October 4, 1968.

McCarthy had stuffed his campaign speeches: Sally Bixby Defty, "Candidates at World Series," *St. Louis Post-Dispatch,* October 3, 1968.

Nearby, David Eisenhower: Game 1, *1968 World Series,* October 2, 1968.

couldn't take his eyes off Gibson: Roger Angell, interview by author, May 4, 2011.

Talbert predicted that the Cardinals would most definitely take the Series: Bob Talbert, "Gibson the Perfect Bore: Like Watching Paint Dry," *Detroit Free Press,* October 3, 1968.

The pain in his arm was constant and unbearable: McLain and Zaret, *I Told You I Wasn't Perfect,* 116.

Examining the faces of the two men, Harry Caray: Game 1, *1968 World Series,* October 2, 1968.

Tom Gorman — would permit McLain the high strike: Cantor, "Denny Blasts Cards."

255 *the Cardinals hitters had made up their minds to stay away:* Associated Press, "Cards' Plan: Lay Off McLains [sic] High Stuff," *Boston Globe,* October 3, 1968.

When one Tigers pitcher complained that McLain: Robert L. Burnes, "The Bench Warmer: The Strike Zone Debate" (editorial), *St. Louis Globe-Democrat,* October 4, 1968.

Cardinals manager Red Schoendienst countered that McLain's high pitches: George Vecsey, "A Question of Strike Zone Looms," *New York Times,* October 6, 1968.

McLain could sense something was wrong: Jack Saylor, "'I'll Correct Control Trouble' — McLain," *Detroit Free Press,* October 3, 1968.

he fell behind early in his counts in the first two innings: "1968: The Year of the Pitcher," *Baseball's Seasons,* January 28, 2009.

256 *McLain was finished:* Ed Wilks, "McLain Stunned at Being Lifted," *St. Louis Post-Dispatch,* October 3, 1968.

After the game, McLain sat in the locker room: Joe Donnelly, "McLain Is Impressed," *Newsday,* October 3, 1968.

terrifying pop of the ball slamming against McCarver's glove: Jon Warden, interview by author, May 2, 2011.

Walking back to the dugout, Kaline: Hawkins, *Al Kaline,* 179.

257 *he had said he didn't give a fuck:* "St. Louis Turns Off, Tunes In on Series Opener," *St. Louis Globe-Democrat,* October 3, 1968; Gibson and Wheeler, *Stranger to the Game,* 199.

History would remember Horton flinching: Willie Horton, interview by author, March 22, 2012.

Watching from the on-deck circle, Jim Northrup: Keteyian and Sarokin, *A City on Fire: The Story of the '68 Detroit Tigers.*

Afterwards, Eddie Matthews tried to steady: Willie Horton, interview by author, March 22, 2012.

Cash compared Gibson to Superman: Gibson and Wheeler, *Stranger to the Game,* 202.

258 *Kaline surmised that Gibson might pitch even better:* Ed Wilks, "'Gibson Will Be Tougher' — Kaline," *St. Louis Post-Dispatch,* October 3, 1968.

how little pleasure Gibson seemed to derive: Angell, *Once More Around the Park,* 129–130.

Meanwhile, Phil Pepe, who was between newspaper jobs: Phil Pepe, interview by author, December 8, 2012.

he'd received a phone call from the vice president: Bob Gibson, "Curves Put Humphrey on Line, Tigers in Line," *St. Louis Post-Dispatch,* October 3, 1968.

Pepe wrote up the column: Bob Gibson, "Bob Fans 17, Blanks Tigers: The Day I Broke Koufax's Record," *New York Daily News,* October 3, 1968.

That evening Denny was back doing what Denny always did: Green, *Year of the Tiger,* 219.

This opinion was also held by young: Gerald Early, interview by author, October 9, 2011.

19. Mudders

260 *Before the fourth game of the World Series:* J. F. ter Horst, "GOP Plots to Reduce Negro Vote, Jackie Robinson Says," *Detroit News,* October 7, 1968.

261 *With the pain in his legs:* Rachel Robinson, interview by author, January 26, 2012.

Afterwards, a dejected Al Kaline: Green, *Year of the Tiger,* 224.

In one cartoon printed in the Detroit Free Press: Dick Mayer, "Dick Mayer's World of Sports" (cartoon), *Detroit Free Press,* October 6, 1968.

262 *Desperate to alleviate the pain in his arm:* Jack Berry, "McLain Through for Series," *Detroit Free Press,* October 7, 1968.

"If you get to Gibson you'll break their spirit": George Cantor, "McLain-Gibson Rematch Is Even More Crucial," *Detroit Free Press,* October 6, 1968.

With over 28 million homes: "It's a New Ballgame" (brochure), NBC, date unknown, A. Bartlett Giamatti Research Center, National Baseball Hall of Fame and Museum, Cooperstown, NY.

Tigers broadcaster George Kell: Game 4, 1968 World Series, NBC, October 5, 1968.

263 *Finally, Mayo Smith came out to speak to his pitcher:* Berry, "McLain Through for Series."

if "you get the shit kicked out of you": Denny McLain, interview by author, November 17, 2012.

264 *"Flipper playing shortstop":* The Bob Hope Show, episode 2, season 19, NBC, October 14, 1968.

The night before, he'd been pranked: Gibson and Wheeler, *Stranger to the Game,* 202.

During the fourth, Norm Cash: Watson Spoelstra, "What Happened in the Stalling Duel," *Detroit News,* October 7, 1968.

When Gibson took the mound in the bottom: Game 4, 1968 World Series, October 5, 1968.

265 *"strike out ten men while treading water":* The Bob Hope Show, October 14, 1968.

"It's unbelievable that a guy can pitch so hard": Feldman, *El Birdos,* 347.

tying his own record of seven steals: Joe Donnelly, "Lou Brock Knows the Ways of Winning," *Newsday,* October 7, 1968.

He felt he had a chance for the record: Ibid.

266 *Throughout the game, Jackie Robinson looked dispassionately out:* John Oppedahl, "Jackie Robinson Says GOP Plotted Against Black Vote," *Detroit Free Press,* October 7, 1968.

20. Anthems

267 *A day after Bob Gibson once again put his team in position:* Jack Saylor, "'Hope It Ends, My Arm Is Tired' — Gibson," *Detroit Free Press,* October 7, 1968.

Gibson listened to the worst thing he'd ever heard: Keteyian and Sarokin, *A City on Fire: The Story of the '68 Detroit Tigers;* Gibson and Wheeler, *Stranger to the Game,* 203.

Game 7 of the 1918 World Series: Bass, *Not the Triumph but the Struggle,* 202.

268 *Tigers announcer Ernie Harwell:* Bill Dow, "Jose Feliciano on Detroit Tigers Legend Ernie Harwell: 'The Best Person I Have Ever Met,'" *Detroit Free Press,* May 9, 2010.

It wasn't until 1983, at the NBA All-Star Game: Pete Croatto, "The All-Star Anthem: Thirty Years Later, Marvin Gaye's Rendition of 'The Star-Spangled Banner' Stands Alone," Grantland.com, ESPN, February 16, 2013, available at: http://grantland.com/features/the-marvin-gaye-national-anthem/ (accessed September 3, 2014).

There were those who enjoyed it: Marvin Miller, interview by author, July 26, 2011; George Vecsey, interview by author, March 2, 2012; Phil Pepe, interview by author, December 8, 2012.

But Michigan governor George Romney: United Press International, "Romney Raps Jose's Anthem," *Kingston Daily Freeman,* October 9, 1968.

A group of Vietnam veterans recovering: Murphy L. Tamkersley et al., "Vietnam Vets Disgusted over Singing of Anthem" (letter), *The Sporting News,* October 26, 1968.

269 *the boos and negative reactions to Feliciano's version:* Marvin Miller, interview by author, July 26, 2011.

He nearly fired Harwell: Ray Lane, interview by author, January 27, 2012; Larry Osterman, interview by author, November 12, 2011.

"If anybody's responsible, it's me": Richard A. Ryan, "Tiger 'Soul' Anthem My Idea, Harwell Says; Defends Singer," *Detroit News,* October 8, 1968.

270 *he believed in tradition:* John Hiller, interview by author, May 17, 2012.

Feliciano had actually brought the Tigers good luck: Willie Horton, interview by author, March 22, 2012.

"Well, it might be our rally song": Al Kaline, interview by author, March 20, 2012.

Mickey Lolich's pregame routine: Keteyian and Sarokin, *A City on Fire: The Story of the '68 Detroit Tigers.*

"a little shit": Jon Warden, interview by author, May 2, 2011.

271 *Charlie Dressen had tried repeatedly:* George Cantor, "In Person, Our Boy, Willie Horton!" *Detroit Free Press,* August 18, 1968.

Cardinals manager Red Schoendienst: Jack Saylor, "Bad-Hop Single over Javier Big Play — Red," *Detroit Free Press,* October 8, 1968.

Only a year before, Brock had lamented: Bill Libby, "Lou Brock's Fight for Fame," *SPORT,* September 1967.

272 *Broadcaster Curt Gowdy wondered out loud:* Game 5, 1968 World Series, NBC, October 7, 1968.
  Earlier in the Series, Horton had expressed his displeasure: Green, *Year of the Tiger,* 220.
  It was a play he had prepped for: Willie Horton, interview by author, March 22, 2012.
  "If you tagged me the first time": Keteyian and Sarokin, *A City on Fire: The Story of the '68 Detroit Tigers.*
  Pointing to Brock's spike marks on the ground: Joe Donnelly, "Brock and Freehan Paint Contrasting Pictures of Same Scene," *Newsday,* October 8, 1968.
273 *They were still up by one run:* Dick Hughes, interview by author, May 9, 2011.
  Roger Angell felt that he'd seen: Roger Angell, interview by author, May 4, 2011.
  Still, Brock believed that he was safe: Donnelly, "Brock and Freehan."
  He wasn't trying to run Freehan over: Tim Moriarty, "Old 'Six' Sends Series to Sixth Game," *Newsday,* October 8, 1968.
  "If he slides, he makes it easy": Donnelly, "Brock and Freehan."
  Tim McCarver believed that not sliding: Tim McCarver, interview by author, January 13, 2012.
274 *Afterwards, Orlando Cepeda, amazed by Lolich's stamina:* Larry Middlemas, "Did He Touch the Plate — 2 Versions," *Detroit News,* October 8, 1968.
  All his life Lolich had felt like a secondary figure: Hawkins, *Al Kaline,* 193.
  Later Smith said that if Wert had gotten a hit: Jerry Green, "Anthem Upsets Lolich," *Detroit News,* October 8, 1968.
  From his post at shortstop: Dal Maxvill, interview by author, October 8, 2011.
  But Kaline wasn't surprised: Al Kaline, interview by author, March 20, 2012.
275 *Standing on third base, Lolich wanted to score:* Hawkins, *Al Kaline,* 189.
  Kaline just wanted to do his job: Ibid., 190.
  In the press box, an exasperated George: George Vecsey, interview by author, March 2, 2012.
276 *Afterwards, as NBC's Tony Kubek began:* Game 5, 1968 World Series, October 7, 1968.
  Kaline didn't think Denny's arm: Ibid.
  Lolich envisioned a scenario: Pete Waldmeir, "Lolich Repeats an Old Refrain: He'll Be Ready Again if Needed" (editorial), *Detroit News,* October 8, 1968.
  "There are a lot of things you can do about pain": Ibid.
  Kaline, for whom Smith had risked everything: Moriarty, "Old 'Six' Sends Series to Sixth Game."

21. Slipping

277 *Before the final game of the World Series in St. Louis:* Freehan, *Behind the Mask,* 190–191.
  Fearing this, Freehan wanted to catch him: Ibid.
278 *Freehan later said that should he ever become a manager:* Ibid.
  Jim Bouton found that out a year later: Jim Bouton, *Ball Four* (New York: World Publishing Co., 1970; reprint, New York: Wiley Publishing, 1990), 190.
  After Game 5, Smith was at a loss about how to proceed: Hawkins, *Al Kaline,* 191.
279 *"How's your arm?":* Ibid.
  McLain said that he fully expected to pitch again: Wells Twombly, "Denny's Sore Shoulder Just a Put-On, He Says," *Detroit Free Press,* October 8, 1968.
  "little, curly-haired Jew cocksucker": Cantor, *The Tigers of '68,* 199–200.
  McLain for once did the responsible thing: Green, *Year of the Tiger,* 233.
280 *Jim Northrup, who'd been moved to center field:* Jack Saylor, "Denny Got Needle, Was 'Scared to Death,'" *Detroit Free Press,* October 10, 1968.
  "Now that we win a game 13–1": Doug Gilbert, "Once Again, It Boils Down to Gibson," *Chicago American,* October 10, 1968.

Smith settled on Lolich: Hawkins, *Al Kaline*, 191.

281 *One of Lolich's most vocal supporters was Sain:* Gilbert, "It Boils Down to Gibson."
McCarver believed that having Gibson in this spot: Studio 42 with Bob Costas, June 15, 2009.
"You go out there and there's 50,000 people": Dal Maxvill, interview by author, October 8, 2011.
Looking back to Game 5: Johnny Edwards, interview by author, November 12, 2011.
An intangible shift had taken place: Al Kaline, interview by author, March 20, 2012.
As he looked forward to the matchup: Roger Angell, interview by author, May 4, 2011.
the "fat guy" — Lolich — couldn't possibly win: Gerald Early, interview by author, October 9, 2011.

282 *Dick Tracewski felt a shared unease:* Dick Tracewski, interview by author, March 2, 2012.
Even Mayo Smith sought to temper expectations: Hawkins, *Al Kaline,* 192.
But Gibson would be the first to admit: Studio 42 with Bob Costas, June 15, 2009; Jack Saylor, "Same Play Worked," *Detroit Free Press,* October 11, 1968.
Even after recording the game's first out: Leonard Koppett, "Mayo Smith Put His Judgment on Line — and Won," *New York Times,* October 11, 1968.
he could tell that Gibson was getting worn down: Daryl Patterson, interview by author, July 7, 2011.
Lolich's true weapon was his three-quarter delivery: Jim Kaat, interview by author, June 22, 2012.
Even pitching on short rest: John Devaney, "Mickey Lolich and the Pride Within," *SPORT,* September 1972.

283 *"To pitch on two days' rest actually meant you had a better sinker":* Jim Lonborg, interview by author, April 23, 2012.
Lolich noticed the change early on: Watson Spoelstra, "What Lolich Wants Lolich Gets — Lots of Go," *The Sporting News,* October 26, 1968.
Concerned, Freehan approached the mound: Freehan, *Behind the Mask,* 75.
a good 20 feet off the bag: Jack Berry, "Cash on Brock: 'Don't Know Why He Did It,'" *Detroit Free Press,* October 11, 1968.

284 *Gibson was admittedly exhausted:* Jack Saylor, "Same Play Worked," *Detroit Free Press,* October 11, 1968.

285 *Watching Flood from behind the plate:* Tim McCarver, interview by author, January 13, 2012.
Looking back from shortstop: Dal Maxvill, interview by author, October 8, 2011.
Sitting in the upper deck on the first-base side: Ray Lane, interview by author, January 27, 2012.
because it was a line drive rather than a fly ball: Larry Jaster, interview by author, July 10, 2011.
the ball was just hit too hard: Fred Lasher, interview by author, September 9, 2011; Daryl Patterson, interview by author, July 7, 2011; Dick Tracewski, interview by author, March 2, 2012.
"That's the ball game right there": Larry Osterman, interview by author, November 12, 2011.
His widow, the actress Judy Pace Flood: Greenburg and Bernstein, *The Curious Case of Curt Flood.*

286 *Flood tried apologizing to Gibson:* Gibson and Wheeler, *Stranger to the Game,* 206.
"You know. Shit happens": Greenburg and Bernstein, *The Curious Case of Curt Flood.*
Knowing him as he did, Wead believed that Gibson would be frazzled: Rodney Wead, interview by author, October 10, 2011.
He simply couldn't forgive Denny: Gibson, Jackson, and Wheeler, *Sixty Feet, Six Inches,* 137.

287 *And he had a World Series Most Valuable Player Award:* Fred Lasher, interview by author, September 9, 2011.

By one estimate, a crowd of 150,000: George M. Boyd, ". . . But Looters Prey on Downtown Stores," *Detroit News,* October 11, 1968.

"biggest spontaneous celebration in peacetime American history": The Year of the Tiger '68: *Official Detroit Tiger Film.*

The party continued into the evening: "Tigers Avoid Welcoming Mob," *Detroit Free Press,* October 11, 1968.

22. After the Fall

288 *On the evening of October 12, 1968:* Episode 3, season 21, *The Ed Sullivan Show,* CBS, October 13, 1968.

289 *Jim Henson's Muppets with Mickey Lolich:* Green, *Year of the Tiger,* 248.

being restrained in his tone and language: Episode 3, season 21, *The Ed Sullivan Show.*

Gibson emerge in a light brown, double-breasted suit: Ibid.

290 *After the 1968 World Series, Gibson would later lament:* Gibson and Wheeler, *Stranger to the Game,* 208.

just not every night: Rick Hummel, interview by author, August 30, 2011.

The following spring you could see McLain working with Sain: McLain and Zaret, *I Told You I Wasn't Perfect,* 139.

For McLain, the lowered mound combined with his shorter frame: Phil Hersh, "Life in the Halls of Shame," *Chicago Tribune,* July 12, 1985.

Previously the uppermost strike call: Gibson and Wheeler, *Stranger to the Game,* 209.

291 *This last change was especially disheartening to Johnny Sain:* Jerome Holtzman, "Sain Sporting a Completely New Look," *Chicago Tribune,* June 6, 1985.

Before the 1968 World Series, the Cardinals were the highest-paid: Cover, *Sports Illustrated,* October 7, 1968, 2, available at: http://www.si.com/vault/issue/40890/2/1?cover_view=0 (accessed December 9, 2016).

Gibson would see the team coming apart: Gibson and Wheeler, *Stranger to the Game,* 210.

Flood had no interest in playing for Philadelphia: "Curt Flood's Letter to Bowie Kuhn" (December 24, 1969), posted at *MLB.com,* March 15, 2007, available at: http://mlb.mlb.com/news/article.jsp?ymd=20070315&content_id=1844945 (accessed May 29, 2014).

292 *With these words, Flood took the thankless first step:* Greenburg and Bernstein, *The Curious Case of Curt Flood.*

The camaraderie and spunk that defined the Cardinals': Katz, "Bob Gibson: A Man Who Challenges You in Every Way."

the 1968 Tigers built around its minor league system: Al Kaline, interview by author, March 20, 2012.

Jim Campbell, who had shaped and groomed the 1968 Tigers team: Dan Ewald, interview by author, January 16, 2012.

Regret. That was what Willie Horton felt: Willie Horton, interview by author, March 22, 2012.

293 *When it came time to negotiate, Campbell offered:* McLain and Zaret, *I Told You I Wasn't Perfect,* 124.

the rookie Jon Warden got a call from McLain: Jon Warden, interview by author, May 2, 2011.

McLain was determined to build his paint business: Gelna McWhirter, "McLain a Very Big Man in Market Place, Too," *The Sporting News,* August 23, 1969.

he seemed more interested in talking up the company: Freehan, *Behind the Mask,* 202.

Once, while on a trip to the West Coast, McLain directed: Harwell and Keegan, *Ernie Harwell,* 160.

294 *he would admit to his stupidity*: Eliot Asinof, "'I Snap Back Real Quick,'" *SPORT*, June 1970.
      teammates chafed at McLain's constant flaunting: Freehan, *Behind the Mask*, 223.
      untenable contempt between Smith and Johnny Sain: Dave Nightingale, "Sain Exits Swing-
      ing on Mayo's '70 Pitch," *New York Post*, August 11, 1969.
      Everything finally came to a head when the team sold Dick Radatz: Freehan, *Behind the
      Mask*, 108.
      "If my advice isn't used and there are no results": Nightingale, "Sain Exits Swinging."
295 *"I won over 60 games pitching for Sain"*: Watson Spoelstra, "Tiger Players Rap Sain's Dis-
      missal," *The Sporting News*, August 23, 1969.
      Lolich was more hesitant initially: Nightingale, "Sain Exits Swinging."
      Back in Arkansas, his marriage was all but finished: Spoelstra, "Tiger Players Rap Sain's Dis-
      missal."
      settlement would force Sain into bankruptcy: Jim O'Donnell, "Mind over Batter," *Chicago
      Tribune*, October 10, 1993.
      It was the same cover image of McLain as in July 1968: "Denny McLain and the Mob: Base-
      ball's Big Scandal" (cover), *Sports Illustrated*, February 23, 1970, available at: http://www
      .si.com/vault/issue/40991/1/1?cover_view=0 (accessed December 10, 2016).
      All the rumors were true: Morton Sharnik, "Downfall of a Hero," *Sports Illustrated*, Febru-
      ary 23, 1970.
      After weighing the accusations against him, Kuhn announced: Associated Press, "McLain
      Can Return for Play on July 1," *Atlanta Constitution*, April 2, 1970.
      By now, Jim Hawkins, just beginning his career as a sportswriter: Jim Hawkins, interview by
      author, February 7, 2012.
296 *In fact, rookie Elliott Maddox was amazed when he watched*: Elliott Maddox, interview by
      author, February 4, 2012.
      McLain was going through a hard time, Campbell said: McLain and Zaret, *I Told You I
      Wasn't Perfect*, 154.
      Three months to the day after his suspension began: Jim Hawkins, interview by author, Feb-
      ruary 7, 2012.
      it wasn't even McLain's idea: Elliott Maddox, interview by author, February 4, 2012.
      As he came into the locker room, one Tiger teammate called Hawkins over: Jim Hawkins, in-
      terview by author, February 7, 2012.
      Later in the press box, Hawkins got a call from Jim Campbell: Ibid.
297 *Maddox has always felt that there was no gun*: Elliott Maddox, interview by author, Febru-
      ary 4, 2012.
      And McLain and Hawkins both contended that backup catcher Jim Price: Denny McLain, in-
      terview by author, November 17, 2011; Jim Hawkins, interview by author, February 7, 2012.
      "I want to be traded," McLain groused: Joe Falls, "Denny Is a Pathetic Case," *The Sporting
      News*, September 12, 1970.
      "when you know if you spit in the wrong way": Ibid.
      he threw out his antacids: Jerome Holtzman, "Owners Peeved at Kuhn," *The Sporting News*,
      January 13, 1968.
      Only Short couldn't see it: Ed Linn, "The Man Who Begs, Buys, and Borrows Trouble,"
      SPORT, May 1971.
298 *When McLain arrived at spring training in 1971*: Greenburg and Bernstein, *The Curious
      Case of Curt Flood*.
      The cover of a spring 1971 issue of SPORT introducing the three men: Linn, "The Man Who
      Begs."
      All of them were grimacing, unsmiling: McLain and Zaret, *I Told You I Wasn't Perfect*,
      178.
      Flood told the team via telegram that his layoff time: Snyder, *A Well-Paid Slave*, 231.

Elliott Maddox, who had grown close with McLain: Elliott Maddox, interview by author, February 4, 2012.

299 *Bob Gibson finally met Jackie Robinson:* Gibson and Wheeler, *Stranger to the Game,* 214.

Agnew's presence on the 1968 Republican ticket: Rampersad, *Jackie Robinson,* 430.

As early as January 1969, Robinson had gone to the White House: Ibid., 432.

Robinson's relationship with Nixon wasn't entirely over: Ibid., 454.

Robinson continued to press the president on issues of race: Ibid., 432.

Though Robinson should have been ready to give up the fight: Ibid., 452, 440.

He confronted Nixon on busing: Robinson, *First Class Citizenship,* 313.

He was accosted by a white New York City policeman: Rampersad, *Jackie Robinson,* 452.

300 *Still, Robinson wasn't too worn down to take to task one of his closest allies:* Robinson, *First Class Citizenship,* 314.

"Times have changed, Jackie": Ibid., 315.

When his daughter Sharon looked at her father: Rampersad, *Jackie Robinson,* 449.

He was alone, submerged by physical and emotional darkness: Burns, Burns, and McMahon, *Jackie Robinson.*

After Jackie Jr.'s death, Robinson's onetime ghostwriter: William Branch, interview by author, February 23, 2012.

301 *For Jackie, this was his family's "last hurrah":* Robinson and Daniels, *Jackie Robinson,* 216.

"see a black face managing in baseball": Burns, Burns, and McMahon, *Jackie Robinson.*

302 *In 1970, after he'd parted ways with the Tigers:* Jordan, "In a World of Windmills."

The following season Sain was back: Ibid.

303 *Sain's personal life:* O'Donnell, "Mind over Batter."

"This time Denny, you've got a whole city in the palm of your hand": Furman Bisher, "Atlanta Welcomes McLain," *The Sporting News,* July 22, 1972.

"I'm proud to say Denny McLain is a good friend of mine": Dave Nightingale, "Riches to Rags!" *Cincinnati Enquirer,* March 30, 1973.

304 *In no way did he think Gibson was finished:* Doug Feldman, *Gibson's Last Stand: The Rise, Fall, and Near Misses of the St. Louis Cardinals, 1969–1975* (Columbia: University of Missouri Press, 2011), 61.

In an effort to jump-start the Cardinals' offense: Gibson and Wheeler, *Stranger to the Game,* 213.

Then, in 1973 in Shea Stadium, as he attempted to pivot: Neal Russo, "Gibson's Fate in Doubt — May Undergo Surgery," *St. Louis Post-Dispatch,* August 6, 1973.

"When I go out to pitch, I'm angry": Rich Koster, "Bob Gibson," *St. Louis Globe-Democrat,* September 2, 1975.

305 *"Maybe I should have walked Jorgensen":* Bob Broeg, "Hall of Famer Gibson: Memorable Intensity," *The Sporting News,* January 31, 1981.

He admitted that he no longer had the same level of concentration: Koster, "Bob Gibson."

a middling pinch hitter named Pete LaCock hit a fastball: Gibson and Wheeler, *Stranger to the Game,* 249.

if he couldn't get out Pete LaCock, well, fuck it: Rick Hummel, interview by author, August 30, 2011.

After the game, Gibson met up with Rodney Wead: Rodney Wead, interview by author, October 10, 2011.

306 *Five years earlier, Gibson had envisioned a different kind of ending:* Feldman, *Gibson's Last Stand,* 200.

Five years after Gibson retired, Roger Angell came out to Omaha: Angell, *Once More Around the Park,* 132.

Gibson, following his divorce from his first wife Charlene: Rodney Wead, interview by author, October 10, 2011.

Gibson confided to Angell that he was worried about his place in baseball history: Roger Angell, interview by author, May 4, 2011.

307 *what exactly was Gibson's job description?*: Jack Lang, "Mets Hope Gibby Can Light a Fire," *The Sporting News*, November 15, 1980.

owner Ted Turner seriously contemplated having Gibson return: Gibson and Wheeler, *Stranger to the Game*, 267.

He fought openly with his former teammate Dal Maxvill: Ibid., 268.

He also clashed with Sain: Herm Weiskopf, "Inside Pitch," *Sports Illustrated*, May 16, 1983.

308 *"It's kind of bad to see Johnny go out"*: "Johnny Sain/Baseball Hall of Fame file," Giamatti Research Center, Baseball Hall of Fame, Cooperstown, NY.

he revealed the book in his hand—Machiavelli's The Prince: O'Donnell, "Mind over Batter."

309 *"And if you can think, you can succeed"*: Ibid.

Even after his debilitating stroke in 2002: Michael Hirsley, "Baseball Pals Pulling for Great: Ailing Sain a Battler," *Chicago Tribune*, June 9, 2002.

"I just wish that everything that came to me at such a young age had come later": Mark Kram, "The Dark Side of a Loser," *Inside Sports*, October 1984.

310 *By the time McLain entered Courtroom 3*: Ira Berkow, "Sports of the Times: A King No Longer," *New York Times*, April 27, 1985, and Michael Maddon, "Loss: McLain," *Boston Globe*, March 16, 1985.

When one borrower couldn't pay: Associated Press, "McLain Convicted, Faces a Sentence Up to 75 Years," *Los Angeles Times*, March 17, 1985.

Just 29 months later, however, McLain was free again: Associated Press, "Denny McLain Walks Out of Tampa Court a Free Man," *Los Angeles Times*, December 16, 1988.

McLain pleaded guilty to reduced charges: United States v. McLain, 701 F. Supp. 1544, M.D. Fla. 1988, Courtlistener.com, https://www.courtlistener.com/opinion/1473970/united-states-v-mclain/ (accessed May 4, 2017).

311 *McLain was reportedly earning $400,000*: Mark Armour, "Denny McLain," Baseball Biography Project, Society for American Baseball Research, last revised July 1, 2015, available at: http://sabr.org/bioproj/person/6bddedd4 (accessed December 11, 2016).

could do nothing: Eli Zaret, interview by author, March 30, 2012.

McLain soon returned to his old habits: Armour, "Denny McLain."

After he was released, he lived in a halfway house: Ira Berkow, "In a Lifetime Full of Second Chances, Denny McLain Receives His Biggest," *New York Times*, December 29, 2003.

underwent bariatric surgery and lost 162 pounds: Paul Caron, "Former MLB Pitcher Drops 162 Pounds," *CNN*, April 7, 2014, available at: http://www.cnn.com/2014/04/07/health/mlb-weight-loss-denny-mclain/ (accessed December 11, 2016).

By the time of his remarriage, he'd begun paying restitution: Berkow, "In a Lifetime Full of Second Chances."

312 *there are still those who are willing to overlook everything*: Eli Zaret, interview by author, March 30, 2012.

for winning when it matters most: Gerald Early, interview with author, October 9, 2011.

313 *Hummel always feels a measure of happiness*: Rick Hummel, interview by author, August 30, 2011.

"How quickly they forget": Roger Angell, interview by author, May 4, 2011.

Epilogue

314 *it was at a similar event at the Holiday Inn O'Hare in 1987*: Jerome Holtzman, "A Sign of Good Times for McLain," *Chicago Tribune*, December 1, 1987.

315 *"I hope this town is happy"*: Boyd, ". . . But Looters Prey on Downtown Stores."

"The deepest meaning of this victory": Ewald, *John Fetzer,* 151.

316   *"Your fighting, winning team is the best tonic"*: Ibid.

"I believe that the 1968 Tigers were put here by God": Cantor, *The Tigers of '68,* 75.

acknowledged that the Tigers' success may have eased racial tensions: Dick Tracewski, interview by author, March 2, 2012.

George Wallace found great support during his presidential runs: Sugrue, *The Origins of the Urban Crisis,* 265.

317   *"The stuff about it pulling the city together is a white person's view"*: Gary Gillette, interview by author, January 14, 2012.

a divide has grown between the people who actually live in Detroit: Joe Drape, "Bankruptcy for Ailing Detroit, but Prosperity for Its Teams," *New York Times,* October 13, 2013.

318   *"Who is this?"*: Denny McLain, email correspondence, February 6, 2012.

I was waiting for Rodney Wead at a restaurant: Rodney Wead, interview by author, October 10, 2011.

319   *"But you have to play along with it"*: Eli Zaret, interview by author, March 30, 2012.

320   *Both men were initially cited:* "Hall of Famer Gibson Won't Be Charged in Fist Fight," Associated Press, March 8, 2002, http://a.espncdn.com/mlb/news/2002/0308/1347728.html (accessed March 30, 2017).

SELECTED BIBLIOGRAPHY

Books

Angell, Roger. *Once More Around the Park: A Baseball Reader*. New York: Ballantine Books, 1991.

Bass, Amy. *Not the Triumph but the Struggle: The 1968 Olympics and the Making of the Black Athlete*. Minneapolis: University of Minnesota Press, 2002.

Besag, Frank. *The Anatomy of a Riot: Buffalo, 1967*. Buffalo, NY: University Press at Buffalo, 1967.

Bouton, Jim. *Ball Four*. New York: World Publishing Co., 1970; reprint, New York: Wiley Publishing, 1990.

Brock, Lou, and Franz Schulze. *Stealing Is My Game*. Englewood Cliffs, NJ: Prentice-Hall, 1976.

Bryant, Howard. *Shut Out: A Story of Race and Baseball in Boston*. New York: Routledge, 2002.

Cantor, George. *The Tigers of '68: Baseball's Last Real Champions*. Dallas: Taylor Publishing, 1997.

Cepeda, Orlando, with Herb Fagen. *Baby Bull: From Hardball to Hard Time and Back*. Dallas: Taylor Publishing, 1998.

Clarke, Thurston. *The Last Campaign: Robert F. Kennedy and 82 Days That Inspired America*. New York: Henry Holt, 2008.

Clavin, Tom, and Danny Peary. *Roger Maris: Baseball's Reluctant Hero*. New York: Simon & Schuster, 2010.

Dexter, Dave. *Playback: A Newsman–Record Producer's Hits and Misses from the Thirties to the Seventies*. New York: Billboard Publications, 1976.

Drysdale, Don, with Bob Verdi. *Once a Bum, Always a Dodger: My Life in Baseball from Brooklyn to Los Angeles*. New York: St. Martin's Press, 1990.

Eisele, Albert. *Almost to the Presidency: A Biography of Two American Politicians*. Blue Earth, MN: Piper Publishing, 1972.

Ewald, Dan. *John Fetzer: On a Handshake: The Times and Triumphs of a Tiger Owner*. Champagne, IL: Sycamore Publishing, 1997.

Falkner, David. *Great Time Coming: The Life of Jackie Robinson from Baseball to Birmingham*. New York: Touchstone, 1995.

Feldman, Doug. *El Birdos: The 1967 and 1968 St. Louis Cardinals*. Jefferson, NC: McFarland & Co., 2007.

——. *Gibson's Last Stand: The Rise, Fall, and Near Misses of the St. Louis Cardinals, 1969–1975*. Columbia: University of Missouri Press, 2011.

Fetzer, John. *America's Agony*. Kalamazoo, MI: Fetzer Institute, 2007.

Fine, Sidney. *Violence in the Model City: The Cavanagh Administration, Race Relations, and the Detroit Riot of 1967*. East Lansing: Michigan State University Press, 2007.

Flood, Curt, with Richard Carter. *The Way It Is*. New York: Simon & Schuster, 1971.

Freehan, Bill. *Behind the Mask: An Inside Baseball Diary*. Edited by Steve Gelman and Dick Schaap. New York: World Publishing Co., 1970.

Gibson, Bob, with Phil Pepe. *From Ghetto to Glory: The Story of Bob Gibson*. New York: Popular Library, 1968.

Gibson, Bob, with Lonnie Wheeler. *Pitch by Pitch: My View of One Forgettable Game*. New York: Flatiron Books, 2015.

——. *Stranger to the Game: The Autobiography of Bob Gibson.* New York: Penguin Books, 1994.

Gibson, Bob, and Reggie Jackson, with Lonnie Wheeler. *Sixty Feet, Six Inches: A Hall of Fame Pitcher and a Hall of Fame Hitter Talk About How the Game Is Played.* New York: Doubleday, 2009.

Golenbock, Peter. *The Spirit of St. Louis: A History of the St. Louis Cardinals and Browns.* New York: HarperCollins, 2000.

Grant, Jim "Mudcat," Tom Sabellico, and Pat O'Brien. *The Black Aces: Baseball's Only African-American Twenty-Game Winners.* Farmingdale, NY: Aventine Press, 2007.

Green, Jerry. *Year of the Tiger: The Diary of Detroit's World Champions.* New York: Coward-McCann, 1969.

Halberstam, David. *October 1964.* New York: Villard, 1994.

Harwell, Ernie, with Tom Keegan. *Ernie Harwell: My 60 Years in Baseball.* Chicago: Triumph Books, 2002.

Hawkins, Jim. *Al Kaline: The Biography of a Tigers Icon.* Chicago: Triumph Books, 2010.

Hirsch, James S. *Willie Mays: The Life, the Legend.* New York: Scribner, 2010.

Hoffer, Richard. *Something in the Air: American Passion and Defiance in the 1968 Mexico City Olympics.* New York: Simon & Schuster, 2009.

Kahn, Roger. *The Boys of Summer.* New York: Harper & Row, 1972; reprint, New York: Harper Perennial Modern Classics, 2006.

——. *The Head Game: Baseball Seen from the Pitcher's Mound.* New York: Harcourt, 2000.

——. *Into My Own: The Remarkable People and Events That Shaped a Life.* New York: St. Martin's Press, 2006.

Kaiser, Charles. *1968 in America: Music, Politics, Chaos, Counterculture, and the Shaping of a Generation.* New York: Weidenfeld & Nicolson, 1988.

Leavy, Jane. *Sandy Koufax: A Lefty's Legacy.* New York: HarperCollins, 2002.

Lipsyte, Robert. *An Accidental Sportswriter: A Memoir.* New York: Ecco, 2011.

MacCambridge, Michael. *America's Game: The Epic Story of How Pro Football Captured a Nation.* New York: Anchor Books, 2004.

McCarthy, Eugene J. *1968: War and Democracy.* Red Wing, MN: Lone Oak Press, 2000.

McLain, Denny, with Eli Zaret. *I Told You I Wasn't Perfect.* Chicago: Triumph Books, 2007.

Mead, William B. *Two Spectacular Seasons: 1930: The Year the Hitters Ran Wild, 1968: The Year the Pitchers Took Revenge.* New York: Macmillan, 1990.

Miller, Marvin. *A Whole Different Ball Game: The Inside Story of the Baseball Revolution.* Chicago: Ivan R. Dee, 2004.

Moffi, Larry, with Jonathan Kronstadt. *Crossing the Line: Black Major Leaguers, 1947–1959.* Lincoln, NE: Bison Books, 2006.

Museum of Broadcasting, ed. *Bob Hope: A Half-Century on Radio and Television.* New York: Museum of Broadcasting, 1986.

Pattison, Mark, and David Raglin, eds. *Sockit to 'em Tigers: The Incredible Story of the 1968 Detroit Tigers.* Hanover, MA: Maple Street Press, 2008.

Persico, Joseph E. *The Imperial Rockefeller: A Biography of Nelson A. Rockefeller.* New York: Simon & Schuster, 1982.

Poston, Ted. *A First Draft of History.* Edited by Kathleen A. Hauke. Athens: University of Georgia Press, 2000.

Rampersad, Arnold. *Jackie Robinson: A Biography.* New York: Alfred A. Knopf, 1997.

Robinson, Jackie. *Baseball Has Done It.* Edited by Charles Dexter. Philadelphia: Lippincott, 1964; reprint, Brooklyn, NY: IG Publishing, 2005.

——. *Beyond Home Plate: Jackie Robinson on Life After Baseball.* Edited by Michael G. Long. Syracuse, NY: Syracuse University Press, 2013.

——. *First Class Citizenship: The Civil Rights Letters of Jackie Robinson.* Edited by Michael G. Long. New York: Henry Holt and Co., 2007.

Robinson, Jackie, as told to Alfred Duckett. *I Never Had It Made: An Autobiography of Jackie Robinson.* New York: Putnam, 1972; reprint, New York: HarperCollins, 1995.

Robinson, Rachel, with Lee Daniels. *Jackie Robinson: An Intimate Portrait.* New York: Harry N. Abrams, 1996.

Rothmyer, Karen. *Winning Pulitzers: The Stories Behind Some of the Best News Coverage of Our Time.* New York: Columbia University Press, 1991.

Russell, Bill, and Taylor Branch. *Second Wind: The Memoirs of an Opinionated Man.* New York: Random House, 1979.

Snyder, Brad. *A Well-Paid Slave: Curt Flood's Fight for Free Agency in Professional Sports.* New York: Penguin Group, 2006.

Sugrue, Thomas J. *The Origins of the Urban Crisis: Race and Inequality in Postwar Detroit.* Princeton, NJ: Princeton University Press, 1996.

Thielman, Jim. *Cool of the Evening: The 1965 Minnesota Twins.* Minneapolis: Kirk House Publishers, 2005.

Thorn, John, and John B. Holway. *The Pitcher.* New York: Prentice-Hall, 1987.

Tygiel, Jules. *Baseball's Great Experiment: Jackie Robinson and His Legacy.* New York: Oxford University Press, 1997.

Vecsey, George. *Stan Musial: An American Life.* New York: Ballantine Books, 2011.

Veeck, Bill, with Ed Linn. *Veeck — as in Wreck: The Autobiography of Bill Veeck.* New York: Putnam, 1962; reprint, Chicago: University of Chicago Press, 2001.

Wainwright, Loudon. *The Great American Magazine: An Inside History of Life.* New York: Alfred A. Knopf, 1986.

Wendel, Tim. *Summer of '68: The Season That Changed Baseball, and America, Forever.* Boston: Da Capo Press, 2012.

Westcott, Rich. *Masters of the Diamond: Interviews with Players Who Began Their Careers More Than 50 Years Ago.* Jefferson, NC: McFarland & Co., 1994.

White, Theodore H. *The Making of the President 1968.* New York: Atheneum, 1969; reprint, New York: Harper Perennial Political Classics, 2010.

Zachter, Mort. *Gil Hodges: A Hall of Fame Life.* Lincoln: University of Nebraska Press, 2015.

Author Interviews

Angell, Roger, May 4, 2011, March 11, 2014
Baldwin, Dave, February 20, 2012 (conducted via email)
Bouton, Jim, February 21, 2012
Branch, William, February 23, 2012
Carey, Paul, January 23, 2012
Chapin, Dwight, March 26, 2013
Chass, Murray, February 9, 2012
Early, Gerald, October 9, 2011
Edwards, Harry, February 23, 2012
Edwards, Johnny, November 12, 2011
Eisele, Al, December 1, 2011
Ewald, Dan, January 16, 2012
Fieux, Nancy, March 4, 2012
Fitch, Bill, January 16, 2012
Gillette, Gary, January 14, 2012
Grant, Mudcat, September 14, 2011
Green, Jerry, May 9, 2011
Groat, Dick, January 19, 2012
Hawkins, Jim, February 7, 2012

Hiller, John, May 17, 2012
Horton, Willie, March 22, 2012
Hughes, Dick, May 9, 2011
Hummel, Rick, August 30, 2011
Jaster, Larry, July 10, 2011
Jones, Sam, January 12, 2012
Kaat, Jim, June 22, 2012
Kaline, Al, March 20, 2012
Koosman, Jerry, February 16, 2012
Lake, Eric, June 28, 2012
Lane, Ray, January 27, 2012
Lasher, Fred, September 9, 2011
Lipsyte, Robert, March 2, 2012
Logan, Chip, February 13, 2012
Lonborg, Jim, April 23, 2012
Luy, Mike, March 4, 2012
Maddox, Elliott, February 4, 2012
Maloney, Jim, February 29, 2012
Marshall, Mike, November 2, 2011
Matchick, Tom, September 13, 2011
Maxvill, Dal, October 8, 2011
McAuliffe, Dick, February 25, 2012
McCarver, Tim, January 7, 2012, January 13, 2012
McDowell, Sam, March 3, 2012
McLain, Denny, November 16, 2011, November 17, 2011
McLaughlin, Gerald, February 2, 2012
Mihelich, Dennis, May 17, 2012
Miller, Marvin, July 26, 2011
Murphy, Lee, February 14, 2012
Naragon, Hal, August 3, 2011
Nelson, Mel, October 28, 2011
Osterman, Larry, November 12, 2011
Pappas, Milt, September 15, 2011
Patterson, Daryl, July 7, 2011
Pepe, Phil, December 8, 2012
Rains, Rob, April 23, 2012
Richert, Pete, February 7, 2012
Robinson, Rachel, January 26, 2012
Sain, Mary Ann, February 29, 2012
Schofield, Dick, October 17, 2011
Serrin, William, June 25, 2012
Sherman, Norman, May 22, 2012 (conducted via email)
Simon, Ron, October 5, 1912
Stokes, David, June 21, 2012
Stolley, Richard, August 23, 2011
Swoboda, Ron, February 27, 2012
Tracewski, Dick, March 2, 2012
Tucker, John, October 7, 2011
Underhill, Jerry, February 28, 2011
Vecsey, George, March 2, 2012
Warden, Jon, May 2, 2011

Washburn, Ray, August 29, 2011
Wead, Rodney, October 10, 2011
Weston, Mary Ann, November 11, 2011
Wheeler, Lonnie, November 26, 2011, and October 3, 2012 (which was conducted via email)
Zaret, Eli, March 30, 2012

Television and Film

Baseball Classics: 1948 World Series, Cleveland Indians vs. Boston Braves. Rare Sportsfilms. 1988.

Baseball's Seasons. "1968: The Year of the Pitcher" (episode 4). MLB Network. January 28, 2009.

Baseball's Seasons. "1967: The Impossible Dream" (episode 11). MLB Network. January 13, 2010.

Black Journal. Episode 20. Museum of Television and Radio, New York. January 1970.

The Bob Hope Show. Episode 2, season 19. NBC. October 14, 1968.

A City on Fire: The Story of the '68 Detroit Tigers. HBO Films. July 2002.

The Curious Case of Curt Flood. HBO Sports. July 2011.

The Ed Sullivan Show. Episode 3, season 21. CBS. October 13, 1968.

Gentle Ben. "Batter Up." CBS. February 4, 1968.

Jackie Robinson. Florentine Films for PBS. April 2016.

Namath. HBO Sports, NFL Films. January 2012.

1968 World Series. Games 1–7. NBC. October 1968.

Studio 42 with Bob Costas. Episode 2, season 1. MLB Network. June 15, 2009.

Super Bowl III. NBC. January 12, 1969.

The Year of the Tiger '68: Official Detroit Tiger Film. Coordinated by Burton Sohigian Advertising, Inc., and produced by Associated Film Contractors, Inc., as a special project for the National Bank of Detroit. Release date unknown.

INDEX